The Structure of American Industry

ELEVENTH EDITION

Walter Adams

Late Professor of Economics
Trinity University (Texas) and Michigan State University

James W. Brock

Moeckel Professor of Economics
Miami University (Ohio)

PEARSON
Prentice
Hall

Upper Saddle River, New Jersey 07458

Library of Congress Cataloging-in-Publication Data

The structure of American industry / [edited by] Walter Adams, James W. Brock—11th ed.
   p. cm.
   Includes bibliographic refrences and indexes.
   ISBN 0-13-143273-7 (alk. paper)
   1. Industries—United States.   I. Adams, Walter [date]   II. Brock, James W.

   HC106.S85 2004
   338.6'0973—dc22

                                                        2004050278

AVP / Executive Editor: David Alexander
VP / Editorial Director: Jeff Shelstad
Editorial Assistant: Katy Rank
Project Manager: Marie McHale
Marketing Manager: Sharon Koch
Marketing Assistant: Melissa Owens
Managing Editor: John Roberts
Production Editor: Suzanne Grappi
Manufacturing Buyer: Michelle Klein
Design Manager: Maria Lange
Cover Design: Bruce Kenselaar
Manager, Print Production: Christy Mahon
Composition: Laserwords
Full-Service Project Management: Jennifer Welsch, BookMasters, Inc.

Credits and acknowledgments borrowed from other sources and reproduced, with
permission, in this textbook appear on appropriate page within text.

Pearson Education LTD.
Pearson Education Australia PTY, Limited
Pearson Education Singapore, Pte. Ltd
Pearson Education North Asia Ltd
Pearson Education, Canada, Ltd
Pearson Educación de Mexico, S.A. de C.V.
Pearson Education–Japan
Pearson Education Malaysia, Pte. Ltd

10 9 8 7 6 5 4 3 2
ISBN 0-13-143273-7

*for Leslie M. Agee and colleagues
and their pioneering work in efficiency*

Contents

Preface

Each day our lives intersect with major industries that comprise the American economy—from the agriculture that provides our food and the petroleum industry that supplies our gasoline, to the banks through which we conduct our financial affairs, the telecommunications we rely on, the beer that we (of legal age) imbibe, the acrid second-hand cigarette smoke we inhale, and the college sports that thrill us.

Individual industries also raise public policy challenges that are front-burner issues: accounting fraud that misrepresents the financial health of firms and bilks investors of billions; the exploding cost of health care; geopolitical events in Iraq, Venezuela, and elsewhere that trigger spikes in gasoline prices; the price and security of airline travel; the recording industry's relentless pursuit of those who download music; and concerns about global warming and fuel consumption in an automotive age of sport utility vehicles.

These issues, in turn, raise a host of economic questions: How are these industries individually organized and structured? What is their history? Who are their major producers and providers, and what market shares do they account for? What is the nature of competition in each of these fields, and how effective is it as a regulator of economic decision making? How well do these industries perform in terms of efficiency, innovativeness, and the allocation of resources? What are the major public policy issues in these fields, and what options are available for addressing them?

Unfortunately, these questions raise considerable interest, but economic treatments of them typically focus on putting theoretical expositions first, so that understanding of the industries themselves is haphazard and disjointed, with a glimpse of one here and a side glance at another there but no coherent understanding of an individual industry in its entirety.

Eleven editions of this book have been published to address this imbalance by treating each selected industry in a comprehensive way as an organic whole. Each edition has sought to invert the conventional economic-analytic paradigm by putting the industry front and center in order to provide a panoramic portrait. Methodologically, it is as much an exercise in induction—reasoning from the particular to the general—as it is a deductive process of deriving reality a priori from abstract postulates and assumptions. The approach, as Walton Hamilton put it in his classic *Price and Price Policies*, "is that of every day, of experience, of finding out"—of proceeding "by way of sample and type, of incident and detail"—based on the premise that "as a temptation to human curiosity industry can have few rivals." Each edition of this book also has striven to be fresh, with thorough updates of industries continued from preceding editions, and with new industries added to reflect changing contemporary interests and issues.

This latest edition once more offers a kaleidoscopic collection of individual industry studies that, it is hoped, readers will find useful for analyzing and understanding major industries in the American economy. Each chapter, written by an expert in the field, continues to offer a "live" laboratory for clinical examination and comparative analysis, as well as for evaluating public policies and options. The collection thus continues to serve as a useful supplement, if not a necessary antidote, to the economist's penchant for the abstractions of theoretical model-building.

In assembling this issue, the editor is appreciative for the contributors' conscientiousness in comprehensively and engagingly addressing their fields; for the production and marketing efforts of Gladys Soto, Jen Welsch, and their colleagues at Prentice Hall and BookMasters; and, especially, for Professor Pauline Adams's willingness to permit the book to continue to be published as a jointly-edited product—something it is hoped will be meaningful for the contributors, adopters, and readers who knew, worked with, and learned from Walter Adams.

James W. Brock
Oxford, Ohio
May 2004

About the Authors

Peter J. Alexander is Senior Economist at the Federal Communications Commission, where he analyzes the economics of broadcast and cable media. He also has taught economics on the faculties of Ohio Wesleyan University and Hartwick College, and publishes widely on communications, media, and industrial economics.

Randall W. Bennett is Professor of Economics at Gonzaga University, Spokane, Washington, where he has published numerous articles on the economics of sports and served as a consultant on antitrust issues.

James W. Brock is Moeckel Professor of Economics at Miami University (Ohio). He is the author of a number of books and articles on industrial organization and public policy, and has testified before various congressional committees on antitrust issues.

Philip G. Cottell, Jr. is Professor of Accountancy at Miami University (Ohio), where he teaches and publishes in the areas of financial accounting, pensions and retirement plans, and accounting pedagogy.

Kenneth G. Elzinga is Professor of Economics at the University of Virginia. He has served as Special Economic Advisor to the Justice Department's Antitrust Division, has published extensively on economic issues of antitrust policy, and has been an expert witness in numerous antitrust cases.

John L. Fizel is Professor of Economics at Pennsylvania State University. He has published numerous articles and books on the economics of professional and collegiate sports, and has served as a consultant on antitrust and sports-related issues.

John Goddeeris is Professor of Economics at Michigan State University. He has published widely on the economics of health care, has served as an expert consultant for the state of Michigan on issues of public finance and access to health care, and has been a visiting scholar at the Congressional Budget Office.

George A. Hay is Edward Cornell Professor of Law and Professor of Economics at Cornell University and a special consultant to Charles River Associates. He was formerly Director of Economic Policy for the Justice Department's Antitrust Division, writes regularly on antitrust law and policy, and has been an expert witness in numerous antitrust cases.

Stephen Martin is Professor of Economics and Faculty Director of the Technology Transfer Initiative at the Krannert School of Management, Purdue University. He is Co-Managing Editor of the *International Journal of Industrial Organization,* has served on the faculty of numerous European universities, and has published widely on industrial economics.

James McConnaughey is Senior Economist at the National Telecommunications and Information Administration, in the Office of Policy Analysis and Development, where he analyzes issues in telecommunications competition, regulatory reform, and universal service and Internet access.

Steven J. Pilloff is Economist in the Division of Research and Statistics of the Board of Governors of the Federal Reserve System, where he is involved in analyzing the competitive effects of bank mergers. He has published numerous articles on the economics of various aspects of commercial banking.

William G. Shepherd is Professor Emeritus of Economics at the University of Massachusetts. He was Special Economic Assistant to the chief of the Antitrust Division at the Justice Department, and edited the *Review of Industrial Organization*. He has served as an economic expert in numerous antitrust and regulatory cases and has published widely in the industrial organization field.

Daniel B. Suits is Professor Emeritus of Economics at Michigan State University. A fellow of the Econometric Society and the American Statistical Association, he has published extensively in the areas of quantitative economic analysis and forecasting.

CHAPTER

Agriculture

—DANIEL B. SUITS

As the supplier of most of the food we eat and raw materials for industry, agriculture is clearly an important sector of the economy. However, its importance extends even beyond this. In nations where farmers are unproductive, most workers are needed to grow food, and few can be spared for education, production of investment goods, or other activities required for economic growth. Indeed, one of the things that correlates most closely with rising per capita income is the declining fraction of the labor force that is engaged in agriculture. In the poorest nations of the world, 50 percent to 80 percent of the population lives on farms, compared with less than 10 percent in Western Europe, and barely more than 1 percent in the United States.

In short, economic development in general depends on the performance of farmers, and this performance, in turn, depends on how agriculture is organized and on the economic context, or market structure, within which agriculture functions.

I. MARKET STRUCTURE AND COMPETITION

Number and Size of Farms

The United States is home to about 2 million farms today. This is roughly a third of the peak number reached 70 years ago. As the number of farms has declined, the average size has increased. Farms in the United States now average fewer than 440 acres, but this average can be misleading, because modern American agriculture is a large-scale business. Although only 5 percent of all farms contain 1,000 acres or more, these include more than 40 percent of the total farm acreage. Nearly a quarter of all wheat, for example, is grown on farms of 2,000 acres or more, and the largest 2.6 percent of all wheat growers raise half of all our wheat.

Size of farm varies widely by product, but even where the typical acreage is small, production is concentrated. Nearly 65 percent of the tomato crop is grown on small farms, but the remaining 35 percent is marketed by the largest 9 percent of growers. Broiler chickens can be raised on small farms, but the largest 2 percent of growers produce 70 percent of all broilers.

In this age of large-scale commercial agriculture, the family farm, once the American ideal, is no longer common. Today, only about half of all farmers earn their livelihood entirely from the operation of their farms; the rest must supplement their farming with other jobs. Moreover, large-scale agriculture is increasingly carried out by large corporations. Although only 2 percent of farms are incorporated, these corporate farms operate 12 percent of all land in U.S. farms and market 22 percent of the total value of farm crops. In states like California, corporate farms operate a quarter of all farm acreage and market 40 percent of the value of all field crops (including 60 percent of all California sweet corn, vegetables, and melons). Even in a state like Kansas, more than a third of all farm products are grown by corporations.

Competition in Agriculture

Despite the scale and concentration of production, modern agriculture remains an industry whose behavior is best understood in terms of the theory of pure competition. Although production is concentrated in the hands of a small percentage of growers, total numbers are so big that the largest 2 percent or 3 percent of the growers of any particular product still constitutes a substantial number of independent farms. For example, although the largest 2 percent of producers grow half of all U.S. grain, this 2 percent consists of some 27,000 farms.

Numbers like this are a far cry from those for manufacturing. Fewer than 300 firms produce men's work clothing, and only 200 cotton-weaving mills exist here, but both of these industries are recognized as highly competitive. Even if we ignore the competitive influence of the thousands of smaller farms growing each crop, we are still talking about nearly 100 times as many independent producers as can be found in the most competitive manufacturing industries.

In addition, the number and size of existing farms are only partial indicators of competitiveness, because no special barriers apply to setting up and operating a new farm. In addition, most farms are adapted to a variety of crops and can easily shift production from one to another when the outlook for prices and costs changes.

Because of this competitive structure, even a huge modern farm is too small a part of the total to influence price or total output by its individual action. Each can decide only how much of which crops to grow and by what methods. The combined result of these thousands of individual decisions determines the total supply that reaches the market, and supply, in conjunction with demand, sets the market price.

Demand for Farm Products

Demand is an important element in the structure of agricultural markets. Potatoes are fairly typical and can be used as a convenient illustration.

Demand for Potatoes

In Figure 1-1, the average farm prices of potatoes in the United States for the years 1992 through 2001 are plotted vertically against annual per capita consumption, which is measured horizontally. Each point represents the data for a recent year. The downward drift of points from upper left to lower right confirms the everyday observation that people tend to buy more at low prices than at high prices. During 1992, for example, when 100 pounds of potatoes sold at a price of $3.93, Americans on average ate only 168 pounds, whereas when the price fell to $3.13, average consumption rose to 190 pounds.

However, a glance at the figure is enough to show that price is not the only influence on buying habits. In 1998, for example, Americans bought an average of 182 pounds of potatoes at a price equivalent to $3.41 per 100 pounds, but they bought only 176 pounds the next year, although the price was almost unchanged. Part of this variation can be traced to changes in buyers' incomes and in the prices of other vegetables that can be

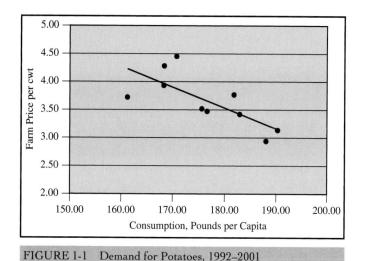

FIGURE 1-1   Demand for Potatoes, 1992–2001

SOURCE: *U.S. Department of Agriculture, Agricultural Statistics, various years.*

substituted for potatoes in the diet. Some of it arises from the appearance in the stores of packaged dried potatoes and in the shifting popularity of such things as fries at fast-food outlets. Statistical procedures make it possible to abstract from the influence of these other things and to estimate the effect of price alone. The result is shown by the line drawn through the midst of the observations. Such a curve, called a *demand curve*, represents the quantities that buyers would be expected to purchase at each price, all other influences held constant.

Demand Elasticity

The response of buyers to changes in price is measured by the *elasticity of demand*, which expresses the percentage change in amount purchased that would be expected from a 1 percent rise in price. Elasticity of demand can be estimated from demand curves by selecting two prices that are close together and reading the corresponding quantities from the curve. Elasticity is then the ratio of the percentage difference in quantity to the percentage difference in price. Applying this procedure to the demand curve in Figure 1-1 yields an estimated elasticity of –0.55. (Price elasticities are negative numbers because consumption tends to decline as price rises.)

An exact measurement of elasticity is rarely needed, but we often need a general idea of how responsive buyers are to price. For this purpose, it is convenient to put elasticities into broad categories, using elasticity of –1, called *unit elasticity*, as the dividing point. Demand with elasticity smaller than 1 (in absolute value) is termed *relatively inelastic* demand. If elasticity exceeds 1 in absolute value, it is referred to as *relatively elastic*. Accordingly, the demand for potatoes, with elasticity roughly estimated at –0.55, is relatively inelastic. In contrast, the elasticity of demand for lettuce (see Table 1-1) has been estimated at about –2.58, so the demand for lettuce is relatively elastic.

Differences in Elasticity

The way buyers respond to changes in price depends on the characteristics of products and on the buyers' attitudes toward them. Things like potatoes, which most people

TABLE 1-1   Elasticity of Demand for Selected Farm Products

Product	Elasticity of Demand	
	Price	Income
Cabbage	−0.25	n.a.
Potatoes	−0.27	0.15
Wool	−0.33	0.27
Peanuts	−0.38	0.44
Eggs	−0.43	0.57
Onions	−0.44	0.58
Milk	−0.49	0.50
Butter	−0.62	0.37
Oranges	−0.62	0.83
Corn	−0.63	n.a.
Cream	−0.69	1.72
Fresh cucumbers	−0.70	0.70
Apples	−1.27	1.32
Peaches	−1.49	1.43
Fresh tomatoes	−2.22	0.24
Lettuce	−2.58	0.88
Fresh peas	−2.83	1.05

n.a. = not available.
SOURCE: Estimated by the U.S. Department of Agriculture.

view as food staples, have relatively inelastic demands. People believe they need a certain amount in their diet, so they are reluctant to cut back when price rises. By the same token, because they are already consuming about as much as they want, they find little use for more when price falls.

In contrast, things viewed as luxuries have relatively elastic demands, because people easily cut back when price rises and are delighted at the chance to enjoy more when lower prices permit. Among farm products, the demand for fruits and fresh vegetables tends to be relatively elastic. The demand for fresh peaches, for example, is estimated to be −1.49, nearly five times that of potatoes.

Demand elasticity also depends on how products are related to each other. Products that have good substitutes tend to have relatively elastic demands, because even small increases in price lead large numbers of consumers to desert the product in favor of the now cheaper substitute. A vegetable like fresh peas has a relatively elastic demand because a family can eat many other fresh vegetables when peas are expensive. These factors are reflected in the demand elasticities recorded in Table 1-1. We see that staple products like potatoes and corn have relatively inelastic demands, but the individual fruits and vegetables that are deemed less essential or that have many close substitutes have relatively elastic demand.

Elasticity of Derived Demand

So far, we have been discussing the elasticity of demand when raw farm products are purchased directly from the farm. Most of these products are bought by canneries, flour mills, cotton mills, and other processors. Even unprocessed fruits and vegetables require transportation, packaging, and retailing costs before they reach the table.

TABLE 1-2   Percent Farm Share in Final Retail Value of Food Products

All Food	Bakery and Cereal	Meat	Fruits and Vegetables	Dairy Products	Poultry
20	5	30	18	30	39

NOTE: *Figures are percent of final retail price received by farmers.*
SOURCE: U.S. Department of Agriculture, *Agricultural Statistics*, 2002 (Washington, D.C.: Government Printing Office, 2002).

As Table 1-2 shows, on average, the original farm value is only about 20 percent of the retail price of food items. This small proportion further reduces the elasticity of demand for farm products. To see why this is so, consider frozen peas, a processed product with demand elasticity at retail of about –2.0. This elasticity means that a 5 percent reduction in the price of frozen peas at the supermarket will tend to induce buyers to increase their consumption of frozen peas by about 10 percent. However, if frozen peas are typical, the value of the raw peas is only about 20 percent of the retail price, and a reduction of 5 percent in the *farm* price of peas will produce only about a 1 percent reduction in the retail price of frozen peas. Given the retail elasticity of –2, the 1 percent reduction in price at the supermarket will induce consumers to buy only 2 percent more frozen peas, and frozen food processors need purchase only 2 percent more raw peas to satisfy the demand. At the farm level, then, the 5 percent decline in price brought only a 2 percent increase in the sale of raw peas, and elasticity of demand for raw peas is only –0.4, despite the highly elastic retail demand for frozen peas.

This relationship holds for all derived demands. In general, the smaller the farm share in retail price is, the lower the elasticity of demand is for the farm product, and demand for raw farm products tends to be inelastic even when retail demand for the final product is highly elastic.

Commodities with Several Uses

When products are used for more than one purpose, demand elasticity varies among uses, depending on whether buyers consider the particular use a necessity or a luxury and on whether the product has good substitutes for that particular use. For example, wheat is used for bread flour and for poultry feed. In its use for flour, wheat is a necessity, and because of its gluten content, it has no good substitute. In fact, recipes for rye, corn, and other non-wheat breads call for the addition of wheat flour to make the dough cohesive. As a result, demand for wheat by flour mills is relatively inelastic. As poultry feed, however, wheat is readily replaced by corn, oats, sorghum grains, and a raft of other substitutes, so the demand for wheat as feed grain is relatively elastic.

The overall elasticity of demand for the product is the average of elasticities in the several uses, weighted by the quantity purchased for each use. Because most wheat is used for flour, its overall demand is relatively inelastic, despite the relatively high elasticity of its demand for use as poultry feed.

Elasticity and the Allocation of Available Crops

When the output of any crop declines, price rises and buyers purchase less, but not all uses are cut back equally. Consumption is reduced the most in uses with the highest elasticity, meaning in the less essential uses, or where the product can be readily replaced

TABLE 1-3 Allocation of Wheat in 2000 and 2001

| | Total Food and Feed | | Human Food | | Animal Feed | |
Year	Million Bushels	Percent Change	Million Bushels	Percent Change	Million Bushels	Percent Change
2000	2,223		956		298	
2001	1,958	−22	950	−1	225	−25

SOURCE: U.S. Department of Agriculture, *Agricultural Statistics*, 2002 (Washington, D.C.: U.S. Government Printing Office, 2002).

by close substitutes. Conversely, when output expands, price falls and consumption increases, but the increase is relatively smaller where demand is inelastic, and it is relatively larger for lower-priority uses and for uses where the now cheaper product can replace expensive substitutes.

This principle can be seen in Table 1-3. When the wheat crop declined 22 percent between 2000 and 2001, only 1 percent less wheat went into human food. In contrast, the use of wheat for animal feed declined by 25 percent.

Other Factors That Affect Demand

In addition to price, purchases are affected by the total number of consumers; by the incomes they have to spend; by the prices of substitutes; by fads, fashions, and consumer tastes; and—for things like soybeans that have important industrial uses—by the state of industrial technology.

Income Elasticity

As with prices, the effect of changes in income on buying is expressed in terms of elasticity. Income elasticity of demand is the percentage change in quantity purchased to be expected in response to a 1 percent rise in real income. An income elasticity of 1 is characteristic of a commodity whose purchase expands in proportion to rising income. When income doubles, so does the amount purchased. Income elasticity less than 1 means that the amount purchased rises less than in proportion to income. When income doubles, the amount purchased does not double. Income elasticity less than 1 is characteristic of staples that even low-income families consume in quantity. When income rises, consumption of the commodity rises little, if at all. Income elasticity greater than 1 means that amounts purchased rise more than in proportion to income. When income doubles, the amount purchased more than doubles. Elasticity greater than 1 is characteristic of fancy products and luxury goods—lobster, for example, whose consumption expands greatly with rising income. (Unlike price elasticity, most income elasticities are positive numbers because consumption of most commodities rises with income.)

Income elasticities for a number of farm products are given in Table 1-1. It is clear that demand for basic staples like potatoes and onions has low income elasticity, whereas demand for cream, fruit, and fresh vegetables is characterized by high income elasticity.

We should note, however, that rising income affects the *composition* of the diet more than it does the total amount of food consumed. Among families that are so poor that they have difficulty getting enough to eat, food consumption grows rapidly when their earnings increase. Once earnings exceed the poverty level though, families tend to shift to more expensive food. For example, although high-income families eat, on average, very little more food than do poor families, they eat nearly three times as much sirloin steak.

Demand Elasticity and Farm Incomes

Low elasticity of demand has important consequences for the behavior of farm incomes. Unlike most manufactured goods, which are priced first with production adjusted to whatever sales materialize, farm crops are grown first and then thrown on the market for whatever prices they will fetch. As production varies from year to year, low demand elasticity causes the prices of farm products to rise and fall more than in proportion to production, so the total dollar value of a smaller crop is greater than that of a larger crop.

This can be tested in Figure 1-1: According to the demand curve, the production of 168 pounds of potatoes per capita would bring a price of about $4 per hundredweight, which would make the value of the crop about $6.72 per consumer. On the other hand, a crop of 180 pounds per consumer would bring the price down to about $3.50, and the crop would be worth only $6.30 per consumer. In short, an increase in production would reduce the total value of the crop to farmers. For this reason, natural year-to-year fluctuations in growing conditions make farming very much a boom or bust proposition.

II. SUPPLY

Just as demand represents the reactions of buyers to prices, incomes, and other factors, *supply* represents the reactions of producers to prices and costs. However, an important difference is found in the speed at which these reactions occur. Buyers tend to adapt quickly to new conditions, but producers often need time to revise plans and production schedules or to acquire new facilities and equipment. For this reason, it is useful to distinguish three different supply situations facing farmers.

Harvest Supply: The Very Short Run

Once crops are mature and ready for market, the maximum quantity available is already standing in the fields, and no action by farmers can yield output beyond that quantity. This sets an upper limit to what can be sold, but the physically available maximum is rarely harvested. It seldom pays farmers to strip fields so thoroughly that every last particle is collected. Some crops mature over a period of several weeks, and growers must decide when the time is best for harvest and whether it is worthwhile to return to the fields for a second harvest a week or so later. Clearly, high prices at harvest time make it profitable to harvest a greater proportion of the potential crop, whereas low prices make careful harvest unprofitable and often lead to outright abandonment of low-yield acreage, because it would cost more to harvest than sale of the crop would bring. In general, however, once a crop is standing in the field ready for market, the harvested supply is extremely inelastic.

Short-Run Supply and Production Costs

Cost Structure

Like those of any business, the costs of farming are of two general types. Some costs, once incurred, are fixed regardless of output. Such *fixed costs* include taxes, interest on farm mortgage, depreciation of equipment, and similar expenses that are not affected by the number of acres planted. Indeed, fixed costs would remain as charges against the farm even if production were abandoned entirely.

Variable costs, on the other hand, are zero as long as nothing is produced, but they rise sharply when production is undertaken. This sharp initial increase includes the costs of planting, acquiring materials, and other costs that would not be incurred if the farm remained idle. An important component of this initial variable cost consists of the labor of the farm owner and family members, or the salaries of hired managers of corporate farms.

Once these start-up costs have been incurred, output can be expanded by relatively small increases in outlay for seed, fertilizer, herbicides, labor, fuel, and similar items. These costs rise slowly as more output is produced, but a limit does apply to what can be grown from given facilities. As this limit is approached, additional output can be obtained only by more intensive labor to provide greater care of the crop, the application of extra fertilizer, or by increases in the application of other inputs. All of this means sharp increases in variable costs.

Costs of a Corn Grower

Typical costs of growing corn on U.S. farms are given in Table 1-4. Clearly, the more acreage that is planted, the more seed, fertilizer, and similar inputs are required, so these are variable costs. Altogether, variable costs amounted to $160.71 per acre planted.

Fixed costs are costs such as interest on farm debt, depreciation of farm equipment and facilities, the rental value of land devoted to production, and other charges that

TABLE 1-4 Costs of Growing Corn, Average of U.S. Farms	
ITEM	COST (1996 $)
Variable Costs per Acre Planted	
Seed	$24.06
Fertilizer, lime, gypsum	53.13
Chemicals	26.82
Fuel, lube, electricity	21.14
Repairs	17.00
Hired labor	8.37
Other variable costs	10.19
Variable Costs per Acre Planted	**$160.71**
Fixed Costs	
General farm overhead	$7,520
Taxes and insurance	11,350
Depreciation	17,475
Interest	8,760
Land	42,740
Operator's labor	13,390
Fixed Costs	**$101,235**

SOURCE: Adapted from Resource Economics Division, Economic Research Service, *Farm Business Economic Report*, 1996 (Washington, D.C.: U.S. Department of Agriculture, April 1999).

once incurred do not vary with acreage planted. The fixed costs in the table are estimated for a typical farm of 500 acres.

Average and Marginal Costs

Total cost is translated into average and marginal cost in Figure 1-2. *Marginal cost*
(MC) is the rate at which total cost rises as production is increased. Once production is
under way, additional corn can be raised for only the variable cost required to plant the
additional acreage. This keeps the marginal cost low until all of the acreage available to
the farm has been planted. In the illustration, this yields about 65,000 bushels. To raise
still more corn, greater and greater outlays are needed to extract additional output
from existing land and facilities, and the marginal cost rises more and more sharply.
Average variable cost (AVC) is high at low levels of production because start-up costs
are spread over limited output. As production expands, however, these start-up costs
are spread over more and more bushels of corn, pulling down the average variable cost
per bushel. As production enters the range where marginal cost rises steeply, the average variable cost stops falling and begins to rise.

Because fixed costs do not change as output expands, *average fixed cost* is inversely
proportional to output. *Average total cost* (ATC) is merely the sum of average variable
and average fixed costs.

Profit Maximization and Supply Elasticity

The most profitable production plan for the farm is to produce the output at which marginal cost is brought into equality with the price the farmer expects to get when the crop
is finally harvested. When the price of corn is expected to be $3.50 per bushel, the farmer
would plant a crop of about 92,000 bushels, and because this price is well above the average total cost, if all goes according to plan, a substantial profit will result. On the other
hand, if the farmer expects a price of $2.50, the most profitable plan is to harvest about
85,000 bushels. Because the resulting average total cost is about $3.60 a bushel, even if
everything works according to plan, the farmer will lose money. Despite the expected loss,
however, the farm continues to operate because fixed costs will be accrued regardless of
how much is planted. Because the expected price more than covers the variable cost of

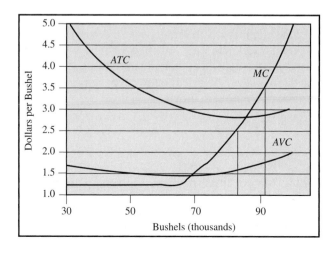

FIGURE 1-2   Costs of a Corn
Grower

*SOURCE: Based on estimates by
U.S. Department of Agriculture,
Economic Research Service, vari-
ous years.*

planting 85,000 bushels, the farmer will lose less by growing the crop than by abandoning production entirely. If the price falls below about $1.50, however, it would be impossible to recover even the variable costs, so the farmer would be better off producing nothing. At the price of $2.99 that prevailed during 1996 when the data of Table 1-4 were gathered, the farm would produce about 87,000 bushels and would reap a small profit.

The cost curves in Figure 1-2 are consistent with the data in Table 1-4 and are typical of agricultural production. Marginal cost rises so steeply after all land is engaged in production that even wide year-to-year swings in price exert little influence on the output of any individual grower, at least so long as the farm continues in operation. In other words, if a farm operates at all, it produces nearly the capacity output obtainable from land and facilities. The result is a low elasticity of supply. According to the figure, a 40 percent price increase from $2.50 to $3.50 induces only an 8 percent expansion of output. This amounts to a supply elasticity of only 0.2.

In fact, supply is more elastic than the costs would suggest, because many farms produce more than one crop. For example, corn and soybeans grow on the same type of soil, and many farms grow both. Hog growers also typically grow corn. Some farms diversify production to protect against the failure of any one crop, and some grow several crops that mature at different times so that more efficient use can be made of harvesting equipment.

In any case, the proportions in which the different crops are grown vary in response to expected prices. For instance, the expectation of higher prices for soybeans compared to corn leads farms that grow both to devote more land to soybeans and less to corn. The expectation of high prices for hogs relative to corn leads hog growers to increase the number of hogs and to buy, rather than grow, the extra corn.

Market Equilibrium

The interaction of short-run supply with demand governs the year-to-year behavior of production and prices. Equilibrium price and output comprise a sort of target in the market, indicating values toward which actual price and output are continually pushed, but it should be understood that equilibrium prices and outputs are rarely observed in practice. For one thing, supply deals with production *plans* rather than the eventual outcome of the plans. The most farmers can do is plant and cultivate crops in a manner calculated to earn the greatest return under normal conditions. How these plans turn out depends on weather, insect damage, blight, and other growing conditions.

In addition, planting decisions are based on *expected* prices as they depend on expected demand, but consumers frequently do the unexpected. A shortage of substitutes, an unexpected rise in popularity, or the introduction of new ways to use the product—including new industrial uses—increases demand and raises prices above expectations. Likewise, declining demand leads to prices below expectations. An example of the resulting oscillation in price and output is shown in Figure 1-3.

Long-Run Supply

The Role of Average Total Cost

When low prices enable farms to recover more than their average variable costs but leave insufficient margin to recover total cost, farms will continue to operate at a loss. They can remain in business by letting buildings and equipment go without adequate

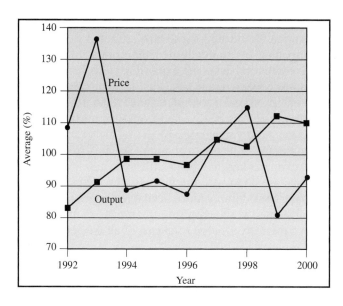

FIGURE 1-3   Price and Output of Onions

SOURCE: U.S. Department of Agriculture, Agricultural Statistics, various years.

repair and by digging into financial reserves to meet family living expenses. Sooner or later though, buildings become unusable and equipment wears out. At this point, farmers must decide whether to continue in operation. Unless the prospects are strong enough to promise recovery of the needed additional investment together with a satisfactory profit, it is clearly better to abandon the farm than to waste more money on a losing proposition.

This means that although the initial response to a fall in agricultural prices is small—we have estimated the elasticity of the short-run supply of corn at 0.2—if the outlook for lower prices continues for several years, output will decline much more as farms abandon production. This makes long-run supply relatively elastic.

Response to Shifts in Demand

Because of the three different supply situations that characterize agriculture, adjustments of prices and output to changes in consumer demand involve a sequence of events that takes several years to complete. Buyers whose demand has risen find themselves initially confronted by an inelastic harvest supply. Although rising prices signal greater demand, growers can market only the result of production plans laid many months previously. The most they can do is to strip fields with greater care than would have been profitable at lower prices and to harvest low-yield acreage that otherwise would have been abandoned.

Despite their small immediate effect, the rising prices perform two important functions. First, rising prices reallocate available supplies among alternative demands. Buyers who can do so shift to (now) cheaper substitutes. The reduction of purchases by these buyers leaves more of the scarce crop for essential uses. Second, the higher prices encourage growers to plan for a larger crop next season by increasing the intensity of cultivation and by shifting some fields from other crops to the more valuable use. By the time of the next harvest, these plans will have materialized in greater output, and prices will drop from the peak they had reached.

If the higher prices continue over several years, production is further expanded as farms invest in additional equipment and new farms are attracted to the profitable crop. This expansion is accompanied by gradually declining prices but continues as long as prices remain above average total cost. The expansion slows and approaches a halt as prices fall to levels that just cover average total cost.

This adjustment process has profound economic significance. Raising crops requires that land, labor, and other resources be diverted from manufacturing and other uses. Consumers who want the commodity signify this by paying higher prices. However, time is needed to transfer resources from one use to another. The most growers can do at harvest time is to employ a few extra workers and buy a little extra gasoline to squeeze as much as possible from crops that are already in the field. By the next season, growers can expand production and make considerably more available. Over a period of years, still more resources can be transferred to the crop, and the transfer will continue until price falls to the level that just covers the average total cost of all the resources used in production.

Reduced demand produces a sequence of responses in the opposite direction. Declining demand is signaled by falling prices, indicating that consumers would prefer fewer resources devoted to the crop. However, most resources have been irretrievably sunk into production of the current crop. The most growers can do at this point is to save some small amount of labor and gasoline by the abandonment of low-yield acreage and by less intensive harvest of the remainder. This saves few resources, but in planning for the next season, growers who find that they can no longer expect to recover their average variable costs shift labor, fuel, and materials to other crops or release them for employment elsewhere. Nothing can be done at this point about resources already sunk into buildings and farm equipment. As time passes though, these wear out and are not replaced. Labor and other resources that would otherwise be employed in fabricating buildings and farm equipment are freed for employment elsewhere in uses that are more valuable to consumers.

III. IMPROVEMENTS IN TECHNOLOGY

It is not enough for an industry merely to move resources in response to changes in demand. It must also keep the productivity of those resources as high as possible. The most important source of increasing productivity is the introduction of new, more efficient methods.

The rate of technical improvement in any industry involves two distinct aspects: (1) how rapidly firms in the industry originate and develop new production methods, and (2) how rapidly firms adopt and put to use new methods as they become available.

At first glance, agriculture has a poor record. The intensely competitive structure and the relatively small scale of operation characteristic of farming simply do not lend themselves to research and development. Expensive laboratories and large research budgets, commonplace in many large industrial firms, are beyond the means of even the largest grower. If improvements had to wait until they could be developed on farms, agricultural productivity today would not be much ahead of what it was a century ago.

Fortunately, it has not been necessary for farmers to develop their own technical improvements. Part of the job has been undertaken by the laboratories of state universities and government agricultural research stations. To a far greater extent, improvements have arisen from the work of farm equipment manufacturers, chemical manufacturers, and other suppliers to the field of modern agriculture. Although farmers originate little themselves, they do provide a ready market for improvements once they have been developed and demonstrated. The result has been a rate of growth in productivity that has outstripped other industries.

The Profit Incentive

The strong incentive to adopt better farming methods is the profit available to the first growers who introduce them. Suppose a corn farmer finds that by the outlay of, say, $4,000 for a new fertilizer, he can grow 3,000 more bushels of corn on his acreage. At a price of $3 per bushel, this adds $9,000 to the value of his crop and $5,000 to his annual net income. Because his individual contribution to the total supply of corn is negligible, his action will not affect the price of corn, and until others take up the new method, the entire $5,000 is pure profit.

Innovation and Prices

Unfortunately for the corn grower, the new profitable situation carries within it the seeds of its own destruction. When other growers see the advantages of the new method, their eagerness for greater profit will lead them to imitate it. As more and more farms adopt the new method, the increase in supply becomes substantial and prices fall. The price decline continues until a new equilibrium is approached at the new, lower cost of production.

The long-run decline in price following technical innovation has a number of important consequences. First, it means that growers must be quick to change, for exceptional profits are available only to the first growers to introduce the new method. As other farms follow suit, the rising supply lowers prices and wipes out the extra gains. Just to break even, all farmers must now adopt the cheaper new method. Ultimately, growers have no real choice about whether or not to adopt the new method. As prices fall toward the new lower-cost level, farms still using the old higher-cost methods are no longer able to cover their costs of production. They must adopt the new method merely to survive, and if they hold back too long, they are driven out of business by losses.

Above all, as prices fall to the new lower level, the entire gain from the new method is passed on to consumers. Growers who first adopted the new method for the sake of extra profits and those who followed along in self-defense have combined in an action that has not only increased the productivity of resources but, with production at the new lower average total cost, has also eliminated the extra profit and has delivered the entire cost savings to society at large in the form of lower prices.

Broiler Chickens: An Example of Innovation

Continual improvement in production methods is one of the most striking features of American agriculture. A good example is the revolution in the production of broiler chickens shown in Table 1-5. It is probably difficult for modern readers to realize that 50 or 60 years ago, chicken was too expensive for everyday use and was generally served only on holidays and special occasions. In fact, during one presidential campaign, one of the candidates expressed his devotion to the prosperity of the voters by the

TABLE 1-5   Production Costs, Production, and Price of U.S. Broiler Chickens, 1934–2000

| Year | Required per 100 Pounds of Chicken | | Production (pounds per capita) | Price[1] (per pound) |
	Feed (in pounds)	Worker-Hours		
1934	n.a.	n.a.	0.76	2.24
1940	420	8.5	3.13	1.92
1950	330	5.1	12.82	1.67
1960	250	1.3	32.76	0.802
1970	219	0.5	52.27	0.660
1980	192	0.1	68.48	0.553
1990	n.a.	n.a.	103.44	0.406
2000	n.a.	n.a.	151.51	0.336

n.a. = not available
[1]*Price of chicken divided by the Consumer Price Index to adjust for inflation.*
SOURCE: Adapted from U.S. Department of Agriculture, *Agricultural Statistics*, 2002 and preceding years (Washington, D.C.: U.S. Government Printing Office, 2002).

promise of "a chicken in every pot." In those days, broiler chickens were raised on farms where they ran freely in yards, competing with one another for food, with heavy losses from accident, predators, and disease, and with high labor costs for care. It took 16 weeks and 12 pounds of feed to raise one 3.5-pound chicken, and it took as much as 8.5 worker-hours to produce 100 pounds of output.

In about 1950, a revolution began in commercial broiler production. Chickens were raised indoors in individual cages. This eliminated wasteful competition for feed, reduced disease and depredation, permitted automated delivery of feed, and substantially reduced labor costs. By 1980, the labor time required per 100 pounds of chicken was barely 1 percent of what it had been 40 years earlier, and it now took only 7 weeks to bring a bird to market weight. These lower costs expanded supply, with a resulting fall in the market price of chicken. Adjusted for inflation, the price of chicken fell from $2.24 per pound in 1934 to $0.336 by 2000. With the decline in price, consumers ate 200 times as much chicken in 2000 as they had 65 years earlier. Chicken, no longer a holiday dish, is now the cheapest meat in the store, and chicken has become the rival of hamburger in fast-food outlets.

Table 1-6 emphasizes that the story of broiler chicken is typical of what has happened to agricultural productivity. The continual introduction of new methods has reduced the production cost of virtually every crop. Today, it takes less than a tenth as much labor to grow an acre of corn as it did 80 years ago, and the acre yields 5 times as much corn. Three times as much wheat can be raised with one-sixth the labor, and a worker-hour of effort yields 13 times as much milk and 100 times as much turkey as it did 90 years ago.

Scale of Operation

When technical innovation reduces farming costs by replacing labor with machinery, the result is lower variable costs but higher charges for interest, depreciation, taxes, and other fixed costs. If lower average total cost is to result, these higher fixed costs must be spread over a larger output.

The influence of technical development on the scale and number of U.S. farms is shown in Table 1-7.

TABLE 1-6 Productivity of Labor and Land in U.S. Agriculture: Selected Crops and Livestock, 1910–2001

Crop	1910–1914	1945–1949	1965–1969	1982–1986	1996–2001
Corn					
labor-hr per acre	35.2	19.2	6.1	3.1	n.a.
bu per acre	26.0	36.1	48.7	109.3	132.9
Wheat					
labor-hr per acre	15.2	5.7	2.9	2.5	n.a.
bu per acre	14.4	16.9	25.9	37.1	40.7
Potatoes					
labor-hr per acre	76.0	68.5	45.9	32.6	n.a.
cwt per acre	59.8	117.8	205.2	283.9	356
Sugar beets					
labor-hr per acre	128.0	85.0	35.0	20.0	n.a.
tons per acre	10.6	13.6	17.4	20.4	21.6
Cotton					
labor-hr per acre	116.0	83.0	35.0	5.0	n.a.
lbs. per acre	201.0	273.0	505.0	581.0	656.5
Soybeans					
labor-hr per acre	n.a.	8.0	4.8	3.2	n.a.
bu per acre	n.a.	19.6	24.2	30.7	38.3
Milk					
labor-hr per cow	146.0	129.0	84.0	24.0	n.a.
cwt per cow	38.4	49.9	82.6	127.3	172.9
Hogs					
labor-hr per cwt	3.6	3.0	1.6	0.3	n.a.
Turkeys					
labor-hr per cwt	31.4	13.1	1.6	0.2	n.a.

n.a. = not available.
SOURCE: U.S. Department of Agriculture, *Agricultural Statistics* (Washington, D.C.: U.S. Government Printing Office, various issues).

When farms grow larger, what happens to the total number in operation depends on demand for the product. As prices fall, total consumption increases in keeping with demand elasticity. Consumption also rises with growing population and increasing incomes. If demand is sufficiently elastic, and if income and population grow fast enough, the market for farm products can expand enough to maintain, or even to increase, the number of farms in operation, despite the larger scale of operations.

Displacement of Farm Labor

Until about 1920, population and income grew faster than farm productivity, and the number of farms increased despite the growth in average size. After 1920, as technical improvements accelerated and population grew more slowly, the number of farms shrank as the average size increased. In the last 40 years, the average size of U.S. farms has doubled, but the total number of farms has been cut by more than half. As the productivity of

TABLE 1-7 Number and Size of Farms and U.S. Farm Employment, 1880–2000

Year	Number of Farms	Average Acreage per Farm	Farm Employment (in thousands)
1880	4,008,000	133.7	10,100
1900	5,740,000	146.6	12,800
1920	6,453,000	148.5	13,400
1940	6,104,000	174.5	11,000
1960	5,388,000	215.5	7,100
1970	2,730,000	389.5	4,200
1990	2,140,000	461.0	2,891
2000	2,172,000	434.0	2,930

SOURCES: U.S. Department of Commerce, *Census of Agriculture* (Washington, D.C.: U.S. Government Printing Office, appropriate years). 2000 from U.S. Department of Agriculture, *Agricultural Statistics,* 2002; Washington, D.C.: U.S. Government Printing Office, 2002.

farm labor rises, any given amount of crop can be grown with the help of fewer people. Unless consumption expands proportionately, rising productivity means fewer people are needed on farms. The history of declining farm labor is shown in the last column of Table 1-7.

It is the market that keeps the number of people engaged in agriculture in balance with productivity and demand. Increasing supply reduces farm prices and the earnings of farm workers. Farm people with marketable skills, especially young people, leave the farm for more profitable opportunities elsewhere. Those without other skills find themselves trapped in low-income farming or are forced off the farm into the city where, without marketable skills, many are added to the welfare rolls.

The fate of farmers is an excellent illustration of two important aspects of competitive markets. Competition generates inexorable pressure to extract greater output from available resources and passes these productivity gains on to consumers in the form of lower prices and higher standards of living. However, in doing so, the market operates without regard for the fate or the feelings of the people involved. The supply and demand for farm labor are rigorously balanced by the competitive market, regardless of what happens to families caught in the adjustment. Nowhere does the market, left to its own devices, take into account the human cost of this process.

Other Social Costs of Modern Agriculture

The increasing size of modern farms has brought profound changes to agriculture. Increasingly, commercial farming of specialized crops is replacing the more diversified agriculture of the old-fashioned family farm. Intense specialized farming, in turn, creates problems. It increases the danger of soil exhaustion as intensive use of fertilizer and single-crop operations replace crop rotation. In addition, contamination of streams and groundwater by runoff from chemical fertilizers and insecticides puts water supplies at risk and jeopardizes wildlife habitats. The lower cost of mechanical harvesting has led to the adaptation of many varieties of food to the requirements of machines, often at the expense of nutritional value and flavor.

Some of these problems reflect more on the tastes and preferences of consumers than they do on farm technology. If people are willing to buy cheap tomatoes with the flavor and consistency of red baseballs rather than pay a little more for flavorful tomatoes that are too delicate for anything rougher than hand harvesting, competitive agriculture will provide for their preferences. By the same token, more and more modern consumers are willing to pay for food raised organically without the use of artificial fertilizers, chemical herbicides, and pesticides. In addition, the supply of such products is increasing steadily as farmers see the profit in the new opportunity.

Other problems are fundamental to the nature of competitive agriculture though, and consumers are powerless to change farming practices. These social costs arise because competitive producers pay attention only to costs that they themselves must pay. Any costs imposed on others count for nothing in the farmer's calculations. If farmers can improve their own position by shifting costs from themselves onto society at large, competition will force them to do so if they want to stay in business. The competitive market provides no mechanism to balance gains in output and lower prices against higher social costs.

Irrigation systems offer an example of the problem. Irrigation provides a stable and ample water supply and does for crops what a lawn sprinkler does for a home garden. Irrigation increases the yield of the individual farm, yet its widespread adoption creates problems for the rest of society. It depletes the water table, lowers the level of lakes and ponds, and increases the problems of the municipal water supply.

Another serious problem is water pollution from farm runoff. This not only contaminates rivers and streams, it also makes a serious contribution to the destruction of fish habitats in ocean beds. A study by the Pew Oceans Commission identified runoff from farms and feedlots as among the fastest-growing sources of oceanic pollution. However, no invoice is presented to farmers for the wider consequences of their actions. Individually, farmers can take account only of the private profit potential of the method, and they find themselves required by competition to adopt it. Yet the collective result is a higher cost to the rest of society.

Concern is increasing that extensive use of agricultural chemicals is dangerously polluting water and wildlife habitats and that consumer health is affected by growth hormones injected into cattle, by antibiotics used in animal feed, and by genetically modified crops. The market cannot prevent individual farmers from engaging in such practices. Indeed, the forces of competition compel individual farmers to employ them. Any limitation or control must be imposed on all farmers from outside the market.

In 1999, methyl parathion and azinphon methyl, two pesticides that had long been used under heavy regulation, were banned outright for use on food crops ranging from apples to turnips. It would have been impossible for farmers themselves to abolish the use of these chemicals. As long as they were available, individual growers had to use them to stay competitive, despite the obvious damage they inflicted. It required action by the government to outlaw their use.

Although a thorough discussion of issues of food safety and environmental pollution far exceeds the scope of this chapter, it is necessary to recognize that product safety and pollution are important aspects of the behavior of any industry. In this respect, untrammeled competition as exemplified by agriculture has a poor record.

IV. GOVERNMENT POLICY TOWARD AGRICULTURE

Price Supports

Left to its own devices, agriculture would function as a nearly perfectly competitive industry. In practice, however, almost nowhere in the world is agriculture free of substantial governmental interference. The problems wrought by technical innovation have generated political pressure on governments everywhere to intervene.

Since it was first instituted in the 1930s as part of the New Deal, U.S. agricultural policy has largely focused on supporting the prices farmers receive for their products at some target level above what would be determined in a competitive market. This has been accomplished by a mixture of techniques. The government has restricted supply by limiting the acreage that could be planted to certain crops—sometimes by outright limitation, sometimes by paying farmers to plant fewer acres than they otherwise would. Sometimes government has bought up enough crops to raise the farm price to the desired level. Under other laws, the government has allowed farmers to produce and market their crops freely and then paid each grower a subsidy to make up the difference between the resulting market price and the target level. Finally, the government has encouraged producers of certain products to join together in monopoly marketing organizations and agree among themselves about how much to produce and bring to market.

Such programs are expensive. Over the 5-year period from 1996 to 2000, the support of agricultural prices directly cost taxpayers an average of more than $14 billion per year. In addition, consumers have had to pay more for some of the food on their tables.

How much do farmers benefit from all this? The rationale for farm policy was to relieve the suffering caused by rapidly increasing agricultural productivity. Yet the history of agriculture has been a continuous story of small farmers being driven out, and clearly those no longer on farms can hardly benefit from higher farm prices. Even most of those who remain on farms gain little from the program. The nature of price supports directs the benefits toward the largest, most successful growers rather than toward the poor and weak who really need help.

A recent analysis by the Environmental Working Group indicated that over the 5-year period from 1996 to 2000, the smallest 80 percent of all farms received less than 16 percent of total agricultural payments. This amounted to an average of only about $1,000 per farm. In contrast, the largest 1 percent of farms received 19 percent of payments, which amounted to an average of almost $11,000 per farm. The 8 largest recipients of the government's agricultural largess received annual payments that exceeded $1 million each. The largest recipient of all gathered in an average of $4.6 million a year over the 5-year period! (On their Web site provided at the end of this chapter, the group lists by name every individual in every state and county who receives governmental payments, and it also indicates the amount received.)

This highly unequal distribution of benefits is a direct consequence of programs that pay for reduced acreage, that buy up excess production, and that directly subsidize prices. When the government pays to reduce acreage, the largest payments necessarily go to the farms with the most acreage. When the government buys surpluses or subsidizes prices, the greatest payments go to farms with the largest production. Moreover, this is only part of the picture, because where output is restricted, consumers must pay higher prices for food. Nobody knows how much this amounts to—it has been estimated at many times the value of the direct payments—but whatever the amount is, it is distributed among farmers in proportion to the size of their operations, and so is concentrated in the hands of the largest producers.

Dissatisfaction with a system that subsidized large producers and provided little or nothing for small farms engendered the Agricultural Market Transition Act of 1996. The idea of the act was to wean American agriculture from price supports and to stimulate a return to agriculture governed by market forces. According to the act, farmers who would contract to use their land exclusively for agricultural purposes and who also would agree to certain measures of conservation and wetland protection would be eligible for direct cash "transition" payments with no further strings attached. Farmers would then be free to grow what they liked and as much as they liked in response to the market.

During the first 2 years of the act, commodity prices were high, and farmers were delighted to accept the transition payments in addition to their income from the profitable sale of crops. But when prices dropped in 1998 and 1999, farmers turned again to the government. The Congressional response was the grant of billions of dollars in emergency aid. When the 1996 act elapsed in 2002, Congress completely reversed its policy with the Farm Security and Rural Investment Act of 2002. Not only did the act restore the old system of agricultural subsidies, but it provided a $50 billion increase over the next 10 years. The system of agricultural subsidy has been changed from its traditional version in little but name.

Other Price-Support Measures

The prices of a broad array of commodities, ranging from citrus fruit to nuts, are set by marketing orders issued by the Secretary of Agriculture. These orders enable producers to organize *marketing boards*, which are given broad powers to control the production and marketing of designated commodities. Aside from professional baseball, marketing boards are the only unregulated legal monopolies permitted in the United States. The boards limit production, sometimes by restricting the quality or sizes of product that can be shipped. Some boards prop up prices by assigning quotas to individual producers and requiring that any additional output be placed "in reserve," usually to be exported at low prices. The political advantage of marketing boards is that they impose the entire cost of the program directly on consumers and avoid charges to the government budget.

The price of milk is supported by a combination of marketing order and government intervention. A marketing order by the secretary of agriculture sets the prices that dairies must pay dairy farmers for fluid milk destined for human consumption. The higher this price is set, the less milk dairies will buy, but the marketing order does little to control production. All milk that farmers cannot sell at the fixed price is sold at whatever price it will bring as industrial-grade milk to be manufactured into butter, cheese, and dried milk. The demand for industrial grade milk is, in turn, supported by loans extended to dairies by a government agency, the Commodity Credit Corporation (CCC). The CCC receives the manufactured dairy products in pledge for the loans.

When marketing conditions are poor, producers leave the products with the CCC rather than repay the loans, and the CCC accumulates a stock of the commodities. From time to time, the government passes on accumulated stocks of butter, cheese, and powdered milk to poor families.

Agricultural Policy and International Trade

The United States is by no means alone in its subsidy of agriculture. Intervention in the field of agriculture is part of the policy of nearly every developed country in the world. Japan protects its rice growers by using quotas that restrict imports to 10 percent of consumption and applies a 500 percent tariff to all rice imported in excess of the quota. Under the Common Agricultural Policy (CAP) of the European Union, the 35 percent of European farm income that comes from government subsidies exceeds even the 20 percent in the United States. To protect its sugar growers, for example, the CAP pays farmers 50 euros (a little more than $50) per ton of harvested sugar beets. This is five times the world price. Basing CAP subsidies on each farm's output, moreover, is an incentive for overproduction that regularly results in mountains of surplus farm products.

These extensive agricultural subsidies make it particularly difficult to bring agriculture into conformity with the free market ideals of the World Trade Organization (WTO), an international organization established in 1994 to promulgate and arbitrate the rules of trade among nations. The main function of the WTO is to ensure that trade flows as smoothly and freely as possible. To bring agriculture more into line with competitive global markets, the WTO agreement requires governments to abandon policies that encourage excess production and to eliminate export subsidies that permit farmers to sell surplus production abroad at prices that are below the domestic market price. Domestic policies that have a direct effect on production were to be cut back by 20 percent by the year 2002. Governments may continue to direct payments to farmers as long as this is done in a way that does not stimulate production, but governments can make certain direct payments that are accompanied by the requirement that farmers limit production. Governments also may continue to provide such services as advice to farmers, research, disease control, road construction, and the like, but subsidies that permit farmers to sell abroad at prices below the domestic level must be phased out. Restriction of agricultural imports by quotas and other nontariff measures must be replaced by tariffs, but these tariffs can be set to provide an equivalent level of protection.

Friction and disagreements among nations about trade policies are channeled into an agreed dispute settlement process where trade practices are examined for conformity to WTO agreements. One serious, and so far unresolved, difference between the United States and the European Union deals with the question of genetically modified crops. The Europeans and several African nations refuse to allow them to be imported, largely on the ground that the nutritional safety of the products has not been demonstrated, whereas the U.S. position is that no scientific evidence shows that the products are unsafe.

Despite the fine words embodied in the WTO push for worldwide free trade, the consequences of existing agricultural policies have been disastrous for many farmers in the poor nations of the world. The Philippines, a charter member of WTO, opened its markets wide to foreign trade and investment. Instead of the expected improvement in living standards, however, farms were wiped out as small-scale farmers found subsidized farm products from the United States and Europe selling in Philippine markets at prices below the Philippine cost of production. According to the Institute for Agriculture and Trade Policy in Minneapolis, Minnesota, U.S.-produced corn sells in Mexico at 20 percent below the cost of production. The $3 billion subsidy of American cotton provides U.S. growers with an inflated price for every additional bale grown. Half of the resulting crop is exported, driving down world prices and destroying poor African cotton farmers in Mali, Benin, and Burkina Faso. CAP subsidies have the same effect on African and Caribbean sugar producers, who, despite their natural advantages in cultivation, must struggle to survive in the face of heavily subsidized European beet sugar.

According to estimates by the International Monetary Fund (IMF), withdrawal of farm subsidies and agricultural tariffs applied by rich countries would add about $120 billion to the global income of poor nations. An increase of only 1 percent in Africa's share of world exports would, according to the estimate, amount to $70 billion a year, an amount roughly five times what is provided to the region in foreign aid.

Unfortunately, this is much more easily said than done. Once in place, agricultural subsidies are extremely difficult to remove, or even to reduce, as was clearly demonstrated by the abortive 1996 attempt by the United States to wean agriculture away from subsidies.

Reform of the European CAP is proving equally difficult. The imminent addition of 10 new members of the EU threatens to bankrupt the CAP. The agricultural sector of Poland alone would wreck the EU budget if current farm subsidy rules apply. In view of this, Franz Fischer, agriculture commissioner for the European Union, has proposed a number of reforms including the gradual reduction of agricultural subsidies, their uncoupling from production, and a limit of 300,000 euros (a little more than $300,000) in subsidy payments to any individual farm. But no sooner were these proposals announced than European farmers and politicians rose in opposition. Clearly, changes are urgently needed, but the process will be slow and painful.

Conclusion

Left to itself, agriculture would be a highly competitive industry, and its performance would be, in many respects, almost ideal. Indeed, it is hard to imagine an industry better adapted to carry out the purely technical functions of producing products and allocating them among uses. Although harvest is subject to the vagaries of weather and random events, available supplies are rationed among users in accordance with consumer priorities as expressed by demand elasticities. At each stage of production, the greatest amount is extracted from available resources. In the very short run, when most costs have already been sunk into crops, relatively little can be done to adapt to consumer desires; however, given time, farmers shift output to match demand. Agriculture has a remarkable history of increasing the productivity of the resources it employs and passing on the increases to consumers in the form of lower prices. At the same time, land, labor, and other resources have been released for the production of other products. All of this has been accomplished with virtually no conscious collective planning, administrative direction, or political processes. Competitive pressure toward improvement is inexorable. New methods are not debated; rather, they simply impose themselves on the industry.

The same competitive process, however, sweeps along regardless of the fates of the people involved. The absence of social costs from the accounts of individual farms means that the search for cheaper methods can damage the environment and impose heavy costs on society at large. Moreover, the same rise in productivity that has brought cheaper food and higher living standards to consumers has been accompanied by serious problems of human displacement. When productivity grows more rapidly than the demand for farm products, people who have devoted their lives to agriculture are driven off the farm to fend for themselves as best they can.

Governments the world over have adopted special programs originally intended to alleviate the plight of farmers, but these programs have done little for the people who are most in need of help. Instead, the result has been to subsidize the largest farms, to induce inefficient use of land and labor, and to produce economic chaos in the pattern of world trade in food and fiber. On the international scene, the lavish subsidy of agricultural production by the United States, the European Union, and other developed nations undermines farming communities of the poorest nations of the world. This inhibits economic development in the third world, and contributes to discontent and resentment at the very time the developed countries are battling world terrorism.

Suggested Readings

Adamantopolous, Constintinous. 1997. *An Anatomy of the World Trade Organization.* London: Kluwer Law International.

Bormann, F. Herbert, and Stephen R. Kellert. 1991. *Ecology, Economics, Ethics: The Broken Circle.* New Haven, CT: Yale University Press.

Burger, Anna. 1994. *The Agriculture of the World.* Brookfield, VT: Avebury.

Cameron, James, and Karen Campbell, eds. 1998. *Dispute Resolution in the World Trade Organization.* London: Cameron.

Carlson, Gerald A., David Zilberman, and John A. Miranowski. 1993. *Agricultural and Environmental Resource Economics.* New York: Oxford University Press.

Cramer, Gail L., and Clarence W. Jensen. 1982. *Agricultural Economics and Agribusiness.* New York: Wiley.

Keesing, Donald. 1998. *Improving Trade Policy Reviews in the World Trade Organization.* Washington, DC: Institute for International Economics.

Knutson, Ronald K. et al. 2003. *Agriculture and Food Policy,* 5th ed. Upper Saddle River, NJ: Prentice Hall.

Reed, Michael R. 2001. *International Trade in Agricultural Products.* Upper Saddle River, NJ: Prentice Hall.

Some Useful Web Sites

Environmental Working Group: www.EWG.org

Institute for Agriculture and Trade Policy: www.iatp.org

The European Union Home Page: userpage.chemie.fu-berlin.de/adressen/eu.html

U.S. Department of Agriculture, *Agricultural Statistics, 2002*: www.usda.gov/nass/pubs/agr02/acro02.htm

U.S. Department of Labor, Bureau of Labor Statistics, Consumer Price Index: ftp://ftp.bls.gov/pub/special.requests/cpi/cpiai.txt

WTO Home Page: www.wtothailand.or.th/index.php

CHAPTER

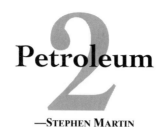

Petroleum

—Stephen Martin

A company's most valuable asset is its customers.

—Business school saying

Just as fossilized footprints mark the passage of a great dinosaur long after the dinosaur is gone, so the record of fluctuations in the price of crude oil marks passages in the world oil market. The tracks of major political events can be seen in Figure 2-1: the Arab-Israeli War of October 1973, the fall of the shah of Iran in January 1979, and the first and second Gulf Wars. Economic changes, which for the most part are less dramatic but have longer-lasting effects, also underlie the movements depicted in Figure 2-1.[1]

Some of these economic changes are:

- the shift in ownership and control over Mideast crude oil reserves from vertically integrated, Western-based international oil companies ("the majors") to national oil companies;
- the development by the majors of new oil supplies that are outside of OPEC control;
- the diffusion of energy-conserving practices on the demand side of the market and of high-technology production techniques on the supply side of the market;
- the vertical integration of national companies into refining and distribution; and
- the return of international majors to nationalized oil provinces.

The market for crude oil is a world market and one that is rich in lessons for students of industrial economics. It illustrates the ease with which firms may engage in limited collusion and the difficulty with which they engage in complete collusion. It illustrates the endogeneity of market structure and the importance of vertical market structure for horizontal market performance. It also illustrates governments' lack of understanding of and lack of faith in market processes.

We will examine the economic and political forces that have determined the performance of the world oil market and the U.S. oil submarket. Some of the questions we shall address are: What industry characteristics have allowed the exercise of market power, and by whom? What industry characteristics limit the exercise of market power? What has been the role of the major oil companies in the market, and what has been the role of smaller, independent companies? How have government policies

---

[1]The source for the nominal price data upon which Figure 2-1 is based is the U.S. Department of Energy, Energy Information Administration, www.eia.doe.gov/emeu/cabs/chron.xls. Accessed April 2, 2004.

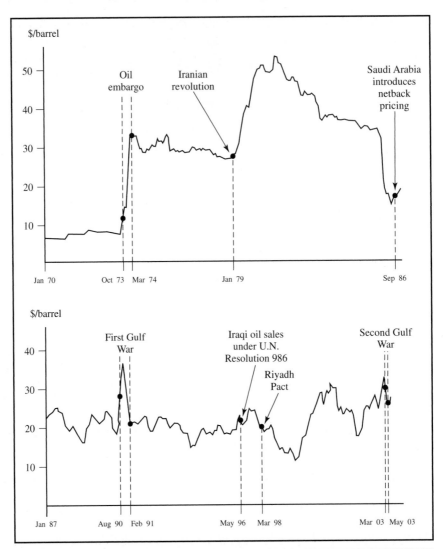

FIGURE 2-1   Real (2002 dollars) Price per Barrel of Crude Oil, January
1970–June 2003

SOURCE: U.S. Department of Energy, Energy Information Administration, "Country Analysis Brief: 2003."

affected the market? What does industrial economics suggest concerning likely future market performance?

I. STRUCTURE AND STRUCTURAL CHANGE

The petroleum industry is made up of four vertically related stages: production, refining, marketing, and transportation. Production involves the location and extraction of oil and natural gas from underground reservoirs; these reservoirs may be so close to the surface that their oil seeps up through the ground, or they may require extensive drilling from platforms located miles offshore. The refinery segment manufactures finished products ranging from petroleum coke to motor gasoline and jet fuel. Wholesale and retail marketers distribute these products to consumers. Connecting these three vertical levels is a specialized transportation industry—including pipelines, tankers, barges, and trucks—that moves crude oil from fields to refineries and finished product from refineries to marketers.

In principle, these four vertically related segments might be supplied by independent firms, and at some times and in some places this has been the case. Throughout the history of the industry though, the tendency has been for firms to integrate vertically and operate all along the line from production to distribution. These vertical links have been and continue to be critical in determining industry structure-performance relationships.

Domination by the International Majors

During the decade or so immediately following World War II, the world oil market was dominated by the seven vertically integrated major oil companies. The Seven Sisters were actually eight,[2] including the French firm Compagnie Française des Pétroles (CFP, later Total). Five of these firms were based in the United States, and three of these five (Exxon, Mobil, and Chevron) were survivors of the landmark 1911 antitrust decision that dismantled the Standard Oil Trust.[3] The other two were British Petroleum (BP) and Royal Dutch/Shell. BP was half owned by the British government. CFP was 25 percent owned by the French government and effectively a public firm. Both are early examples of the continuing government belief that "oil [is] too important to be left to the oil companies." [4]

Together, these eight firms controlled 100 percent of 1950 production of crude oil outside North America and the Communist bloc. Twenty years later, their combined share remained slightly more than 80 percent.

The basis for this control was the system of joint ventures—partial horizontal integration—under which the vertically integrated majors divided ownership of the operating companies that exploited Middle East oil fields, the richest in the world. (See Table 2-1.)

This interconnecting network of joint ventures developed with the support of the home governments of the international majors, each concerned, for reasons of national security, to ensure the access of domestically based firms to crude petroleum reserves. Thus, the U.S. Department of State induced American firms to take part in the 1928 "Red Line Agreement," which formalized control of the Iraq Petroleum Company. The French government set up Compagnie Française des Pétroles to exploit its share of the Iraq concession. The British government was similarly involved in the 1934 agreement that divided the Kuwait operating company between Gulf and BP.

---

[2]Such is the power of alliteration.

[3]In a certain sense, they were second-generation survivors, each being a combination of Standard Oil survivor firms. Exxon combined Standard Oil of New Jersey and the Anglo-American Oil Company; Mobil, for part of its life known as Socony-Vacuum, combined Standard Oil of New York and Vacuum Oil Company; and Chevron combined Standard Oil of California and Standard Oil of Kentucky.

[4]Anthony Sampson, *The Seven Sisters* (Bantam Books, 1976), 68.

TABLE 2-1   Ownership Shares in Middle East Joint Ventures, 1970

	Aramco	Kuwait Oil Company	Iranian Consortium	Iraq Petroleum Company
Exxon	30		7	11.875
Texaco	30		7	
Gulf		50	7	
Chevron	30		7	
Mobil	10		7	11.875
Royal Dutch/Shell			14	23.75
British Petroleum		50	40	23.75
CFP (Total)			6	23.75
Others			5	5.00

SOURCE: S.A. Schneider, *The Oil Price Revolution* (Baltimore: Johns Hopkins University Press, 1983), p. 40.

The U.S. government was instrumental in the 1948 reorganization of the Arabian-American Oil Company (Aramco) as a joint venture of Exxon, Texaco, Chevron, and Mobil to produce Saudi Arabian crude oil. The Iranian consortium—which delivered Persian oil fields into the hands of the seven majors, CFP, and a handful of American independents—was established after a CIA-backed coup returned the shah of Iran to power in August 1953 (reversing the nationalization of Iranian oil by the Mossadegh government). The fact that such a joint venture involving five American firms was contrary to U.S. antitrust law was set aside, at the urging of the Department of State, for reasons of national security.

The ongoing contacts required for the management of these joint ventures resulted in a sharing of information and a commonality of interest that is inconsistent with the kind of independent decision making that is characteristic of competition in a free-market economy:

> [T]he international companies' vertical integration was complemented in practice by a degree of informal but effective horizontal integration. Their joint ownership of operating companies in the Middle East, and their voting rights under the complex operating agreements through which they controlled exploration, development and offtake there, gave them a unique degree of knowledge of each others' opportunities to increase crude offtake, and some leverage to influence each others' opportunities.[5]

The Mideast joint ventures were operated under restrictions that had the effect of ensuring output limitations. For example, partners in the Iraq Petroleum Company were obliged to file their requirements for crude oil 5 years in advance. Each partner

---

[5]J. E. Hartshorn, *Oil Trade: Politics and Prospects* (Cambridge: Cambridge University Press, 1993), 117. The economic and political tensions among the international cartel partners are described in Walter Adams and James W. Brock, "Retarding the Development of Iraq's Oil Resources: An Episode in Oleaginous Diplomacy, 1927—1939," *Journal of Economic Issues* (March 1993): 69–93.

thus gained definite information about the plans of every other partner. A firm that filed requirements for expanded output would telegraph its plans to rivals, exposing itself to immediate retaliation.[6]

With the international majors joined by an extensive network of horizontal and vertical linkages, the world oil market operated as a small-numbers oligopoly in which rivalry manifested itself in development of reserves, in marketing efforts, and in the development of brand names but not, in general, in price competition. The prosperity of the international majors depended on secure access to crude oil deposits. However, with concessions to produce from such deposits in many parts of the world, solid political support from their home country governments, and control over channels of distribution to final consumers, the majors were relatively immune to pressure by the governments of the less developed countries where the highest-quality deposits were located.

The same firms dominated supply on the world market and the U.S. submarket, but government regulations kept the two separate. From the 1930s until the 1950s, controls on oil production by state governments (importantly, the Texas Railroad Commission) held crude oil prices in the United States at artificially high levels.[7] These prices proved attractive to foreign suppliers, and by 1948 the United States became a net importer of refined oil products. Three congressional investigations of the matter in 1950 revealed to the oil companies a congressional preference for low levels of imports. When domestic oil producers raised the price of U.S. crude oil in June 1950, the U.S. coal industry, with the support of the petroleum industry, sponsored a bill to place import quotas on petroleum. The Eisenhower Administration set up "voluntary" import-restraint programs in 1954 and 1958, and when these proved ineffective, imposed mandatory quotas in 1959.

These formal and informal restrictions on the flow of oil into the United States meant higher prices for U.S. consumers, perhaps by as much as $3 billion to $4 billion a year.[8] At a time when the price of crude oil on the eastern seaboard was about $3.75 a barrel, a cabinet task force estimated that the elimination of oil-import quotas would reduce the price of crude oil by $1.30 a barrel.[9]

Although the quotas had been justified on national security grounds, the effect of high U.S. prices in an artificially isolated market was to encourage the extraction of relatively high-cost U.S. crude oil, accelerating the depletion of U.S. reserves and conserving lower-cost reserves elsewhere in the world. It became clear, in 1973, that U.S. national security would have been better served if the pattern of extraction had been reversed.

---

[6]M. A. Adelman, *The World Petroleum Market* (Baltimore: Johns Hopkins, 1972), 84–87. Stigler's theory of oligopoly explains why joint ventures affect market performance: The more rapidly cheating is likely to be detected, and therefore subject to retaliation, the less likely cheating is to occur. George J. Stigler, "A Theory of Oligopoly," *Journal of Political Economy* 72, no. 1 (February 1964): 44–61; reprinted in George J. Stigler, *The Organization of Industry* (Homewood, IL: Richard D. Irwin, Inc. 1968), 39–63.

[7]Decades later, OPEC was to use the Texas Railroad Commission as a model; see Robert Mabro, "OPEC Behavior 1960–1998," *Journal of Energy Literature* 4, no. 1 (June 1998): 8.

[8]S. A. Schneider, *The Oil Price Revolution* (Baltimore: Johns Hopkins, 1983), 46.

[9]U.S. Congress. Senate. Subcommittee on Antitrust and Monopoly, Committee on the Judiciary. The Petroleum Industry: Part 4, The Cabinet Task Force on Oil Import Control (Washington, D.C.: U.S. Government Printing Office, March 1970).

Rise of Independent Oil Companies

One of the most important lessons of modern industrial economics is that market structure is the product of economic forces. The world oil market provides more than one example. Within limits, the Seven Sisters could hold the price of crude oil at artificially high levels, but they could not control entry. Their domination of the world oil market set in motion a process of entry by new firms in search of profit. This process occupied the period from the mid-1950s through 1973 and triggered a transition from a market dominated by the international majors to a market dominated by the governments of producing countries.

The first step in the transition was the 1954 Iranian consortium, when the U.S. government insisted that the majors make room for nine independents. Having gained a toehold in the Middle East, the independents sought to expand their roles. Just as the majors had once been able to play host nation against host nation by shifting production from country to country to resist pressure to expand output, so host nations gained the option of playing independent companies against major companies.

In 1956, Libya granted concessions to 17 firms. Independents subsequently accounted for half of Libyan output, and in due course products refined from this oil found their way to European markets.[10]

The activities of Enrico Mattei, head of the Italian national firm Ente Nazionale Idrocarburi (ENI), had far-reaching consequences. He sought access to oil supplies in Iran and elsewhere, and ultimately found it in the Soviet Union. After 1959, products refined from Russian oil joined the flow of independent oil onto world markets.

The increased flow of oil from these various independent sources created an excess supply at prevailing prices, despite rapidly expanding demand. The result was downward pressure on prices, which the international majors could not resist. However, the governments of the oil-producing nations collected taxes based on a "posted price" for oil, a paper price that was largely divorced from transactions prices. From the companies' point of view, the posted-price system worked well as long as transaction prices were level or rising. Falling transaction prices combined with unchanging posted prices meant that an increasing share of profit went to host countries in the form of taxes that were levied based on the posted price.

In August 1960, Exxon reduced its posted prices for oil. The remaining major firms followed suit. This reduction in the posted prices for oil was no more than a reflection of reductions in transaction prices. The reduction in transaction prices was the natural result of a more rapid expansion in supply than in demand. The more rapid expansion in supply than in demand was, in turn, a result of the actions of the host countries, which had granted independents access to crude supplies as a way of breaking the grip of the Seven Sisters on the world oil market.

The reduction in posted prices was, therefore, an inevitable consequence of the actions of host countries. However, it appeared to them as a unilateral reduction in their own tax revenues, imposed by international corporations. The reaction came at a September 1960 meeting of Saudi Arabia, Iran, Iraq, Kuwait, and Venezuela, when it was agreed to establish the Organization of Petroleum Exporting Countries (OPEC).

The 13 years that followed the formation of OPEC saw a long dance between the two loosely coordinated oligopolies, one of the international majors and one of producing

---

[10]Sampson, *Seven Sisters*, 174–175.

countries. At the start of this dance, the balance of power lay with the companies; at the end, it lay with the countries.

Although OPEC member states were beneficiaries of this shift in power, they did not initiate it. The international companies had a long history of effective cooperation, and they were better at it than the producing countries. By negotiating on a country-by-country basis, the major companies were able to prevent the countries from combining their bargaining power. OPEC was able to prevent further declines in the posted price, but it was not able to reverse the reductions in the posted price that had prompted OPEC's formation.

The catalyst for change was the interaction of independent companies and the revolutionary government of a relatively new oil province—Libya. Colonel Muamer Qadaffi's government took power in September 1969, and soon set about renegotiating the terms of Libyan oil concessions. As we have already remarked, independent oil firms had major roles in exploiting these concessions, and the independents were in a much weaker bargaining position, vis-à-vis the host countries, than the majors. Any one of the integrated majors, faced with an unattractive proposal from a producing country, could credibly threaten to reduce output in that country and turn to supplies elsewhere around the world. Independent companies had no such alternative.

In August 1970, Occidental Petroleum Company agreed to Libyan demands for higher prices and higher taxes. This example inspired other oil-producing nations. In February 1971, oil companies agreed in Tehran to the higher price demanded by the shah of Iran. The major oil companies revised the terms of their arrangement with Libya in April 1971.[11]

The oil-producing countries had demonstrated their ability to control the terms upon which oil was lifted from their territories. However, it was the major companies that owned the operating companies through their joint ventures. (See Table 2-1.) This, too, was to change.

Again it was the radical states rather than OPEC that led the way. Algeria nationalized 51 percent of French ownership in Algerian reserves in February 1971; Libya nationalized British Petroleum's interests in November 1971; Iraq nationalized the Iraqi Petroleum Company in June 1972. Long negotiations between Saudi Arabia[12] and Aramco followed. Aramco agreed to yield an initial 25 percent of its Saudi Arabian concession to Saudi Arabia.[13]

In the absence of intervening political developments, the transfer of control of the world market from the international majors to the producing countries would likely have continued at a gradual pace. The producing countries would have slowly replaced the international majors, with little change in market performance. In such an alternative reality, the Western "man in the street" would have remained blissfully unfamiliar with the nature of the world oil market. Events unfolded rather differently.

OPEC

The 1970s opened with the demand for oil increasing throughout the industrial world. Figure 2-2 shows the steady growth of the U.S. oil demand through the 1960s and early 1970s. Similar growth took place in Europe and Japan. In 1973, with simultaneous

---

[11]Ibid., 253–272.

[12]Represented by Sheik Zaki Yamani.

[13]Ibid., 278–282. On the eventual end of this process, see Youssef M. Ibrahim, "A U.S. Era Closes at Aramco," *International Herald Tribune* (April 6, 1989): 13.

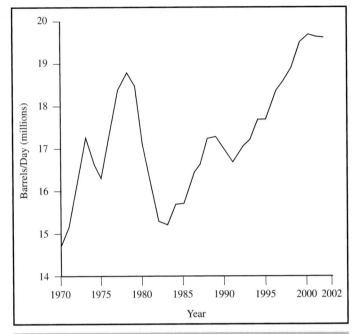

FIGURE 2-2   U.S. Demand for Refined Petroleum Products
(millions of barrels per day), 1970–2002

*SOURCE: American Petroleum Institute, "Basic Petroleum Fact Book,"
2003, Section VII, Table 2.*

booms in North America, Europe, and Japan, world demand for energy—and oil—was at an all-time high.

At the same time, supply and the control of supply were increasingly concentrated in the low-cost Middle East. In 1970, proved reserves[14] of crude oil in the Middle East were 333.5 billion barrels, versus 67.4 billion barrels of proved reserves in the western hemisphere and 54.7 billion barrels in Africa.

The location and development of crude oil reserves is a time-consuming process, particularly when oil fields are located offshore or in other hostile climates. Thus, the 1970s opened with a relatively small short-run supply of crude oil available from fringe, non-OPEC suppliers. These fringe suppliers faced substantially higher development and operating costs than Middle East producers (Table 2-2).

This kind of market is illustrated in stylized fashion in Figure 2-3(a). Here, fringe supply q^F_1, taken to be constant,[15] is small relative to market size; the residual demand

---

[14]The American Petroleum Institute definition of proved reserves is: Proved reserves of crude oil ... are the estimated quantities of all liquids statistically defined as crude oil, which geological and engineering data demonstrate with reasonable certainty to be recoverable in future years from known reservoirs under existing economic and operating conditions.

[15]It is an exaggeration to draw fringe supply as completely inelastic with respect to price—a vertical line— but only a modest one. Most of the cost of oil field development is fixed and sunk, so that price would have to fall very low before fringe firms would reduce output. Given the constraints of location and development, even if price rises very high, it is not possible to expand output much in the short run. Thus, the fringe supply curve will be nearly vertical.

TABLE 2-2	Oil and Gas Production, Finding and Development Costs (\$ per barrel of oil equivalent)	
		\$/barrel
Saudi Arabia		≤ 2
Indonesia		6
Nigeria		7
Venezuela		7
Gulf of Mexico		10
North Sea		11
Russia		14

SOURCE: *The Economist* 6, March 1999, p. 23.

curve left for the cartel, the part of the demand curve to the left of the dashed vertical line at q^F_1, comprises the bulk of the market. In such a market, a dominant firm or perfectly colluding cartel would maximize profit by selecting an output that equates marginal revenue along the residual demand curve—the market demand curve after subtracting fringe output—to marginal cost. In Figure 2-3(a), the corresponding cartel output is q^C_1, which would sell at price p_1. Because fringe supply is small and demand is inelastic, p_1 is much above cartel marginal cost MC_C.

Because the economic interests of the OPEC member nations diverge in fundamental ways, OPEC was (and is) far from being able to act as a monopolist or a perfectly

FIGURE 2-3   Fringe Supply and Cartel Output

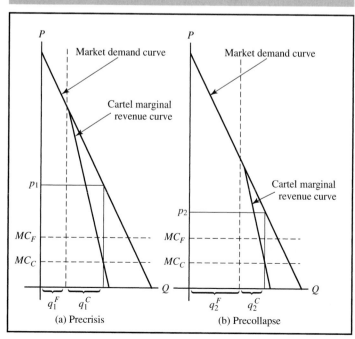

(a) Precrisis

(b) Precollapse

colluding cartel. It was a political rather than an economic event that triggered coordinated OPEC action and allowed it to take advantage of a demand/supply relationship of the kind depicted in Figure 2-3(a). In reaction to Western support for Israel during the Egypt-Israeli War of October 1973, Arab nations imposed production cutbacks and an embargo of crude oil supplies to the West.

The international oil companies were based in the West, and they had long benefited from the political support of their home governments—governments that sought to protect their perceived national security interest in a safe supply of oil. However, the international majors administered the embargo of Western nations according to OPEC directives, going so far as to provide Saudi Arabia with information on the shipment of refined oil products to U.S. military bases around the world.[16]

As the producing countries cut back the supply of crude oil to the international majors, the international majors cut back supplies to independent companies. With their survival threatened, the independents turned to the market for oil that was not tied up by long-term contracts—the relatively narrow spot market. Independents bid up the spot market price of oil, and official OPEC prices soon followed. The immediate result was the 1973 rise in official prices shown in Figure 2-1.

From this price increase flowed longer-run changes. OPEC revenue from the sale of oil rose from $13.7 billion in 1972 to $87.2 billion in 1974. Real U.S. gross national product, which grew 5.2 percent in 1973, fell 0.5 percent in 1973 and 1.3 percent in 1974.

Aside from the accelerated shift in control of production to the producing nations, remarkably few structural changes occurred during the period following the first price increase. U.S. demand for oil fell slightly in 1974 and 1975 but then rose to new heights by 1978 (Figure 2-2). The share of imports in the U.S. market, and specifically imports from OPEC, peaked in 1977 but remained higher than in 1973 (Figure 2-4). The pattern of consumption and supply was much the same in other industrialized countries.

As shown in Figure 2-5 OPEC's share of world crude oil production fell only about 5 percent over the period from 1973 to 1979. World production of crude oil grew throughout this period, but OPEC's production was essentially level: 30,989,000 barrels per day in 1973, and 30,911,000 barrels per day in 1979.

Because of the length of time needed to develop new petroleum reserves and to install energy-saving residential and industrial equipment, the underlying market conditions that greeted the fall of the shah of Iran in January 1979 were essentially the same as those at the time of the Arab-Israeli War of 1973: peak demand, concentration of supply in the Middle East, and absence of spare capacity in the West.

The impact of the course of events on the market was also similar. Supply was disrupted. Independent refiners had their crude supplies cut off. Desperate for crude oil, they turned to the spot market, and the price of oil, shown in Figure 2-1, shot up.

Cultivation of Crude Oil Supplies Outside of OPEC

The response to the second oil price shock, on the demand side and the supply side of the market, was substantially different from the response to the first oil price shock As shown in Figure 2-6, energy use in relation to gross domestic product in the United States was essentially level over the period from the first to the second oil price shock but declined more thereafter. Energy use in the European Union and Japan, consistently

---

[16]Louis Turner, *Oil Companies in the International System* (London: Allen & Unwin, 1983), 136.

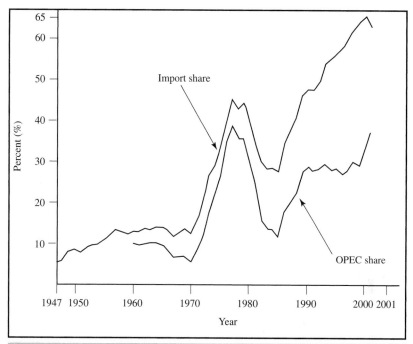

FIGURE 2-4   Import and OPEC Shares of U.S. Crude Oil Supplies,
1947–2001 and 1960–2001, respectively

*SOURCE: American Petroleum Institute, Basic Petroleum Fact Book, 2003, Section IX,
Table 2; Section X, Table 1; Section XIV, Table 4.*

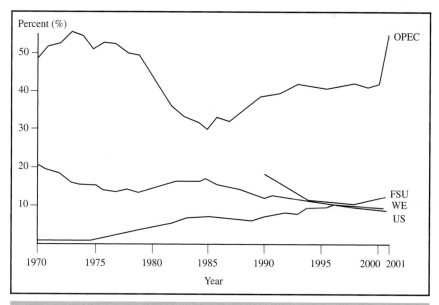

FIGURE 2-5   Shares of World Crude Petroleum Production, 1970–2001

NOTE: FSU = Former Soviet Union; US = United States; WE = Western Europe

*SOURCE: American Petroleum Institute, Basic Petroleum Fact Book, 2003, Section 4, Table 1,
Section 14, Table 2.*

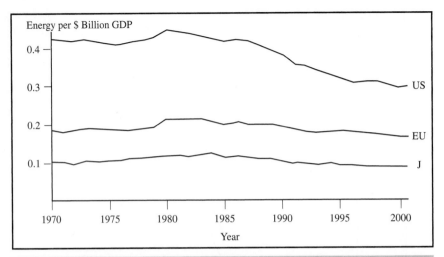

FIGURE 2-6   Total Primary Energy Supply (in millions of tons of oil equivalent) per Billion Dollars of Gross Domestic Product (measured in 1995 U.S. dollars), 1970–2001

NOTE: EU = European Union; J = Japan; US = United States

SOURCE: International Energy Agency, Energy Balances of OECD Countries, internet database.

lower than in the United States, rose slightly over the period from the first to the second oil price shock and has declined slowly since then.

These changes illustrate the long response time required to realize changes in the demand for energy resources. A long-term shift to greater efficiency in energy use occurred, partly due to the higher real price of energy and partly due to increasing concern about the impact of energy consumption on the environment. Demand for energy, and oil, was lower in the 1980s (Figure 2-2) than it would have been without the oil shocks of the 1970s.

A corresponding effect occurred on the supply side of the market, described in Table 2-3 and depicted in Figure 2-5. Crude oil production in the U.S. peaked in 1970 and has followed a downward trend since then. This trend will continue, mitigated by new technology[17] but not by the discovery or exploitation of new reservoirs. Long isolated from the world market by protective quotas, the United States has been thoroughly explored. However, output from Western Europe increased sharply over this period, as the North Sea oil fields of Britain and Norway came into production. North Sea oil output reached a plateau in the mid-1990s and will decline (although technological progress continues to extend its potential beyond original expectations). The North Sea will remain an important source of natural gas.[18]

Output in Latin America rose over this period, and this trend is likely to continue. Venezuela, although a charter member of OPEC, continues to expand its oil reserves. It markets a coal-water mixture that is a good substitute for fuel oil but is exempt from

---

[17]The importance of technological advance in petroleum extraction should not be underestimated. An often prescient geologist, Eckel (*Coal Iron and War*, New York, 1920, 127) predicted in 1920 that the U.S. supply of oil would be exhausted by 1930 or 1935.

[18]See Steve Martin (no relation to the author of this chapter), "North Sea Oil Statistics," *Journal of Energy Literature* 3, no. 2 (December 1997): 32–48.

TABLE 2-3 World Crude Production By Area, 1974, 1985, 2001

	1974		1985		2001	
	Million Barrels	**%**	**Million Barrels**	**%**	**Million Barrels**	**%**
United States	3,203	15.6	3,275	16.8	2,118	8.7
Canada	617	3.0	532	2.7	801	3.3
Western Europe	142	0.7	1,370	7.0	2,260	9.3
Latin America	1,789	8.7	2,285	11.7	3,361	13.8
Asia	816	4.0	1,142	5.9	2,669	10.9
Eastern Europe	3,995	19.5	5,352	27.5	77	0.3
FSU					2,997	12.3
Africa	1,990	9.7	1,772	9.1	2,519	10.3
Middle East	7,987	38.9	3,761	19.3	7,612	31.2
Total	20,538		19,489		24,415	

SOURCE: *American Petroleum Institute, Basic Petroleum Fact Book*, 2003, Section 4, Table 1.

OPEC output quotas. In addition, Venezuela has aggressively acquired networks of refineries and service stations to ensure outlets for its oil. Other Latin American countries, including Peru and Colombia, continue to expand their oil industries; Mexico has increasingly cooperated with international oil companies to exploit its oil deposits.

Crude oil output from the third world, including China and less-developed countries (LDCs) in Africa, will increase. This reflects a convergence of interest between LDCs and the international majors. Nationalizations by OPEC member states cut the international majors off from the Mideast oil fields that were for generations the foundation of their dominant market positions. They will search anywhere outside OPEC's sphere of influence for new reserves, which they can feed into their existing refining and marketing networks. They will do so as long as the new reserves can be developed for a cost at or below the spot market price for oil.

At the same time, LDCs know from bitter experience that it is their development efforts that suffer from dependency on foreign sources of oil. For political reasons, LDCs will encourage the development of local oil supplies even if the cost seems likely to exceed the spot market price of oil. Their national security (and often the lives of their leaders) depends on it.

The same applies to the world's newest group of less-developed countries, the former members of the Soviet Union (FSU). Crude oil output from these countries declined during a transitory period, as the foundations of market economies were laid. Although that process is not yet complete, for these countries petroleum deposits represent a valuable source of foreign exchange and will be exploited accordingly. Major oil companies are gingerly establishing ties in this part of the world, despite the uncertain political and legal environments.[19]

As a result, the international majors will be welcome in the new oil provinces around the world. The supply of oil from less-developed countries will increase, and to some extent this increase will result from political rather than economic considerations.

[19]See, for example, Heather Timmons, "BP Expands Its Interest in Russian Oil," *New York Times* (Internet edition), August 30, 2003.

Along with the substantial increases in crude oil production outside OPEC in the 1980s came the reduction in Middle East output shown in Figure 2-5. By mid-1985, OPEC found itself in the kind of market illustrated in Figure 2-3(b). Fringe supply, after a decade of development efforts, was large in relation to the market. Demand, after a decade of conservation efforts, had grown much less rapidly than expected. The residual part of the market left for OPEC was substantially reduced, compared with the kind of situation shown in Figure 2-3(a). In such circumstances, the best OPEC could do was to set a price p_2, which was much lower than p_1, and market a substantially smaller quantity q^C_2. (See the second set of columns in Table 2-3.)

Just as the international majors' long domination of the world oil market created an incentive for the entry and expansion of independent oil firms, so OPEC's somewhat briefer period of control created an incentive for the development of new oil provinces. The entry of independent firms undercut the resource base of the international majors, and they reacted by seeking new supplies of oil. The entry of new oil-producing countries undercut the power base of OPEC member states, and they reacted by seeking secure outlets for their oil. The result has been a renewed trend to vertical integration, by OPEC member states and by oil companies, with horizontal concentration reduced at all levels of the industry.

The North Sea Oil Markets

Perhaps the most ironic consequence of OPEC's assertion of control over the world crude market is the development of active spot and futures markets for Brent crude blend, which has made the price of North Sea crude a bellwether for the industry. It has also ratified OPEC's inability to do more than move along a shifting residual demand curve.

Sovereignty over North Sea oil deposits lies primarily with Britain and Norway. A large number of international oil companies exploit the North Sea oil fields through a complex web of joint ventures.[20] Concentration of production is high, although declining. Output is dominated by Exxon and Shell, whose combined market share was near 70 percent for much of the 1980s and remained more than 50 percent in 1993.[21]

North Sea oil fields benefit from a location near the major consuming centers of Europe and from a product with desirable physical properties as far as refining is concerned. North Sea oil is a good substitute for U.S. and OPEC products. For these reasons, and because the North Sea supply came about "on line" at a time when international oil companies were scampering to acquire access to oil outside OPEC influence, the spot market for North Sea oil assumed a central place in the interlocking world network of oil markets. The economic importance of the North Sea market is far greater than its share of world oil output (never more than 6 percent). The prices of many other transactions are tied to those on the North Sea market. In times of real or perceived shortage, surges of demand on the North Sea futures market (the market for oil to be delivered 1, 2, or more months in the future) can drive prices up rapidly and often down again just as rapidly. (Examine Figure 2-1 for the time around the Iraqi invasion of Kuwait, which precipitated the first Gulf War.[22]) The role of the price of Brent blend

---

[20]Exxon and Shell, for example, are equal partners in all their North Sea assets.
[21]Paul Horsnell and Robert Mabro, *Oil Markets and Prices* (Oxford: Oxford University Press, 1993), 25–28.
[22]See Steven Butler, "Oil Traders Devise Strategies for the Twenty-First Century," *Financial Times,* May 25, 1990; and Horsnell and Mabro, *Oil Markets and Prices.*

as a marker price for the world petroleum industry confirms OPEC's long-run inability to control the world oil market. However, the picture is not entirely rosy: The spot and futures markets for North Sea oil are subject to speculative binges, and price fluctuations on these markets often have little to do with the fundamentals of supply and demand.

Consolidation and Integration

On balance, changes on the supply side of the world market for crude oil bode well for long-run market performance. Major oil companies are merging and restructuring their activities to reduce costs. State-owned oil firms—the product of the nationalizations of the 1970s—are integrating forward from production into refining and distribution, competing with the international majors at all vertical levels. An increasing number of countries that nationalized their oil industries at the dawn of the OPEC era are allowing the international majors to return, on carefully controlled terms, to develop new reserves. In a fundamental sense, the structure of the world oil market is returning to what it was before the rise of OPEC but with a larger number of players.

August 1998 saw the merger of BP and Amoco (a Standard Oil survivor company). Amoco was short of reserves of crude oil, and the merger would permit the combined firm to scrap outmoded refineries and reduce costs. Six months later, BP Amoco proposed to take over Atlantic Richfield, another Standard Oil survivor and a company pressed by low oil prices and the high cost of extracting oil from the North Slope of Alaska.

In December 1998, Exxon and Mobil, the two largest Standard Oil survivor companies, proposed to merge. Once again, low oil prices and the value of secure access to reserves lay behind the merger.

The Exxon-Mobil merger was approved by the European Commission's Directorate General for Competition, the competition law enforcement arm of the European Union, and by the U.S. Federal Trade Commission (FTC). To obtain FTC approval, Exxon and Mobil agreed to sell off a refinery and nearly 5,000 retail gas stations to avoid substantially increasing seller concentration in regional or local markets.[23] The BP Amoco–Atlantic Richfield merger was approved by the European Union. After initial hesitation (on the grounds that the merger would create too great a concentration of sales of Alaskan crude oil and worsen performance in the West Coast market for supply of crude oil to refiners), the U.S. Federal Trade Commission approved the merger in April 2000, although the FTC required a number of divestitures before giving its approval.

Also in December 1998, the French firm Total (formerly the eighth of the Seven Sisters, Compagnie Française des Pétroles) acquired the Belgian firm Petrofina. In October 1999, TotalFina proposed to take over the French firm Elf Aquitaine, a combination that would ensure European representation among the major private oil firms. The European Commission approved the merger in February 2000, requiring the companies to sell off certain assets, including a number of retail outlets.

---

[23]In this regard, see U.S. Department of Energy, Energy Information Administration, "Price Changes in the Gasoline Market: Are Midwestern Gasoline Prices Downward Sticky?" for a review of the literature on the extent to which upward and downward fluctuations in the price of crude oil are passed on to the price of retail gasoline. The EIA finds that upward fluctuations in the price of crude oil are passed on to the retail price more rapidly than downward fluctuations, but that the full extent of crude oil price changes in both directions is ultimately passed to the retail level.

The pattern of mergers continued into the new century. October 2001 saw the combination of Chevron and Texaco to create what would be the third-largest U.S. oil and gas producer, Chevron-Texaco. In August 2003, Phillips Petroleum and Conoco merged to become ConocoPhillips.

This wave of consolidation among private firms accompanies, and in a certain sense is a consequence of, the diversification of national oil companies out of production and into refining and distribution. Such companies include Saudi Aramco, Venezuela's PDV, Brazil's Petrobras, and Norway's Statoil.[24]

Through a subsidiary of the Kuwait Petroleum Corporation, Kuwait owns two European refineries with a capacity of 135,000 barrels per day, together with 4,800 retail gasoline stations in 7 different European countries. Kuwait has acquired a 22 percent ownership of British Petroleum, much to the British government's concern, and has sought refining assets in Japan.

Venezuela has employed joint ventures to acquire partial interests in refineries in West Germany, Sweden, and Belgium, and has acquired Citgo's refining and distribution operations in the United States.

Other OPEC members also integrated forward into the U.S. market. In November 1988, Saudi Arabia acquired half ownership of Texaco, Inc.'s U.S. refining and distribution network. The three refineries involved had a capacity of 615,000 barrels per day; the distribution network included 11,450 retail gasoline stations. With this investment, the largest source of crude oil in the world moved to secure a market for its product. It also acquires an interest in maintaining profitability at the refining and distribution levels of the market, as well as the crude level.

The motives for this forward integration are partly political and partly economic. A move forward into refining is a way of broadening the local industrial base while taking advantage of existing assets and skills. At the same time, a refinery associated with a national oil company of an oil-producing state has an almost insuperable advantage when compared with an independent refiner. The real cost of crude oil to the integrated refiner is the cost of crude production (regardless of the transfer price from the crude division to the refinery division). However, the cost of crude oil to an independent, nonintegrated refiner is the much higher market price for crude oil. Refining and distribution networks associated with producing nations will always be able to undersell independents. When a surplus of crude oil exists, it will be profitable to do so.

The firms that were created by the merger wave of the late 1990s are large in an absolute sense but small in proportion to the size of the market. A combined Mobil and Exxon, the largest of the lot, would supply about 4 percent of world crude production. Taking the rivalry of state-owned firms into account, the mergers among private firms seem unlikely to worsen performance on the world oil market.

An encouraging structural change is the return of the international majors to oil provinces that were nationalized in the early 1970s. Several OPEC governments have confronted the harsh reality that the development of new reserves, their source of future oil revenues, is risky and expensive. For many such governments, the economic profits collected in the 1980s are gone—spent on wars, welfare, and development efforts—and the option to work with the international majors has become more attractive than it

---

[24]The merger of Statoil with the State's Direct Financial Interest (SDFI) was proposed by Statoil management to strengthen Statoil on the way to privatization.

once was. When the international majors are in place, the discretion of national governments to restrict output will be reduced.[25]

II. CONDUCT

It is sometimes asserted that the price increases of 1973 and 1979 through 1982 were no more than the working of competitive forces. In this view, favored in particular by oil-producing nations, a price of oil at or near extraction cost fails to take into account the scarcity that current consumption imposes on future generations. A price substantially above marginal extraction cost, in this view, is a good thing, because it encourages conservation and spreads consumption of a finite resource over a long time period.

This argument might explain the price increases observed in 1973 and 1979 through 1982. However, it cannot explain the price decline from a real price[26] of more than $53 per barrel in January 1981 to less than $14.50 per barrel in July 1986 (and to $10 per barrel at the end of 1998). Oil is, after all, as much a finite resource today as it ever was, and if future scarcity would produce a high price in 1982, it would seemingly produce an even higher price moving into the twenty-first century. Statistical tests do not support the argument that OPEC pricing is competitive.[27]

Some analysts have suggested that the world oil industry is driven by a single dominant producer—Saudi Arabia. According to the figures in Table 2-4, Saudi Arabia holds about 21 percent of world proven reserves. It is widely believed that Saudi Arabia substantially understates its reserve holdings. This quantitative description does not capture the fact that Saudi crude is by far the least expensive in the world, with an estimated extraction cost of less than $2 a barrel.

These reserve holdings mean that Saudi Arabia will be a factor in the world oil market as long as there is a world market for oil. If Saudi Arabia were to act as a wealth-maximizing dominant firm, it would restrict output and raise the price above the cost of production. It would then gradually give up market share, as other producers expanded output to take advantage of the opportunity for profit created by the price increase.[28]

A variation on this theme suggests that although no single OPEC member has sufficient control of reserves to exercise control over price, OPEC as a group is able to act as a collusive price leader. The predicted market performance is much the same as under the dominant-firm model. OPEC's share of the market should decline over time as independent producers respond to the incentive created by a price above the cost of production.

Figures 2-1 and 2-5 suggest that the dominant-firm and dominant-group models had a certain degree of explanatory power for perhaps 12 or 15 years after the 1973 oil shock. OPEC's share of world crude oil production fell slowly from 1973 to 1979. As

---

[25]The Iranian constitution prohibits granting concessions to foreign firms. Iran has therefore offered so-called "buyback agreements" to foreign firms. Under such an arrangement, foreign firms develop an oil field for a fixed compensation, over a specified period, that is paid by Iranian receipts from the sale of oil. If the price of oil drops, Iran must sell more oil to pay the foreign developer.

[26]Measured in 2002 U.S. dollars.

[27]James M. Griffen, "OPEC Behavior: A Test of Alternative Hypotheses," *American Economic Review* 75, no. 5 (December 1985): 954–963.

[28]Darius Gaskins, "Dynamic Limit Pricing: Optimal Limit Pricing under Threat of Entry," *Journal of Economic Theory* 3 (September 1971): 306–322; Norman J. Ireland, "Concentration and the Growth of Market Demand," *Journal of Economic Theory* 5 (October 1972): 303–305.

TABLE 2-4	Estimated Proven Reserves of Crude Oil, 2003 (billion barrels)
Saudi Arabia	259.3
Canada	180.0
Iraq	112.5
United Arab Emirates	97.8
Kuwait	94.0
Iran	89.7
FSU	77.8
Venezuela	77.8
Russia	60.0
Libya	29.5
Nigeria	24.0
United States	22.4
China	18.3
Mexico	12.6
Algeria	9.2
Brazil	8.3
Angola	5.4
Oman	5.3
Neutral Zone	5.0
Total World	1,213.9

SOURCE: *American Petroleum Institute, Basic Petroleum Fact Book,* 2003, Section 2, Table 4.

already noted, this is a reflection of the long lead times in discovery and development of oil reserves. OPEC's market share fell sharply in the 1980s, bottoming out at 30 percent of the world market in 1985. It has risen to more than 50 percent moving into the twenty-first century as OPEC has taken back market share at the expense of a lower price.

Cartel Dynamics

What the dominant-firm and dominant-group analyses do not capture is the oligopolistic interactions that flavor OPEC behavior. When price is raised above the cost of production, individual OPEC member nations (not just independent producers) have an incentive to increase their output. The problem for OPEC, like any cartel, is to achieve agreement on a course of action (raising price to some level) and then to secure adherence to the agreement. As is the case with any group, differences make for disagreements. OPEC has been plagued by differences in the urgency with which its members wish to turn their asset in the ground, crude oil reserves, into disposable income.

OPEC member states differ substantially in the urgency with which they desire revenue from oil sales. Countries such as Saudi Arabia, Kuwait, and the United Arab Emirates have small populations, high gross national product (GNP) levels per capita, and ruling elites that are well served by modernizing at a slow pace. Their massive oil reserves ensure that they will earn oil revenue for the foreseeable future.

Other OPEC members, such as Indonesia, Nigeria, and Algeria, have larger populations, smaller GNP levels per capita, and substantially smaller oil reserves. Their best hope for economic development is through the maximization of short-run oil revenues. Political pressures reinforce this economic incentive. More than once, governments of OPEC nations have been overturned because of mismanagement of the oil sector, and the ousted leaders often do not survive to collect retirement benefits.

By 1985, OPEC's market share had fallen to 30 percent, mostly on the strength of output cutbacks by Saudi Arabia, which enjoyed an OPEC quota of 4.353 million barrels per day but was estimated to be producing only 2.5 million barrels a day in September 1985. OPEC's official price remained at $28 per barrel, but the spot market price for oil was no more than half that.

At this point, Saudi Arabia introduced a system of "netback pricing." Under this system, the price paid for Saudi crude oil was determined by the market prices of the products refined from the crude. The immediate effect of the netback pricing system was to eliminate risk for the purchaser of Saudi crude: If the price of refined products should fall, the price of crude would fall proportionately. The consequence was a sharp increase in the demand for Saudi oil, output of which reached 6 million barrels per day by July 1986.

Other OPEC members soon adopted their own netback pricing schemes, and oil prices fell as low as $6 per barrel. By August 1986, OPEC members, with the exception of Iraq, which held out for a quota equal to that of Iran, reaffirmed their support for the quota schedule that they were all violating. A series of ineffective agreements followed, and crude prices stayed at levels which, while yielding OPEC members handsome profits, remained below the levels of the early 1980s.

Iraq's August 1990 occupation of Kuwait led to a brief spike in the price of oil (Figure 2-1) but otherwise caused hardly a ripple in the supply of oil to world markets. Supplies from Iraq and Kuwait were abruptly cut to zero, but Saudi Arabia increased output from 5.4 million barrels a day in August 1990 to 8.2 million barrels a day in November 1990, maintaining overall supply at a comfortable level. Saudi Arabia insisted on keeping output at this level for most of the rest of the 1990s.

Judging by its actions, Saudi Arabia perceives its own self-interest to be served by stable oil markets and prices that do not give too much encouragement to conservation efforts or the search for alternative fuels. At the time of the Iraqi invasion of Kuwait, Saudi Arabia was able to act in its own self-interest and expand output because it had excess capacity that allowed it to do so. Other OPEC members with significant petroleum reserves were not slow to draw the conclusion that bargaining power within OPEC is related to production capacity. In the immediate aftermath of the Gulf War, Kuwait (naturally enough), Abu Dhabi, and Iran set in motion substantial investment programs aimed at increasing crude capacity. Not to be outdone, Saudi Arabia initiated an expansion of capacity to more than 10 million barrels a day.

OPEC's pattern of ineffective collusion continued after Iraq was driven from Kuwait in February 1991. Ecuador and Gabon (both small producers) withdrew as OPEC members. Amid bickering over how members would adjust (reduce) their own output as Kuwaiti oil fields returned to production and as Iraq began limited oil sales under U.N. supervision to raise funds for humanitarian needs, OPEC found its residual part of the market increasingly small.

In November 1997, OPEC oil ministers agreed to raise quota output by 1.5 million barrels a day (m b/d), to 27.5 m b/d. A portion of this increase simply acknowledged reality—actual output was reported to be 27.0 m b/d—but the decision also was based on a predicted increase in demand going into winter in the northern hemisphere. By expanding output, OPEC could supply the expected increase in demand rather than letting it go to suppliers outside the organization.

However, the northern hemisphere winter of 1997 to 1998 was mild, a severe economic slowdown in Asia reduced energy demand in that part of the world, and a large stock of crude oil was held in inventory. These three factors meant that crude oil prices fell sharply, and Saudi Arabia reached outside OPEC in pursuit of its long-term goals.

In March 1998, OPEC members Saudi Arabia and Venezuela agreed with non-member Mexico to reduce output by 1.5 m b/d, some 2 percent of world production. Additional output reductions were later pledged by other OPEC members and non-members (in particular, Norway), and producers came closer than in the past to meeting their commitments. The price of crude oil tripled in a little more than a year (from about $9.40 a barrel in December 1998 to peaks of more than $30 a barrel early in 2000). Jawboning by governments of consumer countries was ineffective in persuading OPEC member states to increase output, but in March 2000 the governments of moderate OPEC countries seemed ready to implement such increases to benefit their own perceived self-interest in avoiding disruptions in world economic activity.

The second Gulf War[29] had no more fundamental impact on the world oil market than had the first. Indeed, during this period, continuing unrest in Venezuela unsettled the oil market as much as the situation in the Gulf of Arabia. Prices fluctuated during this period—down in anticipation of increased oil supplies flowing from a liberated Iraq and up when it became clear that these supplies would not materialize as rapidly as some had hoped. OPEC was at most taking advantage of opportunities thrown its way by the market, not controlling the market. The decisions taken at OPEC's April 2003 meeting—to raise target output by 900,000 barrels per day while reducing actual output (which exceeds the target level) by 2 million barrels per day—suggest that it will be business as usual for OPEC in the twenty-first century. For OPEC, "business as usual" is agreements that are more honored in the breach than the observance.

III. PUBLIC POLICY

U.S. Antitrust Activity

The oil industry lies at the foundation of U.S. antitrust policy. It was hostility toward the Standard Oil Trust, widely believed to have acquired control of the post–Civil War U.S. market by means of strategic anticompetitive behavior, that prompted passage of the Sherman Antitrust Act of 1890.[30] Antitrust has been the traditional approach to the preservation of competition in the United States and, as we have noted, in 1911 the Supreme Court upheld a finding that the Standard Oil Company had violated the Sherman Antitrust Act while acquiring a dominant position in the refining, marketing,

---

[29]Taking the end of the second Gulf War to be the declared end of active hostilities, May 2003.

[30]Before the development of the automobile, oil was a source of light rather than a fuel. See George R. Gibon, "A Lampful of Oil," *Harper's New Monthly Magazine* 72, no. 428 (January 1886): 235–257. (This can be downloaded from cdl.library.cornell.edu/cgi-bin/moa/moa-cgi?notisid=ABK4014-0072-26. Assessed March 2, 2004.)

and transportation of petroleum. The Court imposed a structural remedy, ordering the parent holding company to divest itself of controlling stock interests in 33 subsidiaries.[31]

This first case was also the last successful major case involving the U.S. oil industry. To be sure, the oil industry has from time to time attracted the attention of antitrust authorities. In 1940, a case so broad that it became known as the "Mother Hubbard" case was filed.[32] Twenty-two major oil companies, 344 subsidiary and secondary companies, and the American Petroleum Institute were charged, in a Justice Department civil suit, with violating the Sherman and Clayton Acts. The case was postponed because of the onset of World War II and thereafter languished until it was dismissed in 1951 at the request of the Justice Department.

Throughout the postwar period, antitrust action against U.S. oil firms was suspended on grounds of national security. In the closing days of the Truman administration, the government accused the five U.S.-based international majors (along with British Petroleum and Royal Dutch Shell, which were beyond the jurisdiction of U.S. authorities) of seeking to restrain and monopolize crude oil and refined petroleum products, in violation of the Sherman Antitrust Act. However, the State Department urged that the oil companies receive antitrust immunity for their cooperation in setting up the 1954 Iranian consortium, and this immunity weakened the cartel case, which dragged on for years. The cases against Exxon, Texaco, and Gulf were eventually settled by consent decrees, and charges against Mobil and Socal (Chevron) were dismissed. The last parts of the case were dropped by the Justice Department in 1968.[33]

Much of the vitality of American antitrust law derives from the possibility of private enforcement. A private antitrust suit filed in 1978 by the International Association of Machinists and Aerospace Workers (IAM) sought to apply U.S. antitrust law to OPEC. OPEC declined to appear when the case was heard, and the Department of Justice refused to submit the amicus curiae brief requested by the district court. The district court declined to hear the case on technical grounds, among others that the IAM did not have "standing" to sue OPEC because IAM was not a direct purchaser from OPEC.

IAM appealed this dismissal to the circuit court of appeals, which upheld the lower court refusal to hear the case on the grounds that the case would interfere with U.S. foreign relations. Once again, conditions of national security short-circuited the application of the antitrust laws.[34]

Government Policy Responses to OPEC

The fact that the oil crisis of 1973 was repeated just 6 years later is testimony that Western governments generally were unable to develop adequate energy policies the first time around. The founding of the International Energy Agency (IEA) in November 1974 suggests government recognition of the importance of cooperation among consuming

---

[31]See Bruce Bringhurst, *Antitrust and the Oil Monopoly* (Westport, CT: Greenwood Press, 1979).

[32]*U.S. v. American Petroleum Institute et al., Civil No. 8524* (D.D.C., October 1940).

[33]B. I. Kaufman, "Oil and Antitrust: The Oil Cartel Case and the Cold War," *Business History Review* 51, no. 37 (Spring 1977); Sampson, *Seven Sisters*, pp. 150–159.

[34]See Irvin M. Grossack, "OPEC and the Antitrust Laws," *Journal of Economic Issues* 20, no. 3 (September 1986): 725–741. U.S. antitrust laws are effects-based: If actions restrain trade on U.S. markets, those actions are covered by the antitrust laws no matter where they take place. The same is true of the competition policy of the European Union. Although the governments that are members of OPEC might enjoy sovereign immunity for their actions, the same cannot be said for the legally independent companies through which OPEC decisions are implemented.

countries. However, France refused to join the IEA, apparently preferring bilateral government-to-government negotiations with oil-producing nations. Such government-to-government negotiations became common during the tight crude markets of 1978 through 1980, when security of supply was a matter of concern. Since that time, as more and more oil has become available on spot markets, sales with government involvement have declined.

Three interrelated aspects of the continuing debate over proper government policy toward the petroleum industry merit discussion. All reflect a failure to understand the way markets work.

The International Energy Agency   Twenty-one Western nations are members of the International Energy Agency.[35] They have pledged to share oil supplies if it is determined that a shortage of oil has occurred or is likely to occur. Shortage is defined in terms of a physical interruption in supply, and it seems clear that the focus of the IEA is embargoes imposed for political reasons. Price increases, however, have been an important aspect of past oil shocks, and the assessment of market conditions in terms of physical supplies rather than prices reflects a failure to appreciate the role of prices in a market economy. It would be desirable to alter IEA procedures to facilitate a response to a sharp price increase as well as to a sharp supply decrease.

The Strategic Petroleum Reserve   In 1975, Congress established a Strategic Petroleum Reserve (SPR) as insurance against future interruptions in foreign supplies. Targets, set in later detailed plans, were for 500 million barrels in storage by 1980 and a billion barrels by 1985. By March 1988, salt caverns around the Gulf of Mexico housed 545 million barrels. Modest sales from the SPR were made during the first Gulf War, and supplies were added in the period of time leading up to the second Gulf War, bringing the total to just less than 600 million barrels. However, the U.S. government declined to release supplies from the SPR in the face of price increases in the months before the second Gulf War. Although it seems likely that the knowledge that the SPR exists has a calming effect on world oil markets, it would be desirable to let price spikes trigger the release of strategic reserves.

Low Price or Energy Independence?   The debate on U.S. policy toward the petroleum industry has long been bedeviled by a failure to come to grips with the limitations imposed by the way markets work. Figure 2-7 shows a stylized demand curve for the world oil market. U.S. policy makers have long recognized the negative impact of high oil prices on economic activity. Supply shocks mean short-run bursts of inflation. High oil prices raise the cost of all energy-intensive activity, by consumers and by industry. Economic growth is slowed, and the U.S. trade balance—because the high price applies to a good for which the United States is a net importer—is made worse. One might think, therefore, that low oil prices would be welcomed by U.S. policy makers. However, solicitude for the domestic oil industry has led successive U.S. administrations

---

[35]See Douglas R. Bohi and Michael A. Toman, "Oil Supply Disruptions and the Role of the International Energy Agency," *The Energy Journal* 7, no. 2 (April 1986): 37–50; David R. Henderson, "The IEA Oil-Sharing Plan: Who Shares with Whom?," *The Energy Journal* 8, no. 4 (October 1987): 23–31; and George Horwich and David Leo Weimer, editors, *Responding to International Oil Crises* (Washington, D.C.: American Enterprise Institute for Public Policy Research, 1988).

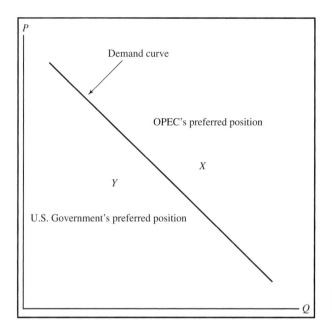

FIGURE 2-7 Wishful Thinking at Home and Abroad

to defend a position that would have the United States at a point like *Y* in Figure 2-7: a low price for oil, but we don't buy much of it, at least not from foreign suppliers.

What is striking is that OPEC member nations suffer from a symmetric failure to come to grips with the way markets work. In the long run, a monopolist or complete cartel can be anywhere that it wants to be on the demand curve. The constraint imposed by the market is that price and quantity are inversely related: A high price means a low quantity demanded, and a low price means a high quantity demanded. It is clear from endless public statements that OPEC oil ministers want very much to be at a point like *X* in Figure 2-7. They want to charge a high price for oil and sell a great deal of oil, but over the long run, the market will not let them.

National Security: The Short Run

The current consumption of U.S. oil always increases future dependence on foreign oil, barrel for barrel. The only way to avoid this is permanent tariffs or quotas that artificially raise the price of oil in the United States and distort input/consumption choices in less efficient and less productive ways. It is not in the national security interest of the United States to be protected from foreign oil that is cheaper than domestic oil.

The specter is raised of unending Middle East reserves and vulnerability to a cut-off of oil supplies from a politically unstable region of the world. The best supply-side response to this possibility is to diversify sources of supply away from politically unstable regions, and this diversification is increasingly feasible as new oil provinces open up around the world. The expansion of oil reserves outside OPEC implies that U.S. security interests lie in an open world market.

No long-run U.S. security interest is achieved in avoiding the current consumption of cheap foreign oil. However, the United States does have a short-run security interest in neutralizing run-ups in the price of oil due to sporadic supply interruptions, and that is a problem that can be addressed, in the event, through proper use of the Strategic Petroleum Reserve.

National Security: The Long Run

Energy security does not come only from finding diversified sources of oil supplies around the world. It also is achieved by finding alternatives to the use of conventional oil and natural gas: shale oil, coal gasification, solar power, nuclear fusion, and others. Experience shows that this sort of research cannot be left entirely to market forces. The costs of commercial-scale plants are far higher, and the development times far longer, than commercial enterprises can support. If government investment in a Strategic Petroleum Reserve to maintain short-run energy security is appropriate, then government support for the long-term (20- or 50-year) research needed to ensure long-run energy security is also appropriate.

On the demand side, energy security lies in conservation and in the efficient use of energy. Yet Figure 2-2 shows that U.S. demand for oil has climbed above the previous peak, between the oil shock of 1973 and the oil shock of 1979. Figure 2-6 suggests that there is still progress to be made in bringing U.S. energy efficiency to the levels of other industrialized countries.

Conclusion

The oil price increases of 1973, 1979, and 1981 reduced the level of world demand for energy below what it otherwise would have been. A decade of moderate prices in the 1990s dulled incentives for the efficient use of energy, and U.S. demand for oil, the primary source of energy, has risen to levels that should evoke concern.

Against this unfavorable evolution on the demand side of the market can be set some favorable developments on the supply side of the market. A critical change in market structure is the expanded number of players. For generations, the world oil market was dominated by the Seven Sisters, the vertically integrated majors. For somewhat more than a decade, the world oil market was dominated by OPEC member states. For the foreseeable future, events on the world oil market will reflect the actions of the OPEC member states (integrating forward toward the final consumer), the international majors (integrating backward through the development of OPEC and non-OPEC reserves), new supplying nations, and independent oil companies. These various firms and nation-firms will collude when they can and compete when they must. The increased number of suppliers reduces the likelihood of successful exercise of control over price.

Nonetheless, when the growth of demand and a reduction in independent supply presents the opportunity to extract monopoly profits, OPEC members or (more likely) a group of high-reserve oil producers who are able and who perceive a common set of interests will take that opportunity. Periodically, supply will be cut back and oil prices will rise. At this writing, the world oil market is more like Figure 2-3(a) than Figure 2-3(b). We will experience future oil price shocks.

Governments can—if they will—mitigate the effects of these shocks. The policy to do so will use the market price as a trigger to release and share strategic reserves over the short run and will promote the development of alternative sources of supply and efficient use of energy over the long run. Policies that fail to use the information provided by the market in the short run, and that rely on the market alone to develop new technology over the long run, will exacerbate future oil shocks.

Suggested Readings

Adelman, M. A. 1995. *The Genie Out of the Bottle.* Cambridge, MA: MIT Press.

Blair, John M. 1976. *The Control of Oil.* New York: Random House.

Boué, Juan Carlos. 1993. *Venezuela: The Political Economy of Oil.* Oxford: Oxford University Press.

Chernow, Ron. 1998. *Titan: The Life of John D. Rockefeller, Sr.* New York: Random House.

Eckel, Edwin C. 1920. *Coal, Iron and War.* New York: Henry Holt and Company.

Hartshorn, J. E. 1993. *Oil Trade: Politics and Prospects.* Cambridge: Cambridge University Press.

Harvie, Christopher. 1995. *Fool's Gold: The Story of North Sea Oil.* London: Penguin Books.

Heal, Geoffrey, and Graciela Chichilnisky. 1991. *Oil and the International Economy.* Oxford: Clarendon Press.

Horsnell, Paul, and Robert Mabro. 1993. *Oil Markets and Prices.* Oxford: Oxford University Press.

Mabro, Robert, Robert Bacon, Margaret Chadwick, Mark Halliwell, and David Long. 1986. *The Market for North Sea Crude Oil.* Oxford: Oxford University Press.

Sampson, Anthony. 1976. *The Seven Sisters.* New York: Bantam Books.

Schneider, Steven A. 1983. *The Oil Price Revolution.* Baltimore: The Johns Hopkins University Press.

Tarbell, Ida M. 1904. *The History of the Standard Oil Company.* McClure, Phillips and Co. (www.history.rochester.edu/fuels/tarbell/MAIN.HTM).

Turner, Louis. 1983. *Oil Companies in the International System,* 3rd ed. London: George Allen & Unwin.

U.S. Congress. Senate. Subcommittee on Monopoly. 1952. The International Petroleum Cartel: Staff Report to the Federal Trade Commission. 82d Cong., 2d sess.

Yergin, Daniel. 1991. *The Prize.* New York: Simon & Schuster.

Some Useful Web Sites

American Petroleum Institute: www.api.org/
Energy Information Administration links page: www.eia.doe.gov/links.html#petroleum
International Energy Agency: www.iea.org/
OPEC: www.opec.org/

Oxford Institute for Energy Studies: www.oxfordenergy.org/
Texas Railroad Commission: www.rrc.state.tx.us/
U.S. Department of Energy: www.doe.gov/

CHAPTER

Cigarettes

—GEORGE A. HAY[1]

Americans purchase some 21 billion packs of cigarettes annually at a retail expenditure of $64 billion. In inflation-adjusted dollars, this represents an increase of nearly 60 percent over the past 3 decades. Yet this gain is due entirely to higher prices and taxes; aggregate physical consumption of cigarettes has actually plunged by about half over this same period. Of the total dollars spent, some $7.4 billion goes to the federal government, and an additional $8.4 billion goes to state governments. Thus, the domestic cigarette industry itself had revenues of about $46 billion in 2001 (a 19 percent increase, in real terms, from 1967). The industry is clearly important in the United States, not only because of the magnitude of consumer expenditures devoted to the purchase of cigarettes, but also because of its significant contribution to government revenues at the state and federal levels.

The cigarette industry is also a fiercely-fought focus of public policy because of the health impacts of smoking. It is estimated that more than 400,000 people die each year due to smoking-related illnesses, representing almost 20 percent of all deaths in the United States and rendering smoking the single largest preventable cause of death in this country. The nation's health care costs due to smoking, according to some estimates, total $75 billion per year.

The health consequences of smoking, in turn, make the analysis of the "performance" of the cigarette industry fundamentally different from that of other industries. Issues related to pricing, advertising, and product development in this industry all have complex public policy ramifications that go beyond the normal analysis of consumer benefit applied to other fields. In addition, the tobacco industry has been involved in litigation related to its health effects that is unprecedented in scope and potential financial impact. In 1998, a group of state attorneys general settled a series of lawsuits seeking reimbursement for the costs of treating victims of smoking-related diseases. This settlement, in conjunction with ongoing federal regulation, will have significant consequences for conduct and performance in the industry in the years ahead.

I. HISTORY

Mass Production and the Tobacco Trust

The economic significance of the cigarette industry and the widespread prevalence of lung cancer in the population are phenomena of the twentieth century. Prior to 1900,

[1]This is a revised version of the chapter in the preceding edition written by Adam Jaffe. Andrew Feng, Murat Hakki, and Jae Kim assisted in updating the data for this revised version. The author has consulted and served as an expert witness in several antitrust matters involving the cigarette companies.

cigars, plug tobacco, and loose-smoking tobacco all enjoyed greater sales than cigarettes. However, the low cost and convenience of cigarettes almost certainly facilitated the spread of the tobacco habit through the population, particularly among women, who had not been major consumers of other tobacco products.

The birth of the modern cigarette industry can be dated to the invention in the 1880s of a practical machine for mass production. Prior to this time, cigarettes were rolled by hand, and commercial cigarettes were produced by relatively small firms. It required skilled workers to roll the cigarettes and significant supervision to oversee the quality of the product. Then, in 1881, James Bonsack obtained a patent for a machine that could produce 12,000 cigarettes per hour, compared to the approximately 3,000 per day that could be rolled by a skilled worker. The patented Bonsack machine was leased to cigarette manufacturers at a price that reduced direct manufacturing costs by about half. Probably more important, the machine produced a standardized output so that many machines could be combined with relatively unskilled operators on a large scale with minimal supervision and quality-control efforts.

Mechanization of production thus removed the barrier to large-scale operation and laid the groundwork for rapid industry growth and industry concentration. In particular, James B. Duke seized the opportunity created by the Bonsack machine, even though his W. Duke Sons &Co. had produced only loose-smoking tobacco prior to 1880. In return for making a large-scale commitment to the new technology, Duke was able to license the machine on favorable terms, giving him a cost advantage over his competitors. He then invested aggressively in manufacturing, and also in advertising and inducements to jobbers and retailers to promote his products. By 1889, Duke was the country's largest manufacturer of cigarettes.

The other firms found it difficult to compete with Duke's cost advantage and aggressive advertising. What ensued resembled the agglomeration that occurred in many manufacturing industries during the closing decades of the nineteenth century. Duke convinced all five major manufacturers of cigarettes to join him in forming the American Tobacco Company in 1890. At the outset, the "Tobacco Trust" controlled approximately 90 percent of U.S. cigarette production.

The trust acted aggressively to preserve its dominant position over the next 20 years. It purchased exclusive rights to the Bonsack machine and accumulated patents on other machines. It was accused of using a variety of tactics to make life difficult for competitors, including attempting to organize strikes among their workers, making exclusive distribution deals with wholesalers and jobbers, and bidding up prices for tobacco leaf in markets where the independents were active. The trust also purchased a number of independents and added their brands to its own. At the same time, in a pattern that has echoes in the modern market, the trust's heavy advertising and promotion succeeded in creating strong brand loyalty to its premier brands. The "Marlboro" of that era was called Sweet Caporal, and it had a market share of approximately 50 percent at the turn of the century. Overall, the trust increased its share of the market to about 95 percent by 1899.

Antitrust Convictions

In its 2 decades of existence, the trust acquired approximately 250 formerly independent firms. Some of these were shut down, but many continued to operate either as members of the trust or as wholly owned subsidiaries. In 1911, however, the Tobacco

Trust suffered the fate of its sisters in oil and other industries, and was found by the Supreme Court to have violated the Sherman Antitrust Act. As a result of this decision, it was ordered that the trust be reorganized and broken up. The cigarette business and principal assets were put in the hands of four companies: the American Tobacco Company, R.J. Reynolds Tobacco Company, Liggett & Myers Tobacco Company, and P. Lorillard Company.

World War I facilitated the spread of cigarette smoking among men. During this period, Reynolds introduced the Camel brand, which incorporated a new and supposedly premium blend of tobaccos. Reynolds abandoned the use of coupons that had previously been a major promotional tool and instead advertised Camels as a more expensive smoke that was worth the higher price. This established the concept of premium brands marketed at premium prices—a concept that continues to characterize the industry today. During the interwar period, the industry was dominated by Reynolds, American Tobacco, and Liggett & Myers, all of which had strong brands that were advertised heavily and priced at levels that yielded high profit margins. In addition, cigarette smoking began to spread among women, who were wooed by advertising campaigns like Lucky Strike's "Reach for a Lucky instead of a sweet."

The onset of the Great Depression set the stage for a series of events that eventually landed the descendants of the Tobacco Trust back at the Supreme Court. Despite falling tobacco-leaf prices and falling consumer incomes, the major tobacco companies raised cigarette prices in 1931 to a level that produced retail prices of approximately 14 to 15 cents per pack.

Because of low leaf prices, however, it was possible for new, small firms to produce a premium-quality cigarette that sold at retail for only 10 cents. The size of the pricing gap and the pressure of hard times allowed these 10-cent brands to make significant inroads into the market, capturing almost a quarter of cigarette sales by 1932. (This pattern in which high prices for premium brands create an opportunity for what we now call discount or generic varieties to get established is one we will see repeated in the 1980s and 1990s.)

The major manufacturers responded to the success of the 10-cent brands. In January 1933, American cut the price of its Lucky Strikes by about 12 percent at wholesale—a cut that was followed by the other premium brands. In February, the price was cut by an additional 10 percent and again matched by the other majors. The majors also pressed distributors to reduce their margins so that the premium brands could sell at retail for 10 cents. The discount brands could not compete at pricing parity, and many of them disappeared.

After a period of intense competition, Reynolds led a price increase in 1934 that brought the price of the premium brands partway back to where it was before. It was later shown that Lucky Strike and Camel had been sold at a loss during the price war.

Despite the aggressive response of the Big Three to the incursion of the 10-cent brands, the former were never able to reclaim the dominant market position they enjoyed at the beginning of the 1930s. In addition to the 10-cent brands, incursions were made by Philip Morris & Co., an independent manufacturer that had never been part of the trust, and Brown & Williamson Tobacco Co., the U.S. subsidiary of the British American Tobacco Co. As a result, the combined share of Reynolds, American, and Liggett & Meyers, which had been 91 percent in 1930, fell to 69 percent by 1939. The advent of Philip Morris and Brown & Williamson in the 1930s represents the last time significant new competitors were established in the field; the "Big Six" of American, Reynolds, Liggett & Meyers, Lorillard, Philip Morris, and Brown & Williamson would collectively dominate the industry through the modern era.

The apparently predatory pricing response of the majors to the growth of the 10-cent brands formed the core of new accusations that the majors had engaged in monopolization and conspiracy in violation of the Sherman Act. The companies were convicted of these charges in 1941 in a decision that eventually was upheld by the Supreme Court. This time though, no structural remedies were imposed on the firms. Instead, they were required to pay fines and were subjected to restrictions on their abilities to communicate and coordinate their actions.

The Cancer Era

The competitive playing field was fundamentally transformed by the emergence in the early 1950s of significant concerns regarding the connection between cigarettes and cancer. Health concerns associated with tobacco and cigarettes were not entirely new; as far back as colonial times (and before), some criticized tobacco as a filthy and dangerous habit, but these concerns had never significantly impinged on the market. This situation changed dramatically in the decade following the end of World War II, however, as the emergence of cigarettes as a mass-produced product, the spread of the smoking habit through the population, and the development of new scientific research techniques led to scientific studies suggesting that cigarette smoking causes lung cancer.

An article in *Reader's Digest* in 1953 summarized this research and sparked widespread discussion and concern about the health consequences of smoking. For the first time, the major tobacco companies perceived these health concerns to be a major threat: The presidents of five of the Big Six companies met for 2 days at a hotel in New York to discuss the situation, the first time since the antitrust conviction of the 1940s that such a meeting had occurred. This meeting was the apparent genesis of an industry agreement on a collective response to the health "problem." With the exception of Liggett & Meyers, the companies joined together to create the Tobacco Industry Research Committee (TIRC), later renamed the Council for Tobacco Research. They published a statement, signed by the company presidents, in major newspapers throughout the United States. The statement was entitled "A Frank Statement to Cigarette Smokers."

In its Frank Statement, the industry disputed the evidence that cigarettes were harmful but nonetheless accepted "an interest in people's health as a basic responsibility, paramount to every other consideration in our business," and promised to fund through the TIRC "research efforts into all phases of tobacco use and health."[2] The statement established a common public industry position on smoking and health that would stand for 40 years. Although the precise expression of this position varied, it amounted to saying that the evidence that smoking was harmful was inconclusive, that more research was necessary, and that the industry was supporting such research in the hope of determining the truth.

---

[2] *State of Minnesota and Minnesota Blue Cross/Blue Shield v. Philip Morris, Inc. et al. (1998).* Trial Exhibit No. 14145.

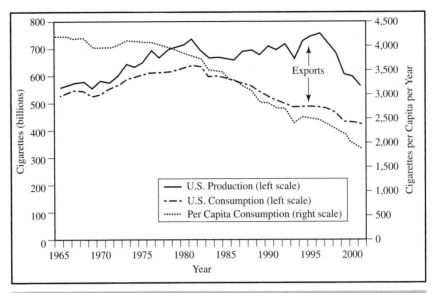

FIGURE 3-1   Production and Consumption of Cigarettes

SOURCE: Federal Trade Commission, 1997 and 2003.

Over the ensuing decade, the industry's position that the danger of smoking was unproven became increasingly untenable. In 1964, the U.S. surgeon general issued a report compiled by a special advisory committee he had convened. After reviewing approximately 7,000 published studies, the report concluded that cigarette smoking was a cause of lung cancer and laryngeal cancer in men, a probable cause of cancer in women, and the most important cause of chronic bronchitis. Subsequent surgeon general's reports have confirmed these findings and added other forms of cancer, heart ailments, and emphysema to the list of diseases whose risk and mortality rates are significantly raised by smoking.

The 1964 surgeon general's report marked a watershed. From that time forward, reducing smoking has become a major public policy objective. In fact, no other legal product has ever been the target of such a large and sustained government effort to reduce its consumption. As shown in Figure 3-1, the incidence of smoking in the United States has declined significantly since the 1960s. Of all the people alive today who were ever regular smokers of cigarettes, approximately half have quit smoking. On the other hand, 40 years after the government found and reported that cigarettes kill people, approximately one quarter of adult Americans still smoke cigarettes, and many of them took up the habit after the publication of the surgeon general's 1964 report.

II. INDUSTRY STRUCTURE

Concentration

As shown in Figure 3-2, the cigarette industry is one of the most concentrated industries in the United States and has been so throughout the postwar period. In 1954, it was the ninth most concentrated manufacturing industry; in 1992, it was the fourth most

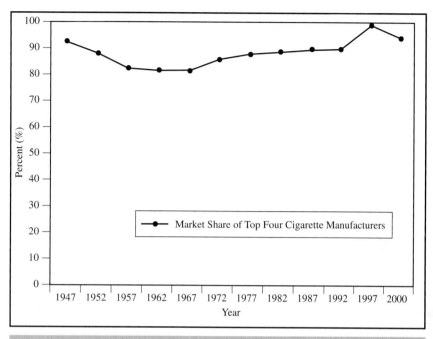

FIGURE 3-2   Four-Firm Concentration Ratio

SOURCES: Federal Trade Commission 1997: U.S. Economic Census; and Information Resources, Inc.

concentrated, and it is the only industry that was among the 10 most concentrated industries in both of these years. In 1996, following the acquisition of American Tobacco by Brown & Williamson, the remaining top 5 firms controlled 99.9 percent of the U.S. market, with the top 4 firms controlling 98 percent. In terms of manufacturing establishments, total U.S. cigarette production in 1997 came from only 13 manufacturing establishments, of which only 10 had 20 or more employees.[3] Pending antitrust review, further concentration in the U.S. cigarette industry is possible; in October 2003, R.J. Reynolds Tobacco Holdings, Inc. and British American Tobacco announced the signing of an agreement to combine the assets and operations of their respective U.S. tobacco businesses: R.J. Reynolds Tobacco Co. and Brown & Williamson Tobacco Corp.

Barriers to Entry

Contributing to the continuing high concentration is the fact that the industry is characterized by significant barriers to entry. With the possible exception of the discount or generic brands that will be discussed later, no significant entry into the industry has occurred during the postwar period. Several reasons account for this: First, smokers exhibit significant brand loyalty that would have to be overcome by a new entrant. Most smokers have a preferred brand; although a smoker might occasionally purchase another brand, the vast majority of a smoker's purchases will be of the same preferred brand.

---

[3]U.S. Census Bureau, 1997 Economic Census, Cigarette Manufacturing.

In fact, it has been estimated that fewer than 10 percent of smokers change their preferred brands in any given year.[4]

This brand loyalty is sustained in part by massive advertising and promotion. Economies of scale in promotion make entry of a major new brand an expensive and risky proposition. In addition, one of the most cost-effective ways of launching a new national advertising campaign was taken away from the cigarette industry in 1970, when the Federal Trade Commission banned advertising of tobacco products on television and radio; the regulatory effects of recent litigation with the states further limit the ability of a new entrant to promote its brand.

Access to distribution channels is another major hurdle for a new entrant. Cigarettes are distributed through thousands of wholesalers and more than a million retail outlets. The major companies have large field-sales staffs that take orders, supervise stocking and point-of-sale displays, and provide a variety of incentives and promotions. A new entrant would have to choose between limited distribution, which would inherently limit brand growth, and a large investment in these distribution activities.

Finally, the fact that industry demand is in a long-run secular decline diminishes entry incentives, even in the face of high current industry profitability. This disincentive is exacerbated by the potential problems of legal liability for health impacts that would have to borne by any new entrant. On the other hand, despite relatively strong brand loyalty, episodes such as the introduction of the 10-cent brands in the 1930s and the recent, albeit limited, growth of the discount segment of the market in the face of large litigation-induced price increases suggest that smokers will switch brands in response to significant price differences. These situations also indicate that opportunities might exist for new entry.

In fact, despite these daunting obstacles, some new cigarette firms have recently entered the market for the first time in decades. Steady, substantial price boosts by the majors have tempted some small, new producers to enter the field by creating a new, "deeply discounted" category. One of these, Carolina Tobacco Company, is headquartered in a residential neighborhood in Beaverton, Oregon, but manufactures its cigarettes at a factory in the former Soviet republic of Latvia. At least initially, it and other similar small firms garnered perhaps as much as 7 percent of the field by 2002, according to some counts.[5] Whether these new entrants can survive is an open question, particularly as the majors have made overtures to acquire them.[6]

Individual Market Shares

Figure 3-3 depicts the evolution of the major firms' market shares in the industry. The dominant long-term trend has been the decline of American Tobacco and Liggett & Myers, and the rise of Philip Morris to almost 50 percent of the field by 1997. Indeed, American, the company that bore the name of the fabled trust, disappeared from the corporate scene when it was acquired by Brown & Williamson in 1996.

Figure 3-4 traces these reversals of fate to particular brands. Chesterfield and Lucky Strike accounted for almost 40 percent of the market in 1950 but had shrunk to insignificance by 1996. Conversely, Marlboro, today's dominant brand with about 40 percent

---

[4]U.S. Surgeon General, Reducing the Health Consequences of Smoking—25 Years of Progress: A Report of the Surgeon General (Washington, D.C., 1989).

[5]Gordon Fairclough, "Four Biggest Cigarette Makers Can't Raise Prices as They Did," *Wall Street Journal*, October 25, 2002, p. 1.

[6]See, for example, Gordon Fairclough, "Tobacco Titans Bid for 'Organic' Cigarette Maker," *Wall Street Journal*, December 10, 2001, p. B1.

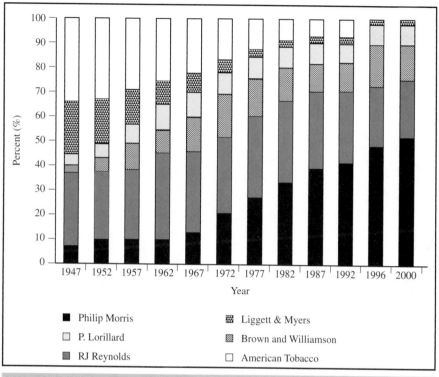

FIGURE 3-3 Cigarette Company Market Shares

SOURCES: Federal Trade Commission 1997; and Grocery Headquarter, 2001. See, for example, Gordon Fairclough, "Tobacco Titans Bid for 'Organic' Cigarette Maker," Wall Street Journal, December 10, 2001, p. B1.

of all sales, was insignificant in the 1950s. Clearly, the industry has been and remains highly concentrated, but substantial shifts have occurred within the field as the leading firms have jockeyed for position.

III. INDUSTRY CONDUCT

Advertising and Promotion

Cigarettes are one of the most heavily advertised and promoted products in the United States. In 2001, the majors spent $11 billion on advertising and promotion, approximately 24 percent of wholesale revenues. This is an astounding expenditure for a product that does not have complicated performance characteristics or design changes that need to be communicated, and whose purchasers have, for the most part, been purchasing the same brand for years. As shown in Figure 3-5, these expenditures have climbed significantly even as the number of smokers has decreased.

Advertising of cigarettes on television and radio was prohibited in 1970, which led to an initial decline in overall advertising and promotional expenditures. However, beginning in the mid-1970s, promotional expenditures grew rapidly, quickly exceeding what was spent previously on broadcast media. Promotional spending now includes coupons and payments to retailers, distribution of specialty gift items, and sponsorship

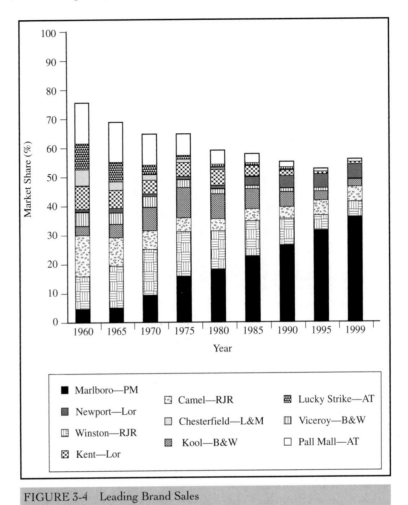

FIGURE 3-4   Leading Brand Sales

NOTE: Lucky Strike and Pall Mall brands were acquired by Brown & Williamson in 1996.
SOURCE: Maxwell Consumer Reports, various years.

of public entertainment. The latter has been especially controversial because of its potential impact on children.

An important aspect of the advertising history of the industry is the "Marlboro Man." Prior to 1954, Marlboro was an unimportant brand, and its owner, Philip Morris, was the fourth-largest of the six major firms. In the mid-1950s, however, Philip Morris repositioned Marlboro as a man's cigarette, modified its tobacco blend to produce a stronger flavor, and changed its packaging from white to the now familiar red-and-white chevron design. At the same time, its advertising began to feature men depicted in tough, action-filled situations. Initially, the nature of these situations varied, but by the mid-1960s, the Marlboro Man was always a cowboy who was photographed in the American West, which was identified as Marlboro Country. The Marlboro Man and Marlboro Country have now been used in ads and packaging in 150 countries; Marlboro has become by far the world's best-selling cigarette and one of the best-known consumer brands of any product around the world.

Advertising and promotion in the field have two general purposes. Defensive advertising and promotion are designed to create or reinforce a smoker's loyalty to his or

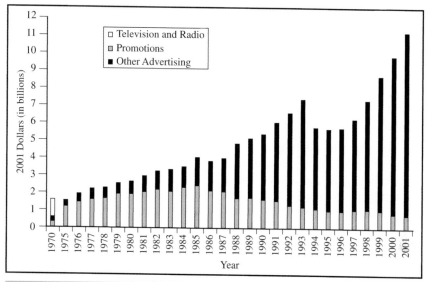

FIGURE 3-5 Cigarette Advertising and Promotional Expenditures (inflation adjusted)

SOURCE: Federal Trade Commission.

her preferred brand. Offensive advertising and promotion, on the other hand, are designed to induce a smoker to try a brand other than his or her preferred brand and, having sampled the alternative brand, to switch loyalties to it. Point-of-sale advertising and promotion, such as counter displays that call attention to special offers (e.g., two packs for the price of one), are primarily designed to serve the second purpose (inducing the smoker to sample an alternative brand).

A related dimension of industry conduct is the large and increasing number of varieties of cigarette brands offered for sale: More than 1,294 varieties of cigarettes were offered for sale in 1998, up from fewer than 600 in 1991.[7] This brand proliferation is due primarily to line extensions, as sellers try to maximize the strength of popular brands by offering them in many different versions. The best-selling Marlboro brand, for example, was offered in 29 distinct varieties in 2003.

Pricing

It is clear that pricing in the cigarette industry, despite the high level of market concentration and significant barriers to entry, does not approximate the level that would occur if the firms were engaging in joint-profit maximization (i.e., setting prices at the level that would be chosen by a single cigarette monopolist). Indeed, a monopolist would never choose a price level at which the elasticity of demand is less than 1 (in absolute value); monopoly profits could always be increased by raising the price until the elasticity becomes greater, and there is no question, at least until the recent round of litigation-induced price hikes, that the elasticity of overall industry demand is significantly less than one. It is difficult to estimate what the monopoly price would be, because it requires extrapolation of demand outside of the range of observed prices, but a recent estimate (although it preceded

---

[7]See annual reports by the Federal Trade Commission on the tar, nicotine, and carbon monoxide of the smoke of domestic cigarette varieties.

litigation-induced cost and price increases) was that a cigarette monopolist would raise the price to approximately twice the then-current level.[8]

On the other hand, evidence suggests that cigarette pricing is above competitive levels. The average real wholesale price of cigarettes rose approximately 200 percent between 1980 and 2002, an increase that cannot be attributed to increased input costs. Historically, wholesale cigarette price changes have occurred infrequently, with no apparent relation to costs, and virtually simultaneously and uniformly among the major manufacturers. As the Supreme Court noted as recently as 1993:

> The cigarette industry has long been one of America's most profitable, in part because for many years there was no significant price competition among the rivals. . . . List prices for cigarettes increased in lock-step twice a year, for a number of years, irrespective of the rate of inflation and changes in the cost of production, or shifts in consumer demand.[9]

An important aspect of pricing in the industry is the division of the market into premium, discount, and deep-discount segments. The modern form of this segmentation was instigated by Liggett & Myers, which pioneered low-price generics in 1980. Liggett was once a major force in the field with a market share in excess of 20 percent, but by 1980 Liggett's share barely exceeded 2 percent. At the urging of a distributor, Liggett took an unusual step to revive its prospects—developing a line of generic cigarettes whose principal competitive characteristic was low price. Liggett's generic cigarettes were an immediate success, accounting for 4 percent of industry sales by 1984. Reminiscent of the 10-cent brand episode of the 1930s, the other majors responded by introducing their own discount brands.

Today all of the majors sell discount brands, although they differ markedly in their dependence on discount sales. Although discount brands account for only about one quarter of industry sales, they do have an important impact on industry pricing. Figure 3-6 shows the pattern of price changes, by segment, over the last decade. In the early 1990s, premium prices increased steadily, notwithstanding the competition from the discount brands. (In addition to Liggett & Myers, discount brands were being heavily promoted by R.J. Reynolds.) Price cuts for deep-discount and discount brands increased the price gap with the premium segment so that by 1992, a price gap of approximately 40 cents had emerged between the premium and discount brands, compared to a manufacturing cost difference of only a few cents per pack.

As a result, the discount segment had grown to about 40 percent of the overall market, and the market share of Philip Morris's flagship Marlboro brand slipped after climbing steadily for more than 2 decades. This resulted in a major realignment of prices in 1993 on what has come to be called "Marlboro Friday." On that day, Philip Morris cut the price of its premium brands by 40 cents, eliminating the price differential between the premium and discount brands. Explained the firm in its 1993 annual report:

> We believe . . . that had we not responded promptly to this discount challenge mounted by our competition, our share losses in premium brands would have accelerated further, and damage to our premium brand franchises would have become irreversible.

[8]Jeffrey Harris, "American Cigarette Manufacturers' Ability to Pay Damages: Overview of a Rough Calculation," *Tobacco Control* 5 (1996): 292–294.
[9]*Brooke Group, Ltd. v. Brown & Williamson Tobacco Corp., 509 U.S. 209 (1993), at 213.*

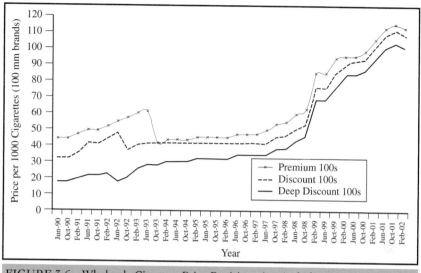

FIGURE 3-6   Wholesale Cigarette Price Revisions (not including taxes)

*SOURCE: U.S. Dept of Agriculture, Economic Research Service, http://www.ers.usda.gov/
Briefing/Tobacco.*

The immediate financial consequences were huge: Philip Morris stock plunged 23 percent in a single day, wiping out $13 billion in shareholder equity. However, the firm's loss of market share was reversed, as can be seen in Figure 3-4.

In 1993, Philip Morris responded to this development with subsequent premium price increases that have restored a significant portion of the pre-1993 gap between the discount and premium brands.

The Battle for Shelf Space

As a result of recent regulations and marketing restrictions, opportunities for the kind of mass advertising and promotion that the cigarette companies historically have used to build overall demand and expand or sustain market share have been substantially foreclosed. This has led to a major shift in the companies' focus toward point-of-sale advertising, especially in convenience stores and gas stations, which account for more than half of all cigarette sales. These are often referred to as "pack outlets," because the majority of purchasers in these outlets purchase by the pack rather than by the carton. (In contrast, in supermarkets and cigarette and tobacco specialty stores, most sales are by the carton.) Pack sales are especially important in the battle for market share because, among smokers of premium or branded discount cigarettes, those who purchase by the pack are most likely to buy a brand other than their usual brand, and thus are the most susceptible to being influenced by the manufacturers' point-of-sale marketing efforts and by the degree of visibility the product enjoys in the retail outlet.

The emphasis on point-of-sale promotion and visibility has manifested itself in manufacturer programs designed to "capture" the most and the best display space in retail outlets. In most convenience stores, the principal display space is on the back wall behind the counter where the cash registers are located. The best space behind the counter is the space above counter height, because this is the most visible to those walking past or waiting in line.

In 1998, Phillip Morris (PM) implemented an aggressive policy of offering retailers enhanced monthly payments and increased opportunities for price discounts in exchange for a commitment to give PM brands a disproportionate amount of the most visible behind-the-counter space, as well as exclusivity or near exclusivity with respect to the placement of signs and other promotional materials throughout the store. R.J. Reynolds and the other majors responded with programs of their own,[10] but PM's dominant market share (and especially the strength of the Marlboro brand) gave it an enormous advantage in dealing with retailers.

Hence, PM's competitors responded in the modern American fashion—by filing a lawsuit against PM, alleging that its marketing programs were akin to "exclusive dealing" (an arrangement where the retailer agrees to carry only a single manufacturer's products) and are illegal under the antitrust laws. After several years of litigation, the suit was dismissed on the grounds that PM's program did not really foreclose rivals' opportunities to compete for the loyalty of retail stores, especially given the short duration of most of PM's retailer contracts. Although it is too early to tell, this competition for the contract is likely to intensify as other opportunities for marketing and promotion of cigarettes continue to be narrowed.

IV. INDUSTRY PERFORMANCE

Assessing the performance of the cigarette industry requires consideration of multiple and conflicting objectives: First is the usual criteria related to allocative efficiency that prices approximate competitive levels in order to maximize consumer surplus; second is the government's fiscal interest in the tax revenues generated by cigarette sales; and third is the public interest in reducing the negative health consequences of smoking.

Exactly what form these concerns should take is unclear. One view would be that adult smokers are aware of the health consequences and choose to smoke because those adverse consequences are more than offset by the benefits they receive from smoking. According to this viewpoint, public policy concern should be limited to adverse health consequences that are not borne by the smokers themselves. These concerns include health care expenditures borne by insurers and other third-party payers, and the health consequences of secondhand smoke.

A broader view would be that smokers are addicted to cigarettes and hence incapable of rationally balancing the costs and benefits of the habit. According to this viewpoint, it should be a goal of public policy to prevent such addictions from forming and to help those addicted to break the habit. A potential intermediate view would allow adults to make up their own minds but would judge that children are often incapable of making well-informed choices about their futures; therefore, it should be a policy goal to prevent them from smoking. Because the overwhelming majority of smokers began smoking before they reached age 18, this view would put a primary policy focus on preventing youth from smoking.

These philosophical issues have an important influence on how the performance of this particular industry is assessed. For most industries, the elevation of prices above cost is viewed as undesirable. If we believe that smokers are rationally balancing the

[10]RJR Tobacco later adopted a similar plan to PM Retail Leader program and was, in turn, sued by Liggett for violating the Sherman Antitrust Act. The case was voluntarily dismissed on May 3, 2001.

risks and benefits of smoking, then this view carries over to the cigarette market, perhaps with a modest adjustment allowing some taxation to compensate for the externalities that smokers impose on others. If, however, we believe that public policy should affirmatively discourage smoking, then high cigarette prices are a good thing, not a bad thing, because they reduce cigarette consumption.

Profits

Despite the long-term decline in industry sales, cigarette manufacturing remains one of the most profitable of all businesses. Figure 3-7 depicts the profits of the major companies. Because the profit margins on premium brands are so much greater than the margins on discount brands, participation in the premium segment is the primary determinant of company profitability. Lorillard and Philip Morris, which both have most of their sales in premium brands, have the highest profit rates. Reynolds and Brown & Williamson are intermediate in their reliance on discount sales; Liggett & Myers derives only 7.2 percent of its sales from premium brands. The industry's overall profit margin of 23 percent of sales is one of the highest of any field.[11]

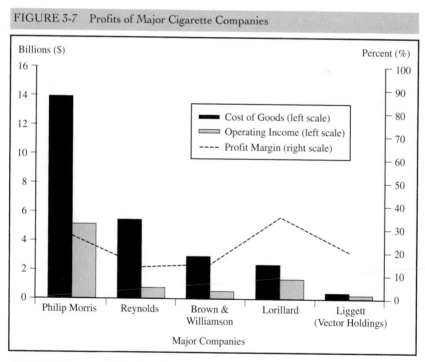

FIGURE 3-7   Profits of Major Cigarette Companies

SOURCE: Company 10-Ks. British American Tobacco Annual Report.

---

[11]Economic theory suggests that profitability should be determined on the basis of the rate of return on assets rather than on sales. Census of Manufacturing data indicate that the investment intensity of the industry is not above average, suggesting that the high profit/sales ratio also corresponds to a high rate of return on assets.

Product Development and the Health Issue

As discussed previously, the industry's public response to the rising concern about cigarettes and health in the 1950s was to question incriminating evidence and call for more research. Privately, however, the companies understood the strength of the evidence against their product and recognized that it had profound competitive implications. For example, a Philip Morris scientist wrote in 1958:

> Inasmuch as the evidence is building up that heavy cigarette smoking contributes to lung cancer . . .
>
> I'll bet that the first company to produce a cigarette claiming a substantial reduction in tars and nicotine, or an ersatz cigarette whose smoke contains no tobacco tars, and with good smoking flavor, will take the market. Further, if he has the intestinal fortitude to jump on the other side of the fence (provided he has some convincing experimental evidence to back him up) on the issue of tobacco smoking and health, just look what a wealth of ammunition would be at his disposal.[12]

Thus, the companies were publicly denying the significance of the health threat, but internally they understood that consumers' desire for safer products created an opportunity to gain competitive advantage. This situation created a fundamental conflict between the industry's collective interest in minimizing the health threat and firms' individual incentive to profitably exploit consumer demand for safer cigarettes. Documents subsequently obtained in legal proceedings formed the basis of allegations that the industry's collective interest prevailed, and that the producers entered into a collusive agreement to suppress research that might have undermined their public position and led to the development of new competition in responding to consumers' health concerns.[13]

If such a collusive agreement existed, it did not eliminate all efforts by the firms to compete in ways that exploited the health issue. The most important product development attempting to reduce the harmfulness of cigarettes was a device called Premier, test-marketed by Reynolds in 1988. Premier was a new concept in cigarette design; indeed, one could question whether it was really a cigarette at all. Instead of burning tobacco, Premier burned a small core of graphite, which heated tobacco extract and a substrate containing nicotine in order to produce a smokelike aerosol containing nicotine and tobacco aroma. Reynolds undertook a substantial research program that demonstrated that the "smoke" from Premier showed dramatically reduced biological activity, using essentially all of the scientific tests that were available and indicative of possible adverse human health effects.[14] Although it is clear that Premier was not a safe cigarette, it is also clear that it represented a major effort to develop a product that was likely to be safer than existing products (and to demonstrate that the smoking hazard could be reduced using available technologies.)

Premier failed in the marketplace for a number of reasons: First, the Premier smoking experience was a major departure for the smoker; it was difficult to light and keep lit, and it was generally perceived to have an odd taste. Second, Premier was

---

[12]Minnesota Trial Exhibit No. 11662.
[13]Minnesota Trial Exhibit Nos. 18904 and 18905.
[14]See Minnesota Trial Exhibit No. 12873.

strongly opposed by public health groups, which seemed uninterested in affording smokers an opportunity to use a potentially safer form of tobacco; instead, they argued that the marketing of a product like Premier would undermine antismoking efforts by suggesting that the health hazard could be reduced. At the same time, Reynolds avoided any marketing attempt to utilize the considerable scientific evidence it had amassed regarding the reduced biological activity of Premier, claiming only that Premier offered a "cleaner" smoke.

For innovation on this front, data produced in litigation indicate that the companies' aggregate expenditure on research and development and product development related to the health effects of smoking totaled approximately $3 billion between 1954 and 1996 (about $2.7 billion of this was in the form of company expenditures, and another $0.3 billion came in the form of funding to the Council for Tobacco Research). Although this might seem like a significant expenditure, it is a small fraction of the almost $50 billion that the firms spent on advertising and promotion over the same period, and a tiny portion of the almost $500 billion of industry revenues over those years.

The Development of "Low-Delivery" Products

The primary product response of the manufacturers to consumers' health concerns has been the development of low-tar/low-nicotine (LTLN) cigarettes, although the companies have consistently denied that these products are designed to reduce the health hazards of smoking. Indeed, they apparently have done no research to determine whether these products provide any reduction in negative health effects. Nonetheless, it is clear that the products are designed to take advantage of the demand for products perceived to be safer without having to admit that any cigarette products are unsafe.

The market response to products perceived to be safer has been clear since the 1950s. That decade saw the introduction and rapid growth of a variety of filter-tipped cigarettes. Filtered brands accounted for less than 1 percent of the market in 1952 but had grown to 51 percent by 1959. Viceroy, which received a favorable rating regarding its tar delivery from an article in *Readers' Digest*, and Kent, which advertised the superiority of its "micronite" filter, enjoyed especially rapid growth. Overall, the sales-weighted average tar delivery has fallen from more than 30 milligrams per cigarette to 12 milligrams in 1998; approximately 86 percent of cigarettes sold in 2001 had machine-measured tar yields of 15 milligrams or less.

The trend toward LTLN products was encouraged by public health authorities, who have suggested since the mid-1960s that reduced deliveries would likely reduce the health risks. It is unclear, however, what, if any, health benefit is associated with LTLN products.

Reduced delivery of tar and nicotine on a testing machine does not necessarily translate into reduced human intake, largely because of the phenomenon of compensation. Because people smoke to get nicotine, they take larger and longer puffs to compensate for a cigarette that delivers less of it. Further, some of the technologies used to reduce deliveries, such as perforating the cigarette paper with tiny holes to draw in additional air, show reduced deliveries on smoking machines but are often ineffective in human smoking. As a result, the health benefit associated with the reduction in machine-measured tar and nicotine yields is probably considerably less than would be implied by the average reduction in yields. Indeed, some experts contend that the compensation phenomenon completely eliminates the potential health benefit of LTLN products.[15]

V. PUBLIC POLICY

Antitrust Action

The advent of low-priced generics in the early 1980s led to an important antitrust decision by the U.S. Supreme Court. This decision has had significant implications that extend beyond the cigarette industry. We have seen that the growth of generics came at the expense of the profitable branded cigarettes. Brown & Williamson, with 11 percent of the market overall, was particularly hard hit. Brown & Williamson responded with its own line of value and generic cigarettes and a price war ensued, primarily in the form of rebates at the wholesale level. The price war became so intense that Liggett sued Brown & Williamson under the antitrust laws, claiming that the company was predatorily pricing its discount brands by setting prices below the average variable costs to produce them.

This claim was significant because, in response to a well-known and widely cited article by Harvard Law School professors Phillip Areeda and Donald Turner,[16] many courts had adopted as a test of unlawful predatory pricing whether prices fell below average variable costs. The key concept here is that when a firm's prices do not even cover its incremental costs, the firm loses more money with every additional unit of output sold and would seemingly be better off by substantially restricting its output and perhaps even by shutting its doors and ceasing to produce altogether. If the firm persists in selling at prices that are below incremental costs, the article suggested, the most plausible rationale would be that the firm expects to achieve the power to charge supra-competitive prices and thereby recoup its short-run losses. However, the significance of the so-called Areeda-Turner test is that the plaintiff does not have to prove that prices eventually will go up; the fact that the defendant is pricing below incremental costs is considered sufficient to permit a court to infer that supra-competitive prices are almost certain to follow. (Because incremental costs are difficult to measure, average variable costs are used as a proxy.)

The question presented to the Supreme Court was two-fold. First, could Liggett win simply by showing that Brown & Williamson's prices were below its average variable costs? Second, if evidence of below-cost pricing was not enough standing on its own, what more would Liggett have to prove, and had they done so? On the first question, the Supreme Court ruled that evidence of below-cost pricing was not enough, and it established an additional test.

In addition to proving that prices were below costs, the plaintiff also had to show that there was a reasonable chance that the defendant eventually would be able to raise prices high enough to offset or recoup its short-term losses. Absent a serious

---

[15]See Federal Trade Commission, Report to Congress for 1997, *Pursuant to the Federal Cigarette Labeling and Advertising Act* (1999); National Cancer Institute, Smoking and Tobacco Control Monograph 8: *Changes in Cigarette-Related Disease Risk and Their Implications for Prevention and Control* (1997).

[16]P. Areeda, and D. Turner, "Predatory Pricing and Related Practices under Section 2 of the Sherman Act," 88 *Harvard Law Review* 697 (1975).

threat of recoupment, it did not matter what prices the defendant charged. What made this part of the opinion particularly significant is that the so-called "recoupment test" is now routinely applied in all predatory pricing cases. Unless the plaintiff can make a plausible argument that the defendant eventually will be in a position to charge prices that are sufficiently above the competitive level to offset whatever losses are incurred during the period of predation, the case can be dismissed even before trial and before the plaintiff can introduce potentially inflammatory documentary evidence ("let's kill our competitors!") to a jury.

With respect to the second question, it is understood that in the context of alleged predatory pricing, a firm can achieve the ability to charge supra-competitive prices either by driving most or all of its competitors out of the market, or by intimidating them into competing less aggressively and cooperating with the predator by matching its prices as they are raised above competitive levels. In this case, no one believed that Brown & Williamson on its own, with an 11 percent market share, could ever achieve control of the market. (Several of the other majors eventually joined in the generic price war, but no allegation was made that they had conspired to do so.) Therefore, the only way that the predatory scheme could succeed would be by intimidating Liggett and the other suppliers of generic cigarettes to compete less aggressively in the hope that the major producers could then cooperate in elevating prices above competitive levels and maintaining them there.

Unfortunately for Liggett, the Supreme Court saw no realistic possibility that the generic threat would subside. Even if Liggett were to pull back somewhat, the market had been opened to the possibility of deep-discount or generic cigarettes and there was little likelihood of turning back. Moreover, even if the generic threat were somehow to subside, it would take an unlawful conspiracy among the major producers or a degree of oligopolistic interdependence that the Supreme Court considered implausible to raise prices high enough to recoup the losses that would be incurred during an extended period of below-cost pricing. Hence, the Supreme Court determined that Liggett had not satisfied its burden, and the jury's award of approximately $150 million in damages to Liggett was thrown out.[17] With the wisdom of hindsight, we can see that the Court was right in being skeptical about the demise of the generic segment of the market, although the Court might have been somewhat more cautious in its prediction that growth of the generic segment would prevent significant price increases in the branded cigarette segment.

Regulation

Concern about the marketing activities of the industry has led to efforts to restrict them to some extent. As early as the 1950s, the Federal Trade Commission (FTC) became concerned that the companies were making exaggerated and unsubstantiated claims related to the use of filters to reduce tar deliveries. The FTC responded by promulgating a regulation prohibiting cigarette advertising from making health claims unless those claims could be scientifically substantiated, and specifically prohibiting any reference to tar and nicotine. Because none of the companies were doing the kind of research that could have conceivably substantiated claims for reduced health hazards

---

[17]The jury had found that Liggett's actual damages amounted to $49.6 million, but under the U.S. antitrust laws, damages are tripled as a deterrent to unlawful conduct.

of particular products, this regulation was interpreted as prohibiting all health claims for cigarettes.

By the mid-1960s, however, the public health community came to believe that reductions in tar and nicotine yield probably would reduce health hazards due to cigarette smoking. As a result, the FTC partially reversed itself, allowing the advertising of tar and nicotine yields as determined by a standardized smoking machine. These tar and nicotine ratings were combined with health warnings that were first required in the 1960s and that have been strengthened since then.

Tobacco advertising on radio and television was prohibited in 1970; in 1997, the FTC filed a complaint against Reynolds's "Joe Camel" advertising campaign, claiming that it was at least partially targeted at underage smokers.

Although the FTC regulates cigarette advertising, it has no authority to regulate the cigarettes themselves. The Food and Drug Administration (FDA) has authority under its authorizing legislation to regulate the safety of drugs and "drug-delivery devices." In 1996, the FDA determined that cigarettes were drug-delivery devices within the meaning of the law, because they delivered nicotine that causes psychoactive effects and is addictive. The FDA also held that the pharmacological effects of smoking were a feature of cigarette design. It also concluded that the most appropriate way to address the adverse consequences of smoking was to prevent minors from smoking.

Accordingly, it began developing regulations to prevent the sale of cigarettes to minors and to restrict advertising that makes cigarette smoking attractive to young people. The cigarette companies challenged these regulations in federal court. A trial judge upheld the regulations but was overruled by the court of appeals and the Supreme Court in early 2000. In the meantime, enforcement of regulations against cigarette sales to minors have been strengthened, but the FDA's advertising restrictions have been suspended.

Legislation is currently under consideration in Congress to give the FDA authority to impose new restrictions on advertising, make it harder for young people to buy cigarettes, and perhaps to even require companies to remove harmful ingredients from their cigarettes. Remarkably, Philip Morris has supported the effort to get this legislation passed. Aside from possibly insulating the cigarette industry from further government criticism, Philip Morris, as market leader, would have the most interest in preserving the status quo, so its support for the measure has been derided by some groups as the "Marlboro Monopoly Act." Smaller manufacturers worry that direct government regulation of cigarette ingredients and manufacturers could lead to higher costs and raise barriers to entry and expansion; larger manufacturers such as Reynolds, Brown & Williamson, and Lorillard seem to believe that additional restrictions on advertising would eliminate their most effective means to gain market share from Philip Morris.[18]

Litigation and Settlement with the States

The cigarette companies have been the target of litigation seeking recovery of smoking-related health costs for more than 3 decades. Until recently, most of these lawsuits were filed on behalf of individual smokers, and until very recently, all such suits were

---

[18]See Vanessa O'Connell, "Why Philip Morris Decided to Make Friends with the FDA," *Wall Street Journal*, September 25, 2003, p. 1; John Carey, "Tobacco Regulation: It's No Pipe Dream," *Business Week* (January 12, 2004): 45.

unsuccessful, because juries often concluded that smokers were aware of the harmful effects of smoking and, therefore, could not blame the manufacturers.[19]

This unsuccessful record led to a new strategy by plaintiffs' attorneys in the early 1990s: A number of lawsuits were filed on behalf of insurers and state Medicaid programs to recover the expenditures these entities had made to treat people with smoking-related diseases. In this way, the issue of smoker responsibility was sidestepped; the smokers might have known that smoking was harmful, but their insurers nonetheless had to bear the costs of treating their illness. The states and insurers argued that the cigarette companies knowingly sold a dangerous product, that they consciously sought to dispel smokers' fears about health risks, that they suppressed information about the addictiveness of smoking, and that they conspired to suppress competition that otherwise would have led to better information about health consequences and the development of potentially safer cigarette products.

These lawsuits presented the industry with the risk of enormous potential legal liability, and the cigarette companies chose to seek an out-of-court settlement. A tentative settlement was reached during the summer of 1997.[20] In return for an initial lump-sum payment of approximately $10 billion, annual payments tied to cigarette sales that amounted to hundreds of billions more over 25 years, and restrictions on their advertising and promotional activities, the cigarette companies would have received immunity not only from the ongoing legal cases but from any class-action lawsuits in the future. In addition, they would have received immunity from the antitrust laws for the purpose of collectively implementing the settlement. Because of these immunity provisions, this initial settlement could be implemented only with a law passed by Congress. After extensive debate and hearings during the spring of 1998, Congress attempted to enact a bill that would have implemented higher cigarette taxes and marketing restrictions, but not the broad immunity against future suits provided for in the original settlement agreement. For the latter reason, the tobacco companies opposed the bill and it was defeated.

As the public debate unfolded, the tobacco companies reached settlements to avoid trial verdicts in four individual lawsuits brought by each of the states of Florida, Texas, Mississippi, and Minnesota. An agreement with the remaining states was finally reached in November 1998. The major features of this "global" settlement are as follows:

- Defendants made an initial payment of $2.4 billion to the states, with each company's payment based on its market value.

- Defendants will make annual payments to the states in perpetuity that ramp up to $9 billion per year by 2018. These payments will be adjusted for inflation and changes in cigarette sales.

- Restrictions are imposed on cigarette marketing, including a ban on the use of cartoon characters, restrictions on sponsorship of sporting events and concerts, a ban on outdoor and transit advertising, a ban on nontobacco merchandise bearing tobacco brand names, and limits on the distribution of free samples.

---

[19]There is reason to believe that this situation is changing. Perhaps in response to the publicity generated by the settlement with the states, several cases on behalf of individual smokers or groups of smokers have resulted in initial findings of manufacturer liability for smoking-related health costs. In a recent case, *Engle v. R.J. Reynolds Tobacco Co.*, punitive damages of $145 billion were levied against the major tobacco companies. The appellate court later overturned the punitive damage amount, but such success can only spur the filing of more lawsuits.

[20]Liggett & Myers, by far the smallest of the major firms, had reached a separate settlement in 1996, in which it agreed to admit publicly that smoking is harmful and to assist the states in their ongoing suits against the other firms.

- The states agreed to pass laws imposing similar payment obligations on any cigarette sellers that are not party to the settlement.
- The states waived all rights to sue on behalf of state agencies (but no restrictions are placed on lawsuits filed by others).

This settlement generates significant revenue for the states, some of which is used for smoking prevention and smoking cessation efforts. However, public health groups have become increasingly vocal in criticizing the states for spending ever-larger portions of their tobacco settlement funds for purposes unrelated to tobacco—especially lately when state budgets have been ravaged by recession. By these groups' calculations, only four states currently fund antitobacco programs at the minimum level recommended by the U.S. Centers for Disease Control and Prevention; collectively, the states' spending on such programs has declined by 28 percent in recent years.[21]

The marketing and promotion restrictions incorporated in the settlement will likely have some beneficial effects. However, the primary market consequence of the settlement is that it has significantly increased the price of cigarettes to consumers. In fact, the overwhelming majority of the monies that will be paid under the settlement will come from higher cigarette prices. By tying the payments to the quantity of cigarettes sold, the settlement, in effect, converts most of the payments into a cigarette excise tax increase. It was expected that cigarette prices would be increased to cover the cost of the settlement payments, and this has in fact occurred. The payments made by each company in the future depend on future sales, not on past sales or any other measure of the harm caused.

In contrast, if the companies had lost any of the lawsuits pending against them, the amounts they would have owed would not have been tied to future cigarette sales, and it is not clear that they could have coordinated the price increases designed to recover from consumers the amounts they would have been required to pay. Indeed, to the extent that existing prices represent the most profitable level that can be sustained given the various firms' market positions and competing interests, one could argue that the assessment of lump-sum penalties unconnected to future market performance would not have affected prices, so all the cost of such a penalty would have been borne by the firms' shareholders.

Settlement-Induced Price Increases

Substantial increases in cigarette prices are a direct result of this settlement. Thus, the end result of litigation with the purported purpose of making the tobacco companies compensate the states and other insurers for increased health costs is that future smokers will compensate the states instead.[22] Figure 3-8 displays the approximate breakdown

---

[21]Campaign for Tobacco-Free Kids, American Heart Association, American Cancer Society, and American Lung Association, "A Broken Promise to Our Children: The 1998 State Tobacco Settlement Five Years Later," November 2003.

[22]The difference between the settlement payments and state excise taxes is that each state's revenues depend on national cigarette sales, not sales in that particular state. This means that any state that aggressively reduces smoking will not suffer a large revenue reduction as a result; this structure thereby minimizes the awkward incentives that are otherwise created when governments simultaneously try to reduce smoking and collect significant tax revenues from cigarette sales. It is worth noting that the same incentive structure could have been achieved by passing a federal excise tax increase, with the resulting revenues returned to the states.

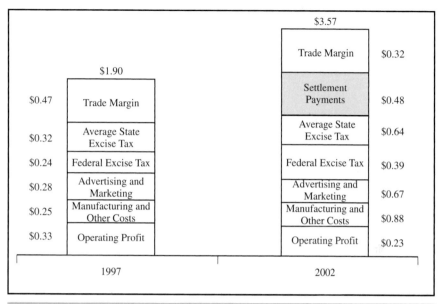

FIGURE 3-8 Estimated Breakdowns of Retail Cigarette Prices

SOURCE: Federal Trade Commission 1997, Company 10-Ks, RJR Tobacco Web site.

of the price of an average pack of cigarettes before the settlement and after it is fully implemented, along with scheduled increases in federal cigarette excise taxes. (The estimates in this figure are based on the assumption that the cost of the settlement is passed along to consumers.) Contrary to early estimates, advertising and promotional expenses and legal costs have gone up, resulting in industry profit margins becoming lower.[23]

The consequences for the tobacco companies, after the initial $2.4 billion lump-sum payment, derive from reduced cigarette sales, including an initial reduction in total cigarette volume of 4.6 percent in 1998 and 9 percent in 1999. After stabilizing in 2000 with a slight increase of 0.1 percent, the reduction was 3.2 percent and 3.7 percent of total volume for 2001 and 2002, respectively, a demand reduction that was offset by higher prices; this has resulted in higher overall revenues for the industry.

Interestingly, one potential consequence of large settlement-induced price increases by the traditional manufacturers may be to expose those manufacturers to competition from new entrants or from other firms that either were not defendants in the original lawsuit or that, like Liggett & Myers, signed their own separate settlements with the states. (Liggett & Myers signed in 1996.) In fact, smaller manufacturers of discount cigarettes have been able to increase their combined market share from 2.5 percent in 1997 to approximately 10 to 15 percent in 2003, with the price increase induced by the settlement acting as a main force driving the recent growth of deep-discount cigarette sales.

---

[23]These are the assumptions used by the FTC in its analysis of the earlier proposed settlement. Federal Trade Commission, *Competition and the Financial Impact of the Proposed Tobacco Industry Settlement*, Washington, D.C., 1997.

The most successful of these new, smaller manufacturers has been Commonwealth with its USA Gold brand. Many of these manufacturers simply opted not to sign the Master Settlement agreement, avoiding the legal cost and allowing them to price their cigarettes much lower. Although the agreement does contain provisions to collect funds in escrow from nonparticipating manufacturers, enforcement has been difficult and the measures themselves have been subject to legal challenges.

Youth Smoking

Public policy has been particularly concerned about the effects of cigarette marketing and promotion in stimulating youth smoking. The majority of all smokers begin smoking before age 18, despite legal restrictions on the sale of cigarettes to minors. Some public health advocates reason from this that if youngsters could be prevented from starting to smoke, the overall rate of smoking initiation in the population would be dramatically reduced. In addition to marketing restrictions, some point to the price increases associated with the settlement as an especially significant antiyouth smoking measure. Some studies have suggested that teen smoking is somewhat more price elastic than adult smoking, which is plausible given that young smokers tend to be less addicted, and cigarette expenditures comprise a larger portion of their disposable income.[24] In addition, part of the revenues from the settlement are being used by some states to fund aggressive counter-marketing measures designed to discourage teen smoking. Again though, public health groups charge that the states' spending on youth tobacco programs has been declining while tobacco company expenditures on marketing, promotion, and advertising have been rising.[25] Unfortunately, no one seems to understand why teens start smoking well enough to know how much difference these measures will make.

Conclusion

The history of the cigarette industry presents a unique and complex challenge to students of industrial organization. One of the most concentrated of industries, resting behind apparently significant barriers to entry, it has enjoyed persistently high profits but also has engaged in periodic price wars. The firms spend huge amounts—absolutely and relative to sales—on advertising and promotion, supposedly in a largely self-defeating effort to steal each others' customers. The industry charges prices that are clearly above competitive levels, but government desire for tax revenue combined with a belief that high prices will discourage smoking have made higher rather than lower prices the aim of public policy.

An epic legal battle over liability for smoking-related health care costs has strained the legal system and produced a significant increase in tobacco taxation. It also has resulted—perhaps much later than anyone in the industry would have guessed 30 years ago—in the companies finally admitting publicly what they knew but admitted only privately decades ago: that smoking is a deadly and addictive habit initially undertaken primarily by youngsters and then continued by adults, most of whom would like to quit.

---

[24]Ibid.
[25]"A Broken Promise to Our Children."

The next phase in the industry's evolution is difficult to predict. The higher prices brought about by the settlement will likely accelerate the decline in smoking some-what. If the FDA is ultimately given authority by Congress to regulate cigarettes, we could see tighter marketing restrictions, and perhaps even limits on permissible levels of tar, nicotine, and other characteristics and ingredients of cigarettes. Yet the very ad-diction that makes smoking such a pernicious public policy problem makes it difficult to identify good solutions, even if legal authority is available. It is clear, for example, that there is no political will for another prohibition era. Mandatory reductions in nico-tine levels are unlikely to work for addicted smokers and could even be counterpro-ductive as smokers smoke more cigarettes to obtain their desired nicotine. The technological potential for cigarette-like products that deliver nicotine without other adverse health effects has never been adequately explored, and it is unclear whether such products are now being pursued by anyone. Therefore, it seems likely that the pe-culiar industrial organization and performance of the cigarette industry will continue to be hotly debated.

Suggested Readings

Adams, Walter, and James Brock. 1998. *The Tobacco Wars.* Cincinnati: South-Western College Publishing.

Bulow, Jeremy, and Paul Klemperer. 1998. "The Tobacco Deal." Brookings Papers on Economic Activity: Microeconomics. Brookings Institution, pp. 323–394.

Federal Trade Commission. Annual. Report to Congress, *Persuant to Federal Cigarette Labeling and Advertising Act.*

Kluger, Richard. 1996. *Ashes to Ashes.* New York: Alfred Knopf.

Tenant, Richard. 1950. *The American Cigarette Industry.* New Haven, CT: Yale University Press.

CHAPTER

Beer

—KENNETH G. ELZINGA

In 1620, as every youngster knows, the Pilgrims landed at Plymouth Rock. Less commonly known is that the Pilgrims had set sail for Virginia, not Massachusetts. What led them to change their destination? They were running out of beer. One voyager recorded the following entry in his diary: "Our victuals are being much spente, especially our beere." We leave to historians the question of how a dwindling beer inventory affected the course of American history. We turn to economics for an understanding of the structure, conduct, and performance of the U.S. beer industry today.

Beer is a potable product with four main ingredients:

1. Malt, which is a grain (usually barley) that has been allowed to germinate in water and then dried.
2. Flavoring adjuncts, usually hops and corn or rice, which give beer its lightness and provide the starch that the enzymes in the malt convert to sugar.
3. Cultured yeast, which ferments the beverage and feeds on the sugar content of the malt to produce alcohol and carbonic acid.
4. Water, which acts as a solvent for the other ingredients.

Because the process of brewing (or boiling) is intrinsic to making beer, the industry often is called the brewing industry.[1]

All beers are not the same. The white beverage (spiced with a little raspberry syrup) favored in Berlin; the warm, dark-colored drink served by the English publican; and the amber liquid kept at a near-freezing temperature in the cooler of the American convenience store are all beer. Generically, the term *beer* means "any beverage brewed from a starch (or farinaceous) grain." Because the grain is made into malt, another term for beer is *malt liquor*, or *malt beverage*. In this study, the terms *beer, malt liquor*, and *malt beverage* are used interchangeably to include all such products as beer, ale, light beer, dry beer, ice beer, porter, stout, malt liquor, and flavored malt beverages.[2] The factor common to these beverages, and which differentiates them from other alcoholic and nonalcoholic beverages, is the brewing process of fermentation applied to a basic grain ingredient.

Beer's production process is not, however, the key to defining beer as a market for economic analysis. The concept of a market entails a group of firms (or conceivably only one firm) supplying products that consumers, voting with their dollars in the marketplace, perceive as good substitutes for each other. Some avid beer drinkers may

---

[1]Non-alcoholic beer is a small but not trivial component of overall beer sales. Domestic shipments in 2002 were about 1.3 million barrels.

[2]Flavored malt beverages (FMBs) also are known as Ready-to-Drink beverages (RTDs), Flavored Alternative Beverages (FABs), and Malternatives. Recall that the alcohol in beer comes from fermentation, not distilling. Some FMBs derive over 70% of their alcohol content from the distilled alcohol that serves as the flavoring agent in the drink. These products, the beer industry maintains, are not true malt beverages and, at least for tax and advertising purposes, should be treated as distilled spirits, not beer.

prefer light beer over malt liquor at the same unit price but might prefer either of these over a glass of skim milk at the same price. For many consumers, the cross-elasticity of demand between different kinds of beer is higher than the cross-elasticity of demand between beer and other beverages.[3] The fungibility among malt beverages distinguishes beer as a separate market. Beer's distinctiveness as an economic market is underscored by the high cross-elasticity of supply between different types of beer and the low cross-elasticity of supply between beer and all other beverages.

The U.S. market for beer is sizable. Among commercial beverages, beer ranks fourth in per capita consumption behind soft drinks, coffee, and milk. Among alcoholic beverages, beer accounts for close to 90 percent of U.S. consumption (by gallons), placing it well ahead of wine and distilled spirits.

I. HISTORY

Beer was a common beverage among the early settlers in America. In 1625, the first recorded public brewery was established in New Amsterdam (now New York City). Other commercial brewing followed, although considerable brewing was done in homes in seventeenth-century America. All that was needed were a few vats for mashing, cooling, and fermenting. The resulting product would not be recognized (or consumed) as beer today. The process was crude, and the end result was uncertain. Brewing was referred to as "an art and mystery."

Brewing was encouraged in early America. For example, the General Court of Massachusetts passed an act in 1789 to support the brewing of beer "as an important means of preserving the health of the citizens . . . and of preventing the pernicious effects of spiritous liquors." James Oglethorpe, trustee of the colony of Georgia, was even blunter: "Cheap beer is the only means to keep rum out."

The 1840s and 1850s were pivotal decades in the beer industry. The product beer, as it is generally known today, was introduced in the 1840s with the brewing of lager beer. Before this time, malt beverage consumption in America resembled that of English tastes—it was oriented toward ale, porter, and stout. Lager beer reflected a German influence on the industry. The influx of German immigrants provided skillful brewers as well as eager customers for this type of beer. At the start of the decade in 1850, a total of 431 brewers in the United States produced 750,000 barrels of beer. By the end of that decade, 1,269 brewers produced more than a million barrels of beer—evidence of the bright future expected by many for this industry.

The latter half of the nineteenth century also saw technological advances in production and marketing. Mechanical refrigeration aided the brewing and the storage of beer. Prior to this, beer production was partly dependent on the amount of ice that could be cut from lakes and rivers in the winter. Cities such as St. Louis, Missouri, with its underground caves where beer could be kept cool while aging, lost this (truly natural) advantage with the advent of mechanical refrigeration.

Pasteurization, a process originally devised to preserve wine and beer (not milk), was adopted during this period. As a result, beer no longer had to be kept cold; it could be shipped into warm climates and stored without refermenting. Once beer was pas-

---

[3]For example, Happoshu is a low-alcohol beer in Japan that, because of a tax loophole, began selling for half the price of regular beer. Happoshu has taken 30% of the regular beer market because of this price differential, indicating the high cross-elasticity of demand between these two types of beer.

teurized, wide-scale bottling and off-premises consumption became viable. In addition, developments in rail and motor transport enabled brewers to sell output beyond their local markets. The twentieth century saw the rise of the national brewer.

The twentieth century also saw beer sales outlawed. The temperance movement, which began by promoting voluntary moderation and abstention from hard liquors, veered toward a goal of compulsory abstention from all alcoholic beverages. The beer industry seemed blissfully ignorant of this. Many brewers thought (or hoped) that the temperance movement would ban only liquor.

In 1919, 36 states ratified the Eighteenth Amendment to enact the national prohibition of alcoholic beverages. This led many brewers to close up shop; some instead produced candy and ice cream. Anheuser-Busch and others built a profitable business selling malt syrup, which was used to make "home brew." Because a firm could not state the ultimate purpose of malt syrup, the product was marketed as an ingredient for making baked goods, such as cookies. Prohibition lasted until April 1933, and brewers reopened rapidly after repeal. By June 1933, 31 brewers were in operation; in another year, the number had risen to 756.

In 1948, the demand for beer in the United States began a slow decline, from a 1947 record sale of 87.2 million barrels. During this period, per capita consumption of beer fell from 18.5 gallons in 1947 to 15.0 gallons in 1958. It was not until 1959 that sales surpassed the 1947 total. In the 1960s and 1970s, total demand began to grow again at an average rate of better than 3 percent per year. In 1965, for the first time, more than 100 million barrels were sold.

The rightward shift in the demand curve for beer was due to the increased number of young people in the United States (the result of the post–World War II baby boom), the lowered age requirements for drinking in many populous states, and the enhanced acceptability of beer among females. Moreover, the number of areas in the United States that were "dry" (i.e., where alcoholic beverages are prohibited) shrank considerably.

In the early 1980s, the market demand for beer stabilized. Demographic patterns reversed themselves as the pool of young people (18 to 34 years of age) declined. Minimum age requirements for the purchase of alcoholic beverages were increased to 21 years. Other factors that cut into demand included the pursuit of physical fitness and the increasing concern about alcohol abuse, particularly drunk driving. In some states, laws restraining the use of one-way (nonreturnable) containers also might have reduced consumption.

The stable market demand for beer stands in contrast with the growing demand for two potential substitutes: carbonated soft drinks and bottled water. From 1980 to 1999, soft drink consumption rose from 35.1 gallons per capita to 49.7; bottled water consumption increased even more dramatically from 2.4 gallons per capita to 17.7 during the same period. In 1980, beer consumption in the United States was 24.3 gallons per capita. It declined to 21.8 gallons by 1995 and has been stable since. In 2000, Americans consumed 21.7 gallons of beer per person.[4]

In the latter part of the 1990s, demographics again favored market growth. From 1998 through 2008, the population in the 21 to 24 age bracket is projected to grow. This group comprises only 8 percent of the U.S. population, but it consumes about 14 percent of all beer. Aggregate consumption is likely to increase moderately as a consequence. In addition, recent medical studies claim that moderate alcohol consumption (including beer) reduces the risk of cardiovascular disease. The *Wall Street Journal* polled 800 readers as to whether such studies would affect their drinking habits: 36 per-

---

[4]Per capita consumption of distilled spirits also fell in the 1980-1999 period. The demand for wine was stable.

cent replied "they lead me to drink a bit more," 18 percent responded "they are a great excuse for drinking a lot more," but 46 percent indicated "I never believe those studies."

II. STRUCTURE

The most important components of the structure of the brewing industry are the nature of demand, the size distribution of firms and trends in industry concentration, entry conditions, and product differentiation.

Demand

The demand for beer is a function of personal income, the weather, government regulations on alcohol consumption, the price and quality of other beverages, demographics, religion, and health concerns. In the United States, demand varies from state to state. Per capita beer consumption in Utah was 12.8 gallons in 2002, and Nevada led all others with a per capita consumption of 30.4 gallons. (The Nevada figure is biased by beer-quaffing tourists.) The highest per capita consumption by natives of a state probably occurs in Wisconsin.

Although economists are not able to measure price elasticity infallibly, statistical estimations indicate that the market demand for beer is inelastic and falls in the range of 0.7 to 0.9. Brand loyalty is not so strong as to make the demand for any particular malt beverage inelastic. Indeed, the demand for individual brands of beer appears to be quite elastic. This places an important limitation on the market power of a brewer's attempt to raise price unilaterally.

Concentration

According to economic theory, consumers facing a monopolist likely will pay higher prices than consumers buying in a competitive market. Consumers buying from an oligopoly will be affected by the nature of competition that takes place among the handful of sellers. For this reason, the size distribution of brewing firms arrayed before consumers is of economic interest. Is the beer industry unconcentrated, with its customers courted by many firms, or highly concentrated, leaving beer drinkers with little choice?

In the first three decades of the post–World War II period, two contrary trends were at work in the industry. The number of major brewers located in the United States declined, but the size of the market area served by existing brewers and the volume of beer supplied by the major brewers increased. Beer drinkers lost some sources of supply but gained access to others.

Then, in the 1980s, the entry of dozens of craft brewers increased consumers' choice of malt beverages. Craft brewers, sometimes called domestic specialties, include microbrewers and brewpubs. The number of craft brewers rose from 1 in 1965 to more than 1,400 in 2002, achieving a critical mass in 1995 by producing more than 1 million barrels of beer.

Some craft brewers no longer can claim micro status because they now sell so much beer. (Current examples would be Boston Brewing and Sierra Nevada.)[5] In 2002, craft brewers included about 1,000 brewpubs (most of these produce fewer than 1,000 barrels of beer annually), more than 400 microbreweries (producing fewer than 15,000 barrels per year), and more than 40 regional specialty brewers (with 15,000+ barrels of capacity).

In recent years, U.S. consumers also have chosen imported beers in increasing numbers. In 2002, imports held more than 11 percent of the U.S. beer market; craft brewers held 3 percent. Thus, although concentration has increased among the largest sellers, craft brewing and imports have caused an explosion in new beer brands that offer consumers different taste signatures.

The Decline in Numbers

In 1935, shortly after repeal of the prohibition, 750 brewing plants were operating in the United States. In 2002, 128 breweries were in operation.[6] From 1947 through 1995, the number of beer companies dropped more than 90 percent, although beer sales doubled. Beer analyst Robert S. Weinberg counts 421 traditional brewers operating in 1947; by 2002, this number had fallen to only 22 firms. Few, if any, American industries have undergone a similar structural shakeup. Recently, due to the growth of the craft beer segment, the number of new plants and independent companies has increased noticeably, though these new entrants are mostly at the small end of the industry size spectrum. The decline in the number of major brewers in the industry has been dramatic.

As the number of once prominent brewers declined, the largest brewers increased their share of the market. As shown in Table 4-1, in 1947, the top five sellers accounted for only 19 percent of the industry's barrelage; in 2001, their share was 87 percent. In 2002, three firms met almost 80 percent of domestic demand: Anheuser-Busch (49.0 percent), Miller (19.1 percent), and Coors (10.9 percent).

Another way economists summarize the distribution of firm size is to compute the Herfindahl Hirschman Index (HHI), which is also shown in Table 4-1. The HHI is each individual seller's market share squared, and these numbers are then summed (a monopolist generates an HHI of 10,000). The rising Herfindahl Hirschman Index testifies to the industry's structural transformation.

The Widening of Markets

In the days of hundreds of brewing companies, most consumers faced an actual choice of only a few brewers because most brewers served a small geographic area. Beer is an expensive product to ship relative to its value, and few brewers could afford to compete in the home markets of distant rivals. Thus, at one time, it was meaningful to speak of local, regional, and national brewers. Of these, the local brewer who brewed for a small market, perhaps smaller than a single state and often only a single metropolitan area, was the most common.[7] The regional brewer served a multistate area but still usually marketed to no more than two or three states. The national brewers, those selling in all (or almost all) states, were few in number and rarely were the largest seller in any particular local area. In addition, it was uncommon for a firm to operate more than one plant.

Today, the terms *local brewer, regional brewer,* and *national brewer* are antiquated.[8] The geographic territory served by the major brewers from one plant grew due to the economies of large-scale production and, to some extent, marketing. A second factor extending the reach of national brewers to serve new geographic regions is their propensity to operate more than one plant.

---

[5]Some craft brewers have their beer produced by other producers (called "contract brewers") where it is made to the craft brewer's specifications.
[6]These are brewing plants of at least 15,000 barrels per year capacity and do not include micro brewers and brewpubs whose capacity falls below a 15,000 barrel annual potential.

TABLE 4-1   Concentration of Sales by Top Brewers: 1947–2001

Year	Five Largest (by percent)	HHI
1947	19.0	140
1954	24.9	240
1958	28.5	310
1964	39.0	440
1968	47.6	690
1974	64.0	1,080
1978	74.3	1,292
1981	75.7	1,545
1984	83.9	1,898
1987	88.1	2,267
1990	88.6	2,555
1992	87.4	2,574
1993	87.3	2,603
1994	87.3	2,637
1995	89.9	2,659
1996	89.2	2,732
1997	88.1	2,729
1998	87.2	2,789
2001	87.2	2,913

SOURCE: Based on beer volume. The HHI includes only the top five brewers in that year. Adapted from A. Horowitz and I. Horowitz, "The Beer Industry," *Business Horizons* 10 (Fall 1967): 14, various issues of *Modern Brewery Age*, and Beer Marketer's Insights 2001 Beer Industry Update.

Size of the Market

Determining the degree of market concentration in brewing entails knowing how far the geographic markets for beer extend. If one national market exists, then concentration statistics for the entire nation are relevant. However, if brewing, like cement or milk, has regional markets, delineating their boundaries is necessary before the industry's structure can be analyzed.

The federal courts have to solve this problem when deciding antimerger cases in the brewing industry. In an early antitrust case involving the merger of two brewers located in Wisconsin, the Antitrust Division asked an eminent economist at Northwestern University to testify in support of the view that the state of Wisconsin alone was a separate market for beer. The economics professor told the government lawyers that such a position was economically untenable. Nevertheless, the lawyers persisted in this view without him and eventually persuaded the Supreme Court that Wisconsin, by itself, is "a distinguishable and economically significant market for the sale of beer."

Although Wisconsin was held to have been a separate market for legal purposes, to single it out as a market in the economic sense is to draw the market boundaries too narrowly (and such a position would not be taken by antitrust authorities today). In

---

[7]According to Timothy McNulty, Chicago alone had 32 independent breweries in 1937, 10 in 1960, 2 in 1969 and none by 1979.

[8]Robert S. Weinberg bifurcates the contemporary beer market into two broad components: the "core" (the major brands of the large domestic brewers) and the "non-core" (imports and domestic specialty brands).

1991, brewers in the state of Wisconsin produced more than 17 million barrels of beer; that year, consumers in Wisconsin consumed fewer than 5 million barrels of beer. Because beer also is "imported" into Wisconsin from brewers in other states, obviously more than two thirds of Wisconsin beer is "exported" for sale outside the state. To say that Wisconsin was a separate geographic market would be to overlook the impact of most beer production in that state, not to mention the impact on the supply of beer coming into Wisconsin in competition with beer produced in Wisconsin. In this case, the court erred by singling out Wisconsin as an economically meaningful market. The geographic market for beer is now nationwide.

Reasons for the Decline in the Number of Brewers

In this section, two possible explanations for the decline in the number of major brewers are considered: mergers and economies of scale.

Mergers

A common explanation for an industry's concentration is a merger-acquisition trend among the industry's firms. At first glance, this seems to be the case in brewing: During the period 1950 through 1983, about 170 horizontal mergers were consummated in the beer industry. However, corporate marriages between rival brewers do not explain the increase in concentration by the leading firms. This is evident when one reviews the merger track record of the top three brewers.

The first antimerger action in the beer industry was taken by the Antitrust Division in 1958 against the industry's leading firm, Anheuser-Busch. Anheuser-Busch had purchased the Miami brewery of American Brewing Company. The government successfully argued that this merger would eliminate American Brewing as an independent brewer and end its rivalry with Anheuser-Busch in Florida.

The impact of this early antimerger action was profound. Anheuser-Busch had to sell this brewery and refrain from buying any others without court approval for a period of 5 years. As a result, Anheuser-Busch did not acquire any rival brewers but instead began an extensive program of building large, efficient plants in Florida and at other locations around the United States. Anheuser-Busch deviated only once from its internal growth policy in 1980 when it acquired the Baldwinsville, New York, brewing plant of the Schlitz Brewing Company. Schlitz's sales had declined so much that it did not need the brewery, and the plant's capacity was so huge that only an industry leader could absorb its output.

Miller Brewing Company, the second-largest brewer, also grew primarily through internal expansion. Miller did purchase brewing plants in Texas and California in 1966 but acquired no other breweries until 1987, when it acquired Leinenkugel, a small, family run brewery located in Wisconsin. Miller Brewing Company itself was the subject of a conglomerate acquisition by Philip Morris in 1970. From that point, Miller, unlike Anheuser-Busch, had a large corporate parent.

In 1972, just after being acquired by Philip Morris, Miller acquired three brand names from Meister Brau, a defunct Chicago brewing firm. Hardly anyone noticed at the time, but out of this acquisition came the low-calorie or "light beer" phenomenon. The Meister Brau trademarks included one called Lite, a brand of low-calorie beer once marketed locally by Meister Brau to upper-middle-class, weight-conscious consumers. The Miller management noticed that Lite had sold fairly well in Anderson, Indiana, a town with many blue-collar workers. In what is now a marketing classic, Miller zeroed in on "real" beer drinkers, claiming that its low-calorie beer allowed them to drink their beer with even less of a filled-up feeling. The upshot of this advertising campaign was remarkable. Lite became the most popular new product in the history of the beer industry.[9]

In 1974, Miller bought the rights to brew and market Lowenbrau, a prominent German beer, in the United States. However, Miller was never able to develop this brand into an important U.S. product.[10] After this event, mergers played no role at Miller until 1993 when it acquired the marketing rights in the United States for the brands of Molson, a Canadian brewer. In 2001, Miller sold these rights back to Molson, which then sold them to Coors.

In 1999, Miller, Stroh (then the number 4 brewer), and Pabst (then number 5) consummated a complex acquisition associated with Stroh's exit from the industry. Miller acquired four brands (Henry Weinhard, Mickey's, Hamm's, and Olde English 800), and Pabst acquired all other Stroh brands (including the former Schlitz and Heileman brands[11]). Miller also acquired Pabst's Tumwater, Washington, brewery (which it closed in 2003), and Pabst acquired Stroh's Lehigh Valley, Pennsylvania, brewery.[12] Miller agreed to produce some of Pabst's beer on a contract brewing basis. Most of the remaining Stroh breweries were to be sold as real estate for nonbrewing purposes.[13] Despite the deal's magnitude in terms of brand ownership rearrangement, it resulted in only a small increase in industry concentration and had no antitrust consequences.

In 2002, Philip Morris sold Miller to South African Breweries, a London-based firm that is the second-largest brewer in the world behind Anheuser-Busch.[14] The venerable Miller Brewing Company is now called SABMiller.

Third-ranked Coors had a long-term policy to brew its Coors brand only in one location: Golden, Colorado. Later, Coors began shipping beer in bulk to Elkton, Virginia, where it is bottled and canned for sale in the East. In 1990, Coors acquired the Memphis, Tennessee, brewery of Stroh. There, as in Virginia, the company only *packages* the Coors brand (but it brews the company's lower-priced Keystone brand there). One reason Coors is a high-cost producer relative to Anheuser-Busch is because its beer travels an average of 1,000 miles; Anheuser-Busch, with its dispersed breweries, ships its beer an average of 200 to 250 miles. In 2002, Coors acquired Carling, Britain's best-selling brand, from Interbrew, marking Coors's first major acquisition outside North America.

Stroh had been a prominent brewer since 1850 and was itself an acquirer until its demise. In 1980, when it was the seventh-largest brewer in the country, Stroh acquired the F. M. Schaefer Brewing Company. In 1982, Stroh acquired the Joseph Schlitz Brewing Company, itself in a sales tailspin but at the time the fourth-largest brewer. This acquisition catapulted Stroh to number three in the industry but also shackled the firm with debt and set the stage for its demise. In 1996, Stroh made another sizable acquisition: the G. Heileman Brewing Company.[15] However, its size did not insulate it

---

[9]Miller failed in its legal campaign to reserve not only "Lite" but also the term "light" to itself; the courts left the generic word in the public domain allowing other brewers to use it to describe their own low–calorie emulations. While Lite enjoyed great commercial success as the first mover in the light beer category, Miller has not been able to maintain Lite's leadership position in the low-calorie market segment the company first pioneered. In 2001, Bud Light became the leading U.S. brand of beer, outselling Budweiser. In 2002, Bud Light and Coors Light outsold Miller Lite. First mover advantages do not insure long-run leadership.

[10]Labatt, a Canadian brewer, currently is attempting to revive the Lowenbrau name in the U.S. beer market.

[11]These would include, in addition to Stroh, Old Milwaukee, Schlitz, Schaefer, Old Style, Schmidt's, Lone Star, Special Export, Schlitz Malt Liquor, and Rainier.

[12]This facility was just acquired by Guinness-Bass Import Co. (GBIC), the U.S. branch of the British firm Diageo, in part to produce Smirnoff Ice, GBIC's best-selling FMB.

[13]Yuengling acquired Stroh's 1.6 million barrel capacity Tampa brewery and will use it to meet current demand in the Northeast and for geographic expansion in the Southeast. Stroh's Portland, Oregon brewery (the former Blitz-Weinhard plant) has ceased operations.

[14]SAB markets such brands as Pilsner Urquell and Castle Lager.

from market competition. In 1999, then the fourth-ranking firm in the beer industry, Stroh exited the market.

Notwithstanding these sizable (and largely unsuccessful) corporate marriages, mergers have not made much of an imprint on the structure of the brewing industry and have not resulted in market power for merging partners. The most actively merging firms, Stroh and Heileman, eventually failed. Much of the increase in concentration in the past three decades was due to the growth of Anheuser-Busch, Miller, and Coors, whose expansion has been largely internal. Indeed, the early enforcement of the antimerger law was partly responsible for the emphasis on internal growth by the leading brewers. Later mergers went largely unchallenged. The antitrust authorities recognized in the mid-1970s that beer mergers they once would have attacked do not merit challenge, even if the merger involves sizable regional sellers.

Most of the mergers in the beer industry did not involve firms of significant stature. Generally, they represented the demise of an inefficient firm that salvaged some remainder of its worth by selling out to another brewer. The acquiring brewer gained no market power but might have benefited by securing the barrelage to bring one plant to full capacity or by gaining access to an improved distribution network or a new territory.

Mergers such as these are not the *cause* of structural change; they are the *effect*, as firms exit or rearrange their assets through the merger route. The trend to concentration in brewing would have occurred even if all mergers had been prohibited. As a consequence, one must look to factors other than mergers to explain the industry's structural shakeup.

Economies of Scale

When teaching the principle of economies of scale, economists generally plot a smooth, continuous average cost curve that is the envelope of a host of similarly curvaceous short-run average cost curves, each one representing a different-sized plant. Economies of scale exist if large plants produce at lower unit costs than small ones. What is seldom mentioned in the discussion of these curves, however, is that great confidence cannot be attached to the location of any point on these cost curves, notwithstanding their precise, scientific appearance in economics textbooks.

With this caveat in mind, Figure 4-1 is a representation of economies of scale in the brewing industry. The figure illustrates the fairly sharp decline in long-run unit costs until a plant size of 4.0 million barrels per year of capacity is reached. Beyond this capacity, costs continue to decline, but less sharply, until a capacity of 10 to 12 million barrels (an enormous brewery) is attained. Only modest cost economies, if any, can be exploited in plants with capacity above 10 to 12 million barrels, and production economies may be offset by the high shipping costs necessary to move so much beer to market.

Figure 4-1 also has a single short-run average cost curve above the long-run average cost curve. A long-run cost curve represents the envelope of different-sized plants, each of which uses the latest production techniques. The short-run average cost curve standing by itself better portrays the situation of many breweries that met their demise in the 1960s and 1970s. These breweries were not only too small to exploit all the economies of scale, but their capital equipment was of such an outmoded vintage that their costs were elevated even more.

---

[15]Heileman had been the industry's fifth-ranking firm, itself the product of over a dozen acquisitions from 1960 on, notably Wiedemann, Associated Brewing, the Blatz brand, Rainier, Carling, and portions of Pabst.

FIGURE 4-1   Economies of Scale in Brewing

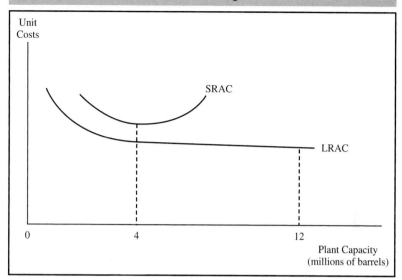

Table 4-2 shows one method, the survivor test, used by economists to estimate the extent of economies of scale. As its name implies, the survivor test considers those plants that have survived over time to be the optimum size. There has been a steady decline (dramatic in some cases) in the number of breweries with a capacity of less than 2 million barrels and an increase in the number of breweries with a capacity of 5 million barrels and more. The fact that large brewing plants not only survived but grew in number is considered, by a survivor test, to be prima facie evidence of their lower unit costs.[16] One understands better the success of Anheuser-Busch and Miller in recognizing that their 18 plants have an average capacity of slightly more than 8.6 million barrels.[17] These are the huge, cost-efficient production units for the U.S. market's leading brands. The only exception to this economies-of-scale thesis is the notable jump in the number of smaller breweries, especially in the 10,000 to 100,000 barrel capacity range. These are primarily new craft brewers.

TABLE 4-2   Surviving Breweries by Capacity: 1959–2001

Listed Capacity Barrels (in thousands)	1959	1971	1986	1992	1998	2001
10–100	68	21	13	8	77	81
101–500	91	33	8	7	19	19
501–1,000	30	32	3	3	1	1
1,001–2,000	18	21	10	5	4	2
2,001–4,000	8	12	10	6	7	5
4,001+	2	7	23	20	20	20

SOURCE: Compiled from plant capacity figures listed in the *Modern Brewery Age Blue Book* (various years); Charles W. Parker, 1984, "The Domestic Beer Industry" and industry trade sources. These figures do not include plants listed only on a company consolidated basis (in the case of multiplant firms) or single-plant firms not reporting their capacity, and these figures exclude microbreweries that produce fewer than 10,000 barrels of capacity.

Table 4-2 does not reflect the appearance of very small breweries in the craft beer segment of microbrewers or brewpubs (if food is served with on-premises beer consumption). In 2002, about 1,200 such firms existed with sales of 10,000 barrels or less. Some of these are small indeed, such as Little Apple Brewing Company in Manhattan, Kansas, capable of brewing about 500 barrels per year.

Microbrewers receive much attention in the business press, in part because there had been, until their arrival, so little de novo entry into the beer industry in the post–World War II period and because they brew beers with different taste signatures than the mainstream lagers produced by the major domestic brewers. Their owners, who often are also the managers and brewmasters, are portrayed as a new breed of entrepreneur in the beer industry. Craft brewers have their own trade journal, *The New Brewer*, and this segment of the industry is promoted by the Institute for Brewing Studies.

Some of the economies from larger brewing operations come in the packaging of the plant's output. The newer bottling lines at the Anheuser-Busch Houston, Texas, brewery have line speeds of 1,100 bottles per minute. Modern canning lines are even faster: 2,000 cans per minute. It takes a brewery of substantial size to utilize such equipment at capacity. Large plants also save on labor costs via the automation of brewing and warehousing and on capital costs, as well. Construction cost per barrel is cut by about one third for a 4.5-million-barrel-capacity plant relative to a 1.5-million-barrel-capacity plant. However, no significant reduction in production costs was detected in a study of multiplant economies of scale by F. M. Scherer and others.

Cost efficiency relates not only to some finite production capacity but also to management's ability to use the capacity efficiently. Shortly after the repeal of prohibition in 1933, new entrants flooded the brewing industry, all expecting to be met by thirsty customers. However, the demand for beer was unexpectedly low after repeal. From a high of 750 brewers operating in 1935, almost 100 were quickly eliminated in only 5 years. Quite a few of these enterprises had operated before prohibition, but many were under new management. Some were family owned firms, and heredity had been cruel to the second or third generations, not endowing them with the brewing or managerial capabilities of their fathers or grandfathers. Competitive pressures, with no respect for nepotism, eliminated such breweries.

A small brewer, producing a quality product and marketing it with minimal transportation costs, can survive in today's industry by finding a special niche for itself. This seems to be the status, by way of examples, of Wisconsin's Stevens Point Brewery; D. G. Yuengling & Son in Pennsylvania (the nation's oldest brewing firm still in business); and the pioneer craft brewer, San Francisco's Anchor Steam Brewery. However, such examples are the exceptions that prove the rule.

In brewing—unlike many manufacturing industries where optimum-sized plants seem to be getting smaller—large, capital-intensive plants are necessary to exploit economies of scale and survive in the industry to meet mainstream beer tastes. In markets where vigorous competitive pressures exist, firms that do not exploit economies of scale or operate with internal efficiency will not survive. This has been the fate of many brewers; they have exited from the industry because of inefficient plants, poor management, or both.

---

[16]For a sophisticated treatment of cost efficiencies in brewing, see the paper by Joe R. Kerkvliet, William Nebesky, Carol H. Tremblay and Victor J. Tremblay.

[17]As examples of scale economies in beer production, Anheuser-Busch recently doubled the production capacity of its Cartersville, GA brewery from 3.4 to 7.5 million barrels of annual brewing and packaging capacity. Anheuser-Busch considers this size to be a more efficient scale. Miller recently closed its Tumwater, WA brewery. This brewery was substantially smaller than Miller's other six breweries and considered suboptimal by Miller cost experts.

The Condition of Entry

The ease with which newcomers can enter an industry is an important structural characteristic for ensuring competitive performance. If entry is not blocked, existing firms will be unable to raise prices significantly lest they encourage an outbreak of new competition. On the other hand, if entry is barred, perhaps by a patent or government license, a dominant firm's market position may be insulated.

Entry into the beer industry is not hindered by the traditional barriers of patents and exclusive government grants. Nor are there key inputs whose supply is controlled or limited by existing firms. Likewise, economies of scale are not so important that an efficient entrant would have to supply an enormous share of industry output. However, the sheer expense of entering the beer industry is considerable. The price of constructing a modern 4- to 5-million-barrel brewery is more than $250 million. Marketing the new brew also is costly because entrants must introduce their products to consumers who are already smitten by vigorous advertising efforts.

Since World War II, no new entrant has cracked the top three sellers of beer in the U.S. beer market. De novo entry has been from imported beer and craft brewers. For example, by 1998, more than 30 new entrants (since 1980) in the craft brewing segment were producing at least 15,000 barrels annually. The lack of new entry at the very top is explained by the relatively low profitability of the industry and the ominous fate of so many exiting firms. Moreover, entry into the industry is risky because breweries have few uses other than producing beer. New entry involves considerable sunk costs.

The 1980s and 1990s were decades in which the market mechanism wrung excess capacity out of the industry rather than inviting new firms and new capacity in. One entrepreneur who recognized the beer industry's excess capacity as an entry opportunity was Jim Koch of the Boston Brewing Co., the leading craft brewer in the United States. This firm has contracts with other brewers who produce, to Koch's specifications, his firm's Samuel Adams brand. The second-largest craft brewer, Sierra Nevada Brewing Co., has taken a different supply tack. It now owns sizable brewing capacity of 600,000 barrels per year.

Import competition merits special mention in any discussion of new entry. Beer imports to the United States—which come mostly from Mexico, the Netherlands, Canada, and Germany—increased more than 26-fold in the period from 1970 through 2002. In 2002, imports represented more than 11 percent of domestic consumption, up from less than 1 percent in 1970. Imported beer no longer can be dismissed as an insignificant part of demand or supply. In 1998, for the first time, an imported beer (Corona Extra) became a top 10 brand. By 2002, this Mexican import was the number 7 brand in the country.

Product Differentiation

When consumers find the product of one firm superior to other market alternatives, the favored firm can raise its price somewhat without losing these customers. Economists call this phenomenon product differentiation. (Marketing specialists call it brand loyalty or brand equity.) Three characteristics of product differentiation in the brewing industry bear mentioning. First, several studies indicate that under blindfolded test conditions, many beer drinkers cannot distinguish among brands of beer. Second, more expensive brands of beer do not cost proportionately more to produce than less expensive brands. Third, considerable talent and resources are devoted to publicizing real or imagined differences in beers, with the hope of producing brand loyalty.

Notwithstanding these efforts, product differentiation in the beer industry has not afforded individual brewers market power to a degree that would be a concern of antitrust policy. Nor have product reviews afforded individual brewers market success. In 2001, *Consumer Reports* ranked Stroh (now owned by Pabst) as the *top-rated* domestic lager and generally gave low marks to imported beers because of their lack of freshness.

The product differentiation of premium beer is important to understand. This phenomenon began years ago when a few brewers marketed their beer nationally and added a price premium to offset the additional transportation costs incurred by greater shipping distances. To secure the higher price, premium beer was promoted as superior in taste and quality, allegedly because of the brewing expertise found at their place of production (notably Milwaukee and St. Louis). At one time, the premium price was offset by higher shipping costs. The construction of efficient, regionally dispersed breweries by firms like Anheuser-Busch and Miller, however, eliminated the transportation disadvantage, but the premium image remained. With transportation costs equalized and production costs generally lower, these firms could wage vigorous advertising (and price-cutting) campaigns in areas where regional and local brewers were once the largest sellers.[18]

One indicator of an industry's advertising intensity is its ratio of advertising expenditures to sales. For some companies in the soap, cosmetic, and drug industries, this ratio is greater than 10 percent. For the malt beverage industry, this ratio is nontrivial but is less than the ratio for such industries as soft drinks, candy, cigarettes, preserved fruits, and other alcoholic beverages.

Nonetheless, the beer industry is a major buyer of television advertising time. In 2002, Anheuser-Busch, Miller, and Coors spent $4.08, $6.90, and $8.63 per barrel on media advertising, respectively.[19] Douglas F. Greer and others have argued that advertising, particularly television advertising, is a primary cause of increasing concentration in the industry. John Sutton offers a variation on this theme, suggesting that advertising is a sunk cost that protects the leading firms from new competition. However, the facts do not permit any tidy explanations or conclusions about the consequences of advertising because no hard-and-fast relationship is evident between dollars spent on advertising and market share gained.

Miller has long been a heavy advertiser. In the period 1967 through 1971, it generally spent twice as much per barrel on advertising as rival brewers. However, Miller's market share did not expand then, nor did other firms feel compelled to emulate Miller's sizable promotional outlays. Schlitz spent more on advertising in 1975 and 1976 than either Anheuser-Busch or Miller, and yet sales of the Schlitz brand declined in that time frame.

Coors experienced expanding sales with small advertising expenditures: In 1968 through 1974, during years of sizable growth, Coors spent an average of only 17 cents per barrel on media advertising. Coors's *growing* use of media occurred when its share position in many states was declining.

Miller was not able to secure more than a toehold in the super-premium segment of the market notwithstanding extraordinary per-barrel advertising expenditures on Lowenbrau. In 1980, Miller High Life was the most heavily advertised brand of beer in the United States; that was the year its sales slowed down, and they declined every year after that until the brand was repositioned at a lower price point.

---

[18]The national brewers also have two other advertising advantages: (1) none of their advertising is "wasted," whereas regional brewers do not always find media markets (especially in television) that coincide with their selling territories; and (2) their advertising investment is less likely to be lost when a customer moves to another part of the country.

Anheuser-Busch significantly increased its advertising expenditures on its Budweiser brand—total and per barrel—from 1991 to 1992, but Budweiser's total sales and share of the market fell. On the other hand, Natural Light has been one of Anheuser-Busch's steadiest performers, even though the company often spends less than a nickel per barrel on its advertising.

To economists, beer is an example of an "experience good," because the product's characteristics can only be evaluated after purchasing the good. With experience goods, advertisements laden with information are of little value to consumers because the validity of the information is largely verified post-purchase. Consequently, advertisements for experience goods tend to emphasize image and the identity of the seller's brand name. This characterizes much beer advertising. For example, SABMiller promotes Miller Lite with the catchphrase "tastes great . . . less filling," and Coors emphasizes its slogan "Rocky Mountain Refreshment."

Critics of these noninformative ads maintain that consumers are manipulated by them, and they create artificial product differentiation for what are essentially homogeneous products. Some critics are particularly concerned that young people will think their own identity depends upon emulating the images portrayed in the ads. Many economists, however, view consumers as rational agents capable of making self-interested decisions regarding the merits of experience goods. Although the content of beer advertisements may appear to be noninformative, consumers are at least made aware of the existence of a product or service if they have observed an advertisement for it, and repetitive advertising increases the likelihood that a potential consumer will encounter such information and alter his or her cache of knowledge.[20]

The total amount of resources devoted to beer advertising is large, but this is not surprising. A brewer wants to inform millions of actual and potential beer drinkers of the availability of its product. New beer customers come of age; old customers might need a reminder. The Supreme Court lent its support to this form of economic reasoning. In the context of another market, the Court opined " . . . advertising, however tasteless and excessive it sometimes may seem, is nonetheless dissemination of information."[21]

Rising per capita income also has contributed modestly to increasing concentration in the beer industry. Premium beer is what economists call a normal good, with a positive income elasticity. The brewers who in the 1970s came to be the major players in the industry are, essentially, producers of premium brands. Popular-priced brands (now often called the budget segment) were once the leading sellers within their respective home states, but this is no longer the case. Premium brands (regular and light) now hold about 65 percent of the market; imports and super premiums have about 13 percent. The loser in the past three decades has been popular-priced beer, dropping from almost 60 percent in 1970 to less than 10 percent in 2002. The traditional domestic super-premium brands also have declined in market share, replaced by a growing emphasis on craft beers and imports.

Specialty brands are not just the offspring of microbrewers. Several major brewers have had modest success with specialty brands, usually priced a notch below craft beers and import brands. Coors (Killian Red) and Miller (Red Dog) are examples of the trend. Product variety generally has a positive income elasticity, and so rising income supports greater product variety. Some beverage sector analysts speculate that the beer industry someday will have the same large array of specialty brands one finds now in coffee and wine.

---

[19]For Anheuser-Busch and Miller, this was an increase over spending in the year 2000 of $3.56 and $4.49 per barrel. Coors' media spending in 2000 was $8.77 per barrel.

Light beer, virtually nonexistent in 1970, has become the largest product segment with about 45 percent of the total market in 2002, almost all of this being brewed by the top three brewers and much of it selling at premium prices. The decline of once prominent brewers like Pabst, Schlitz, and Stroh is explained in part by their lack of success (compared to Anheuser-Busch, Miller, and Coors) in the light-beer segment of the market. Even import brands like Corona and Molson are now available as light beers in the United States.

III. CONDUCT

Pricing

Judging from the early records of the preprohibition beer industry, competition in the industry was vigorous. Entry was easy; producers were numerous. Given these two characteristics, economic theory would predict a competitive industry, and the evidence bears this out. In fact, the early beer industry offers a classic example of the predictions of price theory. Because of the market's inelastic demand, brewers saw the obvious advantages of monopolizing the industry, raising prices, and gleaning high profits. Various types of loose and tight-knit cartels were seen as advantageous, but the difficulty of coordinating so many brewers and the lack of barriers to entry prevented these efforts from being successful, at least for long. The degree of competition is evidenced by this turn-of-the-century plea from Adolphus Busch to Captain Pabst:

> I hope also to be able to demonstrate to you that by the present way competition is running we are only hurting each other in a real foolish way. The traveling agents ... always endeavor to reduce prices and send such reports to their respective home offices as are generally not correct and only tend to bring forth competition that helps to ruin the profits ... all large manufacturing interests are now working in harmony ... and only the brewers are behind as usual; instead of combining their efforts and securing their own interest, they are fighting each other and running the profits down, so that the pleasures of managing a brewery have been diminished a good deal.

In a free-enterprise economy, it is best that rival managers avoid any communications about prices. If such letters are written though, it is best if they decry vigorous market rivalry.

The beer industry also escaped the horizontal mergers that transformed the structure of so many industries such as steel, whiskey, petroleum, tobacco products, and farm equipment during the first great merger movement (1880 to 1904). Attempts were made, mostly by British businessmen, to combine the large brewers during this time. One sought the amalgamation of Pabst, Schlitz, Miller, Anheuser-Busch, and Lemp into one company, a feat that had it been successful would have altered the structure and degree of competition in the industry. The attempt failed though, and the brewing industry entered the prohibition with a competitive structure that responded with competitive pricing.

The Pricing Pattern

Beer is generally sold free on board (f.o.b.) the brewery, meaning that the brewer's costs end at the loading dock, and customers pay the freight. Some brewers sell on a

---

[20]Robert B. Ekelund, Jr. and David Saurman, *Advertising and the Market Process*. San Francisco: Pacific Research Institute (1988), p. 64.
[21]See *Virginia State Board of Pharmacy* v. *Virginia Citizens Consumer Council*, 425 U.S. 748, 765 (1976).

uniform f.o.b. mill basis, but most vary their prices at times to different customers to reflect localized competitive conditions or to test perceived changes in the marketplace.

The present pattern of prices dates back to the start of the twentieth century. For decades, premium beers generally were priced just above the level of popular-priced beers, which in turn were above local (or price or shelf) beer. Because of downward price pressure on premium beer and the decline of independent brewers producing only popular-priced beer, the marketing segments today often are broken down as premium (regular and light), near premium, and budget. A more contemporary category is the super premium, a beer selling at a price above premium. A number of major brewers market their own brand of super premiums, and most imported beers and the output of brewers in the craft segment fall into the super-premium price category.

The demarcation between local/popular/premium has become blurred in recent years, not only because of the introduction of the super premium but also because the price differential between premium and popular-priced brands has narrowed. At the same time, the distinction between local and popular beer on the basis of price has become murky because of pricing specials that regularly appear in either segment of the market and the repositioning of once premium brands, like Pabst Blue Ribbon, into a lower price tier.

Some brands defy categories. Industry expert Robert S. Weinberg provides an example: "Life must be very confusing for a six-pack of Rolling Rock. It comes out of the brewery, and depending on the address it is sent to, it might be popular-priced beer, a premium, a super premium, or a domestic specialty. Same beer, and an extraordinary marketing achievement."[22] Discounting also occurs in the beer industry, even among the premium brands. In 1992, for example, almost 50 percent of the beer sold by Anheuser-Busch, Miller, and Coors included some form of deal: a direct price discount or an advertising or merchandising allowance. In short, beer price differentials are not fully attributable to some identifiable physical characteristic of the product. In the case of malt beverages, price differences also are the result of customers' tastes, market competition, and history.

Marketing

Although all industries are subject to various federal and state laws that affect the marketing of the industry's product, the brewing industry faces an especially variegated pattern of laws and regulations concerning labeling, advertising, credit, container characteristics, alcohol content, tax rates, and litter assessments. For example, Michigan makes optional whether a beer label shows alcohol content, but Minnesota requires an accurate statement of alcohol content. In Indiana, advertising is strictly regulated; in Louisiana, no such regulations exist. Some states require sales from the brewer to the wholesaler to the retailer to be only on a cash basis, whereas other states allow credit. Some states stipulate the maximum and minimum size of containers. States also have varying requirements on the maximum and minimum permissible alcoholic content; in some states, alcoholic content is different for different types of outlets.

In the 1970s, beer advertising was criticized because it allegedly could lead to monopoly problems. This turned out to be unfounded. More recently, beer advertising has been criticized from a public health perspective—the idea that beer advertising increases alcohol abuse among specific populations, particularly underage consumers.

The research of Jon Nelson suggests that advertising does not increase market demand but rather rearranges shares among brands. As a corollary, Nelson concludes that bans on advertising are not sound public policy because the evidence is weak that advertising increases total consumption (and therefore abuse). He does find that bans on *billboard* advertising of alcoholic beverages can reduce the demand for distilled spirits and wine but can increase the demand for beer. Nelson suggests that stricter enforcement of legal drinking age laws is a more effective way of restraining alcohol abuse by young people (Nelson, 2003). The research of Carol and Victor Tremblay (1995) offers a different perspective: that on balance there might be a social gain from restricting beer advertising. Economists do not always see eye to eye.

Government involvement in the beer industry also includes heavy taxation. The federal tax alone on a barrel of beer is $18.00; in 2001, the Treasury Department coffers gathered $3.6 billion in beer taxes.[23] State taxes on beer vary substantially, but in 1999 they averaged $7.91 per barrel. In addition, brewers, wholesalers, and retail outlets pay federal, state, and sometimes local occupational taxes. Federal and state taxes paid by the beer industry amount to more than $27 billion annually, making taxes the largest single cost item in a glass of beer.

Brewer-Distributor Relations

There is little forward integration by brewing firms into the marketing of beer. In the United States, brewers generally are prohibited by law from owning retail outlets, leaving wholesale distribution as the only legitimate forward vertical integration route.[24] Even wholesaling by brewers is prohibited in some states. The retailing of beer is done through two general types of independent outlets: on-premises consumption and off-premises consumption. On-premises sales are the leading retail channel, followed by convenience stores and supermarkets. Brewers generally make higher margins with on-premises sales.

Most brewers rely on independent wholesalers to channel their product to retail outlets. Historically, most wholesalers have been family run businesses. In recent years, the wholesaling of beer has been marked by numerous consolidations and mergers. Some family firms are now big businesses, with many wholesalers today concentrating their distribution on only one or two major brewers. Most Anheuser-Busch volume (62 percent) goes through exclusive distributors; those distributors who are not exclusive have less than 10 percent of their volume in rival brands.

Anheuser-Busch estimates that only 5 percent of Miller's volume and 3 percent of Coors's volume travel through exclusive distributors. Miller and Coors often share the same beer wholesaler (in more than 250 instances). Many localities now have only two beer distributors: one for Anheuser-Busch and one for all others. A typical Anheuser-Busch distributor markets fewer than 30 brands, but a typical non–Anheuser-Busch distributor will handle more than 100 brands from more than 2 dozen different brewers.

Every brewer has an economic interest in what happens to its beer once it leaves the brewery dock, because consumers see the brewer's name on the container, not the name of the wholesaler or retailer. Therefore, brewers negotiate contracts with wholesalers that specify the marketing obligations of each party. Even with the growth in the size of some beer wholesalers, brewers are increasingly involved in channel marketing. For example, large retail accounts often are called upon by the brewer, not wholesalers.

Major brewers almost unanimously support and market through a three-tier distribution system. However, some large retail customers, notably chain stores, would prefer to purchase beer directly from brewers, bypassing the wholesale distributor. Some people worry that the middle man (the second tier of the beer industry's three-tier dis-

---

[22]Robert S. Weinberg, "Talking with Dr. Bob," *Modern Brewery Age*, Nov. 27, 2000, p. 12.
[23]In 2002, as part of legislation establishing the Department of Homeland Security, the Bureau of Alcohol, Tobacco and Firearms was divided into two agencies. Federal regulation of the alcoholic beverage industry regarding taxes and trade regulation now is conducted by the new Tax and Trade Bureau (TTB) of the Department of Treasury.

tribution channel) will be eliminated if large retailers are allowed to deal directly with brewers. The middle person is not really eliminated though if alcoholic beverages do not come to rest in some independent wholesaler's warehouse. From an economic perspective, what is happening is that the middle-person function gets internalized within the parties to the direct-buy transaction.

The trend toward store brands and a closer integration between manufacturer and retailer, already common in food retailing, has not yet affected the beer industry, but the beer industry is not insulated from this trend. In 2003, 7-Eleven contracted with a brewery in El Salvador to supply the convenience store chain with a private label import that will be priced below established import brands.

Just as some retailers might want to buy beer directly, so might some consumers. The prospect of direct sales from brewer to consumer through e-commerce represents a further weakening of the three-tier system. In 2003, the Federal Trade Commission issued a report recommending an end to state bans on direct shipments of wine because e-commerce sales will afford consumers lower prices, more choices, and increased convenience. The FTC dismissed as self-serving the argument of wine wholesalers that direct sales would encourage underage consumption. When the FTC study became public, beer distribution expert Mark Rodman asked rhetorically, "Why is beer different than wine?"[25] The answer is that it is not different, and the prospect for direct sales of beer might be another step in undercutting traditional beer marketing.

Some retail accounts want to bargain with different distributors of the same brand of beer (possibly purchasing from a price-cutting wholesaler in another area). Many brewers have exclusive territories with wholesalers that prevent this. Exclusive territories enable brewers to offer incentives to distributors to cultivate a specific territory with less fear of free riding. An example of free riding would be a distributor who transships dated beer to a territory that has been served by another distributor who, by careful stock rotation, had given that brand a reputation for freshness.

Some critics, however, consider exclusive territorial restraints to be anticompetitive. In an important antitrust case against several major brewers, the New York attorney general once challenged the use of exclusive territories. In 1993, the challenge ended when exclusive territories in beer distribution were found, on balance, to be procompetitive.

At one time, beer wholesalers primarily distributed beer in kegs for on-premises draught consumption. In 1935, only 30 percent of beer sales were packaged; that is, in bottles or cans suitable for on- or off-premises consumption. Since that time, there has been a major shift to packaged beer relative to draught; by 2000, about 91 percent of beer sales were packaged in cans, one-way bottles, and refillables.

The trend to packaged beer once worked to the disadvantage of the small brewer. When beer sales were primarily for on-premises consumption, the small brewer could prosper by selling kegs to taverns in the immediate area; the local brewer offered freshness and transportation economies relative to larger but more distant brewers. Packaged beer from the major brands increased the opportunity for national advertising campaigns though, making on-premises customers more aware of the major brands even if they were brewed many miles away. The mass production of beer in bottles and cans also dovetailed with the desire for convenience that packaged sales offer to off-premises customers.

---

[24]The exception—sometimes hard-won—has been brewpubs which represent vertical integration from brewing to retailing.

More recently, craft brewers have fought this trend by offering specialty beers that could be promoted in restaurants and bars as full-flavored alternatives to the major brands; some craft brewers are integrated vertically into brewpubs and cater to consumers interested in beer that has a different taste signature than that of the major brands.

Beer and the Global Economy

The United States imports far more beer (23.2 million barrels in 2002) than it exports (4.2 million barrels in 2002). In some situations, the trade asymmetry is stark. For example, in 2002 the Dutch sold about 5.9 million barrels of beer to the United States and imported only 2,400 barrels of U.S. beer. Mexico, The Netherlands, Canada, and Germany are the main exporters of beer to the United States (in 2002 order of volume). Mexican and Canadian beers have a transportation cost advantage over their Dutch and German rivals. When asked why Heineken did not build a brewery in the United States to reduce its transportation costs, the firm's U.S. president replied, "I like to have that small word *imported* on the label ... something would get lost" if the bottle read "brewed and bottled in the USA."[26]

The U.S. beer industry is a latecomer to the globalization of markets, but the process is under way. For example, in 1993, Anheuser-Busch purchased an 18 percent stake in the largest Mexican brewer (Cerveceria Modelo) and entered into a joint venture with the leading Japanese brewer (Kirin). As mentioned earlier, Miller was acquired in 2002 by SAB, a London-based, international brewer. In 1991, Coors entered into a joint venture with Jinro to build a large brewery in South Korea and a license agreement with Scottish & Newcastle in Scotland to brew Coors beer for the European market. In 1992, Pabst dismantled its Fort Wayne, Indiana, brewery and shipped it to China, where it once again produces Pabst Blue Ribbon beer.

Although Anheuser-Busch is the largest brewer of beer in the world, it is not truly a global player. Heineken (Holland), Carlsberg (Denmark), Interbrew (Belgium), and Guinness (U.K./Ireland) better define a global brewer. Each produces the majority of its volume outside its home country. Among U.S. brewers with international aspirations, licensing production in foreign markets has been the favored mode of expansion. The export of product from the United States to foreign markets actually declined in the latter half of the 1990s.

IV. PERFORMANCE

Profits

If an industry is effectively monopolized, one might expect to see this reflected in its profits. This is not necessarily so, because (1) demand might be insufficient to yield profits in spite of a monopoly; (2) a monopolist might be inefficient; and (3) accounting records often are imperfect measures of economic costs, so even high accounting profits might not reflect monopoly gains. In spite of these difficulties, economists regularly look at profit data for some insight into an industry's performance.

During the post–World War II period, profits in the beer industry, as measured by accounting records, have been modest, generally falling below the rate of return for all manufacturing firms. In recent years, the rate of return on brewing has exceeded an all-manufacturing benchmark. According to government sources, for the period 1998 through 2000, breweries had a 3-year rate of return of 18.4 percent on net worth compared to an all-manufacturing return on net worth of 13.1 percent.

---

[25]"FTC report supports internet sales and direct shipping for wine," *Modern Brewery Age*, July 14, 2003, p. 1.

As one might expect from the discussion of economies of scale, the largest brewers have been more profitable than the industry average as they exploited these scale economies. Beginning in 1964, the top four companies began to outperform the rest of the brewing industry in terms of accounting profits. Prior to that time, the profit record of the top four brewers approximated that of the rest of the industry and was usually inferior to the firms ranked five through eight who, in those days, were not high-cost producers.

Externalities and Informational Asymmetries

Two kinds of market failure that economists recognize are externalities and information asymmetries. To the extent that an industry is marked by externalities or information asymmetries, the economic performance of that industry is likely to be affected. The existence of market failure raises the question of whether government intervention might remedy the externality or information asymmetry in a policy-efficient manner.

A negative externality occurs when transactions between buyers and sellers reduce the economic welfare of individuals not party to the transaction. Air pollution is the textbook example of a negative externality. The beer industry is remarkably free of the negative externalities often associated with the *production* of products: air and water pollution. Brewing is a clean industry (breweries must be more sanitary than hospitals, in fact), and brewing firms often are courted by localities seeking industry partly for this reason.

The two important negative externality problems in brewing occur in the *consumption* of the product: litter and alcohol abuse. Most citizens are able to restrain their enthusiasm for the beer cans and bottles that end up as litter, and everyone on the roads and highways would like to avoid the negative externality of a drunk driver coming at them head-on.

To deal with litter, legislation banning or restricting the sale of beer containers has been proposed, but only a few states and localities have passed such laws. The most restrictive of these laws was enacted in the college town of Oberlin, Ohio, which simply outlawed the sale or possession of beer in nonreturnable containers. The most well-known of these laws is the Oregon bottle bill, passed in 1971, which banned all cans with detachable pull tabs and placed a compulsory 5-cent deposit on all beer and soft drink containers.

Other states have followed with variations of the Oregon plan. The pull-tab can has disappeared as a result of this legislation, and the deposit cost has offered an inducement to the use of returnable containers or on-premises draught consumption. In Oregon and Vermont, mandatory deposit legislation apparently led to reductions of 60 percent and 80 percent, respectively, in roadside beverage container litter. However, the statewide (or local) approach cannot solve the problem (say, in Vermont) of customers going "over the line" (to New Hampshire) to avoid the deposit requirement and higher prices.

American brewers (with the exception of Coors) historically have opposed all litter taxes and bans on containers, stressing instead voluntary action and other litter-recovery programs. The latter, if generously financed, could solve the litter problem but partially at the expense of nonproducers and nonconsumers.

---

[26] *Beer Marketer's Insights*, December 17, 2002, p. 4, quoting Frans van der Minne.

The negative externality of driving while under the influence of alcohol was responsible for escalating the minimum drinking age in all states to 21 years of age. However, this has had little impact upon young people driving under the influence of alcohol. Economic research suggests that young beer drinkers are more sensitive to price increases. Indexing the federal tax on beer to the rate of inflation since 1951 would, by its impact on retail price, have discouraged enough drunk driving by young drivers to save an estimated 5,000 lives in the period from 1982 through 1988 (more than were saved by raising the minimum legal drinking age). This also would make beer more expensive to all those who do not abuse the product though.

As another strategy, the National Highway Safety Administration has endorsed a blood alcohol content (BAC) level of 0.08 (or above) as a per se driving violation. Most states currently define driving under the influence at a BAC above 0.08, such as 0.10. The American Beverage Institute opposes lowering the BAC but supports stiffer penalties for those caught driving while intoxicated. The costs imposed upon third parties by alcohol abuse go beyond automobile accidents, and alcohol abuse is not limited to the consumption of malt beverages.

Asymmetric information occurs when one party to a transaction knows things about the product that the person on the other side does not know. Asymmetric information is present in the distribution of alcohol. Some consumers, often young ones, might not have as much information about the consequences of alcohol consumption as sellers have, and sellers might not have economic incentives to eliminate this asymmetry. For example, beer advertisements rarely inform consumers of the negative consequences of excessive consumption. Regulations that offset the information asymmetry, as well as privately funded campaigns such as Mothers Against Drunk Driving, might help remedy this market failure. Information that promotes temperance might reduce the market failure associated with beer (or other alcohol) consumption.

Competition

A third kind of market failure occurs when a market is monopolized, either by a single firm or a group of sellers who coordinate their price and output decisions. This is not an economic characteristic of the beer industry. No monopoly brewer exists who, insulated from competition, is able to enjoy the "quiet life."

In some industries, increasing concentration at the national level coupled with inelastic market demand might raise the specter of tacit or direct collusion. However, no evidence of price collusion is seen in the beer industry, nor is the prospect worrisome for the foreseeable future. Even during a period of increasing demand in the 1960s and 1970s, competition among brewers was so vigorous as to force the exit of marginal firms. Furthermore, competition along nonprice vectors is robust, such as new product introductions, promotional activities, packaging innovations, brand advertising, product freshness, and availability. As Gisser has argued, increasing concentration in brewing has enhanced consumer welfare as a handful of firms invested in new technologies that increased the efficiency of an initially unconcentrated market, resulting in lower prices to consumers.

One measure of an industry's rivalry is the extent of changes in market share or turnover in the ranking of its sellers.[27] The beer industry exhibits high mobility in this regard. Schlitz, the nation's second-ranking firm in 1976 and manufacturer of the "Beer That Made Milwaukee Famous," no longer is even brewed there. Pabst was the third-leading seller as recently as 1975, ahead of Miller, and the subject of Antitrust Division action. It has become a shell of its former self. In 2002, for example, Pabst sold only

1 million barrels of its Pabst Blue Ribbon brand. As a consequence of market forces, the once prominent brewing trio of Heileman, Pabst, and Stroh lost more than *22 million barrels* of sales from their brand portfolios during the decade 1988 to 1998.

Miller, the number eight brewer in 1968, bested a number of larger brewers in the marketplace and, by 1977, had become the number two brewer in the United States (a rank it has held since). However, Miller, the darling of the industry in the 1970s, experienced an absence of growth in the 1980s, the 1990s, and into the twenty-first century.

Coors, the number three brewer, attained its current rank in part by changing its status from a regional to a national brewer. (In 1976, Coors only marketed to 11 Western states.) Coors has been bested in a number of states though, where it was once the leading seller. For example, Coors once "owned" Oklahoma and California, with 54 percent and 40 percent of the sales in these states, respectively. By 2002, these percentages had slipped to 16 and 12 percent, respectively.

The one constant in all of this has been Anheuser-Busch: It has been number one since 1957. Even more remarkable than its hold on the number one position has been its relative growth. Throughout the 10-year period from 1992 to 2002, Anheuser-Busch's market share has grown almost every year. Several factors contribute to Anheuser-Busch's strong leadership position. All of its breweries are large, low-cost facilities. Moreover, only two brands comprise much of the firm's output, and these are produced primarily in one package format (Budweiser and Bud Light in 12-ounce cans). This means that Anheuser-Busch does not often incur the cost of changing brewing formulas or reconstituting packaging lines. In addition, because of its enormous volume, the company has per-barrel advertising costs that are significantly below those of many of its rivals. Thus, on the cost side of the competition ledger, Anheuser-Busch is favorably positioned.

On the revenue side of the competition ledger, Anheuser-Busch's pricing strategy builds on the firm's efficiencies in production. Most of its output is sold at premium and super-premium prices, which generate higher margins. The company's general pricing strategy is to change its prices only in line with production-cost changes and to build overall profits through volume gains. TV ads for Anheuser-Busch products are acclaimed for their positive recall. On the other hand, the company has many chips on the Budweiser brand, whose domestic sales have declined in recent years. Should the bloom ever come off the Bud, Anheuser-Busch's position would become vulnerable.

Rivalry from foreign producers never has been as strong a force in the beer industry as in markets like consumer electronic products and automobiles. As described earlier though, the amount of beer imported into the United States has increased substantially in the past decade and now provides an important source of rivalry to domestic premium brands. From 1992 through 2002, imports increased by 15 million barrels, and domestic shipments declined by about 1 million barrels. The growth in beer consumption in recent years has been driven to a significant degree by imports. In addition, the entry and growth of flavored malt beverages has taken sales volume from traditional brewers.

Increases in concentration in brewing are neither the result nor the cause of market power. The reasons, rather, are benign: the exploitation of scale economies and the demise of suboptimal capacity, new or superior products, changes in packaging and marketing methods, poor management on the part of some firms, and the strategic use of product differentiation. As a consequence, Anheuser-Busch, Miller, and Coors no longer

---

[27]Robert S. Weinberg has the most extensive database on the rise and fall of U.S. brewers. I am indebted to him for his counsel and industry statistics. See "Tracking the Winners," *Modern Brewery Age*, Nov. 11, 2002, pp. 20-23.

face an array of robust domestic brewers. Brands like Schlitz, Pabst, Old Style, Stroh, Ballantine, Schaefer, Falstaff, Olympia, Rheingold, Ruppert, Blatz, Lucky Lager, and Hamm's as well as the firms that produced them are gone or are mere shadows of what they once were. The big three domestic brewers now face significant import competition, in some cases from large brewers with operations in many countries, as well as significant competition from craft brewers. In addition, if flavored malt beverages are not a fad but instead consumers increasingly consider these products substitutes for traditional malt beverages, the big three face competition from a different flank with new rivals.[28]

Conclusion

The statistics of the structure of the beer industry, the pricing and marketing conduct of its members, and the profits it has received do not mark it as a monopolized industry. Consumers are pursued by price and nonprice competition. The changing fortunes of even major brewers indicate that the market for beer is no stodgy oligopoly, with firms adopting a live-and-let-live posture toward each other. The number of exits from brewing in the last three decades indicates that this is hardly an industry in which the inefficient producer is protected from the chilling winds of competition.

Suggested Readings

Books, Pamphlets, Monographs, Web Sites

Baron, Stanley Wade. 1962. *Brewed in America.* Boston: Little, Brown and Company.

Baum, Dan. 2000. *Citizen Coors.* New York: Morrow.

Beer Marketer's Insights. Published 23 times per year. West Nyack, NY.

Beer Marketer's Insights—Beer Industry Update. Annual. West Nyack, NY.

Brewers Almanac. Annual. Washington, D.C.: The Beer Institute.

Freidrich, Manfred, and Donald Bull. 1976. *The Register of United States Breweries 1876— 1976.* 2 vols. Stamford, CT: Holly Press.

Modern Brewery Age. Weekly news edition and monthly magazine. Stamford, CT: Business Journals, Inc.

Modern Brewery Age: Blue Book. Annual. Stamford, CT: Modern Brewery Age Publishing Co.

The New Brewer. Bimonthly. Boulder, CO: Association of Brewers.

North American Brewers Resource Directory. Annual. Boulder, CO: Institute for Brewing Studies.

Rehr, David K. 1997. *Political Economy of the Malt Beverage Industry.* PhD diss., George Mason University.

Robertson, James D. 1978. *The Great American Beer Book.* New York: Warner Books.

Scherer, F. M., Alan Beckenstein, Erich Kaufer, and R. Dennis Murphy. 1975. *The Economics of Multi-Plant Operations.* Cambridge: Harvard University Press.

Slosberg, Pete. 1998. *Beer for Pete's Sake.* Boulder, CO: Siris Books.

Sutton, John. 1991. *Sunk Costs and Market Structure.* Cambridge, MA: MIT Press.

Van Munching, Philip. 1997. *Beer Blast.* New York: Random House. www.beerinstitute.org

Articles

Ackoff, Russell L., and James R. Emshoff. 1975. "Advertising Research at Anheuser-Busch, Inc. (1963–1968)." *Sloan Management Review* 16 (Winter).

---

[28]Recognizing this threat, Anheuser-Busch, Miller and Coors introduced their own FMBs.

_____. 1975. "Advertising Research at Anheuser-Busch, Inc. (1968–74)." *Sloan Management Review* 16 (Spring).

Clements, Kenneth W., and Lester W. Johnson. 1983. "The Demand for Beer, Wine, and Spirits: A Systemwide Analysis." *Journal of Business* 56 (July).

Chaloupka, F. J., M. Grossman, and H. Saffer. 1993. "Alcohol Control Policies and Motor Vehicle Fatalities." *Journal of Legal Studies* 22 (January).

Consumer Reports. 2001. "Which Brew for You?" (August), 10–16.

Culbertson, W. Patton, and David Bradford. 1991. "The Price of Beer: Some Evidence from Interstate Comparisons." *International Journal of Industrial Organization* 9 (June).

Gisser, Mica. 1999. "Dynamic Gains and Static Losses in Oligopoly: Evidence from the Beer Industry." *Economic Inquiry* 37 (July).

Greer, Douglas F. 1998. "Beer: Causes of Structural Change." In Larry L. Duetsch (ed.), *Industry Studies.* Armonk, NY: M. E. Sharpe.

Hogarty, Thomas F., and Kenneth G. Elzinga. 1972. "The Demand for Beer." *Review of Economics and Statistics* 54 (May).

Horowitz, Ira, and Ann Horowitz. 1965. "Firms in a Declining Market: The Brewing Case." Journal of *Industrial Economics* 13 (March).

Kerkvliet, Joe R., William Nebesky, Carol H. Tremblay, and Victor J. Tremblay. 1998. "Efficiency and Technological Change in the U.S. Brewing Industry." *Journal of Productivity Analysis* 10 (November).

Lawler, Kevin, and Kin-Pui Lee. 2003. "Brewing." In Peter Johnson (ed.), *Industries in Europe.* Cheltenham: Edward Elgar.

Lynk, William J. 1984. "Interpreting Rising Concentration: The Case of Beer." *Journal of Business* 57 (January).

_____. 1985. "The Price and Output of Beer Revisited." *Journal of Business* 58 (October).

McConnell, J. Douglas. 1968. "An Experimental Examination of the Price-Quality Relationship." *Journal of Business* 41 (October).

McGahan, A. M. 1991. "The Emergence of the National Brewing Oligopoly: Competition in the American Market, 1933–1958." *Business History Review* 65 (Summer).

McNulty, Timothy J. 1986. "Image and Competition Keep Beer Industry Foaming." *Chicago Tribune* (August 11), C1.

Nelson, Jon P. 2001. "Alcohol Advertising and Advertising Bans: A Survey of Research Methods, Results, and Policy Implications." *Advances in Applied Microeconomics* 10.

_____. 2003. "Advertising Bans, Monopoly, and Alcohol Demand: Testing for Substitution Effects Using State Panel Data." *Review of Industrial Organization* 22 (February).

Ornstein, Stanley I. 1981. "Antitrust Policy and Market Forces as Determinants of Industry Structure: Case Histories in Beer and Distilled Spirits." *Antitrust Bulletin* 26 (Summer).

_____, and Dominique M. Hanssens. 1985. "Alcohol Control Laws and the Consumption of Distilled Spirits and Beer." *Journal of Consumer Research* 12 (September).

Rodman, Mark. 2000. "An Industry Caught in the Net," (Parts I and II). *Modern Brewery Age* (July 10), 32–40; (September 11), 22–36.

Sass, Tim R., and David S. Saurman. 1993. "Mandated Exclusive Territories and Economic Efficiency: An Empirical Analysis of the Malt Beverage Industry." *Journal of Law & Economics* 36 (April).

Tremblay, Victor J. 1985. "A Reappraisal of Interpreting Rising Concentration: The Case of Beer." *Journal of Business* 58 (October).

_____, and Carol Horton Tremblay. 1988. "The Determinants of Horizontal Acquisitions: Evidence from the U.S. Brewing Industry." *Journal of Industrial Economics* 37 (September).

_____. 1995. "Advertising, Price, and Welfare: Evidence from the U.S. Brewing Industry." *Southern Economic Journal* 62 (October).

Weinberg, Robert S. 1999. "Watching the Market." *Modern Brewery Age* (March 22), 24–31.

_____. 2000. "Talking with Dr. Bob." *Modern Brewery Age* (November 27), 10–15.

_____. 2001. "Taking the Long View." *Modern Brewery Age* (March 26), 16–23.

_____. 2002. "Tracking the Winners." *Modern Brewery Age* (November 11), 20–23.

CHAPTER

Automobiles

—James W. Brock

The proverbial man from Mars, looking at us afresh, would doubtless come to the conclusion that the automobile was the dominant fact in our producing, consuming, and perhaps our fantasy lives; he could plausibly conclude that the four-wheeled creatures run the society and that the two-legged creatures are its servants.[1]

—Douglas Dowd

Reports commissioned by the industry's trade association lend credence to this claim: They estimate that for every worker employed in automotive manufacturing, seven additional workers are employed in supplying steel, aluminum, copper, lead, plastics, textiles, vinyl, and computer components to the industry, and that overall, automobile manufacturing directly and indirectly generates 6.6 million jobs. Beyond this, the Alliance of Automobile Manufacturers lauds "automobility" for affording Americans unparalleled access to more employment opportunities, more goods and services, and more learning opportunities (including visits to concerts, museums, and natural parks). This automobility, the industry says, is "the core of individualism in America"—a cultural icon that has evoked odes to "merry Oldsmobiles," "Mustang Sally," and "the little old lady from Pasadena."[2]

At the same time, automobiles account for nearly half of the 20 million barrels of petroleum consumed daily in the United States, much of it imported from geopolitically volatile foreign sources.[3] Cars and light trucks dump 43 million tons of carbon monoxide into the nation's atmosphere each year, along with 4.4 million tons of nitrogen oxides and 4.5 million tons of volatile organic compounds.[4] In addition, automobile crashes kill 42,000 people annually and injure an additional 2.9 million people, at a total cost of $230 billion each year.[5] Automobiles are a major cause of congestion and frustration, in addition to serving as homicidal weapons of road rage.

An analysis of the structure, conduct, and performance of this industry is imperative in examining these issues and the public policy questions they pose.

---

[1]Quoted in Stan Luger, *Corporate Power, American Democracy, and the Automobile Industry* (New York: Cambridge University Press, 2000), 1.
[2]Alliance of Automobile Manufacturers, "Contribution of the Automobile Industry to the U.S. Economy," Washington, D.C. (Winter 2001).
[3]U.S. Energy Information Administration, Annual Energy Review: 2001, Washington, D.C., Table 5.12c.
[4]U.S. Census Bureau, *Statistical Abstract of the United States: 2002,* Washington, D.C., Table 349, 218.
[5]U.S. National Highway Traffic Safety Administration, 2002 Early Assessment of Motor Vehicle Crashes, Washington, D.C. (April 2003); idem, Economic Impact of Motor Vehicle Crashes 2000 (May 2002).

I. HISTORY

The automobile as we know it first took shape in the 1890s, when early automotive pioneers experimented with gasoline engines, steam engines, and electric motors as sources of propulsion. By 1900, they had sold approximately 4,000 vehicles. Production expanded rapidly thereafter, reaching 187,000 automobiles by 1910. Entry into the industry was relatively easy, because the manufacturer of automobiles was primarily an assembler of parts produced by others. The new entrepreneur needed only to design a vehicle; contract with machine shops and independent producers for the engines, wheels, bodies, and other components; and promote to the public the car's availability.

The next decade marked the emergence of the Ford Motor Company as the dominant firm. Believing the demand for new cars to be price elastic, Henry Ford's goal was to provide an inexpensive car capable of reaching a large potential market. Standardization, specialization, and mass production, he believed, were the keys to lowering manufacturing costs, and he viewed constant price reductions as the way to tap successively larger layers of demand. "Every time I reduce the charge for our car by $1, I get 1,000 new buyers," Ford said. His strategy was profoundly simple: Take lower profits on each vehicle and achieve a larger volume. As Ford saw it, successive

> price reductions meant new enlargements of the market, an acceleration of mass production's larger economies, and greater aggregate profits. The company's firm grasp of this principle ... was its unique element of strength, just as failure to grasp it had been one of the weaknesses of rival car makers. As profits per car had gone down and down, net earnings had gone up and up.[6]

By 1921, Ford's Model T, which remained largely unchanged for 2 decades, accounted for more than half of the market.

The 1920s witnessed a shift of preeminence from Ford to General Motors (GM), the latter a combination of formerly independent firms (Chevrolet, Oldsmobile, Oakland, Cadillac, Buick, Fisher Body, and Delco). GM adopted a two-pronged strategy: First, contrary to Ford's emphasis on a single model, GM offered a broad variety of models to blanket all market segments. (Its motto was "a car for every purse and purpose.") Second, and again contrary to Ford's strategy, GM elected to modify its cars each year with a combination of engineering advances, improvements in convenience, and cosmetic styling changes. GM believed that annual model changes, despite the expense, would stimulate replacement demand and increase sales; indeed, this strategy catapulted the company into unchallenged industry leadership for a half a century. In this era, the groundwork also was laid for the high concentration that became the industry's hallmark.

Beginning in the mid-1950s, however, successive waves of imports increasingly challenged the domestic oligopoly. By the 1970s, imports had captured more than a quarter of the U.S. market and triggered repeated lobbying efforts by the Big Three, in collaboration with the United Auto Workers union, to obtain government protection from foreign competition.

---

[6]Ford Allen Nevins, *Ford: The Times, the Man, the Company* (New York: Scribner, 1954), 493.

In the 1980s, in response to the domestic industry's political campaigns, foreign firms began to build production plants in the United States. The aggregate output of these "transplants" has reached 2.6 million cars and light trucks, more than Chrysler produces in the United States and one-fourth the combined total number of vehicles assembled by GM, Ford, and Chrysler.

II. INDUSTRY STRUCTURE

The most important structural features of the U.S. automobile industry are buyer demand and the nature of the product, the number of rival manufacturers and their relative size (concentration), economies of scale, and barriers to the entry of new competitors.

Demand and the Product

The demand for automobiles is influenced by a variety of economic factors. First, the demand for new cars is predominantly a replacement demand, and because the purchase of a new car usually can be postponed, market demand is volatile. Second, because the purchase of an automobile constitutes a major investment (at an average price of $21,000 recently), the demand for new cars is also highly sensitive to macroeconomic conditions, including income, unemployment, and interest rates. Third, a key determinant of demand is price. Although the demand for new cars generally is slightly price elastic, the demand for particular makes and models is much more price sensitive owing to the availability of close substitutes. Finally, the revolution in the composition of new "car" demand in favor of sport utility vehicles, light trucks, and minivans is noteworthy (Table 5-1). Between 1975 and 2003, the new sales share of conventional passenger cars dropped from 81 percent to 52 percent, and sales of light trucks (sport utility vehicles, minivans, and pickups) have risen to account for half of the new-vehicle market.[7]

Industry Concentration

The domestic industry has long been dominated by a triopoly of immense firms. The advent of foreign "transplants" has eroded domestic concentration in production, and the growth of imports has lessened the Big Three's dominance at the retail sales end.

TABLE 5-1	Composition of U.S. New Vehicle Sales in 2002 (in millions of units)	
New cars		7.8
New light trucks		8.9
Vans	1.3	
Pickups	3.0	
Sport utility	4.6	
Total cars and light trucks		16.7

SOURCE: *Automotive News, 2004, Market Data Book* (Detroit: Crane Publishing Co. 2004).

---

[7]Karl H. Hellman and Robert M. Heavenrich, Advanced Technology Division, U.S. Environmental Protection Agency, "Light-Duty Automotive Technology and Fuel Economy Trends: 1975 Through 2003," Washington, D.C. (April 2003), 3.

Nonetheless, the Big Three firms remain dominant, and the impact of these procompetitive developments has been attenuated by the Big Three's political success in obtaining government restrictions on imports, by a proliferation of joint ventures and alliances linking the American oligopoly with its major foreign rivals, and most recently by mergers among the Big Three and foreign producers.

Firm Size and Concentration

General Motors remains the largest firm in the industry. With assets of $370 billion, annual revenues of $186 billion, and 365,000 employees, GM is the largest industrial corporation in the world; its annual revenues exceed the gross domestic product of all but a handful of nations. As Table 5-2 shows, GM's revenues are approximately equal to those of the top two Japanese producers *combined* (Toyota and Honda) and are far larger than those of most of the world's other leading automotive concerns.

The Big Three's operations span the globe: General Motors ranks first in either automotive sales or domestic production in Australia, Mexico, and Canada; second largest in Germany and Brazil; third largest in the United Kingdom; and fourth largest in France and across Western Europe generally. Likewise, Ford is the top vehicle producer in the United Kingdom; third largest in Australia, South Africa, Germany, Canada, and Western Europe overall; fourth largest in Brazil; and fifth largest in France and Mexico. DaimlerChrysler is the largest producer of autos in Germany; second largest in Mexico and Canada; fifth largest in South Africa; and seventh largest in France and across Western Europe generally.[8] The global reach of the Big Three has expanded further in recent years owing to a number of cross-national mergers and acquisitions, including

TABLE 5-2   World's Leading Automotive Producers

Rank	Company	Global Vehicles Produced (in millions)	Global Revenues (in billions)
1	General Motors	8.2	$ 186
2	Toyota	6.8	129
3	Ford	6.7	164
4	Volkswagen	5.0	109
5	DaimlerChrysler	4.3	172
6	PSA/Peugeot-Citroen	3.3	68
7	Hyundai	3.1	21
8	Honda	3.0	67
9	Nissan	3.0	57
10	Renault	2.4	47
11	Fiat	2.1	63
12	Mitsubishi Motors	1.6	32
13	Suzuki	1.1	52
14	BMW	1.0	20

SOURCE: *Automotive News*, 2004, *Market Data Book* (Detroit: Crane Publishing, 2004), and Hoover's Online Guide (www.hoovers.com).

---

[8]*Ward's Automotive Yearbook 2002.*

GM's purchase of Saab; Ford's acquisition of Jaguar, Volvo, and Land Rover; and the 1998 merger of Chrysler and Daimler-Benz.

Concentration in U.S. production is depicted in Table 5-3, where the Big Three's rise to dominance is evident, reaching a high-water mark of 94 percent to 98 percent over the period from 1956 through 1985. More recently, transplant facilities built by foreign producers in the American market, detailed in Table 5-4, have eroded the Big Three's share of domestic production: These transplants have come to account for approximately

TABLE 5-3 Concentration of U.S. Automobile Production

Year	General Motors	Ford	Chrysler	Other U.S. Producers	Big Three
1913	12%	40%	*	48%	*
1923	20	46	2%	32	68%
1933	41	21	25	13	87
1946–1955	45	24	19	12	88
1956–1965	51	29	14	6	94
1966–1975	54	27	17	2	98
1976–1985	59	24	13	4	96
1992	42	24	9	25	75
2003**	32	26	16	26	74

* Chrysler not yet in existence.
** Passenger cars and light trucks combined.
SOURCE: Lawrence J. White, *The Automobile Industry Since 1945* (Cambridge: Harvard University Press, 1971); *Automotive News*: Crane Publishing Co., *Market Data Book*, various years.

TABLE 5-4 U.S. Transplant Assembly Facilities

Transplant	Ownership	Location(s)	Models Built	Annual Capacity
Auto Alliance	Mazda/Ford	Flat Rock, MI	Mazda 6 Mercury Cougar	256,432
BMW	BMW	Spartanburg, SC	Z4, X5	120,000
Honda	Honda	East Liberty, OH	Civic, Element	244,174
		Marysville, OH	Accura, Accord	455,712
		Lincoln, AL	Odyssey	160,176
Mitsubishi	Mitsubishi	Normal, IL	Chrysler Sebring Dodge Stratus Mitsubishi Eclipse, Galant, Spyder	234,248
Nissan	Nissan	Canton, MS	Altima, Quest	na
		Smyrna, TN	Maxima, Xterra	436,160
NUMMI	Toyota/GM	Fremont, CA	Pontiac Vibe, Toyota Corolla and Tacoma	361,486
Subaru-Isuzu	Subaru/Isuzu	Lafayette, IN	Subaru Baja, Legacy Isuzu Axiom, Rodeo	248,160
Toyota	Toyota	Georgetown, KY	Avalon, Camry, Sienna	473,008
		Princeton, IN	Sequoia, Tundra	149,986

SOURCE: *Automotive News*: Crane Publishing Co., 2004, *Market Data Book;* Harbour and Associates, Harbour Report: 2003 (Troy, MI).

one quarter of total U.S. output; together, they exceed Chrysler's annual U.S. production and are nearly equal to Ford's. In fact, Honda has surpassed Chrysler as the third-largest producer of conventional passenger cars in the United States. (In addition to their American facilities, foreign firms have built additional transplant facilities in Canada and Mexico.) It is important to recognize, however, that because a number of these transplants are cooperative arrangements involving the Big Three (e.g., Ford-Mazda, GM-Toyota, Chrysler-Daimler-Mitsubishi), they do not represent genuinely independent competitors.

Concentration of sales within various vehicle segments is shown in Table 5-5, where it can be seen that the Big Three are relatively more dominant in the light-truck categories, and their combined share of various passenger car segments, although substantial, has subsided. Sport utility vehicles and pickups together have come to constitute 50 percent of GM's annual U.S. vehicle sales (and possibly as much as 90 percent of its profits),[9] 54 percent of Ford's sales, and 47 percent of DaimlerChrysler's sales—a dependence that we will see is rife with problematic consequences in a post–9/11 world of gyrating oil prices.

Despite this variation among market segments, the Big Three continue to account collectively for two thirds of all sales of new automobiles in the United States.

Foreign Competition

The import share of the American market rose from 0.4 percent in the immediate post–World War II decade to 21 percent in the period from 1976 to 1983. Foreign producers—led first by Volkswagen (its original Beetle accounted for nearly half of all U.S. imports), then by Japanese firms—provided a critical, if not the only source of effective competition for the Big Three in the post–World War II era. Initially, foreign firms focused their efforts on the economical, small-car segment of the market. Then, in the 1980s, after the Big Three succeeded in obtaining government restrictions on the number of Japanese imports, Japanese firms moved into the midsize segments of the

TABLE 5-5   Concentration of Sales by Vehicle Segment

	Total (in millions)	General Motors	Ford	Daimler Chrysler	Big Three
Cars					
Small	1.7	26%	15%	7%	48%
Mid-range	4.2	26	10	11	47
Upscale	1.0	20	20	13	53
Light trucks					
Vans	1.3	26	21	31	78
Pickups	3.0	27	35	19	81
Sport utility	4.6	30	21	13	64

NOTE: *General Motors includes Saab; Ford includes Jaguar, Rover, Volvo, Lotus, and Aston Martin; and DaimlerChrysler includes Jeep.*
SOURCE: *Automotive News*: Crane Publishing Co., 2004 *Market Data Book.*

---

[9]David Welch, "The Sun Is Setting on 'Truckish' Sport-Utes," *Business Week* (May 5, 2003): 88.

market, which were, ironically, the traditional mainstay of the domestic oligopoly. Japanese and European producers also began to gain larger shares of the higher-priced luxury end of the market (Lexus, Infiniti, BMW, and Mercedes).

In order to circumvent government trade restraints, foreign producers—led by the Japanese—also began building production facilities in the United States, in which they employed American labor and management to replicate (and even exceed) their initial successes. By 1992, imports comprised 24 percent of U.S. new-vehicle sales. (Although Japanese makers accounted for the bulk of these, the Big Three themselves are major importers of vehicles produced abroad, including those assembled in their Canadian and Mexican plants, as well as vehicles produced by foreign firms and "rebadged" for sale by the Big Three in the American market.) The import share of U.S. sales has since subsided to approximately 20 percent in recent years, as foreign firms have come to rely primarily on U.S. sales of vehicles assembled in their American production facilities.

Needless to say, import quotas and the perennial threat of protectionism jeopardize the salutary effect that foreign competition has had in eroding concentration in the American market. In the 1990s, for example, the Big Three attempted to persuade Congress to impose a fixed numerical cap on Japanese auto sales, including a legislative limit on the number of vehicles they could produce in their U.S. transplant facilities. Transnational mergers between the Big Three and foreign producers can also undermine competition in the American market.

Joint Ventures and Alliances

Further aggravating concentration and jeopardizing competition is the expansive web of joint ventures and alliances spun among the Big Three and their foreign rivals: General Motors, for example, has purchased half ownership stakes in Subaru and Isuzu, has acquired one-fifth ownership of Suzuki and Fiat, and has bought a controlling interest in the Korean automotive firm Daewoo. With Toyota, GM jointly owns and operates the New United Motor Manufacturing (NUMMI) transplant assembly facility in California, and with Suzuki, GM jointly produces vehicles in the CAMI facility in Ontario, Canada.

Ford—in addition to purchasing Volvo, Jaguar, and Land Rover—has acquired effective control of Mazda; with Mazda, Ford jointly owns and operates the AutoAlliance transplant facility in Michigan. Ford also has held substantial ownership stakes in the Korean Kia firm, which has produced vehicles for rebadging in the United States as Ford models.

Chrysler originally allied with Mitsubishi to jointly build and operate the Diamond Star transplant facility in Normal, Illinois; although Chrysler subsequently sold its ownership in that plant, Mitsubishi continues to assemble various Chrysler models in that facility. The merged DaimlerChrysler firm also has purchased a one-third ownership stake in Mitsubishi and holds a 10 percent ownership stake in the Korean Hyundai firm.

Indicative of the interdependence of these cross-corporate connections, consider that Mazda, in which Ford owns a controlling interest, recently shifted production of its small trucks to Isuzu, in which GM owns a substantial stock share; at the same time, the Korean Daewoo firm reportedly will supply GM and Suzuki with 200,000 vehicles per year for sale by the latter two firms in the North American market.[10] In addition, the

---

[10] Ken Belson, "Mazda Pares Its Truck Output and Shifts Production to Isuzu," *New York Times* (July 5, 2003): B3; James B. Treece, "New Models, Plant Talks Fill GM-Daewoo's Plate," *Automotive News* (June 30, 2003): 4.

Big Three have entered into a number of cross-supply agreements with their foreign rivals for various parts and components, such as engines. All told, global alliances involving the Big Three together represent approximately half of the world automotive market.

Reinforcing these ties among the leading auto companies are a number of cooperative research consortiums in the United States and abroad: The United States Council for Automotive Research (USCAR), for example, links the Big Three in a variety of research activities, including activities pertaining to materials, recycling, and computer applications and electronics. The Clinton administration's "Partnership for a New Generation of Vehicles" provided a government-financed umbrella of cooperation and support for the Big Three, as does its successor, the Bush administration's "Freedom Cooperative Automotive Research" program. At the same time, the European Council for Automotive Research and Development (EUCAR) links European producers in a host of cross-company endeavors.

Alliances and partnership pacts of this magnitude conjoin the U.S. oligopolists with each other, as well as with their major foreign rivals. They expand interfirm communication, coordination, and cooperation, and thus threaten the independence of decision making that is essential for effective competition. They raise the question of whether beyond some point, the participants perceive themselves primarily as partners rather than as competitors. As such, alliances and joint ventures suggest that the effective level of concentration in the industry is substantially higher than would be indicated by examining individual firms' market shares alone.

The Question of Economies of Scale

To what extent is the high level of concentration in auto manufacturing necessitated by economies of large-scale operation? The weight of the evidence suggests that, although substantial, economies of large size are not as extensive as might commonly be assumed, and they are becoming less so in some important ways.

First, scale economies have definite limits in auto production. The Big Three assemble their vehicles at numerous plant locations rather than concentrating their production in one or two gigantic plants. The average capacity of these plants is in the neighborhood of 230,000 vehicles per year, suggesting this figure as a good estimate of what the firms consider the optimum-sized production facility.

Second, the Big Three in recent years have significantly reduced their size by divesting large portions of their parts- and components-making operations. General Motors, long the most vertically integrated of the Big Three, consolidated a number of its parts-making operations to form the Delphi division, which it spun off in 1999 in a move that reduced its workforce by fully one third (200,000 employees), removed 208 manufacturing units from GM's administrative bureaucracy, and created one of the world's largest auto parts producers in the process.

"It is not an advantage to be vertically integrated," GM's chairman explained. "We are going to be a much faster company and focused on our core business of building cars and trucks."[11] Ford and Chrysler have taken similar steps to vertically dis-integrate themselves by spinning off their Visteon and Acustar parts-making operations.

---

[11]Rebecca Blumenstein and Fara Warner, "GM to Make Delphi Unit Independent," *Wall Street Journal* (August 4, 1998): A3.

In a related vein, auto companies are increasingly outsourcing the production of entire modules—parts preassembled into complete units, such as prebuilt interiors with seats, instruments, trim, and electronics already installed—to outside suppliers. Modular assembly is even leading some automakers to encourage outside suppliers to work on the auto firms' final assembly lines, installing their outsourced components.[12] Industry experts estimate that this vertical dis-integration, and the corresponding reduction in corporate size, may cut production costs by as much as 30 percent.[13]

Third, smaller, more flexible assembly plants are increasingly seen as the key to production efficiency in a more competitive industry, where an increasingly important role is played by shifting consumer fashions and preferences, and where the design, production, and changeover of shorter runs of more niche-focused vehicles is becoming more compelling.[14] It is especially significant in this respect that the average time required to change stamping dies for different models is two to five times longer for the Big Three than for Mitsubishi, Honda, Toyota, and Nissan in their North American transplant facilities,[15] again suggesting limits to the economies of ever-larger scale.

Finally, the Big Three's own experience strongly suggests that excessive organizational size entails substantial *dis*-economies of scale and that giantism is no guarantor of efficiency in production. For GM, the world's-largest automotive concern, the classic symptoms of diseconomies of excessive size have recently been described by the firm's chairman, Jack Smith. According to Mr. Smith's assessment, GM in the 1990s

> was a mess. We were the high-cost producer. We had unbelievable excess capacity. We had multiple vehicle and component divisions, all of them doing things differently. We had a huge central office. We had over 13,000 people with an elaborate maze of policy groups trying to coordinate the businesses, not to control them ... We were the tattered remnants of what [former president] Alfred Sloan had put together in the early 1920s.[16]

Outside analysts agree, observing that GM "possesses a legacy of inefficiency few corporations can rival."[17] The DaimlerChrysler megamerger of 1998 has shown that bigger is not always better: The cost savings and synergies that were supposed to flow from the merged firm have failed to materialize; instead, Chrysler has assumed the mantle from GM as the least productive American automaker (with two thirds of its stock market value wiped out since the merger, and Daimler's legendary reputation for quality now suffering). For Ford, too, it is striking that the firm's productivity, efficiency, and product quality have eroded in line with its ballooning corporate size following its acquisitions of Volvo, Rover, and Jaguar, as well as its assumption of control over Mazda.

The problem of excessive organizational size in automobiles is summed up by James Schroer, former executive vice president of sales at Chrysler.

---

[12]See James M. Rubenstein, *Making and Selling Cars: Innovation and Change in the U.S. Automotive Industry* (Baltimore: Johns Hopkins University Press, 2001), 114–118; Robert Sherefkin, "GM Handing Off Interiors," *Automotive News* (January 29, 2001): 1.

[13]Joann Muller, Kathleen Kerwin, and David Welch, "Autos: A New Industry," *Business Week* (July 15, 2002): 104; David Welch, "How Nissan Laps Detroit," *Business Week* (December 22, 2003): 58–60.

[14]"Incredible Shrinking Plants," *Economist* (February 23, 2002): 71–73.

[15]Harbour Report: 2003, 95; Alex Taylor, "The Americanization of Toyota," *Fortune* (December 8, 2003): 170.

[16]Quoted in "Just How Bad Was It, Jack?" *Automotive News* (May 6, 2002): 29.

[17]Alex Taylor, "Finally GM Is Looking Good," *Fortune* (April 1, 2002): 69.

If there is one thing that has done the most harm to the Big Three, it is the word *big* . . . you look around the industry and you see that the advantage is where companies are not big.

Little wonder, then, that some analysts conclude that success in automobile manufacturing requires avoiding megamergers, and that for the Big Three, smaller would be more efficient.[18] In other words, automobile production is not immune from the *U*-shaped long-run average cost curve displayed in microeconomics textbooks.

Barriers to Entry

Barriers to the entry of new competition, another important element of market structure, are immense in the automobile industry. First, the cost to build production and assembly plants is daunting: Honda, for example, has invested $2.3 billion in its Marysville, Ohio, plant. Toyota has invested $5.1 billion in building its Georgetown, Kentucky, facility and forecasts that it will invest $800 million constructing a new pickup truck assembly facility in San Antonio, Texas, when production commences there in 2006.

Second, a new entrant must not only assemble vehicles, it also must market them to consumers, another substantial obstacle to new competition. GM perennially ranks as the nation's first- or second-largest advertiser, spending upwards of $3.4 billion yearly; Ford and Chrysler also rank among the top six leading national advertisers, with total advertising expenditures of $2 to $2.4 billion each in recent years.[19]

Finally, in addition to producing and marketing its cars, a new entrant would have to organize a system of dealers to distribute and service its vehicles. This, too, is a daunting challenge, as GM, Ford, and Chrysler vehicles are retailed through some 16,000 dealerships nationally.

It is not surprising, therefore, that over the post–World War II period, few new firms have commenced domestic production, and those that have (the transplants) have been launched by large, established foreign firms.

III. INDUSTRY CONDUCT

Market behavior in the automobile industry validates what industrial organization theory predicts: Decades of high concentration nurtured tacit collusion, uniformity of conduct, and noncompetitive oligopolistic parallelism, and the advent of a more competitive, less-concentrated industry structure has significantly transformed corporate behavior in the field.

Pricing

As the largest seller, General Motors traditionally was the industry's price leader. GM typically initiated general rounds of annual price hikes in the late summer when the industry's new model lineups were being readied for the fall. Ford and Chrysler awaited GM's price disclosures, which they then matched, so that the Big Three's prices differed

---

[18]Schroer quoted in Micheline Maynard, *The End of Detroit* (New York: Doubleday, 2003), 235; Richard Feast, "Automotive Mergers Rarely Meet Expectations," *Automotive News* (December 1, 2003): 32; Diana T. Kurylko, "Wall Street Paints a Grim Picture of Big 3 Prospects," *Automotive News* (August 11, 2003): 1.
[19]*Advertising Age,* "100 Leading National Advertisers" (2002).

by only a few dollars across their range of models. The essence of oligopoly pricing in the field was conveyed by the *Wall Street Journal* in the early 1980s.

> Auto makers can maximize profits because in the oligopolistic domestic auto industry the three major producers tend to copy each other's price moves. One auto executive notes that if one company lowered prices, the others would follow immediately . . . As a result, price cuts wouldn't increase anybody's market share, and "everybody would be worse off," he says.

Sniffed one Big Three official, "We're not in the business of lowering prices; we're in the business of making money."[20] The advent of foreign competition and transplants, however, as well as the erosion of domestic concentration, have disrupted this noncompetitive pattern of pricing. In a sharp break from the past, prices now are continuously altered through the year. Prices also are more flexible—down as well as up—as a result of competition that compels the companies to constantly adjust incentives, rebates, lease terms, and interest rates on new car loans. Thus, in the wake of 9/11, with the economy slumping into recession, GM launched its "Keep America Rolling" program of new-car rebates and interest-free loans. Ford and Chrysler were compelled to follow, with the result that new-vehicle sales remained at near-record levels rather than plunging under the burden of rigid prices as they had in the past.[21] By 2003, with the economy still in recession, the Big Three were offering new-car incentives of more than $3,000 per vehicle, on average, which continued to sustain their sales at near-record rates.[22] By keeping demand and production up, downward price flexibility cushioned layoffs in the auto-industrial complex and prevented them from compounding the economywide recession as they had in the past.

Some automakers have complained bitterly about this advent of price competition. The chief executive officer of Chrysler, for example, has deplored competitive pricing, charging that "All of these policies are just trashing the whole value chain and turning the product into a commodity."[23] Others have characterized pricing in the U.S. market as "crazy." However, GM's chief executive officer seems to have declared an end to interdependent oligopoly pricing: "It's time to stop whining and just play the game," he recently said in articulating the firm's new pricing philosophy. "At GM, we're going to do what works for us. We fully expect our competitors to do what's best for them." This is the epitome of a genuinely competitive market mentality.[24]

---

[20]Amal Nag, "High New-Car Prices Keep Many Lookers Looking," *Wall Street Journal* (August 3, 1983): 1.
[21]Gregory L. White and Karen Lundegaard, "U.S. Auto Sales Accelerated 13%, Driven by Deals," *Wall Street Journal* (September 5, 2002): 1. The chief executive officer of GM, Rick Wagoner, has superbly conveyed the cyclical difference between noncompetitive administered pricing under tight oligopoly versus the pricing characteristic of more competitive conditions in the industry today: "Normally we took [the impact of] recessions in volume. Now, we did not take the volume down. We took prices down." Quoted in Joseph B. White, "GM Hints at Easing of Discounts," *Wall Street Journal* (September 10, 2003): D4. Thus, under competitive conditions, price reductions cushion declining output and employment during recessions, whereas recessionary drops in output and employment are exacerbated under more rigid, administered oligopoly prices.
[22]Peter Brown, "Incentive Wars," *Automotive News* (January 20, 2003): 1; Julie Cantwell, "Car Prices Fall, and an Industry Changes," *Automotive News* (November 25, 2002): 1.
[23]Mary Connelly, "DCX Embraces Rebates," *Automotive News* (April 7, 2003): 1.
[24]Rick Wagoner, "Auto Boom Is Ours to Lose," *Automotive News* (February 17, 2003): 14.

Product Rivalry

A similar revolution has transformed product rivalry in the field. Here, too, decades of tight-knit oligopoly fostered a pattern of mutually interdependent behavior, which, in turn, generated a bland homogeneity in the product offerings of the Big Three. Primary emphasis was on the superficial: two headlights versus four, recessed door handles versus nonrecessed, "fine Corinthian leathers." Beginning in the 1990s, however, the advent of serious competition began to unleash a flood of new vehicles, designs, and concepts. An industry habituated to a time scale more comfortable for geologists began to operate at a quicker pace that was closer to that of fashion clothing. Two specific episodes highlight the magnitude of these changes.

Oligopoly Restraint: The Case of Small Cars[25]

At the conclusion of World War II, the small, lightweight, inexpensive automobile was seen as a prime means for expanding the postwar market in a manner analogous to Henry Ford's Model T decades before. In May 1945, General Motors and Ford disclosed that they were considering the production of small cars; Chrysler announced a similar plan the following year. The Big Three did not seriously undertake to market such a vehicle until the 1970s though, at least in the American market (a small, lightweight car developed by GM was marketed in Australia in 1948 by a GM subsidiary; Ford's light car appeared the same year in France). Attempts were made to meet increases in imports during the 1950s and 1960s, but these efforts seemed halfhearted and uninspired. The full impact of the industry's dilatory response hit with a vengeance in the 1970s, when oil embargoes and skyrocketing gas prices unleashed a torrent of economical Japanese imports into the American market that nearly bankrupted the Big Three.

Lawrence White explains this lethargy in terms of classic oligopolistic behavior: General Motors, Ford, and Chrysler each seemed to recognize that vigorous entry into the manufacture of small cars by any one of them would trigger entry into that segment by the others. Believing that the small-car segment was not large enough to support all three firms profitably and, further, believing that the availability of small cars would undermine high prices and high profits on sales of their large cars, the Big Three refrained from vigorously exploiting the small-car option. Foreign competitors, however, were not immobilized by such considerations, because they had no established oligopoly position to protect. The oil crises of the 1970s thus provided them an entrée into the American market. They opportunistically broke through the logjam of tacit restraint and forced the domestic oligopoly to confront the challenge of building smaller, higher-quality, more fuel-efficient automobiles.

Oligopoly Restraint Dented: The Chrysler Minivan[26]

Chrysler's minivan, introduced in 1983, quickly became one of the most successful automobiles ever built. By the mid-1990s, minivans accounted for more than a quarter of Chrysler's sales and perhaps as much as two thirds of its profits.

---

[25]This account is drawn from Lawrence J. White, "The American Automobile Industry and the Small Car, 1945–1970," *Journal of Industrial Economics* 20 (1972): 179; Paul Blumberg, "Snarling Cars," *New Republic* (January 24, 1983): 12–14.

[26]This account is drawn from Alex Taylor, "Iacocca's Minivan," *Fortune* (May 30, 1994): 56–66.

Pioneering development work on the minivan concept had been done years before at General Motors and Ford. By the late-1970s, in fact, GM designers had constructed a prototype of what has been described as a dead ringer for Chrysler's minivan. Ford designers, too, had developed the concept of a small, radically different front-wheel-drive van. However, Ford's top management dismissed the concept, and GM refrained from commercializing the minivan partly for fear of cannibalizing its sales of station wagons.

A renegade band of ex-Ford executives who were familiar with the minivan concept (led by Lee Iacocca) moved to Chrysler, however, where they faced disaster: Chrysler had narrowly escaped bankruptcy by virtue of a government bailout in 1979 and 1980, and the company desperately needed a new product success. The minivan concept was seized upon because, according to one Chrysler designer, "We didn't have much to lose."

Their desperate gamble paid off. Chrysler survived and prospered, largely due to the minivan's success and the risk taken in introducing it. Instead of viewing the market as fixed and comprising a few traditional product categories, Chrysler had created an entirely new industry segment. Still, it took a near-fatal commercial crisis to overcome the inertia and risk aversion bred by decades of oligopoly dominance.

Product Competition Unleashed

The minivan marked a watershed in the onset of genuine product competition in the industry. The field ceased to be rigidly divided into a few fixed categories of cars and trucks. Structural competition has ignited an explosion of vehicle types and segments: budget and economy cars; lower mid-range, upscale, and luxury cars; small pickups and large; minivans and full-sized vans; small SUVs, sport wagon SUVs, and mid-range and premium SUVs; retros, cross-overs, and crucks (car-truck combinations); as well as a blizzard of Avalanches, Xterras, Vehicrosses, Axioms, Crossfires, and Insights. Consumers choose among hundreds of models across product segments unimaginable only a few years ago. In the process, product competition has transformed autos into a far more fashion-oriented field, in which a premium is put on creativity, flexibility, sensitivity to buyers' shifting tastes, smaller production runs, and entrepreneurial risk taking. In this competitive milieu, of course, bureaucratic size is a serious disadvantage, which may be an important reason why automakers are concentrating more on design and assembly, and vertically dis-integrating themselves and outsourcing the production of parts, components, and modules to others.

IV. INDUSTRY PERFORMANCE

For decades, industry defenders insisted that the automobile field's highly concentrated structure was necessitated by the economies of large-scale production, the expense of modern innovation, and the dictates of effective industrial planning. Testifying before a congressional committee in 1974, GM representatives asserted that the firm's "size has been determined by the product itself, the requirements of efficient manufacture, distribution, and service, as well as market demand . . ."[27] In light of the Big Three's performance

---

[27]U.S. Congress. Senate. Subcommittee on Antitrust and Monopoly. Hearings: The Industrial Reorganization Act, Part 4, Ground Transportation Industries, 93rd Cong., 2d sess., 1974, 2, 468.

over the past 3 decades, few today would have the temerity to make such extravagant claims. In fact, the advent of effective competition revealed just how seriously the Big Three's performance had suffered during their decades of unchallenged oligopolistic supremacy.

Production Efficiency

One indication of the degree to which production inefficiency afflicted the Big Three is provided in Table 5-6, which compares labor productivity for U.S. and Japanese automotive firms in the early 1980s. These statistics show that gigantic firm size is no guarantor of efficiency. They also reveal the extent to which the domestic oligopoly fell behind the state-of-the-art manufacturing practices being innovated by others: By the early 1980s, Nissan and Toyota were three to four times more productive than any of the Big Three.

Confronted with withering foreign competition, the Big Three have struggled over the past 2 decades to raise their level of efficiency and reduce their bloated cost structures. They have been compelled to redesign their production operations, close antiquated plants, reorganize management structures, modernize facilities and purchasing practices, and cut billions of dollars from their costs. They have made substantial gains: Although the Big Three, as a group, continue to be at a substantial productivity disadvantage compared to North American transplants operated by Honda, Nissan, and Toyota, the magnitude of their disadvantage has declined, on average, from about 45 percent in 1995 to approximately 30 percent by 2001 (measured by total labor hours per vehicle produced). In dollar terms, the Big Three's labor productivity shortfall relative to state-of-the-art benchmarks has been narrowed by nearly half over the period from 1997 through 2002, from $2.6 billion to $1.4 billion per firm, on average.[28] The costs of excessive size are long-lived though: As the Big Three shrink their size, their ratio of retired to active workers is steadily rising, so they now face billions of dollars of "legacy costs" attributable to the pension programs they negotiated with labor during their less competitive days.[29]

Dynamic Efficiency

Dynamic efficiency encompasses product innovation, an area in which the domestic industry's performance is distinguished by four features.

TABLE 5-6   Comparative Productivity: Early 1980s

Firm	Vehicles Produced per Worker
General Motors	4.5
Ford	4.2
Chrysler	4.8
Nissan	11.6
Toyota	16.4

NOTE: *Average of data for years 1980 and 1983, adjusted to reflect different degrees of vertical integration among producers.*
SOURCE: Michael A. Cusumano, *The Japanese Automobile Industry* (Cambridge: Harvard University Press, 1985), 197.

---

[28]*Harbour Report*, 1998 (p. 172), 1999 (p. 175), and 2002 (pp. 142, 148).
[29]Janice Revell, "GM's Slow Leak," *Fortune* (October 28, 2002): 105–110.

First, the rate, breadth, and depth of product innovation were great in the era before World War II, when the field was populated by numerous independents. Innovation competition was intense, and new people with new ideas could put their concepts (good and bad alike) into commercial practice.

Second, with the demise of a vibrant independent sector, and with the consolidation of the field into a tight triopoly, the pace of technological innovation slackened. Innovations like front-wheel drive, disc brakes, fuel injection, fuel-efficient subcompacts, and utilitarian minivans languished in the hands of the Big Three. "Since competition within the industry was mild," David Halberstam writes,

> there was no impulse to innovate; to the finance people, innovation not only was expensive but seemed unnecessary. . . . Why bother, after all? In America's rush to become a middle-class society, there was an almost insatiable demand for cars. It was impossible not to make money, and there was a conviction that no matter what the sales were this year, they would be even greater the next. So there was little stress on improving the cars. From 1949, when the automatic transmission was introduced, to the late seventies, the cars remained remarkably the same. What innovation there was came almost reluctantly.[30]

Third, while the domestic oligopoly slumbered, foreign producers took the lead in advancing the frontiers of automotive technology. According to veteran industry observer Brock Yates, foreign firms forged ahead

> with fuel injection, disc brakes, rack and pinion steering, radial tires, quartz headlights, ergonomically adjustable bucket seats, five-speed manual transmissions, high-efficiency overhead camshaft engines, independently sprung suspensions, advanced shock absorbers, and strict crash-worthiness standards.[31]

By 1989, the contrast was striking: Conveying his impressions of the 1989 Tokyo Motor Show, the publisher of *Automotive News* reported that

> Japanese producers display more show cars, concept cars, and new products than can be believed. . . . They continue to innovate, and their execution of new products is nearly flawless."[32]

Of engine technology, another industry analyst remarked that comparing the U.S. and Japanese was like "comparing the Stone Age and today. . . . "[33] Meanwhile, Roger Smith, former GM chairman, bewailed his firm's glacial pace of new vehicle development, noting that GM's 60-month, new-vehicle development cycle was "longer than it took for us to fight and win World War II."[34]

---

[30]David Halberstam, *The Reckoning* (New York: Morrow, 1986), 244–245.
[31]Brock Yates, *The Decline and Fall of the American Automobile Industry* (New York: Vintage Books, 1984), 149.
[32]Keith Crane, "Tokyo: An Interesting Place for a Show," *Automotive News* (October 30, 1989): 12.
[33]Jesse Snyder, "L.A. Show: Analyst Calls Japanese Leaner, Maybe Meaner," *Automotive News* (January 11, 1988): 6.
[34]Quoted in Albert Lee, *Call Me Roger* (New York: Contemporary Books, 1988), 96.

Fourth, the injection of competition from abroad has compelled the Big Three to become more innovative in every aspect of their products: from engines (multivalves, fuel injection) and brakes (computer controlled, antilock), to transmissions (five speed, six speed, continuously variable) and body styles (sport utility and retro vehicles). At the same time, the Big Three have greatly improved the quality of their offerings. Chrysler Chairman Lee Iacocca conceded the deleterious impact of oligopoly on product quality in one of his firm's advertising campaigns:

> All of us—Ford, GM, Chrysler—built a lot of lousy cars in the early 1980s. And we paid the price. We lost a lot of our market to the import competition. But that forced us to wake up and start building better cars.

The hard part, GM admits in a recent marketing campaign, "meant breaking out of our own bureaucratic gridlock. Learning some humbling lessons from our competitors."

Nonetheless, years of lethargy have created a chasm that the Big Three must constantly struggle to overcome. The quality of their vehicles has improved and may even have surpassed that of their European rivals, but it still remains behind the quality of Japanese makes.[35] They have compressed their new-vehicle development time, but so have Japanese producers. In addition, Japanese firms continue to lead in innovating breakthrough technologies like hybrid vehicles powered by a combination of self-charging electric motors and gasoline engines, as well as super-compact micro cars that compel them to further compress their new-product development times while equipping their factories to even more flexibly adapt to shifts in consumer demands.[36]

Social Efficiency

Social efficiency addresses how well the industry has served the broader public interest in automotive pollution, safety, and fuel consumption and the nation's dependence on foreign oil. In these important areas, the Big Three's performance has been marked by indifference and denial, followed by resistance and pleas of technological impossibility.

On tail-pipe emissions, for example, the industry initially denied the problem: "[W]aste vapors are dissipated in the atmosphere quickly and do not present an air pollution problem," Ford Motor Company told government officials in smog-choked Los Angeles in the 1950s. "The fine automotive powerplants which modern-day engineers design do not 'smoke.'"[37] Later, as automotive air pollution worsened and national concerns about the problem grew, the Big Three (in the guise of a research joint venture) conspired to eliminate competition among themselves in developing and commercializing emissions-control technology.[38] When government emission regulations were promulgated in the 1970s, the Big Three insisted that the regulations would

---

[35]J. D. Power and Associates, Long-Term Vehicle Quality 2003, news release, July 8, 2003.

[36]Todd Zaun, "In Japan, Tiny Cars Offer a Laboratory for Very Big Ideas," *Wall Street Journal* (August 5, 2002): 1. On hybrids, see Danny Hakim, "The Hybrid Car Moves Beyond Curiosity Stage," *New York Times* (January 28, 2003): 1; Richard Truett, "Where Are the Big 3 on Hybrids? Back of the Pack," *Automotive News* (October 22, 2003): 14.

[37]U.S. Congress. Senate. Subcommittee on Air and Water Pollution. Hearings: Air Pollution—1967, Part 1, 90th Cong., 1st sess., 1967, 158. Despite these public claims, the Big Three were sufficiently concerned about the problem to have begun privately researching it decades before. See "Smog Control Antitrust Case," *Congressional Record,* House ed. (May 18, 1971), 15, 626–627 92d Cong., 1st sess., vol. 117.

[38]"Smog Control Antitrust Case," *Congressional Record,* House ed. (May 18, 1971), 15, 627.

be impossible to meet, even though Japanese firms introduced innovative engines combining high performance with lower exhaust emissions (e.g., Honda's Compound Vortex Combustion Chamber, or CVCC, engine).

In the 1990s, as some states were implementing tighter emissions standards, the Big Three again attacked them as unattainable, even though foreign producers (led by Honda) were introducing newer engine designs that were able to meet the standards and still offer greater power and acceleration. In 1998, GM and Chrysler were outraged by Ford's declared goal of engineering its light trucks to be no more polluting than its cars; they were livid that Ford had betrayed what industry insiders considered a gentlemen's agreement to refrain from competing to reduce light-truck emissions.[39] Further, in 2002 to 2003, the Big Three were fighting zero emissions standards in California (but researching upholstery scents[40]) as foreign firms, again led by Honda, were introducing hybrids and hydrogen fuel-cell vehicles that were able to meet those stricter regulations.

On the safety front, patents awarded to the Big Three in the 1920s and 1930s for such features as padded dashboards and collapsible steering wheel columns were shelved until their incorporation was mandated by government regulation. The industry insisted that safety should be optional, supplied only in response to consumer demand. Yet it refused to make available the safety information and product options essential for informed and free consumer decision making. The industry spent millions extolling raw horsepower while hiding behind its slogan, "Safety don't sell."

Eventually, a decades-long battle between government and the industry produced results. The Big Three finally conceded the benefits of seat belts and, in the 1990s, after waging what the Supreme Court called the "regulatory equivalent of war" against air bags,[41] the oligopoly discovered that "Safety really does sell" and began engineering air bags into dashboards, seats, doors, and roofs.

Most recently, as the safety threats of ever-more-massive sport utility vehicles have begun to accumulate,[42] the Big Three once again have responded with protestations of ignorance and resistance. They were outraged when the Bush administration's chief of the National Highway Traffic Safety Administration (NHTSA), Dr. Jeffrey Runge, a veteran emergency room physician, warned of the higher rollover/fatality risk to occupants of SUVs (due to their higher center of gravity and greater proclivity to flip), and cautioned consumers not to succumb to the illusion that these vehicles are somehow safer than conventional cars.[43] (His warnings are corroborated by statistics showing that U.S. traffic fatalities rose to a 10-year high in 2002, driven higher by rollover crashes involving SUVs and pickup trucks.[44])

---

[39]Keith Bradsher, *High and Mighty* (New York: Public Affairs, 2002), 268–269.

[40]Danny Hakim, "New Luxury-Car Specifications: Styling, Performance, Aroma," *New York Times* (October 25, 2003): 1.

[41]*Motor Vehicle Manufacturers Association v. State Farm,* 463 U.S. 29, 46 (1983).

[42]Keith Bradsher, *High and Mighty* (New York: Public Affairs, 2002), 268–269. For an opposing point of view, see Douglas Coates and James VanderHoff, "The Truth about Light Trucks," *Regulation* (Spring 2001).

[43]Karen Lundegaard, "Auto Safety Czar Warns Drivers of SUV Dangers," *Wall Street Journal* (January 15, 2003): 1. For an interesting exploration of the driver psychology involved, see Malcolm Gladwell, "Big and Bad," *New Yorker* (January 12, 2004): 28–33.

[44]National Highway Traffic Safety Administration, 2002 Annual Assessment of Motor Vehicle Crashes, Washington, D.C. (July 2003).

In the area of fuel consumption, when asked in 1958 what steps his division was taking regarding fuel economy, the general manager of GM's Buick division quipped, "We're helping the gas companies, the same as our competitors."[45] The Big Three seemed to believe that gasoline would remain forever plentiful at 20 cents a gallon, so the fuel consumption of their fleets steadily worsened. Only months before the first OPEC oil embargo and gasoline crisis of 1973, when the Big Three's fleet averaged a paltry 13 miles per gallon, GM's chairman recommended faster licensing of nuclear electric power plants as a good way to respond to what he dismissively referred to as America's energy "problem."[46]

In 1979, one month before the overthrow of the shah of Iran and the nation's second energy crisis in 6 years, General Motors declared that automotive "fuel economy standards are not necessary and they are not good for America."[47] In the early 1990s, in the wake of the Persian Gulf War and America's military struggle to secure its foreign oil supplies, the Big Three unveiled what the Wall Street Journal called "some of the biggest and brawniest cars in years,"[48] while protesting that further gains in fuel economy were technologically impossible, even as Honda was unveiling lean-burning engines able to get 55 miles per gallon.

Through the remainder of the decade, the Big Three successfully lobbied to freeze mileage standards and gorged themselves on sales of gas-guzzling light trucks and sport utility vehicles (for which government mileage standards are considerably lower), while Honda and Toyota were commercializing fuel-efficient hybrid vehicles able to achieve 50 to 70 miles per gallon. In 2001 to 2003, in the face of political crises in Afghanistan, Iraq, Venezuela, and Nigeria—each of which triggered spikes in gasoline prices—the Big Three were launching their biggest, heaviest, least fuel-efficient SUVs ever, including GM's Hummer, which gets 12 miles to a gallon; Ford's Excursion, which gets fewer than 18 miles per gallon with a 44-gallon fuel tank; and GM's "Cadillac Sixteen" concept car, which offers a 16-cylinder engine that generates 1,000 horsepower. As a result, the fuel economy of the industry's new-vehicle fleet fell to a 22-year low, with most of the decline attributable to the growth of light trucks and SUVs.[49]

These developments prompted *Business Week* to ask, "Just what planet are American auto execs living on?" and to point out that

> Detroit lost dominance in the car market by sticking its head in the sand while imports offered better mileage and quality. The last thing it can afford is to let the same thing happen in the cash-cow SUV business."[50]

The nation's security, its foreign policy, and its military entanglements and commitments are clearly affected when, as Senator John McCain points out, modest improvements

---

[45]Quoted in John Keats, *Insolent Chariots* (New York: Lippincott, 1958), 14.

[46]U.S. Congress. Senate. Committee on Commerce. Hearing: Automotive Research and Development and Fuel Economy, 93rd Cong., 1st sess., 1973, 564.

[47]Ed Cray, *Chrome Colossus* (New York: McGraw-Hill, 1980), 524.

[48]Joseph B. White and Neal Templin, "Gas Price Jump Finds Car Makers Backsliding on Fuel Efficiency," *Wall Street Journal* (September 14, 1990): 1.

[49]Karl H. Hellenrich and Robert M. Heavenrich, Advanced Technology Division, U.S. Environmental Protection Agency, "Light-Duty Automotive Technology and Fuel Economy Trends: 1975 Through 2003," Washington, D.C. (April 2003), 3.

[50]David Welch and Kathleen Kerwin, "Detroit Is Wrecking Its SUV Edge," *Business Week* (March 3, 2003): 42.

in automotive fuel efficiency could substantially reduce America's dependence on foreign oil by saving as much petroleum as is imported from the Middle East.[51]

An important explanation for the Big Three's traditionally lackluster performance in these areas once again may stem from the oligopolistic interdependence and mutual restraint that governed the companies' conduct. As former GM president Alfred Sloan once secretly confided,

> I feel that General Motors should not adopt safety glass for its cars. I can only see competition being forced into the same position. Our gain would be purely a temporary one and the net results would be that both competition and ourselves would have reduced the return on our capital and the public would have obtained still more value per dollar expended.[52]

V. PUBLIC POLICY

Public policy toward the industry can be examined in four areas: antitrust; protection from foreign competition; government regulation of automotive pollution, safety, and fuel consumption; and government/industry partnership programs.

Antitrust Policy

Antitrust policy has never directly challenged the industry's concentrated structure, and the antitrust actions that have been taken have been tangential and peripheral. For example, in 1969, the government charged the Big Three with illegally conspiring to eliminate competition but only in the smog-control field. In the early 1970s, the government charged GM and Ford with collusive pricing but only in the fleet market for new cars sold to businesses and rental car agencies. In the 1990s, the antitrust agencies investigated anticompetitive practices in the industry but only as they affected supplies of used cars and dealer efforts to impede vehicle sales on the Internet. At the same time, the antitrust agencies have allowed a proliferation of joint ventures and alliances to link the domestic oligopoly with most of its major foreign rivals. In addition, in what might be considered "failing company" antitrust policy, the government engineered the Chrysler bailout in 1979, in part to prevent the industry from becoming even more concentrated.

Protection from Foreign Competition

As we have seen, mutual oligopolistic interdependence became solidified among the Big Three in the post–World War II era. This, together with the protection afforded by formidable entry barriers, insulated the Big Three from effective competition. Noncompetitive conduct, including vertical collusion between management and organized labor to generate a steady escalation of wages and prices, flourished in this structural milieu.

---

[51]Senator John McCain, press release, April 18, 2002.
[52]Quoted in U.S. Senate, Select Committee on Small Business. Hearings: Planning, Regulation, and Competition—Automobile Industry, 90th Cong., 2d sess., 1968, 967.

Foreign competition eventually began to disturb this bonhomie and induced the industry to seek government-imposed shelter from imports. Their efforts succeeded in 1981, when the avowedly free-trade Reagan administration forced "voluntary" quotas on Japanese producers. These "temporary" quotas, ostensibly intended to give the Big Three breathing space, were subsequently renewed throughout the decade.

Predictably, the quotas drove up the price of Japanese imports, which in turn enabled the Big Three to push through sizable price boosts of their own. Yet in an ironic twist, these numerical restrictions impelled Japanese firms to take steps to circumvent them, first by upgrading their offerings and moving into the larger, more profitable midsize and luxury segments of the market, and second by constructing transplant assembly facilities in the United States.

Later, in the early 1990s, the Big Three resumed the import restriction game, demanding that government reimpose quotas on Japanese cars and that the quotas include limits on the number of vehicles that Japanese firms would be allowed to assemble in their American production facilities. They also demanded that the government restrict imports of minivans, even though the Big Three accounted for 85 percent of U.S. minivan sales at the time and even though Chrysler was the country's largest importer of minivans (assembled in its Canadian plants). In a variation of the protectionist game, the Big Three also periodically lobby government to manipulate international currencies in order to raise foreign vehicle prices in the American market.

Regulation: Safety, Pollution, Fuel Economy

Have government efforts to regulate automotive safety, emissions, and fuel consumption been too costly compared with the benefits obtained? Is it true, as the industry has long maintained, that excessive

> regulation adds unnecessary costs for consumers, lowers profits, diverts manpower from research and development programs, and reduces productivity—all at a time when our resources are desperately needed to meet the stiff competition from abroad. [53]

Or is it the case, as Henry Ford II once conceded, that "we wouldn't have had the kinds of safety built into automobiles that we have had unless there had been a Federal law. We wouldn't have had the fuel economy unless there had been a Federal law, and there wouldn't have been the emission control unless there had been a Federal law"? [54]

Is it true, as the industry contends, that government automobile regulations deny freedom of choice for consumers? Or do the Big Three exploit free consumer choice when it suits their purposes but with little compunction about violating that principle when consumers might freely choose imported vehicles, or safer, less polluting, or more fuel-efficient automobiles? Is it true, as the industry claims, that government regulations prevent it from obeying consumer sovereignty by supplying the vehicles that buyers

---

[53]U.S. Congress. House. Committee on Government Operations. Hearings: The Administration's Proposals to Help the U.S. Auto Industry, 97th Cong., 1st sess., 1981, 129.

[54]U.S. Senate, Subcommittee for Consumers, Hearings: Costs of Government Regulations to the Consumer, 95th Cong., 2nd sess., 1978, p. 87.

desire? Or if the industry acted more responsibly, might it minimize the need for direct government regulation? Do individual government agencies, charged with regulating different aspects of automobile performance, subject the industry to contradictory requirements by pitting safety (larger, heavier vehicles) against fuel economy (smaller, lighter vehicles)? Or are the Big Three responsible for rendering such regulations contradictory by first lobbying for, and subsequently exploiting, loopholes exempting sport utility vehicles from the safety, fuel economy, and emissions standards covering conventional cars?

Some economists have argued that less coercive forms of regulation—for example, incentive-based measures involving fees imposed on the sale of unsafe, polluting, gasguzzling vehicles—would be more effective. Is it realistic though to assume that the government would impose such fees if doing so would jeopardize the financial viability of a General Motors, a Ford, or a Chrysler? Would the government seriously consider shutting down GM, for example, if the firm simply refused to pay the fees? Conversely, given their massive size and political clout, would a threat by any of the Big Three to shut down almost inevitably force the government to grant regulatory delays, exceptions, and exemptions?[55]

Government/Industry Partnerships

Finally, there is the issue of government/industry partnerships, such as the "Partnership for a New Generation of Vehicles" launched by the Clinton administration in 1993, and its successor, the "Freedom Cooperative Automotive Research" program unveiled by the Bush administration in 2002. These programs bring the Big Three automakers together, under government auspices and with government funding, to work with government agencies to achieve breakthroughs in technology. A major goal of the Clinton administration's partnership program was to develop by 2003

> a vehicle that could achieve up to three times the fuel efficiency of today's comparable vehicle . . . while at the same costing no more to own and drive than today's automobile and while meeting the customer's needs for quality, performance, and utility.[56]

The Bush administration's "FreedomCAR" program has the goal of promoting the development of hydrogen as a primary automotive fuel in order to reduce American dependence on foreign oil, with the long-term objective of producing "cars and trucks that are more efficient, cheaper to operate, pollution-free, and competitive in the showroom."[57]

---

[55]For an extensive analysis of how the Big Three exploit their economic size and the threat of shutdowns to shape public policy, see Stan Luger, *Corporate Power, American Democracy, and the Automobile Industry* (New York: Cambridge University Press, 2000). For recent examples of the ability of the Big Three, acting in concert with organized labor, to decisively influence regulatory policy, see Keith Bradsher, *High and Mighty* (New York: Public Affairs, 2002), 28, 68, 253, 394. For a succinct survey of economic issues concerning the regulation of automotive fuel economy, see Paul R. Portnoy, Ian W. H. Parry, Howard K. Gruenspecht, and Winston Harrington, "Policy Watch: The Economics of Fuel Economy Standards," *Journal of Economic Perspectives* 17 (Fall 2003): 203–217.

[56]Partnership for a New Generation of Vehicles, Program Plan, Washington, D.C., 1994.

[57]U.S. Department of Energy, "Energy Secretary Abraham Launches FreedomCAR," news release, January 9, 2002.

These programs raise a number of questions: First, are they boons or boondoggles? The Clinton program, for example, cost $1.6 billion, but the fuel efficiency of the Big Three's fleet worsened over the period from 1993 through 2002 when the program was in effect. It was Honda and Toyota, not the Big Three acting in concert with government, that introduced revolutionary hybrid-powered vehicles at affordable prices. Second, are these programs likely to achieve real breakthroughs, or do they instead provide political cover for the Big Three, who can point to them as a way of deflecting more effective regulation?[58] Third, are they likely to promote innovation, or do they stifle it instead by providing the Big Three a forum in which to collusively agree on what technological steps they will, and will not, undertake?[59]

Conclusion

Fifty years ago, at a senate hearing to confirm his nomination for secretary of defense, the president of General Motors, Charles E. Wilson, famously suggested that GM was so large and significant that what was good for the firm was good for the country. An analysis of the American automobile industry underscores the central role that market structure plays in supporting, or contradicting, his claim. It provides a laboratory for studying the dynamic interaction between a changing industry structure, on the one hand, and its influence on industry conduct and, ultimately, industry performance, on the other. It also is a reminder, as Sherlock Holmes observed, that sometimes nothing is so unnatural as the commonplace.

Suggested Readings

Automotive News, Market Data Book. Annual and weekly issues. Detroit, MI: Crane Publishing Co..

Bollier, David, and Joan Claybrook. 1986. *Freedom from Harm.* Washington, D.C.: Public Citizen.

Bradsher, Keith. 2002. *High and Mighty: SUV's—The World's Most Dangerous Vehicles and How They Got That Way.* New York: Public Affairs Press.

Crandall, Robert W. et al. 1986. *Regulating the Automobile.* Washington, D.C.: Brookings Institution.

Ford, Henry. 1926. *My Life and Work.* New York: Doubleday.

Halberstam, David. 1986. *The Reckoning.* New York: Morrow.

Harbour and Associates. Annual. *The Harbour Report on the North American Automobile Industry.* Troy, MI.

Iacocca, Lee. 1984. *Iacocca.* New York: Bantam.

Ingrassia, Paul, and Joseph B. White. 1994. *The Fall and Rise of the American Automobile Industry.* New York: Simon & Schuster.

Kwoka, John E. 2001. "Automobiles: The Old Economy Collides with the New." *Review of Industrial Organization* 19: 55.

Luger, Stan. 2000. *Corporate Power, American Democracy, and the Automobile.* New York: Cambridge University Press.

Madsen, Axel. 1999. *The Deal Maker: How William C. Durant Made General Motors.* New York: John Wiley & Sons.

Maynard, Micheline. 2003. *The End of Detroit: How the Big Three Lost Their Grip on the American Car Market.* New York: Doubleday.

Porter, Richard C. 1999. *Economics at the Wheel: The Costs of Cars and Drivers.* New York: Academic Press.

---

[58]See Harry Stoffer, "FreedomCAR: Real Solution or Tax Waste?" *Automotive News* (June 10, 2002): 1; Elizabeth Kolbert, "The Car of Tomorrow," *New Yorker* (August 8, 2003): 36–40.
[59]See Gregg Easterbrook, "Political Mileage," *New Republic* (October 9, 2000): 25–27.

Rubenstein, James M. 2001. *Making and Selling Cars: Innovation and Change in the U.S. Automotive Industry.* Baltimore: Johns Hopkins Press.

U.S. Congress. Senate. Subcommittee on Antitrust and Monopoly. 1974. Hearings: The Industrial Reorganization Act, Parts 4 and 4A, Ground Transportation Industries. 93rd Cong., 2d sess.

U.S. Congress. Senate. Committee on Commerce, Science, and Transportation. 2003. Hearing: Sport Utility Vehicle (SUV) Safety. 108th Cong., 1st sess. February 26.

U.S. Congress. Senate. Committee on Commerce, Science, and Transportation. 2002.

Hearing: National Security, Safety, Technology, and Employment Implications of Increased CAFE Standards. 107th Cong., 2d sess., January 24.

Ward's Automotive Yearbook. Annual. Detroit, MI: Ward's Communications.

White, Lawrence J. 1971. *The Automobile Industry Since 1945.* Cambridge: Harvard University Press.

Wright, J. Patrick. 1979. *On a Clear Day You Can See General Motors.* Grosse Pointe, MI: Wright Enterprises.

CHAPTER

Music 6 Recording

—Peter J. Alexander

T he Recording Industry Association of America (RIAA), the trade association for the music recording industry, has issued hundreds of subpoenas aimed at individual consumers whom they allege to be copyright violators. According to BusinessWeek Online:

> In early September [2003], the U.S. music industry is planning to break every known rule of public relations by suing hundreds of high school valedictorians, pilots, firefighters, entrepreneurs, and other seemingly upstanding citizens for stealing songs online. The legal confrontation will pit a small group of powerful, technophobic oligopolists against a hip, youthful army of digital sophisticates—who are the very heart of the companies' consumer base.[1]

Beyond the hyperbole, the music recording industry is a fascinating intersection of culture, technology, law, and economics. Without question, the ways in which music is produced, distributed, sold, and consumed have changed substantially since the inception of the industry, just as types of popular music have changed over that time. An important recurring theme is that technological change relating to production, reproduction, and distribution has periodically induced entry, which in turn has caused significant structural shocks within the industry. In the past 5 years, the technological transformation of the industry has been particularly sweeping as the cost of producing, reproducing, and distributing the products of the music recording industry has fallen to near zero.

Yet, despite the seemingly modest technological barriers to entry into the industry, five large, vertically integrated firms account for the vast majority of sales. In part, dominance by these firms likely results from the costs of informing consumers, via radio, about the existence and nature of the products in the industry. For several reasons, it appears that radio airplay is an important barrier to entry for new entrants. Given that small, new firms have historically been product innovators in the industry, the implication is that consumers might not receive the full benefits of these innovations. It is possible that another recent innovation in the technology of supply, high-speed Internet, eventually might erode this important barrier to entry.

This economically small (but culturally important) industry has been the center of controversy involving (1) alleged price fixing by the major firms in the industry and (2) massive alleged copyright infringement by consumers, in what amounts to a free-for-all over economic rents. The clash between the firms and their consumers has erupted into legal open warfare, with the Federal Trade Commission and the courts finding the

---

[1]*Business Week* Online, August 29, 2003, "Music Pirates, You're Sunk," www.businessweek.com. Accessed July 2, 2004.

major firms guilty of overcharging consumers by nearly half a billion dollars in a scheme to maintain artificially high prices, and the industry suing hundreds of consumers for copyright infringement (including a 12-year-old girl who paid $2,000 to settle with the RIAA).

I. HISTORY

The music recording industry is approximately 100 years old. For the first 50 years of its existence, the industry was largely dominated by a relatively small handful of firms that created and produced most of the industry's technology and consumer products. During this time, however, small independent firms often pioneered the new musical styles that became popular with consumers.

Intense, atomistic competition at the producer level in the industry emerged in the 1950s, in part because of a significant innovation in the technology of supply. During this period, concentration in the industry fell dramatically, and the number of small, new firms increased rapidly. Subsequent reconcentration of the industry, beginning in the 1960s, resulted from numerous mergers and acquisitions. Historical concentration levels in the industry from 1890 to 1985 (measured by the Herfindahl index, which is the sum of the square of each individual firm's market share) are charted in Figure 6-1.

In the industry's infancy (1890–1900), three firms—Victor, Columbia, and Edison—produced most audio-related products, including playback devices (i.e., wax cylinder and record players) and the audio products themselves (i.e., wax cylinders and records). Patents held by these three firms were a substantial barrier to entry. This initial phase of high industry concentration was followed by a period of technological innovation (1900–1910) and the expiration of key patents (1914), both of which coincided with the entry of new firms and a modest dispersion of market share.

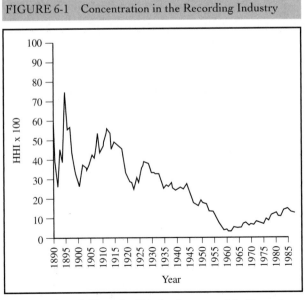

FIGURE 6-1   Concentration in the Recording Industry

SOURCE: *Peter J. Alexander, "Market Structure of the Domestic Music Recording Industry, 1890–1988," Historical Methods 35 (Summer 2002): 130–131.*

From a scale perspective, production (recording) and reproduction (manufacture) of the wax cylinders used for music playbacks were relatively costly, as each cylinder had to be individually produced. To make 10 copies of a recording, the performer either had to perform the song 10 times, or 10 recorders had to be recording simultaneously (or some combination of the two). After recording the performance, the recorded cylinders were replaced with new cylinders, and the song was performed again. If a mistake was made during the performance, all 10 of the recording devices were stopped, the cylinders were discarded and replaced, and the process began anew. Copyrights and scale economies limited the number of competitors and the quantity of new recordings produced. In 1892, for example, only a total of approximately 320 minutes of original musical output was produced. By 1894, that figure reached 1,000 minutes, or approximately 500 two-minute recordings.

Less costly methods for mass-producing cylinders emerged by 1901. One new manufacturing method employed a pantographic technique in which a master recording was used to make copies by replaying the master as a cutting device for reproducing the same sound vibrations on new cylinders. Each original master could be copied approximately 25 times before it wore out. A session using 10 machines to record a single song could ultimately yield 250 cylinders, which represented a 2,500 percent increase over the original technique. Another more efficient technique for mass-producing cylinders utilized a reverse metal master stamper: Several thousand copies could be made from the original before the stamper wore down and had to be discarded. These techniques greatly reduced the cost of reproducing recorded products.

In the period from 1900 through 1920, the number of firms producing record players and records increased. In fact, in the 5-year period between 1914 and 1919, the number of establishments manufacturing phonographs and records grew at an average annual rate of 44 percent (Table 6-1). Unfortunately, these data are aggregated and include the manufacture of records as well as playback devices, and thus obscure the measurement of competition in the production of records at the producer level only. Consequently, these data represent only a rough approximation of the extent of new competition in the music recording industry at the producer level.

TABLE 6-1	Number of Establishments Producing Records and Phonographs, 1909–1929

Year	Number of Establishments
1909	18
1914	18
1919	166
1921	154
1923	111
1925	68
1927	60
1929	59

SOURCE: Peter J. Alexander, "New Technology and Market Structure: Evidence from the Music Recording Industry," *Journal of Cultural Economics* 18: 116 (1994).

This robust, if small-scale, competition at the producer level sparked a great diversity in the industry's offerings, including recordings by black artists. Fink (1989) noted that

> the expansion of recorded repertoire during the 1920s was significant. The first "race" records began to appear. The commercial success [of some of these early recordings] was followed by the release of numerous other black recordings (p. 7).

Smaller new companies often pioneered these product innovations. Shaw (1987) observed that the first popular black female singer to be recorded was signed by Black Swan Records—a small, independent company—in 1920.[2] Indeed, Toll (1982) pointed out that "the innovators did things that were not generally accepted, and sometimes consciously challenged popular trends and tastes" (p. 106).

From 1919 to 1925, the number of firms producing record players or records declined at an average annual rate of 14.8 percent.[3] A handful of the independents grew in size and importance, but in general the number of independent record companies decreased, in part as a result of mergers: As Chapple and Garofulo (1977) noted, by 1929, "most of the smaller companies went out of business or were bought by the larger ones" (p. 92).

From 1930 to 1945, the music recording industry was essentially dormant when measured by industry revenues. This dormancy was a residual of the depression of the 1930s and the hostilities of World War II, because shellac, the prime ingredient for record manufacture at that time, was extremely scarce during the war years.[4] This shortage increased the cost of manufacturing records and their retail price. With the end of World War II, the shortage of shellac abated.

Perhaps more important for the music recording industry, however, was another innovation in the technology of supply: magnetic tape recorders. The pretape recording technology used for recording music was limiting in two ways: First, it was expensive to purchase, and second, it was "unforgiving" in production. By *unforgiving,* we mean that if a mistake was made in the production process, the entire process was stopped, the master disk was discarded and replaced by a new master, and the process had to begin again. According to Gelatt (1954), tape technology radically changed this situation.

> The economic attribute of tape recording transcended all others in its effect on phonographic history. Compared to the old method, tape was enticingly cheap. For an investment of a few thousand dollars one could buy a first-class tape recorder. Between 1949 and 1954, the number of companies in America publishing LP recordings increased from eleven to almost two hundred (pp. 299–300).

In addition to reducing capital costs, tape machines also induced indirect cost reductions by providing an easy way to edit musical performances and thus reduce the costs of recording music. Tape technology made it possible to correct mistakes by rerecording a flawed musical passage properly and then cutting the tape and replacing the

---

[2]OKeh Records, a subsidiary of Columbia, followed Black Swan's release with *Crazy Blues*, a record that "sold so spectacularly that every record company quickly set about finding a female blues singer they could sign" (Shaw, p. 69).

[3]In part, this may be due to the deepening of the new radio broadcast industry. Despite the obvious complementarities that exist between radio and music today, it is possible that the novelty of radio, its lower price, and its free content displaced sales in the music industry.

[4]The industry transitioned to vinyl shortly thereafter.

flawed passage with the correction. As Sanjek (1983) noted, "Magnetic ribbons were easy to edit, and corrections of flawed performances or misspoken lyrics, impossible on the earlier glass-based master recordings, were easy to make and effectively reduced production costs" (p. 38). Consequently,

> as tape equipment became more affordable, new recording studios sprang up around the nation. Many of the independents acquired tape machines themselves and learned recording techniques. As a result of these developments, the free-wheeling independents were now providing competition that could not be disregarded by Columbia, Decca, RCA Victor, and the new Capitol Label, which prior to 1948 accounted for three-fourths of all record sales (p. 39).

By 1956, small, new, independent firms accounted for approximately 52 percent of the recording industry's total market sales; by 1962, these firms accounted for 75 percent of the industry's sales. However, in the period after 1962 and continuing to the present, major firms reacquired market share. Horizontal integration explains much of the current structure of the recording industry, as the mid-1960s marked the beginning of a long wave of mergers and a gradual reconsolidation of the field.

The development and refinement of digital production and reproduction in the 1980s embodies the most recent (and quite likely most provocative) technological change in the industry's history. Prior to the 1980s, the production and playback technologies of the music recording industry were analog based, and music was produced and distributed using vinyl disks and magnetically encoded tape.[5] Compact disks, introduced to consumers in the 1980s, were the first important element in the music industry's shift to digital technology. The transition from analog to digital production and reproduction has had a potentially significant effect on supply-side costs within the industry: With digital products, the incremental cost of producing, reproducing, and distributing perfect copies is functionally zero. Thus, unlike the case where the tape player made production cheaper but did not alter the costs of distribution, digital technology has significantly reduced costs throughout the entire process—production, reproduction, and distribution. It is significant to note, however, that to date, these innovations in supply technology have not triggered an expansion of new competition like that which corresponded to the introduction of magnetic tape recording in the 1950s.

II. MARKET STRUCTURE

Concentration

Five large, international, and vertically integrated firms—Vivendi Universal, Sony Corp., Time Warner, EMI Group, and Bertelsmann AG—collectively account for approximately 85 percent of domestic music industry sales. Market shares for these firms for recent years are shown in Table 6-2.

---

[5]The primary difference between analog and digital signals is that analog is a continuous form of encoding information, and digital is a discrete form. Thus, for analog technologies, information is encoded in a continuous stream, but in digital technologies, sound is encoded in discrete bits.

TABLE 6-2 Domestic Market Share of the Five Largest Recording Firms (in percent)

Year	Universal	Time Warner	Bertelsmann	Sony	EMI	Top Five Share
2003	27.5	17.3	13.8	13.9	10.1	82.6
2002	28.9	15.9	14.8	15.7	8.4	83.7
2001	26.4	15.9	14.7	15.6	10.7	83.3
2000	28.0	15.4	19.4	13.5	8.7	85.0
1999	26.4	15.8	16.1	16.3	9.5	84.1

SOURCE: Nielsen SoundScan, various issues.

With the exception of EMI (which specializes in music), each of these firms is a large, international conglomerate with a far-reaching range of media and other holdings. Total worldwide revenues for these firms in 2002 are shown in Table 6-3.

The Five Majors

The five major firms in the industry share a number of common features. For example, although the firms in the industry have been bought and sold many times, each (excepting Time Warner, which was founded in 1958) can trace a long lineage in the music recording industry dating back to the turn of the twentieth century. In addition, each firm (except EMI) is a part of a much larger (media) conglomerate, with significant interests in motion pictures, television, cable, and book publishing, among other things. Finally, each is vertically integrated into music publishing, production, manufacture, and distribution. Notably, with the exception of some mail-order interests and nascent online stores, the five majors do not have a significant retail presence.

Vivendi Universal Music (which ultimately emerged from the merger of two major firms, Polygram and MCA, in 1998) is a subsidiary of a large French conglomerate, Vivendi Universal, and is currently the largest music company in terms of market share and recorded music revenues. Its operations encompass the production and distribution of recorded music (Polygram Distribution), the licensing of music copyrights, and music publishing. In fact, with more than 1 million titles, Universal Music Group owns the largest catalog of recorded music in the world. In 2002, one out of every four compact disks sold worldwide was a Universal Music Group product. Some of Vivendi's other media holdings include Universal Studios (motion pictures), USA Networks (television), and Houghton Mifflin (book publishing).

TABLE 6-3 Worldwide Conglomerate Revenues of the Major Firms, 2002

Firm	Total Worldwide Revenue (in billions)
Vivendi Universal	$60
Sony	57
Time Warner	41
Bertelsmann	18
EMI	0.36

SOURCE: Various company reports.

Sony Corporation, a subsidiary of the Japanese conglomerate Sony, produces, manufactures (Sony Disk), and distributes (Sony Distribution) recorded music, in addition to holding a substantial interest in music publishing (Sony/ATV Music Publishing). Sony became a major presence in the music recording industry when it purchased CBS Records in 1988. Sony also produces a wide range of well-known consumer electronic products, including the Sony Play Station, compact disk players, and televisions. Some of Sony's other media holdings include the motion picture houses Columbia Pictures and Tri-Star Pictures.

Bertelsmann, a German conglomerate, is the second-largest global media conglomerate measured in terms of total revenue. Like Vivendi and Sony, the Bertelsmann music group produces, manufactures, distributes, and publishes recorded music. Bertelsmann's purchase of RCA in 1985 signaled Bertelsmann's interest in becoming a major presence in the music industry. Bertelsmann's other media holdings encompass extensive book and magazine publishing interests, including Bantam, Doubleday, Random House, and Knopf. Bertelsmann also controls RTL, a major European television/radio broadcaster and content producer.

Time Warner, a U.S.-based conglomerate, produces, manufactures (WEA), and distributes (WEA) recorded music, in addition to holding a substantial music publishing interest (Warner/Chappell Music). Warner/Chappell controls the publishing rights to more than 1 million music titles. Time Warner's other significant media holdings include Warner Brothers (motion pictures), WB Network (television), HBO (television), Time Warner Cable (television), Time-Life (magazines), and Warner Books.

EMI, a British corporation, is the least diversified of the five major firms. Like the other four, EMI produces, manufactures, distributes, and publishes recorded music. The EMI group comprises more than 100 record labels and is the second-largest global publisher of music.

Recently, four of these giants have been in negotiations to merge their recording operations (Sony with Bertelsmann, and EMI to acquire Time Warner's recording business). In early 2004, Time Warner sold its Warner Music subsidiary to a new set of owners led by the Canadian Bronfman interests. Should combinations between any of these firms come to pass, the field would become even more concentrated.

The Competitive Fringe

In addition to the five major firms, many small, independent labels produce music. During the 1950s and early 1960s, small, innovative companies introduced new products to consumers that became popular, and these firms grew into formidable competitors. Among these were Mercury, Dot, Cadence, Atlantic, Roulette, Imperial, Chancellor, Cameo, and Vee-Jay. Most of these firms eventually were purchased by their more established, somewhat diminished major competitors.

Currently, the collective market share of the fringe group is approximately 15 percent, and this includes a vast array of smaller labels and independent artists who produce a handful of products each year. Despite the recent downturn in the industry generally, independent labels report that their profitability is increasing. For example, New West Records—a small label with artists such as Delbert McClinton, the Flatlanders, and John Hiatt—has doubled its business over the past 3 years. Similarly, Rounder Records, a long-established independent label, reports that 2002 was its most profitable year ever.

Distribution

The function of record distributors is to make the products of the music recording industry available to retailers, who then sell the products to final consumers. Physical distribution has significant scale economies, is characterized by high entry barriers, and is dominated by the five vertically integrated music giants.

In the late 1950s and early 1960s, independent distributors were a significant alternative distribution channel for independent recording firms, as the rise in popularity of the products of new record companies induced new entry on the distributor side, as well. However, merger activity in the 1960s and 1970s (and the purchase of many of the formerly successful independent record companies) reduced the volume of many independent distributors, as the merged firms either internalized this function or used their own existing distribution networks. Because national distribution has significant scale features, independent firms did not have enough volume to compete.

Today, the five major producers are also the five major distributors. Thus, a competing company that wishes to create and sell new products must either distribute its product independently (which we have noted has significant scale features) or sign a "pressing and distribution" deal with one of the major labels, whereby the independent firm contracts with a major label for manufacture and distribution.[6]

Digital distribution will likely displace physical distribution in the industry. As Alexander (1994) observed a decade ago:

> Because the products of the music recording industry are produced using digital sequences, a digital distribution network might evolve as computer networks and digital information highways develop and deepen. The costs of distribution should decline dramatically, as physical distribution at a national or international level has significant scale features.

However, industry-organized digital distribution has (at least on the part of the Big Five firms) lagged until recently, although independent digital distribution has become routine. The potential importance of the transition to digital technology from a structural perspective is compelling.

New, industry-sanctioned, online services such as Apple Computer's "iTunes," which introduced its digital downloading service in the spring of 2003, have distributed more than 10 million individual songs to consumers at a price of 99 cents each. In part, current industry efforts to put in place a profitable digital distribution network are largely driven by large-scale, unsanctioned file sharing (that the industry claims is costing it billions of dollars in profits), as well as consumer demand for the convenience of downloading these products.

III. CONDUCT

Pricing

Pricing in the music recording industry varies with the diversity of media formats such as vinyl records, cassette tapes, digital audiotapes, compact disks, and singles. Prices are generally higher on newly issued music products than on the nearly costless reissue of older music material on new formats (e.g., a product that was initially sold on a vinyl

---

[6]Alternatively, the firm might distribute its products digitally via the Internet.

TABLE 6-4 Average (Nominal) Prices of Recorded Music by Format

Year	Vinyl Singles	LPs	CDs	Cassettes	Cassette Singles	CD Singles	Music Videos	DVDs
1997	$4.75	$12.33	$13.17	$8.82	$3.16	$4.09	$17.41	-
1998	4.76	10.00	13.48	8.96	3.58	3.81	18.68	-
1999	5.26	10.97	13.65	8.59	3.38	3.98	19.03	-
2000	5.48	12.59	14.02	8.24	3.54	4.17	15.49	$22.00
2001	5.71	11.91	14.64	8.08	-	4.59	18.60	20.00
2002	5.66	12.06	14.99	6.77	-	4.36	19.62	21.25

SOURCE: Veronis Suhler Stevenson Bank, "Communications Industry Forecast and Report," various years.

disk and then reissued on a compact disk). Table 6-4, utilizing data generated by the RIAA, gives some recent nominal price averages by various media formats.

It is useful to narrow the focus on pricing to compact disks, because they currently comprise 94 percent of the industry's unit sales, making them by far the most important component of the various product formats. In Table 6-5, the pricing analysis from Table 6-4 is extended by converting prices for compact disks from nominal to real values. Using these data, along with unit sales, the price elasticity of demand can be derived. The average price elasticity of demand over the period from 1993 to 2002 is 6.8, which indicates that the demand for compact disks is highly elastic.

It is important to note that a wide range of prices exists, depending on the product and the retailer. Although the major record companies suggest list prices for their products, discounting is widespread, which makes discussion of list prices a tenuous endeavor at best.[7] In particular, electronics firms and nonspecialized chain stores, including Wal-Mart, have been among the biggest price discounters. In the mid-1990s, aggressive

TABLE 6-5 Real Compact Disk Prices and Quantity

Year	Average Price* (real)	Quantity** (units shipped)
1993	$9.09	495.4
1994	8.62	662.1
1995	8.51	722.9
1996	8.13	778.9
1997	8.20	753.1
1998	8.27	847.0
1999	8.19	938.9
2000	8.14	942.5
2001	8.27	881.9
2002	8.33	803.3

NOTE: *1982–1984 = 100; **In millions

SOURCE: Recording Industry Association of America, *Year-end Statistics*, various years.

---

[7]Typically, however, new compact disk releases are priced much higher than reissued older material.

discounting by some of these nonspecialized retailers put significant financial pressure on some of the largest specialty music stores, and it appears that the major recording firms responded by trying to corral this price competition in order to raise prices and preserve distribution profit margins.

According to the Federal Trade Commission, the majors threatened to withdraw cooperative advertising expenditures from retailers if the retailer advertised a discounted price, even if the retailer used its own advertising funds for such advertisements. According to the FTC, this action stabilized retail prices at artificially high levels and eliminated price competition in the retail marketplace for the period from 1995 through 2000. Given that demand in the industry appears to be quite elastic, some of the decline in sales recently experienced by the industry might well be due to prices that were allegedly fixed at artificially high levels.

In the summer of 2003, Universal Music Group, the largest music company measured by market share, stunned the industry by announcing dramatic cuts in its wholesale prices from $12.02 to $9.09, a 24 percent reduction. According to industry reports, UMG hopes these reductions in wholesale prices will be passed along by retailers to consumers, and, assuming the standard inverse relationship between price and quantity demanded holds, that consumers will expand demand and revenues for its products.[8]

Nonprice Rivalry

A prerecorded audio product is a peculiar thing. Unlike most produced goods, its characteristics are not readily apparent to the consumer; that is, buyers in record stores cannot discern and evaluate a prerecorded audio product's attributes by touch, visual inspection, smell, or any of the other means commonly used to inspect products. Instead, a prerecorded audio product must be heard in order to be evaluated, and audio presentation is a prerequisite for the vast majority of purchases. Consequently, radio airplay tends to be one of the most important means for informing consumers of the existence and nature of new products.

Some influence over the content of radio airplay may result from "payola" expenditures.[9] Typically, payola involves firms or their representatives making payments to radio disc jockeys or station managers in return for airplay of the firm's products. According to Coase (1979), payola has been used routinely in the industry, frequently by new entrants attempting to gain market share. Coase noted that in the 1950s,

> there can be no doubt that the new companies ... relied on payola to obtain "exposure" for their records. These companies lacked the name-stars and the strong marketing organization of the major companies, and payola enabled them to expand their sales by making similar efforts in other markets. (pp. 315–316)

However, as a result of subsequent criminal prosecutions, congressional investigations, and increased penalties for engaging in paying payola, the nature and implications of payola appear to have changed by the late 1970s. By that time, Dannen (1990)

---

[8]The stock price of EMI fell more than 10 percent the day Universal announced the price cut, apparently on fears that the move by Universal signaled a possible price war in the industry. EMI's stock price is probably the best benchmark for estimating the effects of price cuts, because of the Big Five companies, it is by far the least diversified and most reliant on sales of recorded music.

[9]Payola (supposedly a contraction of the words *payoff* and *Victrola*) refers to the practice of making illegal payments to radio stations in return for radio airplay. It is not illegal to pay for airplay, per se. It is, however, illegal to take payments for airplay and not reveal that the airtime had been paid for or sponsored.

suggested that the large firms began using payola to obtain radio airplay *and* to exclude small firms from obtaining radio airplay.

> The record companies understood on some level that if radio airplay were not free, it would mean a major competitive advantage. The big companies had budgets sufficient to outbid the small labels for airplay. After 1978, records put out by small labels began to vanish from the Top 40 airwaves. (pp. 14, 15)

The data in Table 6-6 list the number of firms in the industry with only a single hit record over the period from 1976 through 1985. These data do not appear to contradict Dannen's assertion.

According to Dannen, the large firms could outbid the small firms for airplay. Note that a radio station has a finite amount of airtime in any broadcast day, a fraction of which is used for revenue-generating advertising, and the remainder is used to attract customers for advertisers. Assuming that the station operator is indifferent between various musical inputs, the firm willing to pay the most for airtime, *ceteris paribus*, will purchase the airtime and presumably gain a competitive advantage with consumers.[10]

Implicit in Dannen's argument is the idea that in the 1970s, the major firms in the music recording industry recognized that they might use payola as a barrier and an instrument for raising rivals' costs, the rivals being small fringe firms or new entrants. Indeed, Dannen hinted at something beyond simply raising rivals' costs. First, he noted that contact between the major firms and radio stations during the late 1970s had become indirect. The major labels could not allow their staff people to make payments to radio stations, given the increased penalties prescribed by the Racketeer Influenced

TABLE 6-6	Number of Firms with One Hit Record

Year	**Number of One-Hit Firms**
1976	20
1977	21
1978	14
1979	15
1980	7
1981	9
1982	6
1983	7
1984	4
1985	4

---

[10]Why couldn't fringe firms or new entrants simply pay to have their products played over the air, unless their products were inferior? One might argue that smaller firms may have a higher cost of capital. This higher cost of capital might result from the following: (a) a risk premium is attached to their cost of borrowing; (b) credit markets may decline to lend funds to lower-quality borrowers at any rate of interest; (c) lenders may refuse to lend to borrowers who have different levels of risk than the lenders; or (d) banks base their lending rates on the salvage value of the borrower's assets. Assuming that promotion costs for firms are sunk and the salvage values are zero, the interest rate on borrowed funds will tend toward infinity. Thus, one might argue that the incremental cost of capital is higher for smaller firms than for larger firms. To the extent that promotion costs increase, the smaller firm's costs increase at a faster rate.

and Corrupt Organizations (RICO) statute. Instead, a small group of independent promoters, who referred to themselves as the "Network," were paid to represent the major firms' interests directly to radio station operators.

> The term "Network" referred to the tendency of the promoters to work as a loosely knit team. Each member had a "territory," a group of stations over which he claimed influence. If a record company wanted national airplay for a new single, it could choose to hire one of the Network men, who would in turn subcontract the job to other members of the alliance. (pp. 11, 14)

Sidak and Kronemyer (1987) suggested that the rise of independent promoters allowed the major labels to exercise "precautionary ignorance":

> During the mid-1980s, a record company would retain independent promoters under contracts with incomplete and unspecified terms that reflected the record company's need to minimize its knowledge of the promoters' activities. The record company also might avoid inquiring whether the independent promoter uses payola in conducting his business, and particularly whether he intends to use payola to promote the record for which the record company has retained him (p. 538).

In effect, contracting out promotion became the most efficient option given the change in the legal environment. Given a higher penalty and assuming that the probability of being detected in the act of making illegal payments wasn't reduced, the expected cost of engaging in payola increased. According to Dannen, this new market for outside promotional services in effect induced a secondary market for exclusionary rights: "The Network's power came not from its ability to make a hit record but to *prevent* one. This was deliberate, since the Network was the means to deprive small labels of access to the Top 40 airwaves and increase the market share of the major labels" (p. 16, italics in original). Dannen suggested that third-party promotional services purchased radio airplay and excluded new entrants and fringe firms from the airwaves.[11]

In sum, the amount of available airtime at any given radio station is extremely limited and expensive. Industry reports suggest that the number of new "adds" (i.e., songs added to the station's playlist) at major radio stations on a weekly basis is typically in the lower single digits. So, it is possible that relative scarcity of radio airtime, in conjunction with a lower per-unit cost of payola for the major firms, tends to foreclose radio access for smaller firms.[12] According to the *Wall Street Journal* (June 10, 2002),

> To compete for a limited number of open slots on pop radio, labels say they typically pay independent promoters from $200,000 to $300,000 per song, and

---

[11]As Krattenmaker and Salop suggested, "Vertical restraints and contracts can be fertile ground for raising competitors' costs. By contracting with one or more suppliers to exclude rivals, either by dealing with them on discriminatory terms or refusing to deal with them altogether, a firm sometimes can increase its rivals' costs." Thomas G. Krattenmaker and Stephen C. Salop, "Competition and Cooperation in the Market for Exclusionary Rights," *American Economic Review* 76: 109. However, one might argue, as Krattenmaker and Salop noted, that rivals can counteract the exclusionary strategies of the large firms. "It might be argued that such exclusionary conduct would always fail for two reasons: the excluded rivals would have available effective counterstrategies to prevent their own exclusion; and input suppliers would have no incentives to reduce their sales by excluding some customers."

[12]Still, this avoids the question of why small firms couldn't simply pay more than the larger firms and obtain Network services. A simple explanation for this may be that, at the margin, it simply isn't profitable for small firms to pay more than the price being paid by the large firms (i.e., the large firms are paying the monopoly price).

occasionally more than $1 million. These costs have escalated as the radio industry has consolidated, music companies say (p. B1).

Finally, several new developments in the music and radio industry have occurred that might ameliorate or exacerbate this situation. First, the Federal Communications Commission (FCC), the agency that regulates broadcasting, may issue a number of new, low-power radio licenses. This increase in the supply of radio airtime might provide opportunities for small firms and new entrants in the music industry, as well as others. However, these stations will be very low power and hence highly local; thus, the reach of any such station will be modest.

Second, "webcasting," or Internet radio, appears to have become a more significant means of broadcasting music, which opens the possibility of a greater supply of "airplay," as well. Some legal and political wrangling has occurred recently about the price per song that webcasters must pay for using the products of the music recording industry in their webcasts, but it appears that a potentially satisfactory solution might be achieved.[13]

Third, and most important, the structure of the radio industry itself has undergone a significant transformation, with concentration in the industry rapidly increasing in recent years. Moreover, the largest single radio station owner in the country, Clear Channel Communications, which owns 1,233 stations nationwide and claims more than 26 percent of industry revenue, has entered the music promotion field. The increase in radio concentration and Clear Channel's move into promotion will be interesting developments to follow, as both will likely have significant implications for the music recording industry.

IV. PERFORMANCE

The concentrated, vertically integrated structure of recording has important consequences for industry profits, as well as for the quantity and types of products offered to consumers.

Industry Profitability

It is difficult to determine profitability in the industry, although EMI, the least conglomerated of the five majors, reports that operating profits recently were up by 33 percent, despite sales falling by 11 percent. EMI reports that gains in profitability were derived from increased efficiencies. According to the RIAA, revenues in the industry have been falling in recent years. However, to calculate profits, we also would need to know industry costs, and these data are not available. In fact, it is plausible that industry revenues could decrease overall while industry profits increase. In addition, data concerning the number of new releases in the industry are not available. These data are important because aggregate annual revenues will fall, all other things being equal, if the number of new releases falls. Thus, we cannot determine whether the reduction in industry revenue is partly or wholly induced by a reduction in the number of new releases by the industry.

Product Diversity

Among the important (perhaps the most important) performance values of a culture-based industry of this type is product diversity. Although production costs clearly place

---

[13]The Webcasters Alliance, a group with about 400 online music broadcasters, has sued the recording industry in federal court, alleging that the major labels have unlawfully inflated webcasting royalty rates in an attempt to keep independent operators out of the market.

a constraint on the supply side of the market, again all other things being equal, greater product diversity is unambiguously welfare enhancing for consumers, because consumers can obtain products that are closer to their ideal preferences. An important related question is which type of market structure best promotes product diversity?

The empirical evidence relating to industry structure and product diversity is mixed. For example, methods that count the number of hit songs and then relate them to market structure have been employed. These studies unambiguously suggest a strong, negative, linear link between structure and diversity: The more atomistic the structure is, the greater the diversity is, and the more concentrated the structure is, the less diversity there is.[14]

On the other hand, a study using the actual musical characteristics of hit songs, rather than simply the number of songs, suggests that a moderately concentrated industry may better promote diversity than either an atomistic or a monopoly structure.[15] For example, Alexander (1997), working with musicologists, deconstructed the sheet music of hit songs into five dimensions and then applied a measure of (entropic) diversity to the resulting data.[16] When measured against market structure, these results suggest that product diversity is maximized in a structure characterized by a four-firm concentration ratio of about 50 percent. This analysis suggests that an atomistic structure may be characterized by a relatively high level of "me-too" business stealing (i.e., excessive product duplication). Thus, a competitive structure may correlate strongly with product innovation, but it might not best promote product diversity. It is important to note that these data also contradict the hypothesis that a monopoly market structure promotes maximum diversity.

A comparison of these two different measures is shown in Figure 6-2. Note that the counting measure has relatively high levels from 1960 though 1967 (i.e., the number of hit songs was increasing), and thereafter it shows a long, gradual decline. On the other hand, the entropy measure of diversity suggests lower levels of diversity in the pre-1967 period and then an increase through the 1970s. The entropy data imply that although

---

[14]For example, see Bruce Anderson, Peter Hesbacher, K. Peter Etzkorn, and R. Serge Denisoff, "Hit Record Trends, 1940–1977," *Journal of Communications* 30 (1980): 31–43; Richard Peterson and David Berger, "Cycles in Symbol Reproduction: The Case of Popular Music," *American Sociological Review* 40 (1975): 158–73; Eric Rothenbuhler and John Dimmick, "Popular Music: Concentration and Diversity in the Industry, 1974–1980," *Journal of Communications* 32 (1982): 143–149.

[15]Peter J. Alexander, "Product Variety and Market Structure: A New Measure and a Simple Test," *Journal of Economic Behavior and Organization* 32 (1997): 207–214.

[16]The data were derived from sheet music, a visual embodiment of the products' constituent characteristics. A random sample was obtained for the years 1955 to 1988. These years were selected because an abundant supply of sheet music for hit songs is available, and because during this time period, the industry went from a highly competitive market structure (1955–1964) to an oligopoly (1978–1988). Each annual sample consisted of 30 observations that were drawn randomly from *Billboard Magazine*'s Top Pop Singles of the Year. The observations were measured in five dimensions, and a qualitative metric (e.g., 0,1) was used based on the presence or absence of each characteristic. The aggregate observations were entered into a matrix, from which a measure of product diversity (entropy) was derived. The observations used in this study were measured in five dimensions: time and meter, accent, harmonic structure, melody, and form. In each instance, a qualitative metric was utilized. This framework provided a set of n-characteristics ($n = 5$) measured in m-dimensions ($m = 2$). The probability that any product type or variety exists is equal to $1/m^n$ or 1/32. Each annual sample was then deconstructed observation by observation into constituent elements and entered into a 5 by 32 matrix. From the matrix, the number of observations in each of the 32 discrete categories was computed and converted to a percentage of the total. Next, the natural logarithm of the percentage was taken and then multiplied by the original percentage. The sum of the product of the percentages and the natural logarithms of the percentages was then computed. This yielded the level of product diversity for the sample.

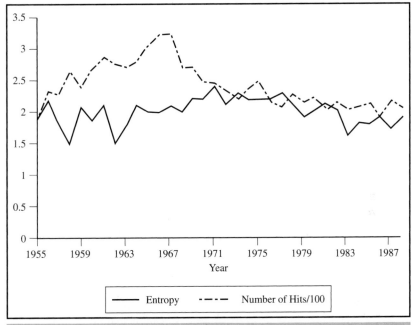

FIGURE 6-2   Measuring Product Diversity in the Recording Industry

SOURCE: Peter J. Alexander, "Product Variety and Market Structure: A New Measure and
a Simple Test," *Journal of Economic Behavior and Organization* 32 (Feb. 1997):
207–214.

the 1950s may be characterized as a period of significant innovation, the characteristics
of the industry's offerings did not display a great deal of diversity or difference relative
to other measured time periods.

V. PUBLIC POLICY

Antitrust Policy

In 2000, the Federal Trade Commission (FTC) charged that the five major recording
companies

> engaged in acts and practices that have unreasonably restrained competition in
> the market for prerecorded music in the United States through their adoption,
> implementation and enforcement of Minimum Advertised Price ("MAP") pro-
> visions of their Cooperative Advertising Programs.[17]

The FTC found that the five major distributors punished retailers for lowering
prices to consumers; as a result, consumers paid almost half a billion dollars in artificially inflated prices between 1998 and 2000. According to a joint statement issued by
all five FTC commissioners, the

> Commission has unanimously found reason to believe that the arrangements
> entered into by the five largest distributors of prerecorded music violate the

---

[17]Federal Trade Commission, "Analysis to Aid Public Comment on the Proposed Consent Order,"
www.ftc.gov/os/2000/05/mapanalysis.htm. Accessed March 5, 2004.

antitrust laws in two respects. First, when considered together, the arrangements constitute practices that facilitate horizontal collusion among distributors, in violation of Section 5 of the Federal Trade Commission Act. Second, when viewed individually, each distributor's arrangement constitutes an unreasonable vertical restraint of trade under the rule of reason.[18]

The economic analysis offered by the FTC warrants quoting at length:

> The MAP (minimum advertised price) provisions were implemented with the anticompetitive intent to limit retail price competition and to stabilize the retail prices in the industry. Prior to the adoption of these policies, new retail entrants, especially consumer electronic chains, had sparked a retail "price war" that had resulted in significantly lower compact disc prices to consumers and lower margins for retailers.
>
> The complaints allege that the distributors were concerned that declining retail prices could cause a reduction in wholesale prices. Through these stricter MAP programs, the distributors hoped to stop retail competition, take pressure off their own margins, and eventually increase their own prices. The distributors' actions were effective. Retail prices were stabilized by these MAP programs. Thereafter, each distributor raised its wholesale prices.
>
> While some vertical restraints can benefit consumers (known as "efficiencies") by enhancing interbrand competition and expanding market output, plausible efficiency justifications are absent in this case.[19]

The Big Five denied the FTC's charges but agreed in September 2003 to settle without a trial and refund $143 million in overcharges to customers.

File Sharing

The music recording industry is currently at the center of an explosive debate about digital file sharing—a debate that in some ways may well be shaping the emerging regulation of the Internet. The industry's trade association, the RIAA, asserts that digital file sharing is destroying industry profits, to the tune of billions of dollars in losses, and has issued subpoenas to hundreds (perhaps thousands) of alleged "pirates"; it is suing 261 of them.[20]

The music industry has been successful in its legal challenges against file-sharing firms such as Napster and MP3.com, but until recently it has been unsuccessful in its attempts to copy protect its products or thwart individual, peer-to-peer file-sharing networks. The

---

[18] Federal Trade Commission, "Record Companies Settle FTC Charges of Restraining Competition in CD Music Market," www.ftc.gov/opa/2000/05/cdpres.htm. Accessed March 5, 2004.

[19] Federal Trade Commission, "Analysis to Aid Public Comment on the Proposed Consent Order," www.ftc.gov/os/2000/05/mapanalysis.htm. Accessed March 5, 2004.

[20] In general, copyright law is designed to protect copyright holders from substantial unauthorized use of copy-protected objects. This legal protection, and the resulting capacity on the part of the copyright holder to exploit the benefits of innovation, is thought to provide appropriate incentives to create.

industry's frustration with this was evidenced by Senator Orrin Hatch, who suggested destroying users' machines if they refused to stop sharing files.[21]

The music industry contemplated similar tactics, but the industry's current strategy for reducing unauthorized file sharing appears to consist of three related tactics: (1) individualized legal actions (e.g., scores of subpoenas and lawsuits) to increase the cost to users of peer-to-peer networks; (2) deep price cuts (Universal's recently announced price reduction); and (3) increased online digital distribution by industry-sanctioned distributors (e.g., Apple Computer's iTunes, and BuyMusic.com). Roughly, this works out to two carrots and one stick: It appears that the industry is attempting to stop unsanctioned sharing and increase legal purchases while transitioning to large-scale digital distribution.

Technical Background

Given that a compact disk player uses a sequence of 0s and 1s to reproduce sound waves, consumers are able to use computers to play compact disks, as well as to transfer songs from compact disks for storage and replay them on their computers. These types of files were, until recently, generally not shared with large numbers of other users, because as late as 1997, the transfer of 3 minutes of music across the Internet required 50 megabytes of hard drive storage space and an enormous amount of time and bandwidth.

However, the development of the MP3 file format dramatically changed these storage and bandwidth requirements. MP3, created by engineers at the German company Fraunhofer Gesellshaft, is shorthand for Motion Picture Experts Group-Layer 3. It is an audio compression format that generates near compact disk–quality sound at approximately one-tenth to one-twentieth the size. For example, each minute of music on a compact disk requires the equivalent of 10 megabytes of computer storage space, but an MP3 format of the same piece could be stored on 1 megabyte or less. To give a practical example of the compression savings, consider that Elvis Presley's *Hound Dog* on compact disk requires 24 megabytes of hard disk space, but when converted to MP3, the storage requirement falls to 2 megabytes. On a 28.8-kilobit-per-second modem, the compact disk version of *Hound Dog* would take at least 1.5 hours to download from another computer; if the file were first converted to MP3, it would take approximately 8.5 minutes.

Clearly, MP3 technology has made digital file distribution more efficient. This increased efficiency is reinforced by the fact that more and more computers are connecting to the Internet via cable rather than modem, which significantly improves the speed at which files can be transferred.

Legal Action against Central Servers

The music industry initially responded to large-scale organized digital file sharing by taking legal action against the most prominent and sizable digital file distributors: MP3.com and Napster.com. These firms claimed protection citing "fair use" and "safe harbor," respectively.

However, in *UMG Recording, Inc. et al. v. MP3.com*, Judge Jed S. Rakoff concluded that "defendant's infringement of plaintiffs' copyrights is clear" (92 F. Supp. 2d 349 [2000]). During the trial, MP3.com argued that its repository of legally purchased copyrighted

---

[21]This type of approach may violate 18 U.S.C.1030(a)(5), which prohibits knowingly causing "the transmission of a program, information, code, or command, and as a result of such conduct intentionally causing damage without authorization, to a protected computer," where damage is defined as "any impairment to the integrity or availability of data, a program, a system, or information."

material, which it distributed to registered users, was protected by "fair use." Judge Rakoff concluded that the "defendant's 'fair use' defense is indefensible and must be denied as a matter of law" (92 F. Supp. 2d 349 [2000]). Moreover, in the Napster.com case, U.S. District Judge Marilyn Hall Patel refused a motion by Napster.com to dismiss the lawsuit against them, ruling that Napster.com was not entitled to "safe harbor" status as provided in the Digital Millennium Copyright Act (DMCA) of 1998. The safe harbor provisions of the DMCA were established to protect Internet service providers from liability and court-issued injunctions regardless of their knowledge, in the event that users of the service committed illegal actions. Judge Patel subsequently issued a preliminary injunction against Napster.com, ordering them to stop distributing copyrighted materials.

Note that MP3.com and Napster.com share common features, the most important of which may be that as distribution systems, they rely on a series of central servers to guide the distribution of digital products. So, for example, if a user of either system sends out a request for a file, the request is routed through one of the firms' servers. Because requests for information relating to the location of MP3 files are routed through their servers, and because a federal judge has held such activity to violate existing copyright law, companies like MP3.com and Napster.com were obvious targets for legal remedy.

Private, Peer-to-Peer, File-Sharing Networks

The architecture of distribution systems like MP3.com and Napster.com is structured around a series of centralized servers that direct electronic traffic and rout requests for files. In contrast, private, peer-to-peer, file-sharing systems like Kazza, Gnutella, and Freenet (to name just a few) are decentralized; that is, they do not utilize a central server. Rather, each individual computer that has the peer-to-peer software installed on it becomes a server via a continuous series of peer-to-peer connections. Therefore, if one machine has the required software and Internet connection, it can connect with another machine, which is connected to another machine, and so on.

The music industry's initial response to this kind of file sharing was to attempt to copy protect its products. Despite many attempts, however, these efforts have failed. The industry's current response to peer-to-peer file sharing is to issue subpoenas to individual consumers for alleged damages, which the industry claims amount to billions of dollars.

Evidence and Estimates of Damages

How economically damaging is digital file-sharing activity to the music recording industry? A lot? A little? None at all? All three of these answers appear plausible, given the paucity of evidence.

The RIAA asked the court to enjoin Napster.com because "Napster is causing irreparable harm to plaintiffs and the entire music industry" (www.cnnfn.com, June 16, 2000). It put the costs of piracy in the billions of dollars. In their motion, the RIAA presented (among other items) a study conducted by the Field Research Corporation that suggested that the use of Napster displaces compact disk sales. Most recently, Josh Bernoff, an analyst at Forrester Research, estimated that the large record companies have lost approximately $700 million to file sharing over the 1999–2003 period.[22]

---

[22]This study appears to measure consumption behavior across different groups of file sharing consumers holding elasticities of demand constant across groups. If so, it calls into question the usefulness of the study. Moreover, the study calculated lost sales using $17 as the price of a lost sale, which is a price the FTC and a United States District Court judge found to be held artificially high. Notably, Bernoff had recently suggested that the reasons for the decline in sales of compact disks were not piracy but rather (1) an economic downturn, (2) competition from other forms of digital entertainment, and (3) shorter playlists on the radio, which implies less information and fewer new products for consumers.

Intuitively, it seems plausible that file sharing might displace some sales. However, the issue is subtle, and the margin for error is potentially great. It is worth noting that despite the industry's legal victory against MP3.com, Judge Rakoff, in establishing damages in the case, noted that "[P]laintiffs have not made any attempt at this trial to prove actual damages they may have suffered. The court views the absence of any proof of actual damages as a mitigating factor favorable to the defendant" (U.S. Dist. LEXIS 13293, CCH p28, 141 [September 6, 2000]).

Evidence also appears to contradict the hypothesis that file sharing has damaged the music industry, at least to the extent claimed by the RIAA. For example, a survey by Jupiter Communications found that Napster users were 45 percent more likely to *increase* their purchases of prerecorded music than those who do not use the service— evidence suggesting that Napster *enhances* demand for these products. In addition, a study by Reciprocal Inc. (commissioned by the RIAA) found that although sales of recorded music fell by 4 percent near college campuses over the past year, sales near 67 colleges that had banned Napster fell by 7 percent. Thus, according to this study, sales fell by a greater percentage in areas near colleges where Napster was banned than in areas where Napster was not banned. Most recently, an unpublished study by economists Felix Oberholzer and Koleman Strumpf finds that dowloading has *no* statistically identifiable effect on sales of recordings.

It is therefore likely that file sharing is both demand enhancing and demand diminishing, although not necessarily in equal proportions. Given the heterogeneity of the customer base in the industry, it appears likely that some users legally purchased a greater quantity of music because they were able to experience it first using a file-sharing network; conversely, it is likely that some potential consumers reduced their purchases because they did not like the products they downloaded after listening to them. It also is likely that some potential customers who might otherwise have purchased the product substituted unauthorized downloads for purchases. In addition, the growing importance of potential substitutes, such as DVDs and new video games, also might be influencing current purchase decisions and inducing a decline in demand for compact disks.[23]

Conclusion

The history of the music recording industry is one in which new technology has sparked entry, and many of these new entrants have been product innovators. However, as we noted, maximum product diversity (as distinct from product innovation) in the music industry may well be achieved when the four-firm concentration ratio is approximately 50 percent. Because radio airplay is a significant factor in exposing consumers to the industry's offerings, the structure and conduct of the radio industry are additional important elements affecting structure, conduct, and performance in the music recording field. Payola has likely been an important impediment to new competition, especially considering the extraordinary reduction in technical scale economies that have been realized.

---

[23]It is not clear whether DVDs, video games, and CDs are substitutes or complements. When DVDs and "new" video games were first introduced, the percentage change in demand for all three was positive. However, while demand for compact disks has fallen in recent years, demand for DVDs and video games has increased over this time. This suggests that compact disks, DVDs, and video games may be substitutable to some degree.

Perhaps most peculiarly, the costs of production, reproduction, and distribution in the industry are close to zero (from a physical standpoint), yet the industry structure in which five firms dominate the field worldwide has been essentially unchanged since the mid-1980s. One implication of this structure is that firms are able to more easily coordinate and carry out anticompetitive activities, such as price fixing. Prices that are held artificially high generate social welfare losses (in the absence of perfect price discrimination), and might have accelerated and amplified the use of file-sharing networks by consumers. The use of file-sharing networks, and the subsequent litigation that has resulted from their use, may also induce welfare losses and will likely influence public policy toward the Internet in ways that may be unforeseen and undesirable.

Suggested Readings

Journal Articles

Alexander, Peter, J. 2002. "Peer-to-Peer File Sharing: The Case of the Music Recording Industry." *Review of Industrial Organization* 20: 151–161. [March]

Alexander, Peter J. 1997. "Product Variety and Market Structure: A New Measure and a Simple Test." *Journal of Economic Behavior and Organization* 32: 207–214. [February]

Alexander, Peter J. 1994. "New Technology and Market Structure: Evidence from the Music Recording Industry." *Journal of Cultural Economics* 18: 113–123.

Black, M., and D. Greer. 1987. "Concentration and Non-Price Competition in the Recording Industry." *Review of Industrial Organization* 3: 13–37.

Coase, R. 1979. "Payola in Radio and Television Broadcasting." *The Journal of Law and Economics* 22: 269–328. [October]

Cunningham, Brandan M., Peter J. Alexander, and Nodir Adilov. Forthcoming, 2005. "Peer-to-Peer File Sharing Communities." *Information Economics and Policy*.

Oberholzer, Felix, and Koleman Strumpf. March 2004. "The Effect of File Sharing on Record Sales: An Empirical Analysis" (unpublished manuscript).

Peterson, R. A., and D. G. Berger. 1975. "Cycles in Symbol Production: The Case of Popular Music." *American Sociological Review* 40: 158–173 [April].

Rothenbuhler, Eric, and John Dimmick. 1982. "Popular Music: Concentration and Diversity in the Industry, 1974–1980." *Journal of Communications* 32:143–49. [Winter]

Sidak J. G., and D. E. Kronemyer. 1987. "The 'New Payola' and the American Record Industry: Transactions Costs and Precautionary Ignorance in Contracts for Illegal Services." *Harvard Journal of Law and Public Policy* 10: 521–572.

Books

Burnett, R. 1996. *The Global Jukebox: The International Music Industry.* London: Routledge.

Chapple, S., and R. Garofulo. 1977. *Rock 'n' Roll Is Here to Pay: The History and Politics of the Music Industry.* Chicago: Nelson-Hall.

Cleveland, B., ed. 1999. *The Recording Industry Sourcebook,* 11th ed. Emeryville, CA: Primedia Information Inc.

Dannen, F. 1990. *Hit Men: Power Brokers and Fast Money Inside the Music Business.* New York: Times Books.

Fink, M. 1989. *Inside the Music Business.* New York: Schirmer Books.

Frith, S., and A. Goodwin, eds. 1990. *On Record.* New York: Pantheon Books.

Gelatt, Roland. 1977. *Fabulous Phonograph.* New York: Appleton-Century.

Lessig, L. 2002. *The Future of Ideas.* New York: Random House, Inc.

Sanjek, David. 1998. "Popular Music and the Synergy of Corporate Culture." In *Mapping the Beat: Popular Music and Contemporary Theory,* edited by Thomas Swiss, John Sloop, and Andrew Herman, 171–86. Malden, MA: Basil Blackwell.

Sanjek, R. 1983. *From Print to Plastic: Publishing and Promoting America's Popular Music (1900–1980)*. Brooklyn, NY: Institute for Studies in American Music.

Shaw, Arnold. 1987. *The Jazz Age*. Oxford: Oxford University Press.

Taylor, Timothy D. 1997. *Global Pop*. New York: Routledge.

Toll, R. 1982. *The Entertainment Machine*. Oxford: Oxford University Press.

Industry Trade Publications and Other Resources

Billboard Magazine
Billboard Rock Monitor
Gavin Report
Music Yellow Pages
Radio and Records
Recording Industry Association of America
Variety

Links to Congressional Hearings, Court Decisions, and Related Resources

Federal Trade Commission Report, "Marketing Violent Entertainment to Children": www.ftc.gov/reports/violence/vioreport.pdf

Federal Trade Commission Press Release: "Record Companies Settle FTC Charges of Restraining Competition in CD Music Market." Follow link on page to additional resources relating to the case: www.ftc.gov/opa/2000/05/cdpres.htm

Information Web site for the FTC/Music Industry Antitrust Litigation Settlement. Follow the various links on the page: www.musiccdsettlement.com/english/default.htm

Media Access Project —A nonprofit, public interest law firm with a large number of useful links to media resources: www.mediaaccess.org/web/

Public Knowledge—General links to information relating to media, technology, and information: www.publicknowledge.org/

U.S. Representative Cannon introduces the Music Online Competition Act. Useful related links on page: www.house.gov/cannon/press2001/aug03.htm

CHAPTER

Banking

—Steven Pilloff

The commercial banking industry provides financial services to a substantial portion of firms and households in the United States and is one of the largest, most important sectors of the nation's economy. Banks provide a wide range of financial products and services, but their traditional activities fall largely into two basic areas: They offer customers safe, liquid, and convenient deposit products; and they lend deposited funds to consumers, governments, and businesses that need to borrow money. Typically, banks pay interest to depositors and collect interest from borrowers. A large portion of their profits comes from the difference in interest received from loans and interest paid on deposits. Therefore, high loan rates and low deposit rates are associated with high profitability. Banks also generate income by charging fees on deposit and loan products.

The industry is made up of commercial banking institutions chartered either by the national bank regulator (the Office of the Comptroller of the Currency) or by the state bank regulator in the bank's home state. Some institutions operate as independent banks that are owned directly and are the only entity in their organization; others operate as part of a bank holding company that owns one or more banking institutions and may also own nonbank subsidiaries such as data processing, specialty lending, investment banking, and venture capital firms. Excluded from this definition of the commercial banking industry are nonbank depository institutions (savings banks, savings and loan associations, and credit unions) and nonbank, nondepository firms (e.g., mortgage companies, consumer finance firms, and mutual fund organizations). Also excluded are nonbank subsidiaries of bank holding companies.

Throughout this chapter, the terms *bank* and *banking organization* are used to refer to an independent bank or to the aggregate of all bank subsidiaries owned by the same bank holding company. The term *banking institution* refers to an entity that has its own bank charter, an independent bank, or an individual bank subsidiary of a bank holding company.

The description of bank activities as collecting deposits and extending loans oversimplifies the definition of commercial banking. For one thing, banks also provide financial services in numerous other areas—trust, investment advisory, and cash management, for example. Moreover, the deposit and loan options available to customers are numerous and varied. Banks typically offer many types of deposit accounts: savings, demand deposit (checking), money market deposit, and certificates of deposit, each with different features such as rate and fee schedules, minimum balance requirements, and withdrawal restrictions. A key feature of bank deposits is that they are federally insured for up to $100,000 and provide a level of safety that cannot be matched by nondepository firms.[1] The credit products provided by banks also are varied and include, for example, automobile, residential mortgage, and consumer loans, as well as commercial and home equity lines of credit.

Each product and service offered by banks could potentially be analyzed as a separate market. Each has unique characteristics, is offered by a different (though often overlapping) set of firms, and is demanded by a different (though again often overlapping) set of customers. For example, mortgage loans, automobile loans, checking accounts, and cash management services could all potentially be considered distinct product markets. Nonetheless, commercial banks are the only firms that provide the broad range of financial services that are commonly thought of as commercial banking.[2] As a result, banks may have the unique ability to form long-term customer relationships that have a special economic importance beyond the actual products and services being obtained. Customers of financial services frequently view a commercial bank as their primary financial services provider and typically obtain multiple financial services from that institution.[3]

In this chapter, commercial banking is considered to involve two distinct markets—retail banking and corporate banking—each of which consists of the set of traditional deposit, loan, and other financial services that are provided by banks to a particular type of customer. The retail segment of commercial banking consists of financial services offered to households and small businesses. Not only does nearly every bank engage in retail banking, but most banks engage exclusively in retail banking.

Evidence suggests that the relevant geographic market for retail banking is local. On the demand side, retail customers strongly prefer to bank locally, so they typically obtain their financial services from a bank located near their home or office. On the supply side, it is relatively costly for banks to provide retail services to customers who do not live or work close to a bank office, because retail accounts typically involve small amounts of money. In addition, the number of bank offices is large and growing, which is consistent with banks continuing to maintain a strong local presence in order to deliver services most effectively.

Corporate banking involves providing financial services to large businesses—commercial deposit and loan products, as well as sophisticated financial services such as foreign

---

[1]The $100,000 federal protection, which is provided by the Federal Deposit Insurance Corporation (FDIC), applies to each separate account registration at a given institution. Therefore, a household or company can fully protect deposits above $100,000 by maintaining several accounts, each with less than $100,000, at an institution under different account holders or by maintaining multiple accounts, each with less than $100,000, under the same account holder at different institutions. Deposits held at savings banks and savings and loan associations are protected by the same insurance, and deposits held at credit unions receive similar protection.

[2]The Supreme Court has recognized that the appropriate product market for evaluating the competitive effects of bank mergers is the cluster of bank products and services offered by banking institutions. For example, see *United States v. Philadelphia National Bank*, 374 U.S. 321, 357 (1963).

[3]These and other findings from the Federal Reserve Board's 1993 Survey of Small Business Finances and 1992 Survey of Consumer Finances are discussed in Myron L. Kwast, Martha Starr-McCluer, and John D. Wolken, "Market Definition and the Analysis of Antitrust in Banking," *The Antitrust Bulletin* (Winter 1997): 973–995. More recent data from the Survey of Consumer Finances are reported in Dean F. Amel and Martha Starr-McCluer, "Market Definition in Banking: Recent Evidence," *The Antitrust Bulletin* (Spring 2002): 63–89.

exchange. A relatively small number of large banks are involved in corporate banking. The accepted relevant geographic market for corporate banking is regional, national, or even international. Because corporate accounts typically involve large sums of money, large firms have a sizable financial incentive to search across a wide range for their best alternative; they are also likely to have the resources and expertise to engage in such a search. In addition, because the potential profits associated with large businesses are substantial, making bank search costs relatively less important, banks generally are not limited geographically in their pursuit of corporate banking business.

Although retail and corporate banking are important components of the commercial banking industry, this chapter focuses on retail banking, which is much better suited for an analysis within the structure-conduct-performance framework. Retail banking has received substantial attention from antitrust authorities, because retail customers are more geographically limited and retail markets are smaller. As a result, extensive research has been done on the proper definition of retail markets and the relationship among market structure, bank performance, and to a lesser extent bank conduct. Corporate banking raises competitive concerns much less frequently, and few studies have been directed at this segment of the industry.

I. HISTORY

For much of its history, the U.S. commercial banking industry has comprised mainly a large number of small, local organizations. Federal and state legal restrictions on bank activities were a major reason for the development of this structure. Restrictions on branching and interstate banking, which limited the ability of state-chartered and federally-chartered banks to grow large and operate over sizable geographic areas, were particularly influential.

Essentially all banks operate a head office where deposits are accepted and loans are originated.[4] Most banks also maintain branch offices. For many years, state-chartered banks were prohibited from operating branches outside their home state. In fact, in many states, state-chartered banks were permitted to operate branches only in a limited portion of the state, such as the bank's home county or its home and contiguous counties; in other states, branching was completely prohibited. A bank that wanted to operate in an area of the state in which it was prohibited from branching needed to form a bank holding company and establish (or purchase) a separate bank subsidiary with its own charter and head office.

Before 1927, federally chartered banks were prohibited from branching. The McFadden Act of 1927 gave national banks some expanded branching rights but still limited them to the same branching restrictions that were imposed on state-chartered institutions. Therefore, national banks were essentially prohibited from interstate branching and in many cases were limited in the extent of intrastate branching they could engage in.

Although no banks could branch across state lines, a loophole in the McFadden Act made it possible for a bank holding company to conduct interstate banking by purchasing a banking institution operating in a different state than the one in which the acquiring holding company's headquarters was located. However, the Douglas Amendment to

---

[4]Exceptions include a small number of Internet banks, which conduct all business without any physical offices and constitute an extremely small segment of the industry.

the Bank Holding Company Act of 1956 prohibited such interstate acquisitions unless the state legislature of the target institution's home state expressly permitted such acquisitions. For many years, no states had laws permitting interstate acquisitions.

The banking industry also faced other restrictions, most notably the Glass-Steagall Act of 1933, which mandated that commercial banking (gathering deposits and making loans) and investment banking (underwriting securities) remain separate activities.[5] Although various restrictions greatly affected the structure of the banking industry, restrictions on branching and interstate banking had the greatest influence.[6]

In recent years, many restrictions on interstate banking have been lifted. In 1975, Maine's state legislature passed a law allowing bank holding companies headquartered in other states to make acquisitions in Maine. Other states followed that lead. By year-end 1984, eight states had enacted enabling legislation, and by year-end 1995, every state had passed legislation allowing some interstate banking.

Restrictions on branching also have been relaxed. Many states have liberalized their branching rules, so it has become easier for banks to expand their operations within their home state. Most states allow statewide branching, with the remaining few permitting limited intrastate branching.

In 1985, the Office of the Comptroller of the Currency also began to facilitate interstate branching for national banks under an existing rule referred to as the 30-Mile Rule. This rule allowed a national bank to relocate its head office anywhere within 30 miles, even if it meant moving the office into a different state. Following the move, the original head office could be operated as a branch. Banks used this type of expansion to enter new states, and many bank holding companies used it to consolidate subsidiaries.

The Riegle-Neal Interstate Banking and Branching Efficiency Act, enacted in 1994, removed many of the remaining limitations on interstate banking and branching. Interstate banking was facilitated as bank holding companies could purchase banking institutions in any state. Riegle-Neal also removed restrictions on interstate branching: A banking institution in one state could merge with an institution in another state, creating a single institution with branches in multiple states. Such mergers could take place among affiliated (owned by the same holding company) or unaffiliated banks. States were given the opportunity to opt out of interstate branching by merger by June 1, 1997, but only two, Texas and Montana, elected to do so. The prohibition on interstate branching expired in Texas in 1999 and in Montana in 2001. In those states that explicitly authorize such entry, banks also can establish new interstate branches. As of March 2003, fewer than half of the states had elected to permit such branching.

II. STRUCTURE

The structure of the commercial banking industry has changed markedly since 1990, largely as a result of extensive consolidation. The number of banks has declined and concentration at the national level has risen; interestingly, average concentration at

---

[5]The Gramm-Leach-Bliley Act (GLBA) was passed in 1999 and removed many of the restrictions on firms engaging in banking and other financial activities. Of particular importance, it repealed restrictions on banks affiliating with securities firms contained in the Glass-Steagall Act.

[6]Although the Glass-Steagall Act legally separated commercial and investment banking prior to passage of GLBA in 1999, regulatory decisions had already blurred the line before the act was passed. For example, the Federal Reserve Board determined that under section 20 of the Bank Holding Company Act, bank holding companies could form subsidiaries that engaged in a limited amount of certain underwriting activities.

the local level has not changed nearly as much. The number and size of very large banks also has increased, a development with potentially important consequences for the industry.

Mergers

Historically, the banking industry has consisted mainly of a large number of small, locally oriented organizations. Although the industry continues to exhibit this basic structure, it has changed dramatically in recent years. Much of the change is attributable to the extensive merger and acquisition activity that has taken place.[7]

Merger Activity

From 1990 to 2002, nearly 3,300 bank mergers involving $2.7 trillion in acquired assets were completed in the United States. (See Table 7-1.) The pace of merger activity generally increased in the early 1990s, remained high through the mid- and late-1990s, and then declined after peaking in 1998.

A small proportion of the deals accounted for a large share of the total acquired assets. These large mergers involving a target with substantial assets generally became more common over time. Mergers in which the target had total assets of at least $1 billion accounted for about 7 percent of all deals but 85 percent of all acquired assets. The 48 deals with a target that had total assets of at least $10 billion involved 66 percent of all acquired assets, and the 10 acquisitions of banking organizations with total assets of at least $50 billion accounted for 32 percent of acquired assets.

TABLE 7-1   Bank Mergers and Acquisitions (1990–2002)

Year	Number	Bank Assets Acquired (in billions of dollars)	Percent of Total Industry Assets[a]	Mergers with Acquired Assets Greater Than		
				$1 Billion	**$10 Billion**	**$50 Billion**
1990	118	68.8	2.0	10	1	0
1991	147	126.8	3.7	11	2	0
1992	240	157.8	4.5	23	3	1
1993	303	106.5	2.9	16	2	0
1994	360	117.5	3.0	16	2	0
1995	357	183.1	4.3	17	4	0
1996	313	322.1	7.1	22	7	2
1997	311	179.5	3.6	17	4	0
1998	379	677.3	12.6	32	8	3
1999	250	243.0	4.3	18	5	1
2000	183	177.0	2.9	16	2	1
2001	179	316.1	4.9	22	7	2
2002	146	54.9	0.8	11	1	0
Total	3,286	2,730.4	—	231	48	10

[a]*Total industry assets for each year measured as of December 31.*
SOURCES: SNL Securities, Federal Reserve Board, and Reports of Condition and Income (Call Reports).

---

[7]The terms *merger* and *acquisition* are used interchangeably throughout this chapter.

In 1998, merger activity reached an unprecedented level, when several of the largest bank combinations in history took place (NationsBank-BankAmerica, Banc One-First Chicago NBD, and Norwest-Wells Fargo). Several other sizable and many smaller deals also took place. Almost 13 percent of industry assets were acquired. In addition, The Travelers Group—a large, diversified, nonbank financial services firm with extensive insurance and securities activities—and Citicorp—a large banking organization—merged to form the largest banking organization in the United States.

Merger Motivations

The gradual removal of geographic restrictions on branching and interstate banking made consolidation in the commercial banking industry possible but does not explain why the merger wave took place. The extensive acquisition activity has been driven by the belief of bankers that substantial gains can be achieved by acquiring other organizations.

A key and commonly cited source of anticipated gains is reduced costs resulting from economies of scale.[8] Economies of scale exist when average costs decline as firm size increases. If scale economies exist in the banking industry, then larger banks would have lower average costs than smaller banks. As a result, they would be able to earn greater profits, either by lowering their prices (raising deposit rates, lowering loan rates, or lowering fees) to attract more customers or by increasing their profit margins (by maintaining prices and enjoying a greater spread between income and expenses) or through some combination of the two.

In the commercial banking industry, economies of scale can come from several sources. Technology is a particularly important potential factor. Banks rely heavily on extensive computer systems, which involve substantial fixed costs and more limited variable costs. Because their total computing and maintenance costs increase relatively little as transaction volume increases, banks may benefit from operations that generate a large number of transactions. Greater size also enables banks to increase employee specialization, possibly resulting in more effective and efficient operations.

Another source of economies of scale is advertising. It might be efficient for large banks, which operate over wide geographic regions, to advertise through radio, television, and large newspapers, which reach broad areas. In contrast, advertising by small banks through those media might reach many individuals who, being well outside the bank's service area, are not potential customers.

Mergers also can eliminate redundancies: Many back-office functions that are performed separately by two independent banks can be performed at lower cost by one consolidated bank. For example, following a merger, it might be possible to eliminate one bank's check-processing facility or payroll department. Likewise, when the acquiring and target banks operate branches in the same neighborhood, some of those branches often can be closed following a merger without greatly inconveniencing customers.

Consolidation also can result in greater market power; that is, a greater ability to sustain prices (service levels) above (below) competitive levels without being forced by market pressures to lower (raise) them. If two banks competing in the same market merge to create a large market share, then (assuming that the post-merger market is sufficiently

---

[8]A somewhat related although less relevant concept in a discussion of retail commercial banking is economies of scope. Scope economies occur when it is less expensive to produce multiple outputs jointly than to produce them separately. Scope economies are more relevant in the context of combining commercial banking with other financial services activities such as investment banking or insurance.

concentrated) the resulting banking organization might be able to exercise market power. Customers of the consolidated bank might be more willing to accept higher prices, because no alternatives may be more attractive than maintaining their existing banking relationship, even with higher prices. If smaller banks in the market recognize that higher prices do not necessarily result in numerous customer defections, they might follow the market leader and also raise prices. In the premerger, less concentrated market, neither merging party might have been able to sustain high prices, because many customers of each partner might have viewed the other partner as a convenient alternative and would have transferred their business if prices were raised or if service quality deteriorated.

The merger of two banks that are not direct competitors also could result in greater market power, because the consolidated bank might benefit from aspects of size that might be associated with greater market power. Large banks generally have substantial resources, or "deep pockets," from which to draw, allowing them more flexibility in pricing strategies. For example, a large bank might decide to set its prices above the competitive level in a market. Smaller banks in that market might try to undercut those prices to attract customers. In turn, the large bank could retaliate by drastically lowering prices, even to the point at which it would incur losses. Because of its substantial financial resources, the large bank likely would be able to sustain losses for a longer time than the small banks. Knowledge that this sequence of events might take place could dissuade small banks from undercutting the prices charged by the large bank. They might elect to be price followers, because failure to do so could invite this kind of pricing discipline. Hence, extensive financial resources might enable large banks to exercise market power by exerting price leadership.[9]

A large bank may increase its market power after a merger if it is able to strengthen its brand identity. Because large banks might advertise more frequently, maintain more offices, and have a more prominent profile as a result of involvement in public activities such as sponsoring a local sporting event, customers might become more familiar with their brand. This familiarity might lead customers to have greater trust in a recognized bank and be willing to pay higher prices for that bank's products and services.

Finally, mergers may benefit banks by reducing risk through diversification. With limited exposure to any particular geographic region, industry, or product type, a large and diversified bank is less vulnerable to economic problems in any single area. Greater diversification also might make large banks better equipped to take advantage of emerging profit opportunities. In particular, geographically diverse organizations are likely to be better suited to allocating resources to new opportunities, because they can easily transfer resources from less profitable to more profitable markets. Smaller, more locally oriented banks do not have similar outside resources to draw on to take advantage of such opportunities.

Failures and New Bank Formations

Although mergers and acquisitions have been the dominant force driving changes in the structure of the banking industry since 1990, the failure and formation of banking institutions also have played a role. There were 460 banking institutions, with total assets of

---

[9]Moreover, the anticompetitive influence of big banks may be reinforced by economies of scale, if they exist, and by the perception of investors that regulators believe very large banks are too big and too important to the functioning of the nation's financial system to be allowed to fail. Bernard Shull, "Banking, Commerce, and Competition Under the Gramm-Leach-Bliley Act," *Antitrust Bulletin* 47 (Spring 2002): 25–61.

TABLE 7-2   Bank Failures and Formations (1990–2002)

	Failures		Formations
Year	**Number**	**Assets (in billions of dollars)**	**Number**
1990	159	10.7	175
1991	108	44.0	107
1992	99	15.6	73
1993	42	2.9	59
1994	11	0.9	48
1995	6	0.8	110
1996	5	0.2	148
1997	1	0.0	207
1998	3	0.3	193
1999	7	1.5	237
2000	6	0.4	192
2001	3	0.1	132
2002	10	2.9	81
Total	460	80.3	1,762

SOURCES: Failure data come from the Federal Deposit Insurance Corporation Web site (www2.fdic.gov/hsob/). Formation data come from various issues of the *Annual Statistical Digest* and *Annual Report* published by the Federal Reserve Board.

$80 billion, that failed between 1990 and 2002. (See Table 7-2.)[10] Most of these failures took place in the first few years of this period. Failures have been fairly rare since 1994, largely as a result of the economic recovery in the southwestern United States and the strong overall expansion of the U.S. economy during most of the 1990s. In recent years, failure rates have continued to remain low, despite an economic slowdown. The decline in failures after the early 1990s is also attributable to generally falling interest rates: Banks have not faced the difficult situation in which their fixed-rate assets are not generating sufficient funds to meet obligations on deposits, for which rates adjust frequently.

During the period when 460 banking institutions failed, nearly four times as many new banking institutions were formed. (See Table 7-2.) However, the large number of new formations may overstate their importance to the industry. New institutions generally start out small and remain that way for many years. Also, some of the 1,762 institutions classified as "new" were formed by established bank holding companies, so they are actually expansions of existing firms.

The number of start-ups undoubtedly has been limited by various barriers to entry into the industry. One barrier has been legal restrictions that have severely limited the potential pool of parties that are allowed to open a banking institution. For example, securities firms, which are already prominent financial services providers, were prohibited from operating commercial banks until fairly recently, when the Gramm-Leach-Bliley Act (GLBA), also known as the Financial Services Modernization Act of 1999, was passed and repealed restrictions on banks affiliating with securities firms. This relaxation of restrictions on the type of firm that can own and operate a commercial bank has

---

[10]In addition, about 485 thrift institutions (savings banks and savings and loan associations) failed.

broadened the pool of potential commercial banking firms. Nonfinancial firms, however, continue to be prohibited from owning commercial banks, so many companies that might want to start a new bank are legally prohibited from doing so.

Even as legal barriers to entry erode, others not attributable to legal restrictions will continue to exist—barriers that discourage not only the formation of start-up banks but also the opening of branches in new markets by existing banks. A lack of accurate and comprehensive information gives rise to one of these nonstatutory barriers. Operating a bank, particularly extending credit, often requires extensive knowledge of market conditions. Although profitable banking opportunities may exist in a given community, a party that is unfamiliar with local businesses and residents may be unable to exploit those opportunities. Evaluating credit risks can involve a great deal of uncertainty, and making bad loans can result in unprofitability and possibly failure. Therefore, prospective bankers may be hesitant to begin operating in a market they are unfamiliar with, even if the market offers potentially profitable opportunities.

Another entry barrier not related to legal restrictions is that attracting customers to change banks can be difficult. Customers face substantial switching costs when they change from one bank to another. Such tasks as opening and closing accounts and arranging for direct deposits and automatic bill payments to be processed differently can be aggravating and time-consuming. As a result, many customers are likely to stay with their current bank, even if another bank offers better prices or service.

Number and Absolute Size of Banks

A key development in the U.S. commercial banking industry has been a large decline in the total number of firms: Between 1990 and 2002, the number fell 30 percent from 9,277 to 6,493. (See Table 7-3.) The decline is expected to continue, with additional firms leaving the industry mainly through merger. However, the common view is that the industry will continue to have a relatively large total number of organizations.

TABLE 7-3   Banking Organizations (1990–2002)

Year	Total	Number with Domestic Banking Assets Greater Than					
		$1 Billion	$10 Billion	$25 Billion	$50 Billion	$100 Billion	$250 Billion
1990	9,277	263	59	26	7	0	0
1991	9,062	257	55	25	7	3	0
1992	8,772	243	55	27	10	3	0
1993	8,358	234	56	30	10	3	0
1994	7,930	237	60	31	12	4	0
1995	7,597	245	63	31	15	4	0
1996	7,333	243	57	30	16	7	0
1997	7,144	261	57	34	18	7	1
1998	6,863	267	57	33	15	7	1
1999	6,744	279	57	34	16	7	3
2000	6,674	297	62	35	18	7	4
2001	6,571	303	62	34	18	10	6
2002	6,493	315	64	36	19	11	6

SOURCES: Federal Reserve Board and Reports of Condition and Income (Call Report). Data for each year are as of December 31.

A major consequence of the consolidation-driven decrease in the number of organizations has been a rise in the number of very large banks, particularly since the late 1990s. At year-end 2002, a total of 11 banks had at least $100 billion in domestic banking assets, including 6 with assets of more than $250 billion. In contrast, before 1996, at most 4 banks had assets exceeding $100 billion, and before 1997, none had assets of $250 billion. Consolidation also has resulted in a rise in the number of moderately large banks, especially since the mid-1990s. Banks with assets above the $1 billion asset threshold have become more numerous as more of these banks have been created by mergers than have been eliminated by mergers. Most of this increase is attributable to a rise in the number of banks with assets of between $1 billion and $10 billion. (In addition to consolidation, the increase in the number of large firms is also somewhat attributable to inflation of asset values.)

The size of the very largest banks may continue to increase in the near future, but at some point their growth is likely to level off. The Riegle-Neal Act of 1994 placed a cap of 10 percent on the share of deposits that a banking organization can control as a result of an interstate acquisition. Therefore, the largest banks will reach a point where extensive additional growth will be legally constrained. In fact, at least one bank has approached this limit: Based on data from year-end 2003, Bank of America Corporation controls just under 10 percent of U.S. deposits, taking into account the firm's acquisition of FleetBoston Financial Corporation in early 2004. However, merger-related growth might not ultimately be limited to 10 percent, because Congress might raise the cap.

Industry and Market Concentration

As consolidation has progressed and the number of moderately large and very large banking organizations has risen, the banking industry has become increasingly concentrated; that is, fewer banks have come to account for a greater proportion of industry deposits. (See Table 7-4.)

TABLE 7-4   Concentration of the U.S. Banking Industry (1990–2002)

| | *Percentage of Total Domestic Deposits Held by the* | | | |
Year	10 Largest Banks	25 Largest Banks	50 Largest Banks	100 Largest Banks
1990	20.3	34.8	49.0	61.1
1991	20.4	36.0	49.0	61.3
1992	24.3	38.8	51.0	62.3
1993	25.0	40.6	53.3	64.1
1994	25.0	41.2	54.0	65.2
1995	24.7	41.0	54.6	66.3
1996	30.0	46.8	58.8	68.5
1997	29.7	46.2	58.9	68.8
1998	32.0	48.4	60.8	69.9
1999	35.6	50.0	61.4	70.0
2000	35.8	51.2	62.3	71.0
2001	38.9	53.9	63.8	71.6
2002	39.8	54.0	64.0	71.8

SOURCE: Summary of Deposits, Federal Deposit Insurance Corporation. Data for each year are as of June 30.

Coinciding with the relaxation of branching and interstate banking laws, deals through which large banks moved into new territory became more common in the 1990s, increasing the prominence of leading banks. Between 1990 and 2002, the share of deposits under the control of the 10 largest banks almost doubled, growing from 20.3 percent to 39.8 percent. The 25, 50, and 100 largest banks also increased the share of deposits under their control. However, these increases are all driven by increased deposit shares for the largest banks, as the share controlled by banks ranked 11 through 25 showed little change, and that of banks ranked 26 through 100 dropped by nearly 9 percentage points.

Although concentration at the national level provides information about the relative roles of large and small firms in the banking industry, that measure does not provide information on the structure of markets that are most relevant for conduct and performance in retail banking. Concentration at the local level provides this information, because banking markets for retail services tend to be local. Urban (defined as metropolitan statistical areas, or MSAs, based on 1999 definitions) and rural (non-MSA counties) local areas are analyzed separately, because the two types of markets differ in some key ways, particularly physical size and density of population and commercial activity, which may influence competitive interactions among banks.

Concentration at the local level can be measured in several ways. The number of banks provides a simple measure of the number of choices customers have. In markets with fewer banks, customers are likely to have fewer convenient choices, and banks are more likely to be able to exercise market power. The three-firm concentration ratio (CR3)—the aggregate share of deposits controlled by the three banks with the greatest individual market shares—provides a measure of the prominence of the leading firms. The Herfindahl-Hirschman Index (HHI) takes into account the market shares of all banks in the market, but larger banks have a disproportionate influence. The HHI is computed as the sum of the squared market shares of every bank in the market and ranges from 10,000 for a monopoly to nearly 0 for a market with numerous competitors, each with a small market share. In markets that have a high HHI, the leading bank or banks have a substantial market share, and in markets that have a low HHI, no single bank has a sizable market share. Therefore, the ability to exercise market power should be positively related to the HHI.

Concentration in urban and rural markets declined between 1990 and 2002. (See Table 7-5.) For both means and medians, the HHI fell, the CR3 fell, and the number of banks rose. During this period, concentration in rural markets was, not surprisingly, much higher than in urban markets. Because they are smaller than urban markets, rural markets can profitably support fewer banks than urban markets. Many banks cannot operate in a rural market with a small market share because they cannot generate sufficient revenues to cover their costs. In contrast, a small share of an urban market involves a greater level of activity, so it is easier to earn sufficient revenues to cover costs.

Using the Department of Justice's definition of a highly concentrated market as one with an HHI above 1,800, rural markets clearly qualify as being highly concentrated. The level of concentration in urban markets is more ambiguous. Although the average urban market can be considered highly concentrated throughout the period, it is unclear whether the change in the median urban HHI, which dropped from 1,903 to 1,702, reflects a meaningful change in the level of competition. The 1990 and 2002 figures are somewhat close to 1,800, but the median HHI in 1990 falls in the low end of

TABLE 7-5   Concentration of Urban and Rural U.S. Banking Markets (1990–2002)

Year	Urban Banking Markets (MSAs)			Rural Banking Markets (non-MSA counties)		
	Number of Banks	CR3	HHI	Number of Banks	CR3	HHI
1990	20.1	67.9	2,022	4.1	90.1	4,342
	(13)	(68.1)	(1,903)	(3)	(100.0)	(3,703)
1991	20.3	66.8	1,980	4.1	89.8	4,303
	(13)	(67.0)	(1,864)	(4)	(97.4)	(3,632)
1992	19.8	67.9	2,041	4.1	89.7	4275
	(13)	(68.2)	(1,958)	(4)	(97.0)	(3,638)
1993	19.3	67.7	2,026	4.1	89.4	4,245
	(13)	(68.0)	(1,937)	(4)	(96.3)	(3,599)
1994	18.9	67.2	1,999	4.2	89.2	4,213
	(13)	(67.0)	(1,876)	(4)	(95.7)	(3,590)
1995	18.7	66.7	1,980	4.2	88.9	4,173
	(13)	(66.1)	(1,841)	(4)	(95.2)	(3,553)
1996	18.4	67.4	2,013	4.3	88.8	4,148
	(13)	(67.1)	(1,859)	(4)	(95.0)	(3,535)
1997	18.9	66.3	1,987	4.4	88.4	4,121
	(13)	(65.3)	(1,843)	(4)	(94.3)	(3,514)
1998	19.3	66.1	1,986	4.5	88.0	4,092
	(13)	(65.6)	(1,850)	(4)	(93.2)	(3,474)
1999	19.8	65.3	1,945	4.5	87.6	4,065
	(14)	(65.2)	(1,800)	(4)	(92.5)	(3,448)
2000	20.3	64.7	1,928	4.6	87.2	4,020
	(14)	(64.3)	(1,744)	(4)	(92.0)	(3,429)
2001	20.6	63.9	1,889	4.7	86.8	3,978
	(14)	(63.5)	(1,723)	(4)	(91.1)	(3,399)
2002	20.8	63.5	1,860	4.7	86.6	3,951
	(15)	(62.9)	(1,702)	(4)	(90.9)	(3,375)

NOTE: *CR3 is the three-firm concentration ratio, and HHI is the Herfindahl-Hirschman Index. The top figure in each cell is the mean, and the figure in parentheses is the median. MSAs are defined using 1999 definitions.*
SOURCE: Summary of Deposits, Federal Deposit Insurance Corporation. Data for each year are as of June 30.

the highly concentrated range, and the median HHI in 2002 falls in the high end of the moderately concentrated range.[11]

Although average concentration in rural and urban banking markets has decreased over time, levels have varied considerably from market to market. For example, Table 7-6

[11]Measures of local concentration cited in the text and tables only include commercial banks. When analyzing proposed bank mergers, antitrust authorities often include, on at least a partial basis, savings banks and savings and loan associations. When measures are computed with thrift institutions receiving at least partial weight, a somewhat different picture of local concentration emerges. For example, computing the HHI with the deposits of thrift institutions included at 50 percent, as is typically done by the Federal Reserve Board in its competitive analysis, yields lower average levels than when thrifts are completely excluded (below 1,600 in urban markets and below 3,800 in rural markets). In urban areas, those levels increased over the full 1990–2002 period, although declines between 1998 and 2002 offset some of that increase. In rural areas, the average HHI with thrift deposits weighted at 50 percent remained stable over the full period, but it also showed variation, increasing from 1990 to 1994 and then decreasing from 1994 to 2002.

TABLE 7-6   Variation in Concentration of Urban and Rural U.S. Banking Markets (2002)

	Urban Banking Markets (MSAs)			Rural Banking Markets (non-MSA counties)		
	Number of Banks	CR3	HHI	Number of Banks	CR3	HHI
Minimum	3	26.1	540	1	33.3	865
25th percentile	11	55.6	1,407	3	75.8	2,371
Median	15	62.9	1,702	4	90.8	3,375
75th percentile	24	71.0	2,103	6	100.0	5,011
Maximum	194	100.0	7,395	16	100.0	10,000

NOTE: *CR3 is the three-firm concentration ratio, and HHI is the Herfindahl-Hirschman Index. MSAs are defined using 1999 definitions.*
SOURCE: Summary of Deposits, Federal Deposit Insurance Corporation. Data for each year are as of June 30.

indicates that in 2002, half of urban markets had 11 to 24 banks, and half had an HHI of 1,407 to 2,103; for each measure, values for the other half of the urban markets were outside these ranges. Although rural markets showed less dispersion in the number of banks (at least half had 3 to 6 banks), they showed considerable dispersion in HHI levels. (The middle half had HHIs in the broad range between approximately 2,400 and 5,000.)

The substantial increases in concentration in the commercial banking industry during the 1990s at the national level and the declines at the local level reflect the influence of consolidation. Mergers have enabled banks to become increasingly larger by enhancing their presence within states and across large regions of the country. However, mergers have not resulted in banks substantially increasing their presence in local markets. These patterns are consistent with the anticipated effects of antitrust policy in banking. Mergers between banks that do not compete with each other in local markets do not raise serious antitrust concerns, and few limits other than interstate banking restrictions have been placed on these so-called "market-extension" mergers. In contrast, mergers between banks that operate in the same local markets do raise antitrust concerns, especially when one or both have a large presence. Antitrust authorities seek to limit the amount of change in the HHI, the post-merger level of the HHI, and the level of the consolidated bank's post-merger market share resulting from these "in-market" mergers. Therefore, banking antitrust policy has, to a large extent, restricted in-market mergers, and most of the substantial consolidation activity in the industry has involved market-extension deals.

Relevant Market Definition

A key issue in applying the structure-conduct-performance framework to an analysis of the commercial banking industry is determining the relevant market, a task that involves defining the product and geographic markets. As previously discussed, the relevant product market is ambiguous, as commercial banking encompasses numerous financial services, many of which might be considered a unique product. For this analysis, the relevant product market is assumed to be the group of financial products and services that constitute retail banking.

The relevant geographic market in retail banking is the area within which banks can reasonably turn for customers and customers can reasonably turn for banks. Surveys show that most retail customers establish relationships with banking organizations that have a physical presence close to where they live or work (in the case of households) or close to where they are located (in the case of small businesses). Therefore, for this analysis the relevant geographic market is assumed to be local. Such an approach is consistent with most research and is the approach taken by antitrust authorities.

In the future, expansion of the area that is considered to be the relevant geographic market might be warranted. Technologies such as telephone banking, ATMs, personal computers, and the Internet may enable banks that lack a physical presence in a geographic region to provide convenient financial services to customers in that region. These technology-based delivery systems allow customers to make deposits, apply for loans, discuss financial needs, and obtain updated account information without having to visit a traditional bank office or, in some cases, interact with a live person.

Although many nontraditional delivery systems are already available, consumer and small business surveys suggest that they are not yet widely accepted. Most customers still appear to prefer that their bank have a local physical presence. Nonetheless, the increasing influence of technological advances on the retail banking industry suggests that the relevant geographic size of retail banking markets should be reassessed regularly. In addition, several recent studies have found that certain state-level measures might be becoming increasingly related to prices and profits, which highlights the current relevance of the issue of market size.[12]

Role of Nonbank Firms

Commercial banks are the largest, most prevalent, most diversified group of depository institutions operating in the United States. However, they are not the only depository institutions in the country. Thrift institutions (savings banks and savings and loan associations) and credit unions also provide depository services, including insured deposit accounts. Thrifts held total assets of $1.3 trillion, and credit unions had $557 billion at the end of 2002, compared with domestic assets of $6.2 trillion for commercial banks. In addition, nonbank, nondepository firms provide some of the same financial services as commercial banks.

Thrift Institutions

Thrift institutions raise funds primarily by collecting consumer deposits, and they invest funds principally in mortgage and other consumer loans. Thrift deposits are protected for up to $100,000 by the same federal deposit insurance that covers bank deposits. For many years, thrifts provided a limited set of consumer-oriented financial services because they were restricted in the types of accounts they could offer and loans they could make. Of particular importance, they were restricted from originating commercial loans. Beginning in the early 1980s, restrictions on their activities, including

---

[12]For example, Lawrence J. Radecki, "The Expanding Geographic Reach of Retail Banking Markets," *Federal Reserve Bank of New York Economic Policy Review* (June 1998): 15–34; Steven J. Pilloff and Stephen A. Rhoades, "Structure and Profitability in Banking Markets," *Review of Industrial Organization* (February 2002): 81–98; Erik Heitfield and Robin A. Prager, "The Geographic Scope of Retail Deposit Markets," *Journal of Financial Services Research* (forthcoming).

commercial lending, were relaxed. However, few thrifts have taken full advantage of these expanded powers.

Although many thrift institutions engage in some commercial lending, relatively few do so in more than a limited way.[13] As of mid-year 2003, 80 percent of savings banks and 60 percent of savings and loan associations held at least some commercial loans, but only 25 percent of savings banks and 10 percent of savings and loans held at least 5 percent of their assets in commercial loans. In contrast, nearly all commercial banks made some commercial loans, and about 75 percent had at least 5 percent of their assets in commercial loans. Because a large proportion of commercial loans is extended to small businesses, the limited involvement of thrifts in commercial lending suggests that they do not provide much competition to banks in at least one important retail banking product—small business lending.

The lack of full competition from thrifts in retail banking is recognized by antitrust authorities. In the competitive analysis of proposed bank mergers, thrifts typically are regarded as market competitors, but their role is generally viewed as limited. However, antitrust authorities often treat those thrifts that provide a full set of bank products and services, including commercial loans, as full members of the commercial banking industry. Thrifts are not included in the analysis in this chapter; as a result, measures of concentration may be somewhat overstated, especially in some markets that have a large thrift presence.

Credit Unions

Credit unions are nonprofit, cooperative financial institutions that collect deposits from and make loans to members. Deposits at credit unions are protected for up to $100,000 by federal insurance, which is administered by the National Credit Union Administration. For each credit union, members must share a "common bond," such as belonging to the same organization or being employed by the same company. Membership requirements greatly limit the competitive importance of credit unions, because they are unable to gather deposits from or make loans to many potential customers. Also impairing the competitive importance of credit unions is their tendency to offer a relatively narrow set of products. Not only are they limited by regulation in the range of products and services they can offer, but many credit unions are small, so they cannot provide more than basic deposit and loan products efficiently.

Other Nonbank Firms

The financial services industry has many specialized firms that compete in certain respects with commercial banks. This competition is limited, however, because specialized firms do not offer as full a complement of financial services as banks provide. For example, nonbank (and nonthrift) mortgage originators compete with banks for residential mortgages but not for other loan products and certainly not for federally insured deposit products. Likewise, many consumer finance companies specialize in lending to consumers but offer no credit services to businesses and no deposit products to anyone. On the deposit side, money market mutual funds, which are not federally insured, offer

---

[13]Steven J. Pilloff and Robin A. Prager, "Thrift Involvement in Commercial and Industrial Lending," *Federal Reserve Bulletin* (December 1998): 1,025–1,037. This article discusses the involvement of thrifts in commercial lending and clearly illustrates that the majority are much less active in such lending than commercial banks.

some competition to bank deposit products but none to loan products. Because non-bank institutions offer a limited set of products and services, their customers are less likely to form the special type of customer relationship with them that they form with banks.

III. CONDUCT

According to the structure-conduct-performance model, market structure affects bank performance by influencing bank conduct; that is, the ways in which banks compete with each other and the intensity of that competition. Like firms in other industries, banks engage in price competition. Unlike prices in many other industries, however, bank prices can be ambiguous, making price comparisons difficult for customers. Banks also compete with each other in several ways that are unrelated to price.

Price Competition

Banks engage in price competition. However, this competition is not nearly as straight-forward as in many other industries, because the price of bank products might not be immediately obvious to customers. First, the price of many financial services involves an interest rate and fees. Because banks tend to charge a variety of fees payable under widely varying circumstances, fees can be particularly difficult for customers to account for as they evaluate a product's price. Some fees, such as monthly account fees, are assessed regularly; others are assessed only when a specific service, such as an ATM, is used; still others are charged only when some condition, such as a minimum balance requirement, is not satisfied. Therefore, two customers having the same type of account at the same institution could pay different prices if their banking practices differed greatly.

Adding to customers' difficulty in evaluating the price of bank products is the nature of the business. Commercial banking is marked by customers maintaining a multi-product relationship with a primary organization, and the most meaningful price for retail banking services is likely to be a composite price of a set of products and services. Such a composite price may be difficult for customers to calculate. Moreover, the products and services included in the set (as well as the weight assigned to each) may differ from customer to customer, depending on individual banking needs. Despite these problems, price competition among banks may be driven by a desire by banks to establish and maintain customer relationships. As such, banks may establish a pricing schedule designed to attract and retain a particular customer base.

Nonprice Competition

Banks also compete in several ways that are unrelated to price. The location of branch offices and, more recently, ATMs is an important form of nonprice competition. Another important area of nonprice competition is customer service: Length of operating hours; length of waiting times for tellers, loan officers, and customer service representatives; and access to senior personnel are just a few of the elements banks can control that determine the level of service they provide. Banks also compete in their provision of services through alternative delivery channels, such as the Internet and the telephone, which may be more convenient than traditional brick-and-mortar offices for some customers.

The set of products offered is another dimension in which banks compete. Product variety directly influences a bank's ability to meet customer needs, because the types of products it offers affect its attractiveness to various classes of customers. Some banks offer many different products to appeal to a broad cross section of customers; others offer a small set of highly specialized products.

Brand recognition is an important component of competition among banks. Through advertising and involvement in community activities such as sponsorship of local events, banks attempt to establish an institutional image such as "integral part of the community," "trustworthy," or "knowledgeable." Much of the brand imaging in the retail banking industry revolves around the fundamental differences between small and large banks: Small banks tend to emphasize their local ownership and management, as well as their ability to provide personalized service; large banks tend to emphasize their wide product offerings, extensive experience, and vast resources as tools to help customers succeed in a complex financial world.

Relationship Competition

Banks compete in developing customer relationships in order to enhance their prospects for cross selling. Cross selling—selling additional products and services to existing bank customers—can be a lucrative and efficient means of expanding business. For example, a bank may encourage its checking account customers to take out a home equity loan, or a bank holding company might try to sell the products of its nonbank subsidiaries, such as insurance or investment products, to its banking clientele.

In attempting to sell additional products, a customer's existing bank or bank holding company has several advantages over other banks. First, because it regularly interacts with customers when customers conduct business at a bank office or ATM, over the telephone, or over the Internet, it has many opportunities to cross sell. Customers might be more responsive to these approaches than to more impersonal or intrusive methods such as media advertising, direct mail, and telephone solicitations that other banks must rely on. Another advantage for an existing bank holding company is the information it possesses about its customers. Such information might enable a bank to identify those products most likely to be desired by particular segments of its customer base, allowing it to better focus its marketing and cross-selling efforts. A third advantage is the trust that an established relationship may engender between a customer and a bank; customers are more likely to place their confidence in a bank they already do business with.

Cross selling, or the potential for cross selling, is viewed by some banks as such an important aspect of competition that they actively seek to increase their opportunities to engage in it. For example, the potential synergies of cross selling were a primary motivation for the 1998 merger of Citicorp and Travelers, which created Citigroup, an extremely large and diversified financial firm. Recently enacted legislation should facilitate continued bank efforts to cross sell to customers, because it has expanded the number of nonbank products and services that may be provided by firms engaged in banking. Although the enthusiasm for cross selling is great, it is not clear that cross selling basic banking services and such diverse products as insurance and investment products can yield large synergies.

Influence of Entry Barriers on Competition

Bank conduct, or competition, may be influenced by the numerous barriers that make it difficult for new and existing organizations to enter markets. These barriers—including customer switching costs, lack of clear information about market conditions, and legal restrictions on who is allowed to operate a bank and where they are allowed to operate—give incumbent firms advantages that might affect their conduct and facilitate the exercise of market power. If entry barriers are sufficiently high, a bank (or potential banker) might still be deterred from entry, even if existing firms in the market are charging high prices and earning high profits.

Special Issues Related to Large Banks

An important development that might influence conduct in the banking industry is the increased prominence of large banks, which might behave differently than smaller banks and might exert a unique effect on competition. In fact, the mere presence of a large bank in a market can affect competition indirectly by influencing the behavior of smaller rivals.

As discussed earlier, large banks that have access to considerable resources might be able to sustain market prices above competitive levels. If large banks benefit from economies of scale, they also might be able to charge lower prices or offer superior service relative to smaller banks. Moreover, if large banks are diversified, they might be able to reallocate their resources to take advantage of profitable opportunities more easily.

Large banks also might have a negative influence on competition as a result of multimarket contact. In banking, multimarket contact occurs when two or more banks compete with each other in several geographic areas, or markets. Consolidation has resulted in increased contact of this nature. Specifically, a bank might be less inclined to act aggressively in an individual market in which rivals that it faces in other markets operate, because those rivals could retaliate against it in those other markets. On the other hand, if a bank faces other banks that it does not encounter elsewhere, then it might be more willing to exploit competitive advantages without such fear of retaliation.

Large banks, particularly those with a small share of a local market, also might increase competition, because they can easily draw on out-of-market resources to exploit profitable opportunities. This ability may restrain other banks that have large shares of the market from exercising market power. If locally dominant banks attempt to raise prices, the large bank may bring in resources from elsewhere to exploit the opportunity. Such a response eventually would drive prices down toward their competitive level. Anticipation that large banks might respond to high prices in this way would discourage locally dominant banks from trying to sustain high prices in the first place.[14]

IV. PERFORMANCE

The structure-conduct-performance paradigm asserts that market structure influences bank conduct, which in turn affects performance. Because direct observation and measurement of bank conduct are difficult, research generally focuses on the relationship between structure and performance.

---

[14]See William M. Landes and Richard A. Posner, "Market Power in Antitrust Cases," *Harvard Law Review* 94 (March 1981): 937–996 for a thorough discussion of this hypothesis.

Influence of Market Structure on Performance

Prices

In unconcentrated banking markets, consumers are likely to have numerous convenient banking alternatives. If any one bank attempts to charge excessively high prices, many of its customers can presumably turn to another bank. For this reason, high prices are generally less sustainable in unconcentrated markets. In more concentrated markets, higher prices might be easier to sustain. Fewer banks operate and market shares are larger, so customers have fewer convenient alternatives. They might accept higher prices or poorer service if transferring to a rival bank that charges lower prices or offers better service is too inconvenient. If all banks in the market know that high prices can be sustained, then they all are likely to charge high prices.

Empirical research has generally found that market structure is related to bank prices in a way that suggests that the exercise of market power increases with concentration. Many studies have found that loan rates rise and deposit rates fall as local market concentration increases.[15] No significant relationship between market concentration and bank fees has been identified in the limited research that has been conducted on that subject.[16]

Efficiency

The market structure in which a bank operates may influence bank incentives for and managerial dedication to cost savings. In less concentrated, more competitive markets, market forces exert pressure on managers to work hard to maximize profits, making efficient operations a top priority. If managers are unable to maximize profits, returns are low and they may be relieved of their duties or forced to sell the bank to a more profitable rival. In the worst case, an inefficient bank could become insolvent and fail.

In more concentrated markets, competition is less intense, so banks have the ability to sustain prices at levels that generate sizable profits. That ability might lead managers to operate inefficiently either for their own or for the bank's benefit. For instance, a manager might direct costly resources toward preserving the existing market structure or pursuing additional market share so that large profits continue or are increased.

Alternatively, a manager might prefer to sacrifice some firm profits in order to live a "quiet life" or to enjoy costly perks such as a large staff or luxurious offices. The additional profit generated by greater efficiency might not, in the manager's opinion, be worth the additional effort. Even if they operate their banks at inefficient levels, above-competitive pricing might make it possible for managers to earn returns for shareholders that compare favorably with other investment alternatives. Finally, managers might operate less efficiently in more concentrated markets because they lack ability and yet are not forced to exit banking; high profits generated from above-competitive prices could mask a lack of managerial skill.

---

[15]For example, Timothy H. Hannan, "Market Share Inequality, the Number of Competitors, and the HHI: An Examination of Bank Pricing," *Review of Industrial Organization* (February 1997): 25–35; Anthony W. Cyrnak and Timothy H. Hannan, "Is the Cluster Still Valid in Defining Banking Markets? Evidence from a New Data Source," *The Antitrust Bulletin* (Summer 1999): 313–331; Erik Heitfield and Robin A. Prager, "The Geographic Scope of Retail Deposit Markets," *Journal of Financial Services Research* (forthcoming).

[16]Timothy H. Hannan, "Bank Fees and Their Variation across Banks and Locations," working paper, Board of Governors of the Federal Reserve System (December 1996).

Empirical analysis indicates that bank efficiency is negatively related to concentration.[17] Managers of banks in markets that are less concentrated and governed more strictly by competitive pressures are more effective at operating efficiently than managers of banks in more concentrated, less competitive markets.

Profitability

Because greater market concentration is associated with higher prices—higher loan rates and lower deposit rates—greater concentration might be expected to lead to a greater net interest margin (the difference between interest income and expenses) and a corresponding rise in bank profitability. However, research findings indicate that as concentration increases, efficiency drops, in which case greater concentration might be expected to lead to a decline in bank profitability. Studies of bank profits and market structure indicate that the concentration-pricing relationship is stronger than, and is only partially offset by, the concentration-efficiency relationship:[18] Banks that operate in more concentrated markets earn higher profits than banks that operate in less concentrated markets.

Influence of Bank Size on Performance

Greater size may enable large banks to operate more efficiently and more profitably than their smaller rivals and to exert a unique influence on market competition. If so, the trend of ever-larger banks controlling ever-larger shares of the industry may have affected the performance of large banks and their smaller rivals.

Performance of Large Banks

Data for commercial banks of various sizes indicate that small banks are less profitable and less efficient than larger banks. (See Table 7-7.) For 2002, the four smallest groups of banks (assets of $1 billion or less) were the least profitable, as measured by an average return on assets (net income divided by average assets) of no more than 1.18 percent. Average profitability within the three groups of larger banks was at least 1.39 percent.

Evidence on the relationship between bank pricing and bank size is mixed. Strong evidence suggests that larger banks charge higher fees than smaller banks.[19] For example, one study found that in 2002, banks with assets of more than $1 billion charged an average fee of more than $23 for a stop payment order, compared with $17 for institutions with assets of less than $100 million; similarly, large banks charged $26 on average for a bounced check, and small banks charged about $20. Because the study summarized fee data for all large banks with assets of more than $1 billion, it is unclear how fees charged by the largest banks differ from those charged by other large banks.

---

[17]For example, Allen N. Berger and Timothy H. Hannan, "Using Efficiency Measures to Distinguish among Alternative Explanations of the Structure-Performance Relationship in Banking," *Managerial Finance* (1991): 6–31; Allen N. Berger and Timothy H. Hannan, "The Efficiency Cost of Market Power in the Banking Industry: A Test of the 'Quiet Life' and Related Hypotheses," *Review of Economics and Statistics* (August 1998): 454–465.

[18]For example, Steven J. Pilloff and Stephen A. Rhoades, "Structure and Profitability in Banking Markets," *Review of Industrial Organization* (February 2002): 81–98; Steven J. Pilloff, "Multimarket Contact in Banking," *Review of Industrial Organization* (March 1999): 163–182; Stephen A. Rhoades, "Market Share Inequality, the HHI, and Other Risk Measures of the Firm-Composition of a Market," *Review of Industrial Organization* (December 1995): 657–674.

[19]Summary statistics of survey data on bank fees are reported in Board of Governors of the Federal Reserve System, *Annual Report to the Congress on Retail Fees and Services of Depository Institutions* (June 2003).

TABLE 7-7   Profitability and Efficiency of U.S. Banks by Size Class (2002)

Asset Size ($ millions)	Mean Return on Assets (as a percentage)	Mean Efficiency Ratio (as a percentage)
Less than 50	1.14	75.1
51–100	1.00	68.8
101–500	1.18	63.4
501–1,000	1.18	61.4
1,001–10,000	1.39	58.6
10,001–50,000	1.67	56.6
More than 50,000	1.46	55.7

SOURCE: Federal Reserve Board Reports of Condition and Income (Call Report).

A study of the relationship between bank size and loan rates provides evidence suggesting that large banks charge lower prices than their smaller rivals. For example, research has found a significant negative relationship between bank size and the rates charged on similar types of commercial loans.[20] However, because loan rates are frequently set to reflect the expected risk of a loan, differences in rates between large and small banks might reflect differences in the types of loans made and the types of businesses served rather than a difference in prices for a similar product. In sum, large banks clearly charge higher fees but, because they charge lower loan rates, whether they charge higher overall prices is not clear. Moreover, it is unclear whether the fees charged by the largest banks differ from those charged by other large institutions.

Although economies of scale have been found for smaller banks, little evidence has been found to support the notion that large-scale economies extend to the largest banks. The precise point at which scale economies disappear is unclear; studies have found benefits from increased size for banks with assets up to somewhere in the range of $100 million to approximately $10 billion or $25 billion.[21] Regardless of where economies of scale cease to exist, the evidence suggests that efficiency gains from economies of scale are more likely and larger for smaller banks than for the larger ones. Therefore, the banks that have been most active in the merger movement and have used acquisitions to grow substantially are unlikely to derive substantial benefits from scale economies.

Average efficiency ratios calculated from 2002 commercial bank data indicate that bank size is positively related to efficiency, but the relationship weakens with bank size (see Table 7-7), which is consistent with gains from economies of scale decreasing with bank size. The efficiency ratio, a measure commonly used by bankers and financial analysts, is calculated as total noninterest expense divided by the sum of net interest income (interest revenue less interest expense) and noninterest revenue. A lower ratio corresponds to greater efficiency. The smallest banks are the least efficient and could

---

[20]See Anthony W. Cyrnak and Timothy H. Hannan, "Is the Cluster Still Valid in Defining Banking Markets? Evidence from a New Data Source," *The Antitrust Bulletin* (Summer 1999): 313–331; David A. Carter, James E. McNulty and James A. Verbrugge, "Do Small Banks Have an Advantage in Lending? An Examination of Risk-Adjusted Yields on Business Loans at Large and Small Banks," *Journal of Financial Services* Research (April–June 2004): 233–252.

[21]For example, Allen N. Berger and Loretta J. Mester, "Inside the Black Box: What Explains Differences in the Efficiencies of Financial Institutions?" *Journal of Banking and Finance* (1997): 895–947; David B. Humphrey, "Why Do Estimates of Bank Scale Economies Differ?" *Federal Reserve Bank of Richmond Economic Review* (September–October 1990): 38–50.

benefit the most from increasing their size, all else being equal: The average ratio for that group (total banking assets of $50 million or less) was 75.1 percent, compared with 68.8 percent for banks in the next-larger size group (assets of $51 million to $100 million). Average efficiency ratios decrease over subsequent size ranges, but the decrease gets smaller as the banks in the range get larger.

Finally, large banks appear to be no better than, and possibly inferior to, smaller banks in attracting and retaining customers. One study found that from 1990 to 1996, the average market share of the approximately 50 largest banks in the industry declined somewhat in markets in which they had engaged in no mergers or acquisitions during the study period.[22] The pattern of declining market share was particularly pronounced in rural areas, but even in urban areas, where large banks maintained constant market shares, large banks demonstrated no special ability to attract customers. These results are consistent with those of other studies, which have shown that large banks are not especially successful at obtaining and holding onto market share.[23]

In summary, large banks appear to perform better than their smaller rivals. Large banks are more profitable and efficient than smaller rivals, but there is little evidence that the largest banks operate much more profitably or efficiently than other, smaller "large" banks. The evidence on pricing is mixed: Large banks charge higher fees, but they also charge lower rates on loans; moreover, it is unclear whether the fees charged by the largest banks in fact differ from those charged by banks of other sizes. Finally, the inability of large banks to grow their share of deposits in local markets is consistent with large banks not having sizable competitive advantages over smaller rivals that enable them to attract and retain customers.

Performance of Other Banks Facing Large Banks

The presence of a large bank might influence the performance of other banks in the market. In particular, if large banks have some unique influence on competition, then the presence of a large bank in a market may affect the performance of smaller, more local banks that also operate in the market. In fact, several studies suggest that large banks might lower the level of competition in markets in which they operate.

One study found that the profitability (as measured by return on assets) of small banks that operate in a single rural market in which a large bank also operates is higher than that of comparable small banks that do not compete with a large bank.[24] This finding is consistent with the idea that large banks exert a special anticompetitive influence on the market, such as disciplinary pricing. It does not support the idea that large banks with small or moderate market shares procompetitively prevent the exercise of market power by smaller banks with large market shares.

One study found that multimarket contact—the extent to which banks in a given market also compete with each other in other markets—is positively related to the

[22]Steven J. Pilloff and Stephen A. Rhoades, "Do Large, Diversified Banking Organizations Have Competitive Advantages?" *Review of Industrial* Organization (May 2000): 287–302.

[23]For example, John T. Rose and John D. Wolken, "Geographic Diversification in Banking, Market Share Changes, and the Viability of Small, Independent Banks," *Journal of Financial Services Research* (March 1990): 5–20.

[24]Steven J. Pilloff, "Does the Presence of Big Banks Influence Competition in Local Markets?" *Journal of Financial Services Research* (May 1999): 159–177. Also, see John D. Wolken and John T. Rose, "Dominant Banks, Market Power, and Out-of-Market Productive Capacity," *Journal of Economics and Business* (August 1991): 214–229.

profitability of all banks in the market.[25] This result suggests that when banks compete with each other in several markets, they might be more willing or able to act cooperatively or, alternatively, less willing to compete aggressively in any particular market for fear of retaliation in the other common markets. This lack of vigorous competition appears to influence all the banks in a market, large and small alike. However, large banks are more likely to be strongly influenced by multimarket contact because they have extensive operations in many markets and are more likely to encounter each other frequently. Therefore, competition in markets in which large banks operate is most likely to be strongly affected by multimarket contact.

V. PUBLIC POLICY

Currently, antitrust policy toward the U.S. commercial banking industry is concerned primarily with mergers, particularly with whether proposed transactions violate antitrust standards. The basic goal is to limit concentration in retail banking markets that are defined to be local in scope. The discussion in this chapter suggests that this approach is appropriate. High levels of local concentration are associated with higher prices, higher profits, and lower efficiency. Prohibiting transactions that would result in high levels of concentration appears to be an effective way of maintaining markets that are sufficiently competitive that customers have adequate choices and banks cannot sustain extremely high prices.

One issue that merits scrutiny, but which is not incorporated in current policy or is only minimally incorporated, is whether large banks have a unique effect on competition independent of their prominence (i.e., market share) in a local banking market. Key differences may exist among banks of different sizes in their behavior, performance, and effect on rivals. The issue is important because the dichotomy between the largest organizations in the industry and the many community banks is increasing as mergers create larger and larger banking firms that have substantial resources and operate over extensive geographic areas. Understanding such issues as whether large banks have unique sources of market power, and whether banks of different sizes differ substantially in their ability to operate efficiently and meet customer needs, is critical in designing and implementing an effective antitrust policy.

Another issue that warrants continued examination is the size of the relevant banking market that should be used when assessing concentration. The relevant geographic market, at least for retail banking, is considered to be local. Expanding the geographic scope of the relevant market might be increasingly appropriate, because with growing use of the Internet and other advanced technologies, banks might be able to serve customers without having a nearby physical presence. If customers can complete all banking transactions through alternative delivery channels and are comfortable doing so, then retail banking markets may not be limited to local areas. However, until customers feel more comfortable about establishing and maintaining a relationship with a bank that does not have a nearby physical presence, technological advances will not effectively extend the borders of retail banking markets. Determining the appropriate size of

---

[25]Steven J. Pilloff, "Multimarket Contact in Banking," *Review of Industrial Organization* (March 1999): 163–182. Also, see Gary W. Whalen, "Nonlocal Concentration, Multimarket Linkages, and Interstate Banking," *The Antitrust Bulletin* (Summer 1996): 365–397.

banking markets is an important issue that could have a substantial effect on antitrust policy, because, if markets were enlarged, fewer mergers would likely raise serious competitive concerns.

A controversial issue in banking for many small customers involves the ATM surcharge fee, which is imposed when a customer of a given bank uses an ATM that is not owned by that bank. The fee is levied by the ATM owner and is charged directly to the ATM user in addition to any other fees imposed by the ATM user's bank. Paying this fee leads many consumers to feel that they are being gouged by ATM operators and forced to pay unfairly to access their own money. Public outrage has been so vehement that some areas have attempted to ban banks from imposing ATM surcharges. Banks contend that they are simply charging a fair price for providing consumers with the ability to access their deposits and that consumers who do not want to pay a surcharge fee can avoid the fee by accessing their accounts through a different channel.

In addition to consumer issues, the ATM surcharge fee also raises antitrust issues. In particular, large banks, which tend to own numerous ATMs located over an extensive area, may be able to use surcharge fees to encourage customers of small banks to switch to larger banks. One way that small bank customers can avoid surcharges is to switch to a larger bank with more widely distributed ATMs. In this manner, customers can increase the likelihood that an ATM owned by their bank will be conveniently located wherever they need or want cash.

Illegal tying is an issue that has increased in importance since the enactment in 1999 of the Gramm-Leach-Bliley Act, which enables banks to expand their range of financial services offerings. With certain exceptions, banks are prohibited by federal law from making the purchase of one product or service a requirement for the purchase of another product or service. Although the removal of many restrictions on the activities of firms engaged in banking has increased opportunities for firms to provide multiple products to customers, it also has increased opportunities for banks to strong-arm customers into buying unwanted products in order to obtain necessary ones. The potential problem is most severe when banks possess substantial market power in a particular product market. Tying has received a lot of attention recently, and bank regulators are attempting to clarify what constitutes illegal tying, with the Federal Reserve Board expected to issue a ruling sometime in 2004.

Conclusion

Commercial banking is one of the largest and most important industries in the United States. A substantial portion of businesses and households rely on commercial banks as their primary source of credit and as a safe and convenient place to keep cash. Since 1990, the industry has been affected by a number of developments—mainly mergers and acquisitions but, to a lesser extent, failures and new formations—that have transformed the industry but that have not substantially affected competition. Although the industry has experienced a large decline in the number of banks and an associated emergence of larger banks that control more of the industry, the evidence is mixed regarding whether substantial size enables large banks to influence competition. Moreover, although competition may be affected by increased market concentration at the local level, changes in (and levels of) average concentration since 1990 do not indicate that mergers have resulted in substantially less competition during this period.

In future years, banks should continue to be the primary providers of financial services to many American households and businesses. Moreover, the industry is likely to experience further structural change as consolidation, regulatory reforms, and technological developments take place at a rapid pace. Therefore, identifying relevant markets and understanding the key factors that influence competition in those markets will continue to be an important element of effective public policy.

Suggested Readings

Adams, Robert M. 2002. "Retail Commercial Banking: An Industry in Transition." In *Industry Studies*, edited by Larry L. Duetsch, 3rd edition, Armonk, NY: M.E. Sharpe, 170–193.

Berger, Allen N., Rebecca S. Demsetz, and Philip E. Strahan. 1999. "The Consolidation of the Financial Services Industry: Causes, Consequences, and Implications for the Future."*Journal of Banking and Finance* (February): 135–194.This paper is in a special edition of the journal in which many other interesting articles on the consolidation of the financial services industry appear.

Edwards, Corwin D. 1955. "Conglomerate Bigness as a Source of Market Power." In *Business Concentration and Price Policy,* Princeton, NJ: Princeton University Press, 331–359.

Group of Ten. 2001. *Report on Consolidation in the Financial Sector*.

Rhoades, Stephen A. 1993. "Commercial Banking: Two Industries, a Laboratory for Research." In *Industry Studies*, edited by Larry L. Duetsch, Englewood Cliffs, NJ: Prentice Hall, 271–305.

Shull, Bernard, and Gerald A. Hanweck. 2001. *Bank Mergers in a Deregulated Environment: Promise and Peril.* Westport, CT: Quorum Books.

Sinkey, Joseph F. 2002. *Commercial Bank Financial Management in the Financial-Service Industry.* Upper Saddle River, NJ: Prentice Hall. Chapter 19 provides a helpful discussion of consolidation.

CHAPTER

8

Telecommunications

—JAMES McCONNAUGHEY[1]

At the dawn of the twenty-first century, American telecommunications bandwidth occupies a role of critical importance. Bandwidth measures communications carrying capacity to deliver voice, data, video, and text to the end user. The United States is in the throes of a bandwidth crosscurrent. In one market, bandwidth is so plentiful that a capacity glut may well lead to a precipitous drop in transmission prices. In another market, a bandwidth shortage threatens to impose a limit on the quantity and diversity of information. The first market is the U.S. long-distance market; the second is the U.S. local telephone market.

The characteristics of each market differ markedly. The long-distance market is relatively open, invites market entry, and resides in an environment of de facto deregulation. Innovation in long-distance facilities and bandwidth proceeds at a furious pace. The local telephone market, by contrast, is dominated by firms that are enjoying monopolist status. Rivalry in this market is at best stunted, entry remains episodic, and government regulation stands as an institutional reality. The local exchange market rests upon some 270 million lines of copper wire—about 80 percent of all such "local loops" today—that connect telephone central office switches to a customer's home or office. The technology of twisted copper wire has changed little over the past 110 years.

It is the local telephone market—the copper wire pair—that emerges as a bandwidth bottleneck in today's economy, and it is local telecommunications that has invited the attention of Congress, regulatory agencies, and Internet users. That the local telephone monopoly is now a top policy priority is illustrated by the following questions: How can the United States promote competition in a market that is concentrated? How can public policy modernize telephone investment to accommodate an apparently insatiable demand for information bandwidth? Which industry should be allowed to compete in local telephony: Line resellers? Equipment suppliers? Long-distance carriers? Cable television firms? Electric power companies? Wireless operators? Suppliers of aerospace hardware? Internet service providers?

Is the current clamor for alternatives to the copper wire based on a technological imperative, or does local telephony constitute the essence of a natural monopoly? If so, does local telephony call for more rather than less regulatory oversight? If the former, which government agency should exercise that oversight: a city, a county, a state, or the U.S. government? How can the public resolve an inevitable jurisdictional clash between state and federal agencies?

[1]The views expressed in this chapter are those of the author and do not necessarily represent the views of the Commerce Department. This writing has benefited immensely from the insights of my former collaborator, Manley R. Irwin, Emeritus Professor of Economics at the University of New Hampshire's Whittemore School of Business and student *extraordinaire* of the eminent Walter Adams.

In the final analysis, bandwidth capacity is not merely a question of more or less, but rather it is an issue of economic incentives. Which institutional setting best delivers future electronic goods and services to the firm and consumer: a competitive market, a regulated market, or admixtures of both? Whatever choice is selected, that policy option will surely configure a twenty-first century online economy. First though, what has the United States inherited from its telecommunications past?

I. HISTORY

Telecommunications over the past 130 years has traversed four somewhat loosely defined stages: monopoly (1876–1894); competition/regulation (1894–1920), monopoly/regulation/antitrust (1920–1956), and antitrust/divestiture (1956–present).

Monopoly

Consider the first stage—monopoly (1876–1894). The filing of two telephone patents on the same day of the same year presents an event that is unique in economic history.[2] Suffice it to say that Alexander Graham Bell's patent prevailed over Elisha Gray's filing. The Boston Bell Patent Association, now in possession of a valuable property right, offered to sell the patent to the largest communication firm in the country—the Western Union Telegraph Company. Western Union management rejected the offer on the grounds that the $100,000 asking price was exorbitant. Today's students of corporate history generally agree that the Western Union Telegraph Company committed a commercial blunder of the first order.

To generate a return on its investment, the Boston Bell Patent Association was forced to offer telephone service to the public. Service commenced in Boston, Massachusetts, and the association assigned franchises in separate, exclusive geographic markets—especially heavily populated cities. In 1878, the Boston Bell Patent Association hired a young manager from the United States Postal Service, Theodore Vail, who took a 50 percent cut in salary and accepted the assignment to convert a telephone patent into a viable commercial venture.

Recognizing its mistake, Western Union gave a research contract to the Thomas Edison laboratory to develop a rival telephone instrument. The Western Union Telegraph Company proceeded to establish a telephone subsidiary, the Home Telephone Company, but Vail was not intimidated by his $50 million rival. In fact, he took the offensive and charged Western Union with patent infringement. Vail not only threatened a patent suit, he pledged that Bell would enter the telegraph market. The mouse roared; the lion blinked. Western Union agreed to withdraw from the voice market and to sell its operating subsidiary to Bell. Vail, in turn, renounced any intention of offering telegraph service. Historians mark the 1879 cartel agreement as the "Magna Carta" of the telephone industry.

Within the next 6 years, Vail put in place the foundation of what was to become known as the Bell System by issuing exclusive franchises to prospective telephone

---

[2]The situation may be even more remarkable than we thought: Recent reports state that a German science teacher may have invented a crude but working "telephon" some 13 years before Dr. Bell in 1863. "Telephone's Real Inventor in Doubt," *Discovery News* (December 9, 2003) http://dsc.discovery.com/news-/briefs/20031208/bell_print.html. Accessed May 7, 2004.

companies. Although Bell assumed an equity stake in each operating company, each company raised its own capital. In 1881, Bell acquired Western Electric Company, a manufacturer that had supplied telegraph equipment to Western Union, and assigned it a license to manufacture telephone apparatus under the Bell patent. Then in 1885, Vail established a company that connected long-distance or toll lines to Bell's local telephone operations. The new American Bell Telephone Company provided local and long-distance service to customers or, in telephone parlance, its subscribers.

For reasons that are not entirely clear, Vail left the company in the late 1880s. By then, the American Bell Company had gone public, the stock was performing well, and Vail was an individual of considerable wealth. However, he did not rest. He became a roving capitalist and started traction and electric power companies in Europe and South America. With his telephone holdings, Vail purchased a retirement farm in Vermont.

The basic Bell patent expired in 1894. Though market entry became the order of the day, the company's structure was positioned to deal with competition. The company was horizontally integrated, vertically tied between long-distance and local service, and vertically connected between telephone service and the manufacture of telephone equipment. In place, too, were the company's policies and practices. For one thing, the company did not sell Bell's telephone instrument; rather, the subscriber leased basic phone service. (At one time, Bell headquarters would not permit individual Bell affiliates to take ownership of the telephone handset.) Bell refused to make its long-distance lines available to competing telephone companies. The result of American Bell's policies was that a non-Bell customer required two phones, one for local calls and one for toll or long-distance calls. To save money, a subscriber could lease a Bell instrument that permitted both local and toll calls. One by one, independent telephone companies found the logic of selling out to Bell compelling.

Competition/Regulation

Bell's patent expiration did foster the growth of independent, or non-Bell, phone companies, particularly in rural areas of the United States. The expiration also saw the rise of independent or non–Western Electric suppliers in the manufacturing market. Thus began an era of telephone competition. The results were predictable: Telephone rates dropped, usage increased, and productivity surged. By the turn of the century, Bell— now known as the American Telephone and Telegraph Company, or simply AT&T— saw its market share reduced to about half of the telephone service in the United States.

By the early 1900s, the J.P. Morgan Company acquired an equity stake in AT&T and prevailed upon Theodore Vail, at that point retired on his Vermont farm, to assume AT&T leadership. Once again, Vail's signature proved indelible. He instituted a personnel meritocracy, cut costs, improved service quality, pushed long-distance facilities to the West Coast, and acquired his old nemesis—the Western Union Telegraph Company. Under Vail, AT&T continued to buy independent telephone companies, denied toll access to local rivals, leased—did not sell—telephone instruments to subscribers, and purchased equipment almost exclusively from its Western Electric subsidiary for Bell operating companies.

Vail also possessed the gift of foresight. He was cognizant that telephone handsets, central office exchanges, and transmission lines had competitive substitutes. Marconi's vacuum tube radio in particular posed a threat to AT&T's investment in wire and cable. By 1910, Vail had centralized AT&T's research activities, laying the groundwork for what was to become a world-renowned private laboratory—Bell Telephone Laboratory.[3]

Vail was aware of public sentiment, if not hostility, toward big business "trusts" as they were called at the turn of the century. The government-driven breakup of the American Tobacco Company and the Standard Oil Companies loomed large on the corporate scene; when AT&T's Western Union purchase was challenged by the U.S. government, Vail deferred to the government and divested the Western Union Telegraph Company from Bell ownership. Vail nevertheless remained convinced that competition in telephony was unworkable. The telephone industry, he maintained, was a "natural" monopoly.

The European response to natural monopoly—nationalization—appeared straightforward enough, and Vail knew that the U.S. Postal Service under the Woodrow Wilson administration coveted AT&T ownership. Vail responded by observing that there was little difference between a private or a public monopoly. Both, in his opinion, remained unaccountable to the consumer. Vail's response to natural monopoly was regulation, government oversight, and a public watchdog—not unlike that of the Interstate Commerce Commission (ICC) in transportation.

Exhorted by the Bell telephone companies, Congress in 1910 amended the Interstate Commerce Commission Act to extend the ICC's jurisdiction over interstate telephone service. The Bell System supported legislation to extend state commission oversight to telephone services and facilities. Populists and monopolists found common cause in a mandate for "universal telephone service" to the public at large.

To solicit, indeed welcome, government regulation was regarded as corporate heresy in the early years of the 1900s. Nevertheless, Vail insisted that a government board, not unlike a jury, would monitor AT&T's service, rates, investments, and earnings. Vail said that his company must tell the truth about itself or someone else would.[4] However, regulatory due process carried a bonus; it immunized a telephone monopoly firm from antitrust assault. The result was that AT&T was to become the largest corporation in U.S. history.

Monopoly/Regulation/Antitrust

U.S. telephony grew and prospered over the next 40 years. In the 1920s, AT&T merged the research and development work of Western Electric and AT&T to form a single research entity, Bell Telephone Laboratories. AT&T also moved into broadcast radio, employing telephone lines to link the company's radio network as far west as Nebraska. Then the Bell System reversed itself and sold its broadcasting operations to RCA in the mid-1920s. Western Electric sold off its European operations to International Telephone and Telegraph (ITT) in order to concentrate on supplying the domestic equipment needs of the Bell operating companies. AT&T not only survived the Great Depression but continued its $9 dividend, a revenue flow so reliable that the company's stock was viewed as a bedrock investment for widows and orphans.

Franklin D. Roosevelt's New Deal inaugurated a series of alphabet agencies: the FPC, SEC, CAB, and FCC. The latter, the Federal Communications Commission was assigned

---

[3]John Brooks, *Telephone: The First Hundred Years* (New York: Harper and Row, 1975), 129.
[4]Ibid., 143.

interstate telephone regulatory oversight. The commission's first major investigation probed AT&T's control of buyers and sellers of telephone equipment. Were such internal transactions, asked the commission, in the interest of the telephone consumer? AT&T obviously said yes, but the commission's staff wasn't so sure. A task force recommended that the FCC seek legislative authority over Western Electric's sales, prices, and earnings. Too radical even for the New Deal, the proposal was dropped in 1939. By then, foreign policy began to supersede U.S. domestic issues as the clouds of another war descended over Europe.

Pearl Harbor brought World War II to the United States, and AT&T, the Bell Telephone Laboratories, and Western Electric made important contributions to the nation's defense effort. By 1946, the war was over and the FCC wrestled with a postwar development: to bring a new signal, television, to homes.

Then, in 1949, another antitrust shoe dropped. The Justice Department charged that AT&T's ownership of an unregulated supply affiliate (Western Electric) violated section 2 of the Sherman Antitrust law, which prohibits monopolization of trade. In 1956, the suit was settled by the Eisenhower administration through a consent decree between plaintiff and defendant. AT&T agreed to open its patent portfolio to all users and to confine its activities to regulated telephone service. Under the agreement, Western Electric was to remain part of the Bell System. The decree was not without controversy, however. The government claimed victory, and AT&T's response was somewhat muted. From Bell's perspective, Vail's structure had been preserved; the institution of private monopoly and regulation was once again validated.

Antitrust/Divestiture

The next 28 years of the Bell System proved equally tumultuous. For one thing, regulators at the federal level began to question the underlying premise of AT&T's structure and policies. Worse, AT&T found itself caught in a crossfire between government antitrust and public utility regulation. Market entry into telephony clearly violated the premise of natural monopoly, and it came from none other than the FCC, often aided by the courts.

This was but a first step. By the 1970s, the FCC had ruled that subscribers could attach their own telephone sets to the Bell System's lines, that new firms could enter private interstate long-distance markets, that satellite communications companies could operate within the domestic United States, and that firms could lease and resell Bell's telephone circuits to end users.

Those decisions, a break from past practices, were opposed vigorously by AT&T and state public utility commissions (PUCs). AT&T protested that entry would thwart economies of scale, raise telephone rates, degrade service quality, and compromise the integrity of the best communications system in the world. AT&T took its case to Congress, where it sponsored the Consumer Communications Reform Act, legislation that, if enacted, would sanction telephone mergers, ban market entry, block competitive substitutes, and reverse the procompetitive policies of the FCC. AT&T's legislative effort failed.

AT&T's response to market entry also had an unintended effect: It elicited private antitrust action. Soon some dozen firms filed complaints in the courts. In November 1974, the Justice Department filed an antitrust complaint alleging that AT&T had blocked the entry of suppliers of telephone service, foreclosed telephone equipment manufacturers from selling to the Bell operating companies, stalled competitors' private branch exchanges (PBXs) from plugging into Bell's networks, and orchestrated a Bell System response to deny local circuits to AT&T's long-distance competitors.

Nor was the department's proposed solution inconsequential. It sought horizontal and vertical divestiture of AT&T, which amounted to a dismemberment of the Bell System in the tradition of the Standard Oil breakup. Although the Bell System found an ally in the U.S. Department of Defense, President Reagan's attorney general insisted that AT&T had manipulated the regulatory process to perpetuate its telephone monopoly. Perhaps more distressing, the suit challenged AT&T's conviction that public utility regulation superseded the nation's antitrust laws. AT&T argued that the company was subject to oversight by 50 state commissions, and its practices and tariffs were sanctioned and approved by those regulatory bodies. Assistant Attorney General Baxter served notice that he would litigate the case to "his eye balls." The government presented its brief before a district court in Washington, D.C. After the plaintiff's case was concluded, AT&T asked that the suit be dropped. However, Judge Harold Greene wrote that the department's brief was not without merit and that AT&T indeed might have violated the nation's antitrust laws.

In January 1982, the parties reached a historic agreement. AT&T agreed to divest its 23 Bell operating companies and to reconstitute them as 7 independent Regional Bell Operating Companies (RBOCs): NYNEX, Bell Atlantic, BellSouth, Ameritech, Pacific Telesis, Southwestern Bell, and US West. Restructured along geographical areas, the operating companies were to confine their activities to local, intrastate telephone services. AT&T retained Western Electric and Bell Laboratories and continued to provide interstate long-distance service to the public. The agreement took effect in January 1984.

AT&T would reimburse local telephone companies—the RBOCs—for the use of local telephone facilities (the "loop" in telephone parlance). Known as an access charge, this payment would ensure that local telephone service would remain affordable to the public at large. Put differently, a universal service support system required that business users subsidize residential subscribers, and that urban subscribers contribute to the telephone bills of rural users. In essence, users in competitive toll markets subsidized consumers in noncompetitive local markets.

The fourth stage of telecommunications experienced the rise of the online computer. A legacy of World War II, the computer was devised to enable the Army Corps of Engineers to calculate artillery tables. Unlike a voice or analog signal, the computer generated digital signals that were transmitted over telephone lines. By the 1950s, computers began to be used in commercial applications such as the generation of payrolls, accounts receivable, and sales data. Later, the intercontinental missile spurred the development of a U.S. early warning system across the north pole. Radar dishes scanned the sky for intruders, fed information into computers, and relayed signals via telephone lines to the United States. The digital signal, modulated as an analog tone for line transmission, was then reconstituted at U.S. Air Force headquarters. National defense needs sired the modulation–demodulation unit, known as the modem, as a device to accommodate a digital signal. AT&T's tariffs, known as the Sage Network, were duly approved by the FCC.

Thermonuclear missiles raised the possibility of electromagnetic bursts capable of knocking out telephone circuits within the continental United States; the Department of

Defense launched studies to address that potential threat. A Rand scientist, Dr. Paul Baran, proposed to assemble binary signals into packets routed through computers over many different telephone lines.[5] Reconstituted as a message at the receiver's terminal, packet switching was designed for digital transmission. In the 1960s, computers permitted remote users to access the arithmetic and memory of a mainframe computer. Sponsored by the Defense Department, computer terminal sharing suggested the possibility of distributed information processing not unlike that of an electricity utility—a computer utility.

In the mid-1960s, an FCC docket asked whether the U.S. analog telephone system could accommodate the impending needs of digital traffic. Did telephone rates and policies comport with growing use of online computers? Was telephone company investment responsive to the imperatives of a digital world?[6] The telephone industry's answer to the FCC's computer inquiry was reassuring: The computer required no fundamental change in the industry's regulation, investment, prices, or subscriber policies.[7] There was one exception: Subscribers could attach computers to phone lines via a modem provided by the telephone company.

The rapid pace of the advancement of technology since then has kept public policy makers busy. Technological change successively made obsolete the FCC's rulings in the original (1970) "Computer I" inquiry and "Computer II" inquiry (early 1980s). The "Computer III" inquiry (latter 1980s and the post-AT&T divestiture period generally) still stands but has been revised frequently to accommodate new technological, political, and legal realities. The attempts to draw a bright line between unregulated computers and regulated telephone service proved frustrating as commissions continually searched for an optimum mix of regulation and market forces.

In the 1980s, the personal computer (PC), born in a California garage, gained legitimacy when IBM and other suppliers entered the PC market. If the 1980s heralded the personal computer era, the 1990s were to become the era of the Internet. The Department of Defense's Advanced Research Products Agency network linked university computers over copper wire bandwidth. The introduction of a graphic user interface (icons and graphic signals) required larger bandwidth—more than the 56 kilobits per capacity of local telephone loops.[8] Copper wire was beginning to impose a limit on computer access speed.

Today, the computer is the driving force behind long-distance fiber networks. Internet speed, nevertheless, is constrained by copper wire loop capacity; the local telephone line surfaced as an issue of public policy in the 1990s. Congress passed the Telecommunications Act of 1996 in an attempt to address local loop congestion.[9] The act promised Regional Bell Operating Companies entry into the long-distance market if competition were introduced into the local telephone market. The legislation represented a landmark endeavor to convert a monopoly market into a competitive market—to alter, in short, the structure of the telephone industry. It is to such structural matters that we now turn.

---

[5]Wilson Dizard, *MegaNet: How the Global Communications Network Will Connect Everyone on Earth* (Boulder, CO: Westview Press, 1997), 146.

[6]Before the Federal Communications Commission, Docket No. 16979, In the Matter of Regulatory and Policy Problems Presented by the Interdependence of Computer and Communication Services and Facilities, Notice of Inquiry, November 10, 1966.

[7]Stuart Matheson and Philip Walker, *Computers and Telecommunications: Issues in Public Policy* (Upper Saddle River, NJ: Prentice Hall, 1970), 153; Appendix C, 242–243.

[8]Comments of Philip J. Sirlin, Schroder & Co., in "Cable Industry," Wall Street Transcript (March 1, 1999): 8.

[9]Dick W. Olufs, *The Making of Telecommunications Policy* (Boulder, CO: Lynne Rienner, 1999), 135.

II. MARKET STRUCTURE

Market structure includes elements of demand, supply, and entry barriers in long-distance and local exchange markets.

Demand

As a derived demand, U.S. buyers consume about $300 billion worth of telecommunication services annually. Of that total, local service revenues account for $125 billion; long distance accounts for almost $100 billion.[10] Cellular and other wireless phone services, which represent a mix of local and long-distance minutes, add another $75 billion, having more than doubled in size since the end of the 1990s—a veritable technological revolution.[11] The divide between voice and data traffic suggests another shift in buyers' tastes and preferences: Whereas voice traffic experiences single-digit growth, nonvoice or data traffic demand increases at some 200 percent per year. Internet demand, a subset of data traffic, is estimated to increase by 500 percent annually.[12]

That the Internet ushers in a new era is seen by the following:

- Eighty percent of Internet traffic is driven by electronic commerce among business firms.
- The Intel Corporation states that its online microprocessor sales now total $1 billion per month.
- Cisco (Internet switches and routers) estimates that 80 percent of its sales are Internet driven.
- Dell computer (personal computers) observes that half of its PC sales originate on the Internet.
- GE's Internet has cut procurement cycles in half and processing costs by a third.
- Amazon (books, music, etc.) sales on the Web are growing at 33 percent per year, and now exceed $5 billion annually.
- U.S. e-commerce revenues are expected to surpass $1 trillion in 2004.

Electronic commerce (e-commerce) is beginning to assume a generic pattern. First, a firm adopts the Internet to multiply customer access and to achieve cost economies. To secure a first mover advantage, the firm reassesses its value chain and outsources high-cost activities. The firm's suppliers, no longer perceived as adversaries, tie their computers to their customer's database, quickening response time to consumer demand. Some e-commerce firms mandate that supplier operations be located within 15 minutes of final assembly lines. Greater transaction economies are passed forward to the customer as reduced prices.

The Internet, by direct access, permits a firm to circumvent traditional marketing or sales channels. Banks, for example, engage in online financial transactions and can bypass a rival's investment in brick and mortar. Online brokerage services today challenge conventional investment houses; an online MBA program can reach students beyond a traditional university classroom. Geography no longer protects or insulates.

Web sites enable a firm to compress response time to buyers' shifting tastes. Ford Motor Company, for example, links 120 design engines worldwide, permitting a 24-hour

---

[10]FCC, Telecommunications Industry Revenues 2001, Table 2.
[11]Cellular Telecommunications & Internet Association. See www.wow-com.com/market_research/. Accessed April 14, 2004.
[12]Reinhardt Krause, "Web Weaving Its Way through Telecom Industry," *Investor's Business Daily* (June 9, 1999): A4.

design cycle.[13] Toyota claims it can deliver a customized car to a customer in 5 days. Once a firm enjoys an Internet-competitive advantage, rivals are sure to follow. Competitors have little choice. Failure to do so can prove traumatic. In an online environment, nouns become adverbs, such as *Amazoned* or *Delled.* (Ford Motor Company's Brazilian experiment to outsource its manufacturing activities has prompted use of the phrase *Ford Amazon.*)[14]

That e-commerce occurs within an environment of accelerating change is seen in the observation of Jack Welch, former CEO of General Electric: The Internet, he said, represents "the greatest change in business in [his] lifetime."[15] The president of Intel commented that "all companies will be Internet companies or they won't be companies at all."[16] Market pressure fuels the adoption of e-commerce in the United States and throughout the world. It is estimated that 90 percent of the global bandwidth was carrying Internet traffic by the year 2003.[17] Bandwidth now constitutes the new paradigm. (See Figure 8-1.)

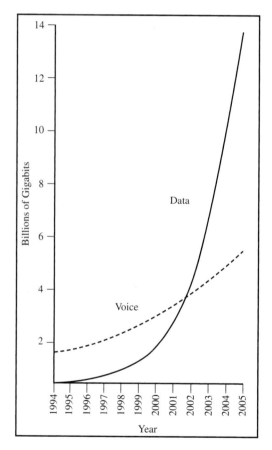

FIGURE 8-1   U.S. Long Distance Traffic

SOURCE: Fortune, 13 October 1997, 112. © Time Inc. Reprinted by permission.

---

[13]Ira Brudsky, "The Case against Making Money the Old Fashioned Way," *Network World* (May 3, 1999): 47.
[14]"Internet Anxiety," *Business Week* (June 28, 1999): 86; Tim Burt, "Ford to Farm out Key Final Assembly Jobs to Contractor," *Financial Times* (August 4, 1999): 1.
[15]Matt Murray, "GE Now Views Internet as Crucial to New Growth," *Wall Street Journal* (June 23, 1999): 15.
[16]Matthew Benjamin, "Surf's Up: International Network Services Prepares to Ride Data Traffic Tidal Water," *Investor's Business Daily* (June 29, 1999): A9.
[17]Thomas Bonnett, Telewars in the States: Telecommunications Issues in a New Era of Competition (Washington, D.C.: Council of Governors Policies Advisors, 1996), 19.

Supply

Long-Distance Market Shares

The $99 billion U.S. long-distance, or toll, market is dominated by three firms, with hundreds of providers sharing the rest of the field. The approximate market shares (based on 2001 long-distance carrier revenues) are depicted in Table 8-1.

MCI struggled for 6 years to enter the market, beginning in 1963. It prospered but was acquired by WorldCom Incorporated in 1997 for $20 billion. Beset by accounting irregularities and other mismanagement, WorldCom spiraled into bankruptcy but has recently reemerged as MCI, reorganized and with $35 billion of its debt eliminated.[18] Sprint, a Midwestern company, has pushed fiber optics transmission, operates a long-distance service, and has moved aggressively into wireless communications. MCI WorldCom, outbidding BellSouth, announced its intent to acquire Sprint but was discouraged in 2000 by a skeptical Justice Department; now, a resilient BellSouth has reportedly made serious overtures to an attentive AT&T.[19] Bursting onto the scene in recent years, wireless carriers as a group garnered about one out of every five long-distance dollars in 2001.

Long-Distance Market Entry

Though classified as a loose oligopoly, the long-distance market has experienced a rash of start-up firms, with corporations investing in high-speed data routers, fast switches, and optical fiber links.

Six companies (Qwest, Global Crossing, Frontier, Williams, IXC, and Level 3) entered the "backbone" toll market several years ago, although some have experienced financial difficulties in recent years. Other firms on the market's edge include the aerospace industry. Even electric power companies are exploring the potential of broadband telecommunications supply. In 2002, more than 1,000 firms identified themselves as toll carriers in the United States.

This entry pattern suggests that traditional market barriers might not be as formidable as they have been over past decades. Scale economies have traditionally been thought

TABLE 8-1 Long-Distance Market Shares	
AT&T	34.2%
MCI	21.4%
Sprint	8.5%
Wireless carriers	21.8%
All other long-distance carriers	14.1%
Total	100.0%

SOURCE: Federal Communications Commission, Trends in Telephone Service, August 2003, Table 9.8 (2001 data).

---

[18] "MCI Ready for Post-WorldCom Life," *Washington Post* (November 1, 2003): E1.
[19] "Is BellSouth Just Window Shopping?" *Business Week* (November 5, 2001), 102; Shawn Young and Almar Latour, "BellSouth–AT&T Talks Face Hurdles," *Wall Street Journal* (October 27, 2003). www.online.wsj.com. Accessed April 14, 2004.

to pose a hurdle to long-distance entry. Apparently, that constraint has diminished as entrants perceive incumbent carrier investment as a handicap rather than an asset to bandwidth efficiency.

Certainly, one constraint that can give pause to any firm pondering market entry is the absolute size of the incumbent corporation. However, in U.S. long distance, neither market share nor corporate assets appears to have arrested the entry process. Government regulation for many years in the twentieth century constituted a barrier to market access. However, federal regulation of toll carriers today is largely benign.

A notable exception concerns the Regional Bell Operating Companies. Section 271 of the Telecommunications Act of 1996 permits RBOCs to supply "in-region" long-distance service, as long as a number of obligations are met. These requirements encompass the establishment of interconnection agreements that comply with a 14-point competitive checklist, such as nondiscriminatory access to RBOC network elements and unbundling of certain functions for use by competitors. The act authorizes the FCC to judge whether the applicants have met these standards. RBOCs have now been permitted to offer long-distance services in almost all their respective home markets and could present significant rivalry to incumbent toll carriers.[20]

Moreover, the burgeoning use of e-mail by Americans and attractive offerings of "free" long-distance minutes as part of bundled-service wireless calling plans already have made inroads into long-distance revenues, thereby also reducing the primary base on which the national universal service system assesses contributions from carriers.[21]

Beyond labor, capital, and administrative expenses, long-distance firms incur other expenses, namely an access charge of 4 cents per minute for local loop facilities and a contribution to a universal service fund that includes an education or e-rate assessment used to support telecom purchases by public schools and libraries, as well as support for Internet access by rural health care providers. Such costs are currently borne by interstate carriers and their customers under the aegis of the FCC.

Competitive substitutes, such as Internet Protocol (IP) telephone services, pose a real alternative to switched voice service. Tied to the Internet, a PC in one location can send a packetized voice message to another PC. Internet service providers (ISPs) deliver "voice" as data transmission. The Telecommunications Act of 1996 exempted Internet traffic from local telephone access charges. Clearly, telephone users are attracted to IP cost savings: One company reports that its telephone bill between its New Jersey and Dallas offices dropped from $2,500 per month to "pennies on the dollar."[22] The head of AT&T Labs compared IP to "Pac-Man—it will eventually eat everything in its way."[23]

---

[20]See www.fcc.gov/Bureaus/Common_Carrier/in-region_applications/. Accessed April 14, 2004.

[21]Federal Communications Commission, "Federal Communications Commission Adopts Interim Measures to Maintain Universal Service Fund," news release, December 13, 2002.

[22]James DeTar, "Hearing a Pin Drop in Cyberspace, Phone Carriers Use Internet More," *Investor's Business Daily* (June 6, 1999): A6; "Telecommunications: Prognosis 1999," *Business Week* (January 11, 1999): 99.

[23]Peter Grant and Almar Latour, "Battered Telecoms Face New Challenge: Internet Calling," *Wall Street Journal* (October 9, 2003). www.online.wsj.com. Accessed April 14, 2004.

Indeed, AT&T and several other firms launched "voice over IP" (VOIP) services at the end of 2003. The import of VOIP and other Internet-based services has not been lost on the FCC: The commission held a VOIP forum in December 2003 and then launched a landmark proceeding to examine this "challenge to established technological, market, and regulatory structures of our analog past."[24]

The RBOCs view IP telephony as a threat as well as an opportunity. Fearing financial bypass around their loop plant investment, BellSouth and QWEST (formerly US West) in the late 1990s imposed a local access charge on Internet service providers offering IP phone service—a charge that implies that thousands of ISPs may fall under the category of long-distance telephone companies.[25]

More recently, BellSouth announced its plan to deploy a form of IP telephone technology, initially to businesses in the Southeast.[26] In addition, QWEST's CEO, reacting to a recent court decision in Minnesota barring that state's PUC from regulating service provider Vonage's IP offering, declared that his firm would soon enter that market. His rationale was that it "might just be the opportunity to break up the massive regulatory logjam that exists today."[27] In the meantime, ISPs now solicit customers by giving away personal computers or rescinding monthly lease charges, or by offering alluringly low rates.

Local Telecommunications

Unlike toll telecommunications, barriers to market entry in local telephone service remain formidable. The local loop plant traditionally has embodied the essence of a natural monopoly, and few communities or towns would let dozens of firms tear up streets in the name of consumer choice. State commissions, seemingly embracing the natural monopoly concept as equivalent to the public interest, have historically erected barriers to local market entry. A firm contemplating offering local telephone service typically must obtain a license of public convenience and necessity, and must receive the "eligible telecommunications carrier" designation before it can draw from the pool of universal service support monies. Entry in the local arena has not been for the faint of heart.

A second barrier to local competition hinges on matters of plant depreciation schedules. Regulatory officials reasoned that stretching plant economic life (i.e., outside wire) to 25 years would result in low annual depreciation expenses. Low expenses translated into reduced monthly telephone bills to the consumer but also distorted price and investment signals for potential entrants.

A third entry barrier derived from a policy brokered between state and federal regulatory agencies. Over time, long-distance costs declined, but local telephone costs increased. State commissions solicited a revenue contribution from long-distance customers to subsidize local service. Prior to the breakup of the Bell System, this toll subsidy was subsumed within a complex cost-separations process. After the breakup, the toll subsidy was recycled as an access charge levied upon long-distance subscribers using a

---

[24]Federal Communications Commission, "FCC to Begin Internet Telephony Proceedings," news release, November 6, 2003.

[25]"Telecommunications: Prognosis 1999," *Business Week* (January 11, 1999): 99.

[26]"Battered Telecoms Face New Challenge: Internet Calling."

[27]"QWEST to Pursue VOIP Services; CEO Cites Regulatory Vacuum," *TR Daily* (November 4, 2003). www.tr.com/newsletters/trd (available only with paid subscription). Accessed April 14, 2004.

local carrier's wire. The result found local costs higher than local rates—a shortfall that was made up by a long-distance subsidy. Few firms would contemplate entering a local market where revenues did not cover costs.

In recent years, the FCC has adopted orders that make universal service assessments, such as those associated with access charges, more explicit and spread out more among service providers. That there remains much to do in adapting the rapidly growing interstate support system to the new realities of competition and technological change is fully grasped by the FCC, industry, and Congress.[28]

Today, the four Regional Bell Operating Companies together with GTE operate some 30,000 circuit switches and 162 million local access lines. With a plant investment of $320 billion, the RBOCs and GTE control about 87 percent of U.S. local lines.[29] Since the Bell System breakup, the RBOCs' aggregate local services market share has remained relatively stable, but AT&T's long-distance share has plummeted. (See Figure 8-2.)

The Telecommunications Act of 1996 embraced the concept of competitive local exchange carriers (CLECs) to compete with the RBOCs and independent local exchange carriers. However, competition thus far remains less than robust. RBOCs' market share reductions are modest. The FCC has found that nationwide, local service competitors such

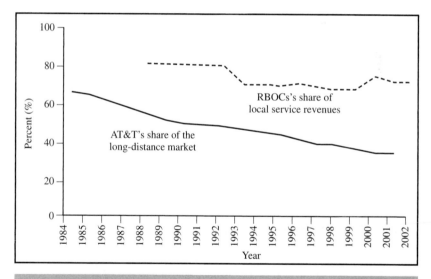

FIGURE 8-2   Share of U.S. Telephone Markets

SOURCE: Author's estimates.

---

[28]See, for example, Written Statement on Universal Service by FCC Chairman Michael K. Powell before the Senate Committee on Commerce, Science, and Transportation, October 30, 2003.

[29]Stephanie Mehta, "Locked Out: Some Bells Less Friendly than Others Toward Newcomers," *Wall Street Journal* (September 21, 1998): C8; Federal Communications Commission, Trends in Telephone Service, August 2003, Table 7.3.

as CLECs and resellers have managed to wrest only 15 percent of local service revenues from incumbent local exchange carriers. The trend has been encouraging, though: In 1997, local competitors accounted for 2.3 percent of local service revenues, meaning the total for 2002 jumped more than sixfold.[30] On the other hand, Dr. Robert Crandall of the Brookings Institution has concluded that local telephony remains concentrated because state regulators have succeeded in restricting entry into most intrastate markets.[31]

However uncertain the entry process is, CLECs and Internet service providers have had some influence on the local bandwidth market, particularly in the realm of high-speed Internet access known as broadband. CLECs have introduced digital subscriber line (DSL) equipment that multiplies bandwidth capacity to 30 times that of a regular telephone dial-up modem; cable modems offered by cable TV companies provide bandwidth capacity that exceeds that of copper wire by as much as 50 times. Other loop alternatives include fixed wireless, satellite dishes, and third-generation (3G) wireless. Most recently, a high-frequency wireless fidelity local area network (WiFi) has been catching on with consumers packing laptops at public "hot spots" such as hotels, airports, and restaurants, and with organizations that need wireless networks to augment their wire line capabilities. Cable modems have captured about two thirds of the broadband market in the United States, though RBOCs have dropped DSL prices in response.[32] Still, competitive substitutes fall short of converting much of local telephony into a "contestable" market.

Today, as the nation moves to e-commerce, the local telephone line persists as a bandwidth bottleneck. Rather than being competitive, the local market is becoming more concentrated. Horizontal merger is the culprit: Verizon, the RBOC formerly known as Bell Atlantic, for example, has acquired NYNEX and GTE. Southwestern Bell Communications (SBC) has purchased Pacific Telesis, Southern New England Telephone Company, and Ameritech. (See Table 8-2.)

Like Verizon, SBC now controls some 30 percent of all local access lines in the United States. As one SBC manager put it, "We love access lines."[33]

Cellular/Wireless Telecommunications

At the same time, the burgeoning cellular telephone business has blossomed into an arena of take-no-prisoners marketing, stiff price competition, and technological gadgetry, which also is being fueled by recent federal rules permitting local phone number portability: Effective November 24, 2003, customers could for the first time keep their existing cell phone numbers as they switched to another wireless service provider, as well as transfer their traditional landline phone numbers to wireless systems. One pundit likened these actions to a "bloody mess, [like] throwing gasoline on a fire."[34] The current structure of this segment of the telecommunications market

---

[30]FCC, Trends in Telephone Service, 2003, Table 8.7.

[31]Robert W. Crandall, "Managed Competition in U.S. Telecommunications," working paper 99-1, AE1 (Washington, D.C.: Brookings Joint Center for Regulatory Studies, March 1999), 15.

[32]See, for example, U.S. Department of Commerce, "A Nation Online: How Americans Are Expanding Their Use of the Internet," February 2002, Figure 4-1; "SBC Yahoo DSL Cuts Prices Again," CNETNews.com, September 30, 2003. www.news.com. Accessed April 14, 2004.

[33]Gautam Naik et al., "Party Line: SBC and Ameritech Send Phone Industry Loud Wake-up Call," *Wall Street Journal* (April 12, 1998): 5.

[34]Matt Richtel, "Opening Pandora's Flip Phone: New Flexibility on Cell Numbers Creates Uncertainty," *New York Times* (November 24, 2003): C1.

TABLE 8-2 Top Telecommunication Mergers

Announced	Target (country)	Acquiring Company (country)	Deal Value (in billions)
10/05/99	Sprint (U.S.)	MCI WorldCom (U.S.)	$127.27
05/11/98	Ameritech (U.S.)	SBC Comm. (U.S.)	72.36
07/28/98	GTE (U.S.)	Bell Atlantic (U.S.)	71.32
01/18/99	AirTouch Comm. (U.S.)	Vodafone Group (U.K.)	65.90
06/14/99	US West (U.S.)	Qwest Comm. (U.S.)	48.48
10/01/97	MCI Comm. (U.S.)	WorldCom (U.S.)	43.65
02/17/04	AT&T Wireless (U.S.)	Cingular (U.S.)	41.00
02/20/99	Telecom Italia (Italy)	Olivetti (Italy)	34.76
04/22/96	NYNEX (U.S.)	Bell Atlantic (U.S.)	30.79
10/19/99	Orange (U.K.)	Mannesmann (Germany)	30.00
04/01/96	Pacific Telesis (U.S.)	SBC Comm. (U.S.)	22.42

SOURCE: *Wall Street Journal*, 20 October 1999, A23; *New York Times*, 18 February 2004, C1.

features six major mobile phone companies, accounting for more than 80 percent of U.S. cell phone users (see Table 8-3); the number of leading firms in this field may fall to five, if the recently-announced merger between AT&T Wireless and Cingular is permitted by regulatory agencies. Interestingly, incumbent local exchange carriers have major holdings in some of these companies. For example, the RBOC Verizon is a 51 percent partner with European giant Vodafone in top-ranked Verizon Wireless; BellSouth and SBC control Cingular, which is ranked second; and Sprint Communications has spawned Sprint PCS, ranked fourth.

These companies find themselves in a world where cell phone revenues are booming while the local voice business erodes. In fact, telecom analysts believe that cumulative revenue growth for wireless services will total $108 billion in the United States from 2004 through 2008, and traditional wire line services are projected to decline by $80 billion over the same period.[35]

TABLE 8-3 The Largest Cell Phone Companies (as of 3Q 2003)

	Subscribers (in millions)	Market Share (%)
Verizon Wireless	36.0	24.6
Cingular Wireless	23.4	16.0
AT&T Wireless	21.9	14.9
Sprint	15.5	10.6
NEXTEL	12.3	8.4
T Mobile	12.1	8.3

SOURCE: *New York Times*, November 24, 2003, C4.

[35]"Bells Urged to Hike Wireless Exposure," *TR Daily* (November 25, 2003). www.tr.com/newsletters/trd (available only with paid subscription). Accessed April 14, 2004.

Broadband also is expected to yield positive returns during the span, perhaps less impressive in magnitude but a key to keeping wire line networks from being cannibalized by the wireless wave.[36] Moreover, many observers expect consolidation to occur among the existing wireless carriers as profit margins shrink, and a merger minuet already has begun.[37]

In sum, the market structure of U.S. telecommunications remains bifurcated. The long-distance market experiences vibrant entry; the local market retains monopoly in much of its business. Technological wild cards such as cellular and the Internet, and who plays them, will have much effect on future outcomes.

III. MARKET CONDUCT

Long Distance

Price and nonprice competition manifest themselves in the long-distance telecommunications market. To the extent that firms in the toll market are aware of rival pricing strategies, carrier prices tend to converge over time. A rate discount by one carrier is invariably countered by rivals. A firm, for example, may offer a discount on Sunday calls, but rivals might then trump the rate by extending discounts for calls to an entire weekend. Price competition is, in fact, so heated that carriers are not above employing "fighting brands" that require tapping digits to secure cheaper rates (e.g. "10-10-321"). Subscribers might be surprised to learn that some of those digit brands are affiliates of either AT&T or MCI.[38] That price rivalry is standard operating procedure can be seen by rates offered by new long-distance suppliers, especially firms that are relying on fiber optics transmission. Here, rates are not determined on the basis of time and distance, but rather they reflect bandwidth quantity used by the customer. New pressures have emerged as wireless firms and local telephone companies have joined long-distance carriers in offering bundles of local, long-distance, and wireless services for a monthly fee, often featuring unlimited or large blocks of minutes for long-distance calling. The increasing use of e-mail also has dampened demand and the price for long-distance offerings.

The long-distance market is characterized by nonprice competition, as well. Long-distance carriers encourage brand and customer loyalty, and "quiet as a pin drop" ads inform subscribers that circuit quality is unmatched by rivals. Marketers increasingly tout bundled services as a standard offering to their subscribers, often obscuring once clear demarcations between local and long-distance traffic. The corporate market enables firms to generate Internet bandwidth for exclusive company use. Here, a firm leases bandwidth and purchases Internet routers or switches to secure a state-of-the-art digital network. Such links, which enable the firm's Web site to link employees as

---

[36]Ibid.

[37]"Telecom Industry Abuzz on Merger Talks," *Atlanta Constitution-Journal* (January 15, 2004). www.ajc.com. Accessed April 14, 2004; "AT&T Wireless for Sale as Shakeout Starts," *New York Times* (January 21, 2004): C1.

[38]John J. Keller, "AT&T Prepares Campaign to Battle MCI's '10-321' Plan," *Wall Street Journal* (April 8, 1998): B7.

well as customers and corporate suppliers, have emerged as a competitive strategy in markets where industry boundaries are now permeable.

Local Telecommunications

Local telephone companies control a critical piece of telecommunications real estate—the line between the end user and the company's central office switch. In the absence of competitive alternatives, local carriers enjoy pricing discretion at this last telecommunications mile—subject, of course, to regulatory approval. Every long-distance call ends or begins on the subscriber's local premises, and each toll user is assessed a fee of several cents per minute. From the perspective of a long-distance toll carrier, the access charge constitutes the carrier's largest expense. AT&T's access charge payments total $12 billion annually; since 1984, AT&T has paid the RBOCs more than $200 billion.

Whether the local access charge is reasonable or not is controversial. Long-distance carriers argue that RBOC fees far exceed cost and are exorbitant. RBOCs, on the other hand, insist that the charges must remain high to ensure telephone availability to all. Be that as it may, long-distance customers contribute $25 billion annually to local exchange users.

In addition to monthly service rates, local exchange carriers offer bandwidth options to corporate users. A local carrier, for example, will provide high-speed, broadband capacity T-1 leased lines that may vary from $1,000 to $3,000 per month. The Telecommunications Act of 1996 attempted to breathe competitive life into local telecommunications services. New entrants either resell RBOC circuits or place multiplex equipment in carrier central office locations. The former lease circuits wholesale at an 18 percent discount and attempt to compete with RBOC customers at the retail level. Lest one regard local competitors as fly-by-night operations, two major CLECs have attempted to lease local circuits and compete in providing basic telephone service: AT&T and MCI.

AT&T invested $4 billion in an endeavor to enter the local lease service business, generating revenue of $86 million. However, AT&T's new CEO halted this strategy of market entry and labeled the leased route option a "fool's errand."[39] MCI spent $2 billion as a CLEC and then backed off lease circuits as a vehicle for local entry. Many CLECs allege that they are vulnerable to an RBOC wholesale/retail financial squeeze that, in effect, precludes them from effective customer access. Still, some competitors cling tenaciously, particularly where they are able to combine their own networks with facilities leased from the Bell companies at economical rates.[40]

Another type of CLEC provides broadband access at the local level by employing digital subscriber line (DSL) equipment in the RBOC's central office and then leasing RBOC lines to the customers' premises. Although DSL CLECs have penetrated the market somewhat, they, too, are beholden to RBOCs positioned in the dual role as supplier and rival. CLECs assert that RBOCs engage in dilatory tactics by claiming that the central office lacks DSL capacity, that CLEC equipment must be checked for safety, that

---

[39]"New Boss, New Plan," *Business Week* (February 2, 1998): 124.
[40]AT&T news release, September 8, 2003.

CLEC filing papers are mislaid, and that contract penalties lock in telecommunications customers.[41] AT&T, in particular, has alleged that 80 percent of RBOC lines have been tardy or late in availability. Moreover, potential entrants allege that RBOCs find central office capacity for their own DSL equipment often of the same make as that of their CLEC rivals. Some CLECs complain that when they approach RBOCs' customers, the RBOCs expedite DSL equipment as a way to foreclose competitive entry.

The FCC recently issued a landmark, and controversial, order that reaffirmed network unbundling requirements for RBOCs' voice telecommunications facilities but eliminated most requirements related to incumbent broadband networks. The latter action was heralded by the FCC's chairman as "taking vital steps across the desert . . . bold steps to promote broadband investment," but castigated by another FCC commissioner as a "broadband policy blackout . . . simply the old system of local monopoly dressed up in a digital cloak."[42] The expected surge of litigation and appeals regarding this order will surely enlist a legion of lawyers, economists, and other consultants, all of which suggests that participation in the local telephone market requires tenacity, deep pockets, and much patience.

Building on a broadband infrastructure, voice over the Internet is rapidly gaining momentum as the new technology of choice for providing voice services. A number of significant advantages are obtained: Internet Protocol equipment is more efficient and costs substantially less than the traditional circuit-switched plant. An IP network also is not charged or assessed for universal service and wireless 911 emergency service. It can be adapted easily by cable companies seeking to offer voice services, and video calls and Web-based telephone messaging cost less under such architecture.

A new-generation technology, called IPv6, promises even more capabilities, better security, and lower operational expenses for Internet users. Downsides can be found, though. Although the sound quality has improved dramatically, VOIP calls still are less reliable and the technology less proven than the traditional mode. IP still does not accommodate E911 connections well and often fails during a power blackout (unlike conventional phone service).

VOIP poses serious issues for policy makers as it becomes widely implemented: The lack of universal service assessments undermines the established support system for high-cost areas, low-income users, and schools and libraries seeking to embrace the Internet Age; the absence of local access charges also deals a significant blow to local carrier revenues. Law enforcement officials now able to tap phone lines for security reasons would not be able to undertake such measures with current versions of IP telephony. Because Internet phone service currently rides over traditional telephone or cable lines, it will not work unless the conventional phone network is intact. Given the huge stakes, it is no wonder that regulators debate among themselves about the right blend of market mechanism and government rules.[43]

---

[41]Henry Goldblatt, "The Real Target Is Your Dial Tone," *Fortune* (November 24, 1997): 116; David Rohde, "RBOC Termination Penalties Challenger," *Network World* (May 10, 1999): 39; Ronald Rosenberg, "AT&T's Armstrong Hits Bell Atlantic," *Boston Globe* (November 6, 1998): C2; Nick Wingfield, "No Mercy: Covad Communications Needs the Bell's Cooperation to Thrive. It Says It Isn't Getting Much," *Wall Street Journal* (September 21, 1998): R10.

[42]News releases of Chairman Michael K. Powell and Michael J. Copps, August 21, 2003, in the FCC's Triennial Review Order (CC Dockets 01-338, 96-98, 98-147). August 21, 2003.

[43]"Internet Telephone Challenges Social Contract," *New York Times* (January 5, 2004). www.nytimes.com. Accessed April, 14, 2004. See also "Telecommunications: Strong Signals the Bad Times Are Over," *Business Week* (January 12, 2004): 100–101.

IV. MARKET PERFORMANCE

Market performance parallels the dichotomy in long-distance and local service.

Long Distance

Although the toll telephone market approximates an oligopoly, the lowering of entry barriers has had a positive influence on carrier price, productivity, cost, and innovation. Rivalry is, in fact, so keen that some experts claim that toll service is in danger of becoming a commodity. In this market, price wars break out periodically. Recently, the average long-distance call was posted at 10 cents per minute. One carrier announced 5-cents-per-minute rates on one or more weekend days. AT&T then countered with a 7-cents-anytime rate in response to a 5-cents off-peak plan by MCI and Sprint. In real terms, toll telephone rates in the United States have dropped by more than 80 percent since 1984.[44]

Falling rates stimulate telecom usage. In 1984, U.S. consumers completed 1.2 billion toll calls. By 1995, toll call usage had exceeded 11.5 billion calls per year. Over that same period, AT&T saw its market share fall steadily. Long-distance rivalry places a premium on cost efficiency. AT&T allocates 22 percent of its revenue to overhead cost, but MCI's smaller overhead has served as a benchmark for all carriers.[45] New optical fiber firms promise to make available further cost savings.

Competitive entry forces modernity of capital spending in the toll market. In the 1980s, MCI and Sprint's adoption of fiber optics forced AT&T to write off $9 billion in investment and to inaugurate its own fiber investment program. Today, new fiber optic firms generate unrelenting pressure on toll costs and prices, with fiber costs approaching a penny per minute.

This suggests that the toll market has experienced immense productivity in transmission. In fact, productivity has been breathtaking: In 1975, a single optical fiber delivered 8,000 circuits; by 1995, a single fiber could accommodate 1.5 million circuits.[46] More recently, new multiplexing techniques have lifted fiber capacity 16 times. According to the Council of Economic Advisers, the cost of transmitting one bit of data over a kilometer of fiber optic cable fell by three orders of magnitude between the mid-1970s and the early 1990s. Productivity gains convert into falling costs and dropping prices and ultimately can contribute to economic growth.[47]

Toll carriers are now providing Internet Protocol equipment access in preference to conventional voice circuit switching technology. Here again, the telecommunications market reaps productivity gains from data routers and packet switching computers whose performance, in turn, follows Moore's Law (which holds that microprocessor

---

[44]FCC Trends in Telephone Service, Ibid.

[45]Seth Schiesel, "Long Distance Giants Report Solid Results for Quarter," *New York Times* (July 30, 1999): 14.

[46]Michael King, "Too Much Long Distance," *Fortune* (March 15, 1995): 107.

[47]President's Council of Economic Advisors (CEA), Progress Report: Growth and Competition in U.S. Telecommunications 1993–1998, February 8, 1999, 35. It is not unusual to find long-distance rates of 3 or 5 cents per minute. In addition, the Commerce Department has recently linked strong productivity growth of the telecommunications and information sector to recent growth in the U.S. economy more generally. Economics and Statistics Administration, Digital Economy 2003, Washington, D.C., December 2003.

productivity doubles every 18 months). The result is that Internet Protocol equipment prices are falling 20 percent to 30 percent annually. This has not gone unnoticed: When Cisco recently announced that it had shipped its 2 millionth VOIP telephone, it noted that shipping the first million required more than 3 years, and the second million took less than 1 year.[48]

Several U.S. toll carriers have a presence in wireless technology and service, and wireless rates are declining: From 1993 through 2002, the average local monthly bill decreased by more than 25 percent, and the average number of minutes used nearly tripled.[49] The cell phone industry now targets the Internet market, permitting subscribers to "surf the net" while on the move. Many have wondered if Finland will serve as a prototype, where wireless has overtaken wire line facilities as the medium for voice communication. Indeed, the International Telecommunication Union, affiliated with the United Nations, estimates that worldwide there are 1.2 billion fixed telephone lines and 1.3 billion mobile phone subscribers.[50]

Meanwhile, AT&T and CLECs employ broadband access in an attempt to bypass RBOCs' local loop wire. Some cable TV companies now offer long-distance, local service, and Internet service packages, a prospect that raises the subversive notion that Internet telephony may well become a "free" good.

Local Telecommunications

Local telephone service prices have increased moderately since 1984. Local rates have not seen any dramatic price reductions, nor has the local telephone user seen price wars of the kind seen in the long-distance market. Indeed, from 1997 through 2002, the annual change in the Consumer Price Index (CPI) for local residential phone service ranged from +1.0 percent to +4.5 percent, while the interstate toll service rate for households experienced price *decreases* of -0.7 to -11.2 percent over the same time span.[51]

The $25 billion in access fees paid by toll subscribers do stabilize local telephone rates. Still, the sunk investment of RBOCs conditions their performance. Huge embedded plant and facilities costs militate against a rapid conversion by RBOCs to new technologies such as IP; it is estimated that it will take years for a full conversion to IP by local incumbent carriers.[52]

Still, entry at the local level has had a therapeutic influence upon RBOC performance. As cable companies Comcast, Time Warner, Cox, and others attract 13.2 million high-speed Internet customers, which is nearly double the DSL total, the RBOCs have undertaken competitive responses with some success: SBC, Verizon, and BellSouth have introduced price cuts to as low as $29.95 a month for a limited time in hopes of wooing new subscribers. The move to add DSL subscribers is a defense against cable companies that now offer broadband access bundled with video and phone services. Realizing they have no video offering to compete with cable, SBC and QWEST Communications recently signed contracts with EchoStar's Dish Network to bundle

---

[48]"Beyond the Bubble," *The Economist* (October 11, 2003): 18.
[49]FCC Trends in Telephone Service, Table 11.3.
[50]"Beyond the Bubble," 1–2.
[51]FCC Trends in Telephone Service, Table 12.3.
[52]"Battered Telecoms Face New Challenge," 2.

video into their service package for phone and data services.[53] In addition, Verizon reportedly has a plan to "leapfrog" the cable companies by supplanting its copper wires with high-capacity fiber optic lines.[54]

RBOCs offer wireless capability across the nation and compete with affiliates of long-distance carriers. Although wireless rates have dropped in the United States, their 40-cents-per-minute cost stands in sharp contrast to an 8-cents-per-minute rate in Toronto, Canada.[55] Rate disparities once again suggest that an industry's economic performance is not unrelated to industry structure.

To sum up, the salutory effects of rivalry on carrier performance are striking: The U.S. long-distance market embraces the productivity gains of computers and telecommunications while coming to grips with commoditization and thin margins. Until recently, in contrast, the U.S. local market has seemed comfortable with its technological lot and its large stream of access revenues. Is this quiet life about to become less quiet? Public policy will surely have a say.

V. PUBLIC POLICY

How should the United States address such questions as RBOC collocation policy, universal service subsidies, local competitive substitutes, and corporate mergers? In answering these questions, the United States confronts three major policy options: maintain the status quo, enlarge regulatory oversight, or promote greater competition in local telecommunications. Each of these has advantages and drawbacks.

Status Quo: Pro

Those who defend a status quo policy marshal several arguments. First, the Telecommunications Act of 1996 introduced competition, CLECs, into the local telephone market. CLECs offer new transmission bandwidth that competes with RBOCs in the retail market. Cable firms now offer a broadband alternative to the copper wire pair and bundle Internet and local and long-distance as a service offering. Proponents of the status quo insist that local access charges are declining and that the annual billion-dollar subsidy ensures the universality of telephone service, particularly to the economically disadvantaged.

Proponents of the status quo also assert that competitive substitutes do intrude into the local market, whether DSL, fixed wireless, cable modems, or satellite relay. Some RBOCs are employing satellite dishes as a device to confer fast Internet access to their customers.[56] The loop market, in short, does not constitute a technological backwater.

A status quo policy insists that RBOC horizontal mergers are monitored to comply with a public interest standard. Adherents to the status quo challenge critics who contend that government oversight—state PUCs, the Federal Communications Commission, and the Department of Justice—is incapable of divining the merits of corporate consolidation. These regulatory bodies can and will determine whether horizontal affiliation

[53]"DSL Gaining at Cable's Expense?" CNET News.com, July 25, 2003. www.news.com.com. Accessed April, 14, 2004. See also "Price War Looms for High-Speed Net Access," *USA Today* (November 14, 2003): B1.

[54]"Internet Services Challenge Definition of 'Phone Company,'" *Washington Post* (October 23, 2003): E1.

[55]Peter J. Howe, "U.S. Cell Phone Costs Fall but Stay above Europe's," *International Herald Tribune* (June 24, 1999): 12.

[56]David Rohde, "Rivals Slam SBC/Ameritech Proposal," *Network World* (July 19, 1999): 29.

generates scale efficiencies that position RBOCs to participate in a worldwide information market. If regulatory opponents disagree, they can pursue their case in the forum of legal due process. Regulatory institutions also possess the expertise and knowledge to monitor RBOC vertical diversification into the long-distance market. The FCC has examined the merits of Bell Atlantic's acquisition of GTE and the SBC-Ameritech merger. Congress, in fact, empowered the FCC to assess whether sufficient competition exists in local telecommunications as a condition for RBOC entry into long distance.

The regulatory machinery, state and federal, can and will strike the right balance between competition and regulation.

Status Quo: Con

Critics of the status quo argue that the intent of the Telecommunications Act of 1996, to bring competition to local telecommunications, has failed. RBOCs and a number of state utility commissions have opposed local competition at virtually every step, including filing briefs stating that the 1996 statute violates the U.S. Constitution. RBOCs, they say, will not tolerate competition in local facilities irrespective of subscriber demand for high-speed Internet access. Critics also remind status quo defenders that the market share of DSL CLECs remains fragile and insignificant as a market force.

Second, critics of the status quo submit that universal service and the local access charge are nothing but an incumbent's ploy to protect its local telephone monopoly. RBOCs that demand that universal service be extended to the Internet are simply asking that their "natural" monopoly status be expanded in perpetuity.

Third, critics observe that local competitive substitutes subsist at the sufferance of RBOC economic power. For one thing, the RBOCs manifest a conflict of interest. They engage in wholesale circuits and retail circuits. The result is that potential entrants are subject to a classic economic squeeze. Regulatory critics ask why AT&T withdrew from leasing RBOC lines after spending $4 billion. The answer, they say, is that RBOCs effectively choked off market entry. Those critical of the status quo remind Congress that not one RBOC merger has ever been enjoined by a state regulatory commission, the FCC, the Department of Justice, or the Federal Trade Commission. The nation's antitrust watchdogs, say critics, are not unlike Rip Van Winkle.

The result is more than disquieting: RBOCs are gathering more and more landlines into fewer and fewer hands. Certainly, RBOC horizontal acquisitions are not grounded on the premise of bringing high-speed bandwidth to the needs of electronic commerce. Rather, say critics, RBOC mergers are merely an accumulation of monopoly assets in an eternal search for guaranteed local subsidies.

Critics of a "steady as she goes" policy question the FCC's approval of SBC's $120 billion acquisition of Ameritech on the condition that SBC serve as a CLEC in 30 non-SBC markets. Presumably, FCC policy rests on the proposition that a marriage of two monopolies will somehow inspire "good" conduct and that FCC oversight will ensure such conduct. Critics of regulation insist that nothing in the past prevented SBC from establishing competitive services in Ameritech's territory or vice versa. Thus, under the guise of pursuing the public interest, the FCC has eliminated two competitors from the marketplace while touting the virtues of an Internet economy. Regulatory critics insist that the Internet was sired not by telephone monopoly but by telephone competition.

Finally, critics of regulation submit that a status quo policy is a case of institutional amnesia. Telecommunications policy today has forgotten why AT&T was broken apart in the first place: The courts approved the 1984 AT&T divestiture because of the obvious failure of government regulation. What, they say, has changed since then to inspire a resurrection of the public utility principle?

Regulatory Option: Pro

Consider next the pros and cons of a second policy choice: more regulation. Those supporting more rather than less public oversight insist that competition at the local facilities level constitutes an elusive dream. The reality, they say, is that the copper loop will long remain embedded in the telephone plant. The loop is, has, and will remain a local monopoly. No market force will dissolve or remove that stubborn fact. In addition, incumbents can acquire or merge with LECs or CLECs, and markets thereby remain concentrated. Proponents of the regulatory option conclude that RBOC control of local facilities mandates more rather than less public oversight.

Regulatory advocates note that the CLEC phenomenon was created by the Telecommunications Act of 1996. CLECs are a creature of Congress; their life can be sustained by artificial means only. Stated differently, promoting competition and regulation under our current policy is a prescription for chaos. Proponents of public oversight insist that state regulatory commissions retain undiluted jurisdiction over local telephone plant. That policy has provided the United States with the best telecommunications system as measured by any standard. Federal intrusion into a local monopoly simply undermines the effectiveness of regulation at the state level.

Adherents to the regulatory option argue that not only has local telephone service been recognized as a universal subscriber right, but that universality can and must be extended to Internet users, as well. The Internet market now reveals a digital divide that segregates those consumers who are financially endowed from those who are financially disadvantaged. Universal service has bridged a voice divide; universal service also can overcome an Internet divide. To ensure consumer equity, regulation must play an affirmative role. The FCC's e-rate makes available subsidies for K-12 schools and public libraries. Those constituencies must share the benefits of affirmative regulation. Moreover, as VOIP becomes more widespread in a world beset by unrest, law enforcement officials arguably will need the same wiretap access they now enjoy with respect to the public switched network in order to protect the public.

Advocates for regulation insist that competitive substitutes are often misconstrued by free-market advocates. New technology complements but does not replace existing telecommunications facilities and services. Regulation ensures a coordinated adaptation of assets by local telecommunications carriers. Moreover, few quarrel with the insistence that the Internet is endowed with elements of the public's convenience and necessity. If nothing else, widespread Internet access accords the United States a comparative advantage in a world of global competition.

According to some regulatory adherents, control over horizontal acquisitions by RBOCs must and should remain the province of state regulatory commissions. They, not the federal government, are ultimately responsible for local telephone performance. Nor do state commissions exercise that mandate alone. Some 30,000 local and county authorities are empowered to define and promulgate the interest of the consuming public. Certainly, no one can deny San Antonio or Detroit's right to judge whether cable modems are to be shared or will remain the exclusive property of cable TV firms.

Finally, regulatory advocates insist that RBOC vertical mergers do not occur in a vacuum. All acquisitions are studied and monitored for their public interest dimension. Only regulation can determine whether the public will benefit from local telephone competition.

Regulatory Option: Con

Critics of the regulatory option insist that the cause of local bandwidth gridlock is none other than regulation itself. Any shortfall in RBOC economic performance rests ultimately upon government disincentives. RBOCs are utilities; not surprisingly, they behave as utilities. In addition, utilities institutionalize cost-plus. Critics suggest that regulation by state commissions masks and protects RBOC malperformance, and the goal of universal access is simply a front for economic privilege.

Regulatory critics contend that local access charges reinforce market power under a public interest fig leaf. RBOCs and state commissions may proclaim local technical diversity, but that is only because they have been unable to stifle new competitors. Regulatory critics contend that it is not the RBOC that is responsible for inadequate bandwidth or obsolete plant. Rather, responsibility rests with a public sector that aids and abets RBOC market power.

Local substitutes, say regulatory critics, have arisen in spite of, not because of, enlightened government oversight. State utility commissions might proclaim local technical diversity, but that is only because they have been unable to stop new entrants. After all, PUCs regard competitive substitutes as the antithesis of scale economies and a threat to the orderly premise of public oversight. Potential rivals are seen as cluttering up otherwise clean regulatory dockets.

Finally, regulatory critics conclude that RBOC horizontal integration promotes market concentration. If nothing else, market concentration guarantees public sector job security. Professor James Buchanan's well-known observations on the economics of public choice or Professor George Stigler's famous capture theory of regulation, suggest critics, merit re-reading in this context.

Competition Option: Pro

The competitive option concurs with the observation that the source of local bandwidth gridlock is regulation. Free-market advocates offer a simple policy remedy: Deregulate the local loop market. In fact, do more. RBOCs manifest a conflict of interest to the extent that they are wholesalers and retailers of local circuits. There should be little wonder that CLECs subsist as bit players on the local telecom stage. RBOCs can throttle rivals through a time-honored vertical squeeze, accelerate new equipment, and then tie up rivals in regulatory due process where RBOCs hold a comparative advantage. That power was the thrust of the Justice Department's 1974 antitrust case against AT&T.

The remedy to the vertical squeeze, say procompetitive advocates, is restructuring (i.e., "divestiture II"). The RBOCs must spin off their retail operations from their wholesale operations.[57] The RBOCs' conflict-of-interest boil must be lanced in the tradition of the AT&T divestiture I. Then and only then will the public have any real opportunity to enjoy the benefits of price, cost, productivity, innovative performance, and, most important, adequate bandwidth capacity.

Free-market proponents insist that universal service is an anachronism. Market forces now ensure customer price, choice, and quality. Internet Protocol telephony holds the promise of making toll calls a "free" service. Under a policy of open markets, bandwidth access will no longer be reduced to a zero-sum game.

Open-market advocates contend that a thousand flowers can bloom in loop substitutes. Few in telecommunications, they argue, can predict which technology will prevail in the industry over the long term. Fewer still are regulatory bodies endowed with the gift of foresight. Rather, the give and take of market forces will yield undistorted signals for investment and pricing, and reveal technical options appropriate to tomorrow's consumer needs.

Finally, free-market proponents question whether RBOCs should be permitted to engage in horizontal acquisitions. Whatever the answer, market advocates suggest that regulatory authorities are the least qualified to make that determination. Rather, RBOC mergers must meet the test of the nation's antitrust laws.

Competition Option: Con

Skeptics of the competitive/antitrust option reply that the odds favoring RBOC structural reform are virtually nonexistent. For one thing, the RBOCs surely possess sufficient political power to block any move toward their own restructuring or divestiture. State regulatory commissions, they argue, accept their mandate to protect local RBOCs, posing a united front against libertarians convinced that a new era of deregulation is upon us.

Skeptics of open competition insist that universal service evokes images of equity and fairness, and reflects regulation at its best. Any proposal to deregulate local telephone service is tantamount to abandoning the telephone subscriber to the illusion of free choice. In any case, they insist, RBOCs and state commissions stand opposed to any move toward open local markets.

Opponents of competition note that local loop subsidies represent the dilemma of the commons. Someone must rise above narrow self-interest and determine the public good. To assault the local access subsidy is essentially to attack those citizens who are most vulnerable in our society. In exercising its mandate to impose an e-rate or Internet tax, the FCC is merely carrying out the wishes of Congress.

To ask the nation to desist from regulatory oversight is to contemplate a nonexistent world. Critics of competition insist that horizontal integration at the RBOC level is now U.S. telecommunications policy. The FCC has conditioned and approved a number of mergers: Bell Atlantic with NYNEX, then GTE; SBC with PacTel, SNET, and Ameritech; and US West with QWEST. In a world of global competition, bipartisan agreement now demonstrates that the nation's antitrust laws are a legacy of a bygone era.

---

[57]Peter Howe, "Breakup, Then Buildup," *Boston Globe* (June 6, 1999): F7.

Critics of competition insist that RBOC and cable company entry into each other's market is increasingly a fact of life. However, if public policy is adamant that RBOCs must share telephone lines, cable firms will be under enormous pressure to do the same. Critics of local competition conclude that any policy must accept the fact that RBOCs exhibit market preeminence, that divestiture is not a serious proposal on any public agenda, that market entry in loop bandwidth will remain impervious to genuine competition, and that technical substitutes to copper wire remain speculative. Public utility regulation, in short, must not be consigned to the ash heap of public policy history.

Conclusion

Two decades after the Bell System breakup, the drift of the American economy toward electronic commerce is in its infancy but accelerating. The long-distance telecom market today experiences quantum jumps in bandwidth growth and productivity. Juxtaposed against that dynamism stands the quiescent but awakening local exchange market. Can these two markets—so distinct in tradition, technology, regulation, and access—be bridged? Thus far, no consensus has emerged. Ultimately, the public must decide which policy options are appropriate. The process is likely to include an admixture of technology, economics, and political maneuvering. To that extent, the issues generated by an e-commerce economy will remain a front-burner controversy on the public policy agenda for the foreseeable future.

Suggested Readings

Brock, Gerald W. 2003. *The Second Information Revolution.* Cambridge: Harvard University Press.

Cairncross, Frances. 1997. *The Death of Distance: How the Communications Revolution Will Change Our Lives.* Cambridge: Harvard Business School Press.

Computer Science and Telecommunications Board of the National Research Council. 2001. *The Internet's Coming of Age.* Washington, D.C.: National Academy Press.

Dizard, Wilson. 1997. *MegaNet: How the Global Communications Network Will Connect Everyone on Earth.* Boulder, CO: Westview Press.

McNamara, John R. 1991. *The Economics of Innovation in the Telecommunications Industry.* Westport, CT: Quorum Books.

Olufs, Dick W., III. 1999. *The Making of Telecommunications Policy.* Boulder, CO: Lynne Rienner.

CHAPTER

Airlines

—William G. Shepherd and James W. Brock

"Deregulation" is a potent rallying cry: Get government off the backs of business! Rein in the "nanny state"! Liberate the invigorating interaction of consumers and producers in the free marketplace to supplant stodgy government bureaucrats in allocating resources and determining the prices, quality, and kinds of goods and services provided.

But what does effective deregulation entail? Does it mean *no* government policy whatsoever? Does it require nothing more than preventing the state from intervening in the marketplace? Will competition automatically flourish as an effective instrument for regulating society's economic decision making? Or can privately contrived mergers, monopolies, and anticompetitive practices subvert competition and thwart the goals of deregulation?

These core questions frame an analysis of the airline industry—a field that had been comprehensively regulated by the state for 40 years before it was deregulated in 1978.

These questions are of more than idle academic interest. As portrayed by airline officials, the industry is crucial for the nation's well-being. It is "a vital infrastructure for U.S. commerce, carrying 620 million passengers and 22 billion ton miles of cargo each year." It directly employs 1 million workers and pays nearly $18 billion in taxes annually. Beyond this, they say, airlines make "a significant contribution to the $700 billion travel and tourism industry, which employs approximately 1 of every 7 people in the U.S. civilian labor force," while providing "an essential social and business link between America's cities and its smaller communities."[1]

At the same time, the industry is the subject of scathing indictments in the media and Congress. Feature articles in prominent business periodicals, as well as scores of witnesses testifying before congressional committees, document charges of "airline hell," plead for an air passenger bill of rights, and decry the depredations inflicted on the flying public, especially businesspeople, who are boiling on the verge of revolt.

Clearly, airline deregulation continues to be hotly debated, especially in the wake of the 9/11 terrorist attacks that triggered the bankruptcy of two major carriers and an outpouring of billions of dollars in government aid for the industry.

---

[1]Leo F. Mullin, chairman and chief executive officer, Delta Airlines, testimony before the U.S. Congress. Senate. Committee on Commerce, Science, and Transportation, October 2, 2002.

I. HISTORY

Every schoolchild learns that the aviation age was launched in 1903 when the Wright brothers piloted their motor-driven contraption through the air for 12 seconds. The brothers covered a distance of 120 feet at Kitty Hawk, North Carolina, a distance shorter than the wingspan of a modern commercial jetliner.

A decade later, the first scheduled air service commenced with the St. Petersburg–Tampa Air Boat Line, carrying a manifest of one passenger twice daily across Tampa Bay for a fee of $5. Intrepid travelers soon could fly from Long Island, New York, to Detroit, Michigan (4 days), or from Chicago to Seattle, Washington (5 days), usually with rail tickets included in the fare "just in case." Seated in canvas yacht chairs, refreshed by windows that could be opened and closed, and outfitted with "burp bags," passengers would tip pilots for safe landings and have them sign "certificate of flight" stubs attached to their tickets.

Early air passengers thrilled to the roar of hand-cranked aircraft engines and grass landing fields, while braving the loss of body heat (and sometimes consciousness) in unpressurized aircraft climbing over mountain ranges. They could fly the "Route of the Conquistadors" or contemplate the consequences of patronizing the evocatively named "Fireball Air Express."[2]

To stimulate the fledgling field, the federal government began funding contracts in the 1920s to carry mail via air. Initially, these contracts were competitively bid for by carriers and were strictly limited in coverage. Subsequently, however, government air mail contracts became instruments of privilege, providing a handful of carriers with permanent operating rights over major routes and cities—monopoly rights that were officially grandfathered in the Civil Aeronautics Act of 1938.[3] The 1938 act created the Civil Aeronautics Board (CAB) and charged it with regulating interstate air travel in order to promote a high degree of safety; sound economic conditions; and proper adaptation of air transportation to the country's commercial, postal, and national defense needs. To carry out its mandate, the CAB was given four key powers: (1) The entry power to grant or deny the certificates of public convenience and necessity that an airline was required to hold in order to fly interstate routes; (2) the rate power to approve or reject airfares; (3) the power to approve or deny mergers involving certificated carriers, with approval conferring immunity from the antitrust laws; and (4) the power to approve (or disapprove) collusive agreements among carriers, with approval again conferring immunity from the antitrust laws.

Unlike the regulation of such "natural monopolies" as telephone service and electricity, competition was supposed to play an important role in achieving the goals set forth for the CAB. Thus, the commission whose recommendations shaped the 1938 legislation urged that there "must be enough competition to serve as a spur to the eager search for progress," and that there "must be no arbitrary denial of the right of entry of

---

[2] Carl Solberg, *Conquest of the Skies: A History of Commercial Aviation in America* (Boston: Little, Brown and Co., 1979); R. E. G. Davies, *Rebels and Reformers of the Airways* (Washington, D.C.: Smithsonian Institution Press, 1987).

[3] For details, see Horace M. Gray, "Air Transportation," in *The Structure of American Industry*, rev. ed., ed. Walter Adams (New York: Macmillan, 1954), 466–469.

newcomers into the field where they can make an adequate showing of their readiness to render a better public service than could otherwise be obtained. There must be no policy of a permanent freezing of the present air map, with respect either to the location of its routes or the identity of their operators. The present operators of airlines have no inherent right to a monopoly of the routes that they serve."[4]

The 1938 act made clear that "no certificate shall confer any proprietary, property, or exclusive right in the use of any air space, civil airway, landing area, or air navigation facility."

Air travel grew spectacularly, as Table 9-1 shows, from 6,000 passengers in 1926 to 400,000 in 1930, and reaching 3 million by 1940. A cynic might say the modern age of air travel had arrived by 1946, when *Fortune* magazine published a feature article asking "What's Wrong with the Airlines?" The article reported "To travel by plane, a passenger must now sacrifice his comfort, his sleep, and often his baggage. He must endure inconveniences that rise to the level of punishment" while spending countless hours waiting with only his sins to "drearily contemplate."[5]

Perhaps this was because the CAB had come to conceive its primary mission to be protecting the field—including the dominant grandfathered carriers American, United, Eastern, and TWA—from competition. Thus, by 1975, despite a 200-fold increase in air traffic over the preceding decades, the CAB had refused to authorize a single major new trunk carrier to compete in the field. Nonscheduled carriers attempting to enter the industry after World War II by combining postwar surplus military aircraft with droves of de-commissioned pilots, and offering deeply discounted fares to

TABLE 9-1	U.S. Scheduled Airline Travel 1926 – 2000
Year	**Passengers Emplaned (thousands)**
1926	6
1930	418
1940	2,966
1950	19,220
1960	57,872
1970	169,922
1980	296,903
1990	465,560
2000	665,513

SOURCE: Steven A. Morrison and Clifford Winston, *The Evolution of the Airline Industry* (Washington, D.C.: Brookings Institution, 1995), 7; Aviation Week, *Aviation & Aerospace Almanac* (Washington, D.C., 2003), 16.

---

[4]Quoted in U.S. Congress. Senate. Subcommittee on Administrative Practice and Procedure. Report: Civil Aeronautics Board: Practices and Procedures, 94th Cong., 1st sess., 1975, 213.
[5]*Fortune* (August 1946): 73–201.

promote traffic, were harassed and tightly circumscribed by the CAB. Carriers other than the majors were rigidly compartmentalized within regional geographic areas and relegated to subsidiary "feeder" status. At the same time, the CAB restricted the number of major carriers that were allowed to compete on routes. The board seemed to abhor the prospect of price competition: It rejected proposed fares when they were below the fares of other carriers, especially when they threatened to reduce the profits of incumbent airlines. Over time, it came to function as a cartel forum where carriers could discuss and agree on the fares that the CAB subsequently would validate and enforce. The board permitted anticompetitive mergers, and at times encouraged them, while steadily expanding the range of airline practices that were exempted from the antitrust laws.[6]

By the 1970s, the consequences of 40 years of CAB regulation were becoming clear: The industry was artificially concentrated in the hands of a few major airlines, despite the fact that the explosion in traffic could support far more carriers. Routes were inefficiently gerrymandered among carriers in order to placate incumbent operators. Airfares on regulated interstate routes were as much as twice the fares charged on comparable but unregulated *intra*state routes within large states, particularly Texas and California, where price competition was allowed by state aviation agencies. The CAB seemed congenitally compelled to regulate each area in which carriers might attempt to compete, including carry-on luggage and free alcoholic drinks, while planes wastefully flew half empty.[7]

The case for deregulating the industry began to reach critical mass. Bolstered by economic studies demonstrating that CAB regulation stifled competition, institutionalized inefficiency, and inflated fares, the appeal of airline deregulation began to spread across the political spectrum. By 1975, free-market Republicans and consumer-oriented Democrats supported deregulation and its promise to reduce airfares, expand consumer choice, enhance efficiency, and "get government out of the marketplace."

In 1978, the Airline Deregulation Act was passed. The act called for free entry by 1980 (subject to safety and technical requirements), free pricing by 1983, and the abolition of the CAB by 1985. The act declared that henceforth, the paramount goal of public policy would be the

> encouragement, development, and maintenance of an air transportation system relying on actual and potential competition to provide efficiency, innovation, and low prices, and to determine the variety, quality, and price of air transportation services.[8]

Highlighting the emphasis on competition, the act underscored the importance of the "prevention of unfair, deceptive, predatory, or anticompetitive practices in air transportation," including "the avoidance . . . of unreasonable industry concentration, excessive market domination, and monopoly power . . ."[9]

---

[6]See Walter Adams, and James W. Brock, *The Bigness Complex,* 2d ed. pp. 210–12. (Palo Alto, CA: Stanford University Press, 2004), and the sources cited therein.
[7]Ibid.
[8]Airline Deregulation Act of 1978, Public Law 95-504, 92 Stat. 1706, 1707 (October 24, 1978).

Thus liberated, major carriers quickly began adjusting their routes and schedules, and a number of regional airlines (USAir, Piedmont, and Delta) vigorously expanded into nationwide operations. More than 60 new carriers had entered interstate service by 1983, including People Express, Southwest, New York Air, and World Airways. They cut fares by 20 percent to 40 percent and offered "few frills" service, with the result that air travel increased at a rate significantly above the historical trend.

Soon, however, a number of developments transpired that would decisively shape the course of the industry.

First, a rapid-fire series of mergers and acquisitions in the mid-1980s enabled the majors to strengthen their dominance by eliminating promising new competitors: Northwest acquired Republic Airlines, one of its major regional rivals in the upper Midwest. TWA acquired Ozark Airlines, an expanding regional carrier in the lower-Midwest region. Delta acquired Western Air Lines, another formidable regional carrier in the Rocky Mountain West, and USAir acquired Piedmont and Pacific Southwest, two more expanding regional carriers. At the same time, Texas Air acquired Continental, Eastern, and People Express.

Second, the major carriers further solidified their collective dominance by gaining control (either directly or indirectly) of most of the nation's leading commuter airlines—small carriers which, had they remained independent, could have expanded their operations and become more competitive regionally and even nationally.

Finally, the majors implemented hub-and-spoke route systems for funneling passengers into central hub airports, where they were transferred between planes and dispatched again to their final destinations. The result, as we will see in the next section, was to divide the country into a patchwork of powerful, regional "fortress" monopolies.

II. STRUCTURE

The most important elements of the industry's structure are the nature of demand, the relative size and concentration of carriers, the proliferation of alliances and cooperative agreements among airlines, and barriers to competition.

The Nature of Demand

For distances of 300 miles or more, no close substitutes exist for the speed of air travel. Another important characteristic of demand is the urgency of the trip and the flexibility of the flyer's schedule: Leisure travelers have considerable leeway in planning their trips. They can travel near or far away; at one time of the year or another; and can do so by car, train, or bus instead of by air. As a result, this group is sensitive to price; in economic parlance, its price elasticity of demand is high.

In contrast, passengers flying for professional purposes (such as business trips) typically do not have such flexibility in their scheduling; they must travel long distances, frequently on short notice, so their price elasticity of demand for air travel is low. These differing groups and price elasticities of demand create a powerful incentive for carriers to engage in price discrimination by charging higher fares to professional travelers and

---

[9]Ibid.

lower fares to leisure passengers, contingent on the carriers' ability to limit competition among themselves for the lucrative high-fare, low-elasticity passengers.

Relative Firm Size and Concentration

More than 100 certificated air passenger carriers operate in the United States. They are classified into three main categories. The majors are the largest carriers, operating extensive national and international routes. (They are sometimes referred to as network carriers.) National carriers are smaller lines that operate route systems that are less extensive and more focused. (For example, Delta, a major carrier, serves 263 cities, but JetBlue and AirTran serve 25 to 45 cities.) Most of these lines also are referred to as low-cost carriers, owing to their low-cost, low-fare policies. Commuter/regional carriers are the most numerous category, encompassing approximately 90 operators; these firms fly smaller aircraft on thinly traveled routes to and from smaller communities, then feed passengers into the larger carriers' systems.

The majors represent the lion's share of traffic, accounting for approximately three-quarters of U.S. commercial air travel, with the remainder divided between national (19 percent) and regional carriers (5 percent). The economic physiognomy of the leading carriers in each of these three categories is depicted in Table 9-2, where the disproportionate relative size of the largest airlines is evident.

Concentration in the industry can be analyzed along a number of dimensions. Table 9-3 depicts trends in airline concentration at the national level, where it can be seen that the initial impact of deregulation in 1978 was to reduce the level of concentration as new carriers entered the field and as existing regional carriers expanded the scope of their operations. The rash of mergers during the mid-1980s, however, reversed this trend and raised concentration, with the top eight carriers coming to account for approximately 96 percent of the nation's air passenger traffic by 1992. Since then, concentration at the national level has drifted downward somewhat, but the four largest carriers continue to control nearly two thirds of the field collectively, with the top eight accounting for nearly 90 percent (sustained, in part, by American's acquisition of TWA in 2001).

Closer inspection reveals that concentration is considerably higher in some geographic regions of the country, on major city-pair routes, and especially at major airport hubs. Regionally, concentration (measured by the combined market share of the four largest carriers) varies from a low of 55 percent in the East North Central area to a high of 82 percent in the South Central region.[10]

Table 9-4 shows that concentration is high on the largest, most heavily traveled routes, with the two largest carriers together accounting for a 67 percent share of passenger traffic, on average, for the major routes shown.

At the local airport and city levels, the monopolizing impact of the hub-and-spoke route systems instituted by the majors is apparent: As Table 9-5 shows, the degree of single-firm dominance has dramatically increased at many of the nation's major airports, with the dominant carrier typically accounting for two thirds or more of local air transportation. In fact, the General Accounting Office recently found that one of the major carriers transported more than half of all passengers at 16 of the nation's 31

---

[10]Aviation Week, *Aviation & Aerospace Almanac* (Washington, D.C., 2001), 242–247.

TABLE 9-2   U.S. Airlines 2002

	Operating Revenues (millions)	Passengers Carried (thousands)	Number of Aircraft	Employees
Major Carriers:				
American	$15,871	94,048	819	97,760
United	13,916	68,350	567	78,727
Delta	12,410	90,799	573	65,566
Northwest	9,152	51,743	444	44,254
Continental	7,353	39,486	366	36,496
USAir	6,915	47,155	280	33,321
Southwest	5,522	72,448	375	33,056
Leading National Carriers:				
ATA	1,150	7,846	69	6,826
AirTran	733	9,700	67	5,000
JetBlue	635	5,672	37	2,924
Frontier	445	3,069	36	3,380
Spirit	405	3,673	32	2,700
Midwest Express	359	2,164	32	2,460
Leading Regional Carriers:				
American Eagle	1,199	11,835	239[a]	n/a
Continental Express	1,089	8,593	188	5,100
SkyWest	774	2,213	149	5,079
Atlantic Coast Air[c]	761	7,160	142	4,815
Atlantic Southeast	752	8,071	131[a]	5,500[b]
Mesaba	417	5,380	109	3,800
Comair	n/a	8,349	110[a]	5,500[b]

[a] *Data for 2000*
[b] *Data for 2004*
[c] *Renamed Independence Air*
SOURCE: Air Transport Association, Economic Report: 2003 (Washington, D.C.); Bureau of Transportation Statistics, Department of Transportation, "Air Carriers: T-100 Domestic Market" (www.transtats.bts.gov); and company Internet Web sites.

largest airports; in only 6 of these cases did another carrier account for more than 10 percent of the remaining traffic.[11]

Joint Ventures and Alliances

Interwoven through these overlapping layers of concentration is a steadily expanding web of affiliations, alliances, and joint ventures among the major carriers. First, a host of partnerships link the nation's leading regional airline operators with the major carriers. American Airlines, for example, operates American Eagle (the nation's largest

---

[11]JayEtta Z. Hecker, U.S. General Accounting Office, "Aviation Competition: Challenges in Enhancing Competition in Dominated Markets," testimony before the U.S. Congress. Senate. Committee on Commerce, Science, and Technology, March 13, 2001.

	TABLE 9-3	Industry Concentration: Nationwide	

Year	Top Four Airlines	Top Eight Airlines
1978	57.7%	80.4 %
1983	54.7	74.1
1992	69.9	95.7
2002	61.9	87.2

NOTE: *Based on revenue passenger miles flown.*
SOURCE: U.S. Congressional Budget Office, Policies for the Deregulated Airline Industry (Washington, D.C.: July 1988), p. 15; Aviation Week, *Aviation & Aerospace Almanac* (Washington, D.C.), various years; and Air Transport Association, Economic Report: 2003 (Washington, D.C.).

TABLE 9-4   Industry Concentration: Major City-Pair Routes Fourth Quarter 1999

Route and Traffic Rank	Largest Carrier and Market Share (%)		Second Largest Carrier and Market Share (%)		Top Two Carriers Combined (%)
1. Los Angeles-New York	American	(31.8)	United	(22.2)	54.0
2. Chicago-New York	United	(35.9)	American	(31.4)	67.3
3. Boston-New York	Delta	(44.9)	US Shuttle/ USAir	(29.4)	74.3
4. New York-Washington	Delta	(40.2)	US Shuttle/ USAir	(25.1)	65.3
5. Atlanta-New York	Delta	(66.9)	Continental	(19.1)	86.0
6. New York-Orlando	Delta	(43.2)	Continental	(28.2)	71.4
7. Ft. Lauderdale-New York	Delta	(33.4)	Continental	(26.4)	59.8
8. New York-San Francisco	United	(41.3)	American	(18.1)	59.4

SOURCE: Aviation Week, *Aviation & Aerospace Almanac: 2001* (Washington, D.C.), p. 375.

regional carrier), and has ticket-writing and passenger-sharing (code-sharing) agreements with a number of other regional carriers. Delta operates the nation's second-largest system of commuter/regional carriers (Delta Connection, comprising Atlantic Southeast Airways and Comair), and also has code-sharing partnerships with American Eagle Airlines, Atlantic Coast Airlines, and SkyWest (the nation's fifth-largest regional carrier). Likewise, USAir operates the fourth-largest network of regional carriers, encompassing Allegheny Airlines, Piedmont Airlines, PSA Airlines, and Potomac Air, with additional code-sharing agreements with Air Midwest, Mesa Airlines, and Shuttle America, among others.[12]

Second, the majors have forged cooperative scheduling, ticketing, and marketing agreements among themselves in recent years. Most notably, United and USAir, the

---

[12]Aviation Week, *Aviation & Aerospace Almanac: 2003* (Washington, D.C.), 323–325.

TABLE 9-5   Industry Concentration: Hub Airports

Hub Airport	2001 Top Two Airlines and Market Shares (%)		1980 Top Airline and Market Shares (%)	
Atlanta	Delta	79.2	Delta	52.5
	AirTran	10.3		
Chicago O'Hare	United	45.9	United	31.6
	American	29.8		
Cincinnati	Delta	92.2	Delta	38.1
	Mesaba	1.4		
Denver	United	65.1	United	27.3
	Frontier	8.9		
Detroit	Northwest	77.1	Republic	20.9
	Spirit	3.3		
Minn./St. Paul	Northwest	80.4	Northwest	41.7
	Sun Country	3.8		
Pittsburgh	USAir	75.9	USAir	53.4
	Delta	2.3		
Salt Lake City	Delta	61.8	Western	28.4
	Southwest	11.9		
St. Louis	American	73.0	TWA	43.3
	Southwest	12.7		

NOTE: *Market shares include shares of subsidiary and affiliated commuter carriers, where available.*
SOURCES: Aviation Week, *Aviation & Aerospace Almanac* (Washington, D.C.), 2003, pp. 373–380, and Julius Maldutis, "Airline Competition at the 50 Largest U.S. Airports— Update," Salomon Brothers, May 6, 1993.

second- and sixth-largest carriers in terms of revenues, implemented an agreement in 2003 to reciprocally issue tickets for travel on the other carrier's flights, to cross list each other's flights as their own, and to honor frequent-flyer miles accumulated by passengers traveling on either airline. Delta, Northwest, and Continental—the third-, fourth-, and fifth-largest carriers—have struck a similar marketing partnership agreement among themselves, as have American Airlines and Alaska Airlines.

Third, on a global scale, the major carriers have entered into alliances with leading foreign airlines that have evolved into the three major international groupings depicted in Table 9-6. Clearly, these are significant cooperative arrangements that combine as partners the dominant American airlines with most of the leading carriers outside the United States. The OneWorld alliance, for example, is a partnership involving American Airlines (the world's second-largest carrier measured by passenger kilometers), with the 1st-, 6th-, 10th-, and 13th-largest carriers outside the United States (British Air, Quantas, Cathay Pacific, and Iberia, respectively). The Star alliance joins United and USAir (the 1st- and 10th-largest carriers worldwide) with each other, as well as with the 3rd-, 7th-, 9th-, 11th-, and 17th-largest carriers outside the United States (Lufthansa, Air Canada, All Nippon, Thai Air, and Varig, respectively). Similarly, the SkyTeam alliance joins Delta, the 3rd-largest carrier worldwide, with the 2nd-, 12th-, and 14th-largest carriers outside the United States (Air France, Korean Air, and Alitalia, respectively). The recently

	Annual Passengers		
Alliance	**(millions)**	**American Partner(s)**	**Foreign Partners**
OneWorld	228	American	Aer Lingus
			British Airways
			Quantas
			Cathay Pacific
			Iberia
			LanChile
			Finnair
Star	292	United	Air Canada
		USAir	Lufthansa
			Air New Zealand
			Austrian Airlines
			British Midland
			Mexicana
			Singapore Airlines
			Varig
			All Nippon Airways
			Thai Airways
SkyTeam	228	Delta	Air France
			Alitalia
			Korean Air
			AeroMexico

TABLE 9-6   Global Airline Alliances

SOURCE: Daniel Michaels and Scott Neuman, "Global Partners May Get Roiled by Turbulence," *Wall Street Journal*, December 6, 2002, B5, and "US Airways Joins Star Alliance," *New York Times*, June 2, 2003, C2.

disclosed merger between Air France and KLM is expected to bring KLM into this third major global alliance, perhaps along with KLM's American partners, Northwest and Continental, as well.

Finally, the nation's five-largest carriers—American, United, Delta, Northwest, and Continental—have combined to launch a jointly owned, jointly operated Internet Web site, Orbitz, for online ticket sales. Organized by carriers representing 70 percent of the industry, this joint sales agency affords a tantalizing opportunity for the carriers to closely monitor each other's fares. It also provides a means to undermine price competition from independent Web sites (e.g., Travelocity, Expedia), which may be denied equal access to the dominant carriers' fare information and lowest available rates.

These affiliations and alliances require a considerable degree of cooperation among major actual and potential rivals. As such, they suggest that concentration in the field is higher than market-share statistics alone would indicate.

Barriers to Entry

At the time of deregulation, some economists heralded the airline industry as a "contestable" market in which market shares, mergers, and concentration levels would be irrelevant due to the high mobility and flexibility of resources in the field: Existing carriers, they believed, could quickly move planes and alter schedules to compete on different routes; by the same token, new carriers could swiftly put new aircraft into operation on selected routes. Monopoly and oligopoly market power, they concluded, would be fleeting and inconsequential.[13]

Alas, a host of daunting barriers, many of them constructed by incumbent carriers, subsequently refuted this contestability theory. First, the nation's largest, most congested airports (Chicago O'Hare, Washington National, and New York's LaGuardia and Kennedy) are accessible only to carriers holding government slots to land and depart aircraft at particular times throughout the day. The bulk of these slots originally were given to the dominant carriers that already were operating at these airports, and these carriers have increased their share of them over the years. At Chicago O'Hare, for example, American and United together control 90 percent of the total number of landing and takeoff slots available; at Washington National, 98 percent of the available slots are held by American, Delta, Northwest, United, and USAir. By hoarding slots (or charging high fees to sell or lease them), dominant carriers can prevent new or existing carriers from competing on routes to and from these major airports.[14]

Second, dominant carriers also control access to these and other hub airports through exclusive-use agreements negotiated with local airport authorities for control of gates, terminals, and baggage and ground-handling facilities. In one in-depth analysis, the General Accounting Office found that the major carriers control 94 percent of all gates leased at the nation's largest airports, with 86 percent of these leased on an exclusive-use basis. As a result, dominant carriers can limit competition either by refusing to lease their gates to other carriers (even if they are underutilized) or by leasing them only at onerous rates. In addition, majority-in-interest contracts empower dominant carriers to veto physical airport expansions that could provide the additional terminals and gates needed by new competitors.[15]

Third, the majors have transformed their ticketing and reservation systems into yet another barrier to competition. During the 1980s and 1990s, computer reservation systems operated by American and United came to be utilized by virtually all travel agents and corporate travel departments for their scheduling needs; by manipulating the on-screen presentation of flights, these carriers could disadvantage other airlines and compel them to pay exorbitant fees to have their flights included in computer displays.

---

[13]See William J. Baumol, John C. Panzer, and Robert D. Willig, *Contestable Markets and the Theory of Industrial Structure* (San Diego: Harcourt Brace Jovanovich, 1982); Elizabeth E. Bailey, "Contestability and the Design of Regulatory and Antitrust Policy," *American Economic Review* 71 (May 1981): 178–183; Elizabeth E. Bailey and John C. Panzar, "The Contestability of Airline Markets during the Transition to Deregulation," *Law & Contemporary Problems* 44 (Winter 1981): 125–145. For a trenchant criticism of this theory, see William G. Shepherd, "'Contestability' versus Competition," *American Economic Review* 74 (September 1984): 572–587.

[14]U.S. Congress. Senate. Subcommittee on Antitrust, Business Rights, and Competition. Hearing: Airline Competition: Clear Skies or Turbulence Ahead? 106th Cong., 2d sess., 2001, 67; John H. Anderson, U.S. General Accounting Office, "Domestic Aviation: Service Problems and Limited Competition Continue in Some Markets," statement before the U.S. Congress. House. Subcommittee on Aviation, April 23, 1998; U.S. General Accounting Office, "Airline Deregulation: Barriers to Entry Continue to Limit Competition in Several Key Domestic Markets," report to the Chairman. U.S. Congress. Senate. Committee on Commerce, Science, and Transportation, October 1996.

[15]The classic study of the gate/terminal barrier is U.S. General Accounting Office, "Airline Competition: Industry Operating and Marketing Practices Limit Market Entry," Washington, D.C., August 1990, 36, 42, 47–54. For more recent studies, see U.S. General Accounting Office, "Airline Deregulation: Barriers to Entry Continue to Limit Competition in Several Key Domestic Markets," 1996; Transportation Research Board, *Entry and Competition in the U.S. Airline Industry* (Washington, D.C.: National Academy Press, 1999). For some specific recent examples, see Bruce Ingersoll, "Gateless in Detroit," *Wall Street Journal* (July 12, 1999): 1; Edward Wong, "Denver's Idle Gates Draw Covetous Eyes," *New York Times* (August 5, 2003): C1.

More recently, similar charges of manipulation have been leveled against the Orbitz online ticketing system that is jointly operated by the largest carriers.[16]

Bonus payments and commission "overrides" paid by major carriers to travel agents and corporate travel departments for booking preset percentages of their flights on a particular carrier create another obstacle to competition, as do frequent-flyer programs that reward travelers for not patronizing other carriers, including new entrants.[17]

Finally, as we shall see, the prospect of devastating price cuts by the major carriers in response to new competition can serve as yet another powerful barrier to entry.

The Question of Economies of Scale

Little evidence is available to indicate that high concentration in airlines is dictated by any extraordinary economies of scale or scope of operations. In fact, to the contrary, the evidence suggests that the largest airlines are the highest-cost carriers, a diseconomy of excessive size that has grown more pronounced in the post-9/11 period.

Table 9-7 records the sizable cost disadvantage of the largest carriers relative to Southwest, the eighth-largest carrier in terms of revenues and the one generally considered the industry's benchmark for efficiency. These statistics show, for example, that American, United, and Delta have operating costs that are 25 percent to 62 percent higher than those of Southwest in recent years. This diseconomy of scale has been evident for at least a decade and began growing greater after 1996, well before the industry slump following the 9/11 attacks.[18] In fact, it has been estimated that the Big Three carriers (American, United, and Delta) could reduce their costs by 25 percent to 33 percent if they were able to operate as efficiently as Southwest Airlines. Another recent

TABLE 9-7   Airline Operating Costs

Index of Unit Operating Costs (Southwest = 100)

Size-Rank of Carrier	1999	2001
1. American	125	161
2. United	125	162
3. Delta	125	136
4. Northwest	121	141
5. USAir	185	173
6. Continental	127	135
7. Southwest	100	100

NOTE: Unit operating costs are defined as total operating expenses per available seat mile flown.
SOURCE: Calculated from data contained in Aviation Week, *Aviation & Aerospace Almanac,* 2001 and 2003 editions (Washington, D.C.).

---

[16]"Southwest Air's Suit Says Travel Web Site Misleads Consumers," *Wall Street Journal* (May 7, 2001): A10.
[17]On bonuses and discounts, see General Accounting Office, "Airline Deregulation"; Scott McCartney, "Continental Air Loses Some Accounts after Data-Disclosure Demand," *Wall Street Journal* (February 6, 2001): B1.
[18]William Swelbar, "Growth of Low Fare Carriers," presentation at the Second Annual MIT Airline Industry Conference (Cambridge, MA, April 8, 2003).

analysis finds that for identical cross-country flights and aircraft, including the same crew size, United's costs are nearly double those of vastly smaller JetBlue.[19]

To an important degree, these diseconomies of scale seem to stem from the monopoly hub systems implemented by the majors following deregulation: By requiring airlines to schedule large numbers of flights to arrive and depart at hub airports within narrow time periods, the carriers that operate hub systems have large numbers of gates, facilities, and ground crews that are idle during most of the day.[20] (Some experts suggest that it was the prospect of monopoly profits that rendered these high-cost hub systems financially attractive in the first place.)[21] In addition, smaller, lower-cost carriers operate fewer different types of aircraft (Southwest flies only Boeing 737s), which simplifies their maintenance and parts operations, and enables them to hold down their costs. Large mergers like American's acquisition of TWA in 2001 also have raised some big carriers' costs, as has their accommodation of labor unions in driving up salaries (while showering management with munificent stock options, pensions, and severance agreements).[22] It is these cost inefficiencies that Southwest and some new low-cost carriers (e.g., JetBlue, AirTran) have exploited in recent years to capture a growing share of industry revenues.

III. CONDUCT

Pricing in the industry is characterized by a tacitly collusive pattern of mutual interdependence and parallelism at the national level. It is reinforced by monopoly pricing at the monopoly regional hub level, and sustained by strategic price cutting that contains or eliminates new competitors while maintaining pricing discipline among the majors.

Tacit Collusion Nationally

As industrial organization theory predicts, mutually interdependent behavior emerged as concentration rose in the field following deregulation. As the industry became more oligopolistic, the major carriers came to recognize that a significant pricing move by any one of them could be expected to elicit a quick response from the others and, especially, that a price cut would be quickly matched, reducing profits for all.

Thus, when the former chairman of American Airlines, Robert Crandall, was asked why his carrier did not offer lower fares to attract major corporate customers, his response reflected a classic oligopoly mentality: "Because it would be dumb. The reality is that you will go to Detroit because you have to go to Detroit whether the fare is $175, $275, or $375." The same mentality was evident in the response of a USAir vice

[19]Scott McCartney, "Southwest Sets Standards on Costs," *Wall Street Journal* (October 9, 2002): A2; Susan Carey, "Costly Race in the Sky," *Wall Street Journal* (September 9, 2002): B1.

[20]Peter Coy, "The Airlines: Caught Between a Hub and a Hard Place," *Business Week* (August 5, 2002): 83; Melanie Trottman and Scott McCartney, "The Age of Wal-Mart Airlines," *Wall Street Journal* (June 18, 2002): 1.

[21]Scott McCartney, "Big Three Airlines Face Tough Tasks," *Wall Street Journal* (October 24, 2002): D5.

[22]Scott McCartney, "On Brink of Chapter 11, American Reaches Deal with Unions," *Wall Street Journal* (April 1, 2003): 1; Steven Greenhouse, "Unions Are a Victim of Their Own Success at the Nation's Airlines," *New York Times* (April 26, 2003): B3.

president when asked why his airline did not attempt to gain more traffic by pricing below the identical fares charged by other major carriers on their Denver to Dallas routes: "If I know that if I cut my fare $20 today, you're going to cut yours $20 tomorrow, then it's stupid for me to do it." As a Delta official said of the years immediately following deregulation: "We went through a period of bashing each other's heads in over fares. It took us a while to learn how to compete."[23]

"Learning how to compete" meant learning how to set the general structure of fares through a tacitly collusive pattern of price leadership/price followership: One of the majors takes the lead in communicating its intentions concerning a change in airfares, and the others either follow the leader and adopt similar fare changes themselves, or, alternatively, refuse to follow the leader, thereby compelling the initiator to scale back or abandon its pricing change. In either event, fares are uniform across the major carriers and move together in lockstep.

This recognition of mutual interdependence enables the majors to fly in remarkably close pricing formation. Consider, as one example, the following series of events: Throughout the spring of 1998, the majors repeatedly attempted to raise fares, but Northwest refused to follow (perhaps for fear of disrupting wage negotiations with its pilots). Northwest's resistance prevented the other carriers from raising fares and repeatedly forced them to rescind their price hikes. In mid-August, however, Northwest signaled to the others its willingness to cooperate by announcing a general increase in its leisure fares of 4 percent, an increase that was immediately matched by the other majors. Thirty-six hours later, however, Northwest abruptly canceled its price hike and reduced its fares by 4 percent; the other majors immediately followed and rescinded their 4 percent fare hikes. A few days later, Northwest reconsidered its pricing, tailored its price increase to fewer travel categories, and announced a price hike of 4 percent once again—an increase that was immediately matched by the other major carriers![24]

The centralized computer system into which airfare information is fed facilitates constant communication and signaling among the majors through the way they elect to file their fare plans (start date, stop date, price change, routes and passenger classes affected, and so forth). Using the specific characteristics of the fare information they file with this central clearinghouse, the majors are able to track each other closely—and, at times, to communicate their dismay with one another (including the infamous *FU* letter code attached to fares filed to signal displeasure about a rival's competitive price cutting). The majors are able to enforce a great deal of pricing discipline among themselves by, for example, selectively targeting fare cuts on a rival carrier's most lucrative

---

[23]Quoted in Christopher Winans and Jonathan Dahl, "Airlines Skid on Bad Moves, Bad News," *Wall Street Journal* (September 29, 1989): B4; "Flying the Unfriendly Skies," *Philadelphia Inquirer* (special edition, December 1989): 4.

[24]"Northwest Changing Its Mind Again," *Wall Street Journal* (August 24, 1998): C19. For a similar episode involving United, see Susan Carey, "All in a Day's Flying: Fares Rise, Fall, Rise 5% Again in 24 Hours," *Wall Street Journal* (September 9, 1997): A6.

routes in order to pressure it to abstain from competitive pricing in other routes and regions.[25]

Tacit collusion among the majors permeates their other pricing and marketing activities, as well. Through a process of leadership-followership, for example, the majors uniformly lowered the compensation they pay to travel agencies for booking flights in 1995, 1997, 1999, 2001, and again in 2002, each time by identical amounts. Similarly, when American recently altered its rules governing the use of nonrefundable tickets, the other majors followed American's lead exactly.[26]

Monopoly Pricing Regionally

At the regional level, the majors are able to price monopolistically at the hub airports and regions they dominate. Table 9-8 shows one estimate of the extent to which fares at dominated hubs exceed airfares at airports that are more competitively served. It shows, for example, that passengers flying from Pittsburgh (dominated by USAir) pay

TABLE 9-8   Fare Differentials: Dominated vs. Nondominated Airports

	Fare Differential for:		
Dominated Hub	**Short-Haul Routes**	**Long-Haul Routes**	**All Routes**
Cincinnati	+ 78%	+ 35%	+ 57%
Pittsburgh	+ 86	+ 18	+ 57
Minneapolis	+ 46	+ 63	+ 55
Charlotte	+ 75	+ 23	+ 54
St. Louis	+ 38	+ 61	+ 49
Memphis	+ 57	+ 29	+ 43
Atlanta	+ 49	+ 28	+ 41
Detroit	+ 51	+ 21	+ 40
Denver	+ 37	+ 28	+ 29
All	+ 54	+ 31	+ 41

NOTE: Dominated hubs *are defined as hub airports where no low-fare carrier operates. Fare differences are controlled for route distance and density differences.*
SOURCE: JayEtta Z. Hecker, U.S. General Accounting Office, Testimony before the U.S. Senate, Committee on Commerce, Science, and Transportation, March 13, 2001.

---

[25]For especially informative reports of this tacit collusion and disciplining process in action, see Scott McCartney, "Airfare Skirmish Shows Why Deals Come and Go," *Wall Street Journal* (March 19, 2002): B1; Melanie Trottman, "America West Is Pressed by Rivals," *Wall Street Journal* (April 22, 2002): A3; Asra Q. Nomani, "Fare Warning: How Airlines Trade Price Plans," *Wall Street Journal* (October 9, 1990): B1; Asra Q. Nomani, "Dispatches from the Air-Fare Front," *Wall Street Journal* (July 11, 1989): B1.

[26]U.S. Congress. House. Committee on Small Business. Hearing: Issues in the Travel Agency Business, 107th Cong., 2d sess., 2002; Edward Wong, "Most Big U.S. Airlines Ease Policy on Nonrefundable Tickets," *New York Times* (August 22, 2003): C3. Marketing alliances among the majors may reinforce this tacitly collusive pricing discipline. "When you have 20 percent of the market [Continental and Northwest combined]," says the CEO of Continental about that airline's affiliation with Northwest, "United will say … 'Screwing with one might be the same as screwing with the other.' Now, as a joined-at-the-hip partner with Northwest, you better watch out if we do get upset. We have a lot of different ways that we can pay you back." Quoted in U.S. Congress. Senate. Subcommittee on Antitrust, Business Rights, and Competition. Hearing: Airline Competition: Clear Skies or Turbulence Ahead? 106th Cong., 2d sess., 2001, 62.

a monopoly premium of 86 percent on short-haul flights, and long-haul passengers at Minneapolis (dominated by Northwest) pay a monopoly premium of 63 percent. Overall, 24.7 million passengers at dominated hubs pay 54 percent higher fares for short-haul flights, 31 percent higher fares for long-haul flights, and an average of 41 percent higher fares for flights of all lengths combined.[27]

A second manifestation of monopoly pricing at dominated hubs is the dramatic effect that the entry of a low-fare carrier has on a dominant airline's fares: With a monopoly on nonstop service from Atlanta to Los Angeles, for example, Delta's fare was $1,151 for a one-way walk-up ticket; when AirTran and JetBlue launched competing service on the route, Delta slashed its fare to $249. Similarly, the entry of AirTran into Wichita, Kansas, compelled Delta and American to cut their fares from $1,600 to $460 on service from Wichita to Washington, D.C. In one recent study, the Department of Transportation found that on routes from Atlanta (dominated by Delta) where AirTran entered, airfares fell 43 percent and passenger traffic rose 65 percent; conversely, when AirTran exited these routes, Delta raised fares by an average of 55 percent, with a corresponding 25 percent decline in air travel.[28]

Finally, the ability of the majors to simultaneously charge high fares to passengers with less price-elastic demand (i.e., business, professional, last-minute) and far lower fares to passengers with more price-elastic demand (i.e., leisure, vacation) further attests to monopoly pricing power. This price discrimination is, as Table 9-9 shows, sizable and growing: Full fares have grown to more than triple the available discount fares (with full fares much higher in particular cases) and have increased in relative importance in generating revenues for the major carriers.[29] Given that there is no evidence of any remotely comparable differences in the cost of carrying each class of passenger, effective

TABLE 9-9   Price Discrimination in Airfares

Year	Ratio: Full Fare to Discount Fare
1990	2.89
2000	3.46
2002	3.59
Change 1990–2002	+ 24.2%

NOTE: *Data for 2002 are for January through August only. Data are for all major airlines, excluding Southwest.*
SOURCE: Derived from data provided in *Airline Monitor,* "Yield Trends: Major Airlines, Domestic Operations," October 2002.

---

[27]U.S. Department of Transportation, Office of the Assistant Secretary for Aviation and International Affairs, "Dominated Hub Fares," Washington, D.C., January 2001.

[28]Edward Wong, "Delta Gets Some Stiff Competition on a Key Route," *New York Times* (May 28, 2003): C1; Martha Brannigan, "Discount Carrier Lands Partners in Ill-Served Cities," *Wall Street Journal* (July 16, 2002): 1; U.S. Department of Transportation, "Domestic Airline Fares: Fourth Quarter 1998 Passenger and Fare Information," Washington, D.C., July 1999, 40.

[29]Transportation Research Board, *Entry and Competition in the U.S. Airline Industry* (Washington, D.C.: National Academy Press, 1999), 30.

competition for the patronage of each group would prevent carriers from engaging in this kind of price discrimination. In fact, evidence indicates that the gulf between full and discount fares is greatest in the most monopolized hubs and that the entry of a new competitor significantly narrows the full-to-discount price differential.[30]

Predatory Pricing

A third important feature of conduct in the industry is the resort by the major carriers to sharply targeted price cuts and capacity increases to contain, and frequently eliminate, a new carrier that is attempting to compete.

Examples abound: When Frontier initiated service from Denver (hub dominated by United) to Billings, Montana, it offered an average fare of $100, which was half the prevailing fare charged by United. United slashed its fare to match that of Frontier. When Frontier exited the route, United raised its fare *above* the original level.[31] Similarly, when start-up Spirit Airlines attempted to enter Northwest's Detroit hub with an unrestricted one-way fare between Detroit and Philadelphia of $49 (compared to Northwest's average fare of $170), Northwest slashed its Detroit-Philadelphia fare to $49 and added 30 percent more seat capacity to the route. When Spirit subsequently abandoned the route, Northwest raised its fares to $230 (higher than its original fare) and cut its seat capacity.[32] Similarly, when Western Pacific Airlines entered the Dallas–Colorado Springs route, American cut its average fare on the route by approximately half and more than doubled the number of seats flown; Western Pacific's exit enabled American to boost its fare to the level it had set prior to Western Pacific's entry.[33]

A general analysis of the response of incumbent carriers to new competition prepared for the Department of Transportation has found that in 10 of 12 cases examined, the new entrant's fare was at least 50 percent below the average fare of the incumbent(s) prior to entry, and that in three fourths of the cases, the average fare of the incumbent fell by one third or more within 6 months after entry. Within 2 years, however, the new entrant had abandoned the routes, enabling the incumbent carrier(s) to raise fares.[34]

The study found that dominant carriers were able to exploit a variety of additional weapons to reinforce the lethal pricing pressure brought to bear on new competitors, including sandwiching flights closely around those scheduled by a new entrant; boosting frequent-flyer awards to passengers flying those particular routes; and raising the commissions overrides paid to travel agents for scheduling passengers on the dominant carrier's flights.

---

[30]U.S. Department of Transportation, Office of the Assistant Secretary for Aviation and International Affairs, "Dominated Hub Fares," Washington, D.C., January 2001.

[31]U.S. Congress. Senate. Committee on Commerce, Science, and Transportation. Hearing: Aviation Competition, 105th Cong., 2d sess., 2000, 29.

[32]W. Zellner, "How Northwest Gives Competition a Bad Name," *Business Week* (March 16, 1995): 34. For additional examples, see U.S. Congress. Senate. Committee on the Judiciary. Hearing: Airline Hubs: Fair Competition or Predatory Pricing? 105th Cong., 2d sess., 1998; U.S. Department of Transportation, Office of the Secretary, "Enforcement Policy Regarding Unfair Exclusionary Conduct in the Air Transportation Industry," Findings and Conclusions, January 17, 2001.

[33]*United States v. AMR Corp.*, 140 F. Supp. 2d 1141, (D.C. Kansas, 2001). Judge Marten considered neither this, nor sharp declines in American's profitability on such routes, to constitute evidence of illegal predatory pricing under the antitrust laws.

[34]Clinton V. Oster and John S. Strong, "Predatory Practices in the U.S. Airline Industry," study prepared for the U.S. Department of Transportation, January 15, 2001.

In general, the major carriers cannot have it both ways: If their pre-entry fares are competitive (as they claim), then their sharp price cuts in response to entry must be below the competitive level. If, on the other hand, their sharply lower post-entry fares are competitive (as they also claim), then their pre-entry prices must be monopolistic.

IV. PERFORMANCE

In *The Wealth of Nations*, Adam Smith delineated the adverse performance consequences of monopoly: The price of a monopolized item is "the highest which can be squeezed out of the buyers." According to Smith, potential competitors are excluded from a business "which it might be both convenient and profitable for many of them to carry on." Inefficiency bred by lack of effective competition "seldom allows the dividend of the company to exceed the ordinary rate of profit in trades which are altogether free," and the monopolist is constantly contriving what Smith called "absurd and oppressive" schemes. In the case of the airline industry, Smith's assessment of two centuries ago seems prescient.

First, as shown in the preceding section, fares on dominated routes and at monopolized hubs exceed by large margins the fares charged on routes and airports where competition is effective.

Second, these high fares induce a misallocation of resources by engendering an under consumption of service (what Smith called "understocking the market"), as well as by inducing a substantial waste of time, effort, and gasoline on the part of air passengers attempting to evade such fares. The extent of misallocation due to under provision of service is revealed when a new carrier enters a dominated route: The immediate consequence is a plunge in price and a sharp increase in the amount of air travel. According to one recent study, competitive entry and the corresponding decline in airfares typically triggers air travel increases of 61 percent to 86 percent—a direct measure of the degree to which service is artificially understocked in the absence of competition.[35] At the same time, considerable resources are wasted as passengers drive to board flights at nondominated hubs (frequently flying back to the dominated hub city they drove away from) and rent cars and hotel rooms for unnecessary overnight and weekend stays, all in an effort to escape the monopoly fares charged by dominant carriers. In the process, the inherent technological advantages of air travel—speed, ease, and convenience—are significantly nullified.

Third, the monopolistic hub systems implemented by the majors have inflated costs and undermined operating efficiency. As Table 9-7 shows, it is the largest carriers that have the highest operating costs. It is also telling that two of the biggest carriers recently declared bankruptcy (United and USAir), and one of the largest has skated perilously close to it (American); meanwhile, smaller carriers that have generally spurned hubs (Southwest, AirTran, and JetBlue) have prospered in the post-9/11 period. Compounding this cost inefficiency is the coalescence of power between dominant carriers and powerful

---

[35]U.S. Department of Transportation, Office of the Assistant Secretary for Aviation and International Affairs, "Dominated Hub Fares," Washington, D.C., January 2001. Also see Scott McCartney, "Airlines Neglect the People of Their Hub Cities," Wall Street Journal, March 10, 2004, p. D3.

labor unions, which further inflates the majors' costs. (Pilots at American Airlines, for example, reportedly fly an average of 39 hours per month, compared to an average of 62 hours per month for Southwest pilots.)[36]

Fourth, evidence suggests that the quality of service is significantly better on more competitive routes than on less competitive routes.[37]

Finally, on the innovation front, the record is mixed. On the one hand, most major carriers have been quick to incorporate newer, quieter, more fuel-efficient aircraft into their fleets. They also have been quick to computerize their operations and to capitalize on the advantages of the Internet. On the other hand, these new technologies have been transmuted into instruments of monopoly by manipulating computer reservation systems to favor the operators' airlines, by exploiting computer systems to better communicate and collude on airfares, and by manipulating the Internet to possibly lessen competition from other airlines and other ticket distribution channels. Smaller carriers, especially Southwest, have been far more innovative in designing and managing their routes and ground operations for maximum efficiency, undoubtedly an important reason why a number of them have been profitable over the 2001 to 2003 period, while the majors were suffering huge financial losses.

V. PUBLIC POLICY

Major public policy issues in the industry concern reregulation of the field, antitrust, and direct government aid to airlines in the wake of the 9/11 terrorist attacks.

Reregulation?

Was deregulating the airlines a mistake? Do technology and cost characteristics render competition inherently unworkable in this field? Should the industry be reregulated, as some contend?

The answer is *no* on all three counts. No credible evidence demonstrates that airlines are subject to such overwhelming economies of scale as to render monopoly and tight-knit oligopoly inevitable. To the contrary, it is the largest carriers and the most monopolized hub systems that exhibit the highest costs, not the lowest. In fact, experience during the initial years following deregulation demonstrated that competition was feasible, workable, and desirable as new carriers flocked into the field, as existing carriers rearranged their routes and fares in accordance with consumer preferences, as competition spread throughout the air transportation system, and as airfares declined and air travel jumped.

---

[36]Melanie Trottman and Scott McCartney, "The Age of 'Wal-Mart' Airlines Crunches the Biggest Carriers," *Wall Street Journal* (June 18, 2002): 1; Keith L. Alexander and Jonathan Finer, "A Blueprint for the Future," *Washington Post* (national weekly ed., August 19–25, 2002): 21; Scott McCartney, "On Brink of Chapter 11, American Reaches Deal with Its Unions," *Wall Street Journal* (April 1, 2003): 1; Bill Swelbar, "Ten of the Things We'll Be Watching Closely that Will Impact the Structure of the U.S. Airline Industry," presentation, ESI-Sloan Aviation Forum, Washington, D.C., January 14, 2002.
[37]Michael J. Mazzeo, "Competition and Service Quality in the U.S. Airline Industry," *Review of Industrial Organization* 22 (June 2003): 275.

Antitrust Policy

The policy failure was not in deregulating the field but in failing to recognize that strict enforcement of the antitrust laws would be imperative in nurturing competition and combating private efforts to subvert it. The failure was not one of deregulation but, instead, the mistake of assuming that an absence of government intervention would ensure that effective competition would automatically prevail.

First, as we have seen, a watershed of acquisitions was permitted in the mid-1980s that enabled the dominant trunk carriers to absorb rapidly expanding, highly competitive regional carriers. The 1978 deregulation statute gave the Department of Transportation authority to disapprove anticompetitive mergers, but the department approved these and other mergers, a number of which were opposed by even the Reagan administration's merger-friendly antitrust division. Congress subsequently transferred antitrust authority over mergers to the Antitrust Division of the Justice Department. The Justice Department finally did block the merger between United and USAir that was proposed in 2000; however, at the same time, it allowed American to acquire TWA and its St. Louis hub monopoly, apparently without encouraging the acquisition of financially troubled TWA by a smaller, low-cost carrier like Southwest, which could have enhanced competition in the field.

Second, the antitrust agencies and the Transportation Department have allowed a proliferation of affiliation and partnership pacts that have concentrated the majors' control over most of the nation's leading regional and commuter carriers—smaller carriers whose independence could enable them to grow in importance as a source of new competition in the field. The agencies also have permitted the majors to steadily concentrate control over international air travel in a handful of global alliances (frequently with an accompanying exemption from the antitrust laws), acting only recently to block American's effort to tighten its affiliation with British Airways (an alliance that would have monopolized air travel between a number of major American cities and London's Heathrow airport).[38] In recent years, the agencies even have allowed the majors to affiliate among themselves by integrating their routes and ticketing, including the affiliation between United and USAir, as well as an affiliation encompassing Delta, Northwest, and Continental Airlines—two partnerships involving five carriers that together account for 60 percent of domestic air travel.

Third, the agencies have done little to prevent the majors from constructing a host of formidable barriers to competition (e.g., slots, gates, airport ground facilities), or to dissolve these obstacles once they have been built. An exception is the majors' manipulation of computer reservation systems, where the Transportation Department promulgated rules regulating the nondiscriminatory presentation of flight information on screens and displays. However, this initiative may have been rendered moot by the rise of Internet ticketing, which the five largest carriers have been allowed to offer collectively in a joint venture that is rife with anticompetitive concerns.

Fourth, the Justice Department prosecuted collusive behavior among the majors in the early-1990s by challenging their methods of communicating and signaling each

---

[38]See, for example, U.S. Department of Justice, Public Comments before the Department of Transportation, U.S.-U.K. Alliance, Docket OST-2001-1029, December 17, 2001.

other through their fare-filing practices.[39] However, the Justice Department did not challenge the highly concentrated industry structure that makes such collusion (whether tacit or explicit) virtually inevitable in a field dominated by a few large oligopolists, who rationally recognize the fact of their mutual interdependence.

Finally, the Justice Department at last moved to prosecute predatory practices in the field in 1999 by filing an antitrust suit against American Airlines, charging the carrier with illegally eliminating new competitors from its Dallas–Fort Worth hub. Despite evidence that American slashed its fares on targeted routes, inflated seating capacity on them, deliberately elected to suffer temporary losses in profitability, had higher costs than new entrants, and raised fares after new competitors were eliminated, the court dismissed the government's charges without allowing the case to proceed to trial. American, the court held, had "engaged only in bare, but not brass, knuckle competition."[40] The court apparently was unable to distinguish pricing that reflects the competitive process from predatory pricing that destroys the competitive process.

9/11 and Government Aid

In the wake of the 9/11 terrorist attacks and in response to the industry's pleas for government financial aid in a time of crisis, legislation was passed providing direct government subsidies to air carriers. The Air Transportation Safety and System Stabilization Act was enacted on September 22, 2001, to provide $5 billion in cash grants to be paid to airlines in proportion to their size. The act established an additional fund of up to $10 billion in government-backed loan guarantees for carriers deemed financially deserving by a newly created Air Transportation Stabilization Board (ATSB) composed of the secretary of transportation, secretary of the Treasury, comptroller general, and chairman of the Federal Reserve or their designees. In early 2003, Congress provided an additional $2.4 billion in subsidies for security measures to the industry.

As of May 2003, $4.6 billion in emergency direct payments had been disbursed to air carriers, with $3.2 billion of this total (70 percent) flowing to American, United, Delta, Continental, Northwest, and USAir. As of mid-2003, 16 carriers had applied for government loan guarantees: 6 of these were either approved or conditionally approval by the ATSB, and the other 10 were rejected. The largest applications approved were submitted by USAir ($900 million) and America West ($380 million); the largest submission that was rejected by the ATSB was United's original application for $1.8 billion in government loan guarantees, an application that was rejected again in 2004.[41] (In addition to these programs, the government's pension guaranty agency assumed $2.8 billion of the pension obligations of TWA and USAir, while legislation was approved in Congress in early-2004 that would further ease the major carriers' pension payments.)

Such government aid raises a number of nettlesome public policy issues. First, does such aid represent an essential response to a national crisis that was tragically focused on air transportation, including the shutdown of the nation's air system, as well as increased

---

[39]*United States v. Airline Tariff Publishing Co. et al.*, Complaint, Civ. Action No. 92-2854, filed December 21, 1992. The carriers subsequently settled with the Justice Department without contesting these charges.

[40]*United States v. AMR Corp.*, 140 F. Supp. 2d 1141 (D. Kan. 2001), affirmed by the Tenth Circuit Court of Appeals, 2003-2 Trade Cas. (CCH) P74,078 (July 3, 2003).

[41]Statement of Jeffrey N. Shane, U.S. Department of Transportation, before the Senate Committee on Commerce, Science, and Transportation, January 9, 2003.

airline insurance and security costs? Or did 9/11 and its aftermath exacerbate trends that already were underway in the industry prior to that event, especially among the major carriers, which already were experiencing losses in profitable business traffic due to high fares, high costs, expensive mergers, billions spent buying back their own stock shares, and lavish executive compensation packages?

Second, was the creation of the ATSB to disburse government loan guarantees an admirably pragmatic response to a catastrophic event? Or did it invest a small board with immense power to choose winners and losers, thereby subjecting its determinations to suspicions of political lobbying, favoritism, and "rent seeking"? Will future government actions almost unavoidably be influenced by considerations of their effect on the particular carriers whose multimillion dollar debts the federal government has guaranteed?

Third, was a unique opportunity to promote competition lost by not making billions in government grants and loan guarantees contingent on dominant carriers taking steps to relinquish their stranglehold on slots, gates, ground facilities, and routes to and from their fortress hub monopolies? Would that not also promote the public interest? Conversely, does disbursing billions in government payments to carriers in proportion to their size serve to reward monopoly and oligopoly rather than combat them?

Conclusion

The purpose of deregulating the airlines was to replace pervasive government control with competition as a better regimen for regulating economic decision making—to substitute the invisible hand of the competitive marketplace for the visible fist of the state. However, a failure to enforce the antitrust laws has allowed the industry to jump from centralized government control to centralized private control without taking root in the region of effective competition in-between these extremes. The success of some rapidly-growing independent carriers like JetBlue and AirTran over the post-9/11 period offers a glimmer of hope, although these two carriers together account for only 3.5 percent of the field, and their success might be attributable in important part to cash-strapped majors that temporarily have lacked the financial resources with which to bludgeon them.[42] Overall, then, the potential benefits of effective competition remain unrealized, and the industry attests to the consequences of antitrust inaction in a newly deregulated field.[43]

---

[42]*See* Melanie Trottman, "Big Airlines Cut Fares, Add Routes to Fight Newer Low-Cost Carriers," *Wall Street Journal,* February 6, 2004, 1.

[43]For a more sanguine view, see Alfred E. Kahn, *Lessons from Deregulation: Telecommunications and Airlines after the Crunch* (Washington, D.C.: AEI-Brookings Joint Center for Regulatory Studies, 2004).

Suggested Readings

Books

Bailey, Elizabeth E., David R. Graham, and Daniel P. Kaplan. 1985. *Deregulating the Airlines.* Cambridge: MIT Press.

Caves, Richard E. 1962. *Air Transport and Its Regulators: An Industry Study.* Cambridge: Harvard University Press.

Dempsey, Paul S., and Andrew R. Goetz. 1992. *Airline Deregulation and Laissez-Faire Mythology.* Westport, CT: Quorum Books.

Douglas, George, and James Miller. 1974. *Economic Regulation of Domestic Air Transport: Theory and Practice.* Washington, D.C.: Brookings Institution.

Morrison, Steven A., and Clifford Winston.1995. *The Evolution of the Airline Industry.* Washington, D.C.: Brookings Institution.

Petzinger, Thomas. 1995. *Hard Landing.* New York: Random House.

Government Reports and Other Sources

Air Transport Association. Annual Report. Washington, D.C.

Aviation and Aerospace Almanac. Washington, D.C.: Aviation Week.

Hecker, JayEtta Z. 2001. U.S. General Accounting Office. "Aviation Competition: Challenges in Enhancing Competition in Dominated Markets." Testimony before the U.S. Congress. Senate. Committee on Commerce, Science, and Transportation. March 13.

_____. 2001. "Airline Competition: Issues Raised by Consolidation Proposals." Testimony before the U.S. Congress. Senate. Subcommittee on Antitrust, Business Rights, and Competition. February 7.

Transportation Research Board, National Research Council. 1999. *Entry and Competition in the U.S. Airline Industry.* Washington, D.C.: National Academy Press.

U.S. Congress. Senate. Subcommittee on Antitrust, Business Rights, and Competition. Hearing: Aviation Competition and Concentration at High-Density Airports, 107th Cong., 1st sess., 2002.

U.S. Congress. Senate. Committee on Commerce, Science, and Transportation. Hearing: Airline Passenger Fairness Act, 106th Cong., 1st sess., 2000.

U.S. Congress. Senate. Committee on the Judiciary. Hearing: Airline Consolidation: Has It Gone Too Far? 107th Cong., 1st sess., 2002.

U.S. Congress. Senate. Committee on the Judiciary. Hearings: State of Competition in the Airline Industry, 106th Cong., 2d sess., 2000.

U.S. Congress. Senate. Committee on the Judiciary. Report: Civil Aeronautics Board Practices and Procedures, 94th Cong., 1st sess., 1975.

U.S. Department of Transportation, Bureau of Transportation Statistics (www.bts.gov/oai)(Provides access to a wide variety of airline statistics.)

U.S. Department of Transportation, Office of Assistant Secretary for Aviation and International Affairs. http://ostpxweb.dot.gov/aviation/intro (Provides statistical information and reports relating to domestic and international competition issues.)

U.S. Department of Transportation. 1996. The Low Cost Airline Service Revolution. Washington, D.C.: April.

U.S. General Accounting Office. 1999. "Aviation Competition: Effects on Consumers from Domestic Airline Alliances Vary." Washington, D.C.: January.

U.S. General Accounting Office. www.gao.gov. ("Reports" link contains recent studies of the industry under the general "transportation" subject heading.)

Wayne, Leslie, and Michael Moss. "Bailout for Airlines Showed the Weight of a Mighty Lobby," *New York Times,* October 10, 2001, 1.

CHAPTER

10

Health Care

—John Goddeeris

No U.S. industry is larger or more important than health care. National health expenditures currently account for 14.1 percent of gross domestic product (GDP). In other words, more than $1 out of every $7 spent on final goods and services produced in the United States is devoted to health. Collectively, we spend more than $1.4 trillion, and on a per capita basis, more than $5,000 annually for every man, woman, and child in America.

The health care industry encompasses an immense variety of goods and services. An expectant mother's visit to her doctor for a prenatal checkup; a pair of contact lenses; a surgical operation to replace a failing hip; or the drug cocktail that keeps a potential AIDS patient relatively symptom-free are among the outputs of the health care sector. Figure 10-1 shows the major components of national health expenditures, as defined by the U.S. Centers for Medicare & Medicaid Services (CMS). The largest categories, in order, are hospital care, physician and clinical services, prescription drugs, and nursing home care. The "other" category includes a wide range of goods and services, such as dental care; home health care; the services of other professionals such as chiropractors and optometrists; over-the-counter medications; durable medical equipment such as eyeglasses, hearing aids, and wheelchairs; the costs of administering government health programs and private health insurance; and government-funded public health services and medical research.

The sheer size of the health care sector makes it a key component of the U.S. economy. In addition, some of our most intense policy debates revolve around health care issues. In the early 1990s, continuing rapid increases in health care spending along with growth in the number of uninsured Americans led to calls for a major overhaul of our health care system. President Clinton proposed a sweeping reform in 1993, which was hotly debated in Congress and the national media. That effort ultimately stalled. For a time, the emergence of managed care health insurance seemed to slow the growth of spending, and general economic prosperity made health care reform a less pressing need. However, in the early twenty-first century, the combination of a sluggish economy, resurgent health care spending, demands to include prescription drug coverage in Medicare coverage for seniors, and increases in the number of uninsured focused renewed attention on the health care economy.

Even aside from its size and policy importance, the health care industry is a fascinating field for students of industrial organization to examine. Traditional relationships among patients, doctors, health insurers, hospitals, and other suppliers of care have undergone much change in the last 20 years, with no equilibrium yet in sight.

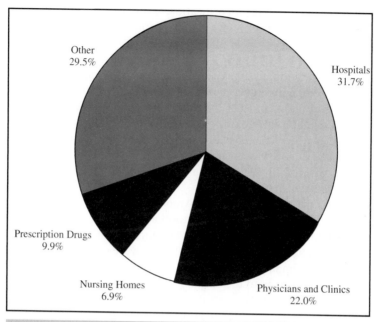

FIGURE 10-1   U.S. Health Care Expenditures in 2001, by Type of Service

SOURCE: Centers for Medicare & Medicaid Services, National Health Accounts, cms.gov/statistics/nhe.

I. HISTORY

Today, we take it for granted that medical care is expensive but that it also can be powerful. A typical day in the hospital cost about $1,300 in 2001 and several times as much for intensive care. However, modern hospital care can often save the lives of heart attack victims or those suffering from severe burns or trauma from an automobile accident. People need a mechanism, either private insurance or support through public programs, to enable them to obtain care without the risk of staggering financial losses. The fact that 44 million Americans (15.2 percent of the population) are uninsured and lack such a formal mechanism is widely viewed as a serious public policy problem.

Things were not always this way. A century ago, medical care was not expensive, and medical insurance was virtually nonexistent in the United States. The workers' compensation system was developing in the early twentieth century, making employers responsible for the costs of work-related injuries, but workers were much more concerned about income reductions from lost work time than about the costs of medical care.

By 1929, the first year for which we have reasonably good data on national health expenditures, health spending was only about 3.5 percent of GDP. One important reason that the health care industry was much smaller is that the capabilities of medicine at the time were limited. In 1976, the President's Biomedical Research Panel wrote:

> Fifty years ago the term technology, and for that matter science, would have seemed incongruous in a discussion of medical practice. The highly skilled practitioner was a master of diagnostic medicine, but the ultimate intentions of

his skill were limited to the identification of the particular illness, the prediction of the likely outcome, and then the guidance of the patient and his family while the illness ran its full, natural course.[1]

That situation gradually changed. As technology improved, hospitals began to evolve from charitable institutions used only by the poor to facilities for the treatment of serious illness or injury. In 1929, the first prototype for a Blue Cross health insurance plan was developed at Baylor University, enabling subscribers to pay a little each month to avoid large bills when hospital care was needed. The idea spread, backed by groups of hospitals that saw it as a way to increase revenue during the Great Depression. Blue Shield plans, organized by doctors as a mechanism for prepaying for physician care, began to emerge a decade later.

Still, by 1940 only 9 percent of the American public had any private health insurance, and national health expenditures stood at about 4.1 percent of GDP. A remarkable transformation was beginning, however. During World War II, a time of tight labor markets in this country, employee fringe benefits were exempted from wage-price controls and became an important tool for attracting and retaining workers. The fact that the cost of health insurance to the employer was not counted as part of the employee's taxable income made insurance a preferred form of compensation even after the war ended. At the same time, advances in surgery and increases in the cost of hospital care increased the financial risks associated with not having insurance coverage.

This combination of circumstances led to the rapid spread of health insurance. By 1950, more than half the population had some private coverage. The numbers continued to grow, reaching 82 percent of the population by 1975.[2] Private insurance has remained closely tied to employment: In 2002, 88 percent of those with private insurance got it through their own job or that of a family member (usually a parent or spouse).[3] For a variety of reasons, health insurance is less expensive if purchased by large groups than if purchased by individuals, and place of employment is one natural basis for grouping. The favorable tax treatment of employer-provided health insurance also encouraged the link between health care insurance and jobs.

In the era of the War on Poverty and President Johnson's Great Society, new government programs extended coverage to groups that had difficulty obtaining it. Medicare and Medicaid were enacted in 1965 and grew rapidly. Medicare is a federal program that provides substantial, though incomplete, health insurance coverage to nearly all of those aged 65 and older. Medicaid is a federal–state matching program aimed at providing coverage for the poor. In practice, it reaches far from all of the poor, and coverage varies considerably across states. Both programs made significant contributions to reducing the residual number of Americans with no source of insurance.

Although the overall trend in the last 60 years has been toward expanding insurance coverage, private coverage has eroded in recent years. The share of the population without either public or private coverage has increased. The most widely accepted estimates show that 86.1 percent of the population had health insurance in 1990, with 73.2

---

[1]President's Biomedical Research Panel, Report of the President's Biomedical Research Panel (Washington, D.C.: Government Printing Office, 1976).
[2]Health Insurance Association of America, *Source Book of Health Insurance Data, 1990* (Washington, D.C.: Health Insurance Association of America, 1990).
[3]Robert J. Mills and Shailesh Bhandari, Health Insurance Coverage in the United States: 2002 (Washington, D.C.: U.S. Census Bureau, September 2003).

percent having some private coverage, but that the shares had fallen to 84.8 and 69.6 percent, respectively, in 2002.[4]

Even more striking than the spread of public and private insurance has been the growth of health care spending. Between 1950 and 2001, health care spending per capita went from $476 (in 2001 dollars, using the GDP deflator to adjust for changes in the price level) to $4,819, an increase of 913 percent over and above the general increase in prices.[5] By comparison, real GDP per capita grew by about 190 percent over the same period.

Figure 10-2 displays the growth of health care spending since 1960 in a slightly different way. It shows for each year the percentage increase over the previous year in per capita spending on health care, after adjusting for general inflation. Over the entire period, health care spending per capita grew faster than the general price level in every year, and in all but 5 years it increased at least 3 percentage points faster. The average of the net annual changes over the period is 4.9 percent. Interestingly, the 5 years of slowest growth all occurred between 1994 and 1998, though rapid increases have since returned.

What can account for such dramatic growth of spending, sustained over such a long period? Surely several factors have contributed, but most economic experts stress that the growth of insurance and spending are closely entwined, each feeding on the other, along with a third factor—the advance of knowledge. New knowledge creates new capabilities for diagnoses and treatments, often at high cost.[6] The health care financing system in place for most of the second half of the twentieth century, increasingly

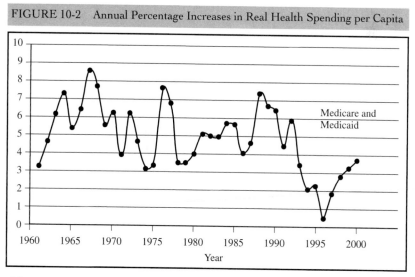

FIGURE 10-2   Annual Percentage Increases in Real Health Spending per Capita

SOURCE: *Author's calculations using data from Centers for Medicare & Medicaid Services (health services and supplies), U.S. Census Bureau (resident population), and U.S. Bureau of Economic Analysis (GDP price deflator).*

---

[4]Mills and Bhandari, Health Insurance Coverage in the United States: 2002.
[5]Health care spending is measured here by "health services and supplies," which is national health expenditures minus spending on research and construction of new facilities.
[6]Joseph Newhouse, "An Iconoclastic View of Health Cost Containment," *Health Affairs* 12 (Supplement 1993): 152–171; Burton A. Weisbrod, "The Health Care Quadrilemma: An Essay on Technological Change, Insurance, Quality of Care, and Cost Containment," *Journal of Economic Literature* 29 (June 1991): 523–552.

dominated by third-party payment as time went on, imposed little restraint on the adoption and application of innovations in health care that, however costly, offered some hope of medical benefit.

II. INDUSTRY STRUCTURE

We focus on three key components of the health care industry: health insurance (now predominantly provided in some form of managed care), physicians, and hospitals.[7] Before we turn to these components of the supply side of the industry, a brief look at its current sources of revenue will provide helpful background. Figure 10-3 breaks down national health expenditures by source of funds. It shows that nearly half (45 percent) of all spending on health is publicly funded, and that Medicare and Medicaid each individually account for a substantial fraction of the total.

The "other public" category includes spending on a number of things, the largest of which are public health activities, programs of the Veterans Administration and the Department of Defense (including health care coverage for the dependents of armed services personnel), state and local government hospitals, and medical research. On the

FIGURE 10-3   U.S. Health Care Expenditures in 2001, by Source of Funds

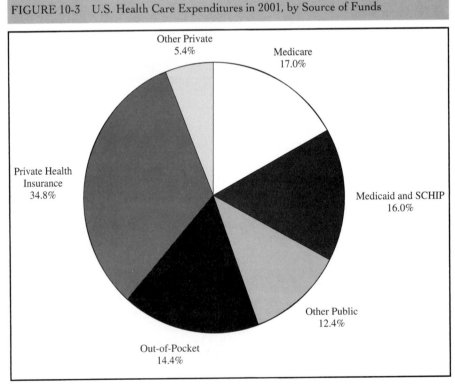

Other Private 5.4%

Medicare 17.0%

Private Health Insurance 34.8%

Medicaid and SCHIP 16.0%

Other Public 12.4%

Out-of-Pocket 14.4%

SOURCE: Centers for Medicare & Medicaid Services, National Health Accounts, cms.gov/statistics/nhe.

[7]The most significant omission is any special consideration of prescription drugs. Drugs are increasingly important to health and as a share of health care expenditures. The pharmaceutical industry is an important area of study in its own right.

TABLE 10-1 Sources of Revenue by Type of Service: 2001

	Hospital Care	Physicians Services	Prescription Drugs	Nursing Homes
Out-of-Pocket	3.1%	11.2%	30.7%	27.2%
Private Insurance	33.7	48.1	47.4	7.6
Other Private	4.9	7.1	0.0	3.7
Total Public	58.3	33.6	21.9	61.5
Medicare	29.9	20.4	1.7	11.7
Medicaid and SCHIP (State Children's Health Insurance Program)	17.3	7.1	17.4	47.5

SOURCE: Centers for Medicare & Medicaid Services, National Health Accounts, cms.gov/statistics/nhe.

private side, payments by way of private insurance are more than twice those that come directly from consumers' pockets.

The breakdown in Figure 10-3 is true on average, but as Table 10-1 shows, sources of revenue vary a good deal by type of service. For hospital care, for example, the out-of-pocket share is much smaller than the overall average, at about 3 percent; Medicare alone accounts for 30 percent of revenues. Medicaid is especially important for nursing homes, accounting for nearly 48 percent of their revenues; private insurance accounts for only 8 percent. The absence of an outpatient prescription drug benefit under Medicare and incomplete private insurance coverage for drugs leaves a relatively high share of those expenses paid directly out-of-pocket. (Partial prescription drug coverage was added to Medicare in late-2003, to become effective in 2006.)

Health Insurance

Health insurance is the point of contact for access to most health care services for most of the population; as such, it is a good place to start examining the structure of the health care industry. Most health insurers in the United States prior to the mid-1980s played a passive role in the provision of health care. The insurance contract defined the financial terms of the policy, including the premium, scope of services covered, and cost-sharing arrangements for the enrollee. Decisions about which services to provide were left to the enrollee and his or her doctor. Choice of doctor also was unrestricted.

Health insurance was at first dominated by Blue Cross and Blue Shield plans, which were nonprofit organizations established by hospital and doctors' associations. Later, companies operating in other lines of insurance—so-called commercial insurers such as Aetna, Travelers, New York Life, and Prudential—entered the market. By the early 1950s, they had as a group surpassed Blue Cross–Blue Shield in total number of people covered.

For policies written by commercial insurers, sometimes called indemnity policies, the doctors, hospitals, and other providers of covered services would bill the enrollee, who would pay the bill and then recover the insured amount from the insurer. In the case of policies written by Blue Cross and Blue Shield, as well as for individuals covered by Medicare and Medicaid, coverage was more commonly in the form of "service benefits." The insurer agreed to cover a specified set of services when needed, with perhaps some cost sharing on the part of the enrollee. Providers would be paid (or "reimbursed") directly by the insurer. For doctors, this usually meant they were paid according to what they charged for services, with some screens applied to assure that a doctor's charge was not out of line with customary fees in the community. Hospitals and other providers usually were reimbursed for costs incurred. Regardless of whether the indemnity or service benefit approach was used, the insurer took little active role in treatment decisions.

In the last 20 years, the health insurer's role has changed dramatically. Managed care emerged and largely swept the marketplace, though its more intrusive forms have become less popular lately. Although the concept of managed care encompasses a broad range of organizational forms and management tools, its various manifestations have in common an attempt to go beyond consumer cost sharing and benefit package design to influence the nature of the care that an enrollee receives, as well as the choice of provider.

At one end of the managed care spectrum is the staff model health maintenance organization (HMO). In a staff model HMO, the doctors caring for the enrollees are employees, or part owners, of the organization that is providing health insurance. Because the HMO agrees to provide care to its enrollees for a fixed premium, the organization has an incentive to minimize the cost of providing that care. Given that additional services do not generate additional revenue (except consumer cost-sharing payments, if any are used), each additional dollar of cost reduces the organization's net profits. If the organization's incentive to minimize cost can be translated to its medical staff, then the staff can be expected to manage the care of enrollees in a cost-conscious way.

The staff model HMO has been in practice for many years. The term *health maintenance organization* was coined in the early 1970s, but the most successful example of the staff model, the Kaiser Health Plan, dates back to the collaborative efforts of medical entrepreneur Dr. Sydney Garfield and the industrialist Henry Kaiser in the 1930s.[8] The Kaiser Plan grew to more than 1 million enrollees by 1962 and more than 2.5 million by 1972. Another early example of this model, which used to be called prepaid group practice, is the Group Health Cooperative of Puget Sound, founded in 1947 and today serving more than 500,000 enrollees in the state of Washington.

Other types of HMOs contract nonexclusively with groups of doctors or Independent Practice Associations (IPAs) of individual doctors. This form integrates the insurance plan less tightly with physicians than the staff model, as the same doctors might contract with several other HMOs and also see patients not affiliated with any HMO. The insurer, however, can still attempt to influence the provision of care by a variety of methods, including monitoring the use of services (e.g., requiring preapproval of nonemergency hospital admissions, reviewing length of hospital stay), requiring that enrollees be approved for specialty care by a "gatekeeper" primary care physician, selectively contracting with doctors and hospitals rather than allowing enrollees unrestricted choice, or using payment methods other than straight fee-for-service to influence provider incentives. For prescription drug coverage, the set of drugs covered and the manner in which they can be obtained also may be limited.

Other forms of managed care use some or all of these tools in various forms and combinations. The lines between different types of organizations are increasingly blurry. In a preferred provider organization (PPO), the insurer contracts selectively with a preferred set of providers at discounted rates and creates incentives in the form of reduced cost sharing for enrollees to use those providers. Typically, PPOs also use some forms

---

[8]Paul Starr, *The Social Transformation of American Medicine* (New York: Basic Books, 1982). The Kaiser Plan is technically a group model rather than a staff model HMO. Rather than employing its doctors, the health plan contracts in each region where it operates with a single medical group, which serves only Kaiser patients.

of utilization management. Many HMOs now also include a point-of-service (POS) option, which allows enrollees to see providers outside the regular network, usually with considerably higher cost sharing by the enrollee.

Figure 10-4 shows the rapid evolution of health insurance markets. In 1980, managed care meant only HMOs, which had less than 10 percent of the group insurance market nationally. By 1988, PPOs had emerged, but conventional insurance still accounted for 73 percent of enrollment. From that point, the market share of conventional health insurance declined rapidly in favor of the various forms of managed care, falling below 10 percent by the year 2000.

In addition to the decline of conventional insurance, Figure 10-4 displays another important trend. In the late 1990s, insurance premium increases had moderated, and the economy was growing at a good pace. Consumers began to turn away from the more intrusive forms of managed care. The total market share of HMOs, including POS plans, has declined recently in favor of PPOs, which now account for more than half of the group insurance market.

The use of managed care also increased in the 1990s in the publicly funded Medicare and Medicaid programs. Since 1985, Medicare has been willing to contract with HMOs on a risk-contract basis, paying a fixed amount per enrollee, often referred to as a capitation (per-head) payment. The HMO then bears the risk that the enrollee's expenditures might be higher or lower than the capitation amount. Medicare paid HMOs 95 percent of the average of what it spent on fee-for-service Medicare enrollees in the same geographic area.

The number of enrollees participating in risk contracts grew slowly. About 1 million participated in 1987, which at that time was about 3 percent of Medicare enrollees.

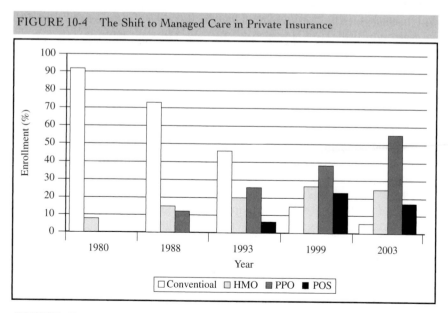

FIGURE 10-4   The Shift to Managed Care in Private Insurance

SOURCE: Kaiser Family Foundation, Employer Health Benefits 2003 Annual Survey, Exhibit 5.1, www.kff.org/insurance/ehbs2003~abstract.cfm; 1980 numbers taken from D.M. Cutler and R.J. Zeckhauser, "The Anatomy of Health Insurance," in A.J. Culyer and J.P. Newhouse eds., Handbook of Health Economics (Amsterdam: North-Holland, 2000), Fig. 4.

By the end of 1995, the number was 3.1 million, and by the end of 1999, it was about 6.3 million, or 16.4 percent of enrollees. By 2001, however, a number of HMOs had stopped participating, due in part to changes in Medicare's payment methods, and enrollment had fallen to 13.8 percent of the Medicare population.[9]

Although Medicare has thus far made managed care participation a matter of enrollee choice, many states require that their Medicaid beneficiaries enroll with a managed care plan. Initially, federal law prohibited states from restricting the choice of medical providers for Medicaid beneficiaries, though the low payment rates characteristic of Medicaid often made it difficult for beneficiaries to find doctors who were willing to see them.

The law was changed in 1981, allowing states to experiment with managed care and other innovative approaches. Managed care participation was still low going into the 1990s, but it has expanded rapidly since then.[10] In 1991, fewer than 10 percent of Medicaid beneficiaries were in managed care. By 1995, the number had grown to nearly 30 percent, and by 2002 to nearly 58 percent, or about 23 million enrollees. Some of this enrollment is in a mild form of managed care called primary care case management, in which a primary care doctor agrees to manage the care of a set of enrollees but is not at risk for the cost of hospital and specialty care. However, this model has been shrinking relative to capitated models, in which the managed care organization is at risk for the costs of all covered services. Primary care case management accounted for 30 percent of Medicaid managed care enrollment in 1996 but only 24 percent in 1998.

A notable trend among HMOs and health insurers is a movement away from nonprofit organizational forms toward entities organized as for-profit businesses. Early HMOs were organized predominantly as nonprofits, the only type eligible for federal subsidies under the HMO Act of 1973. When direct federal subsidies ended in the early 1980s, market share began to swing heavily toward for-profits, partly as a result of entry of new for-profit HMOs and their growth, but also from conversion of nonprofit HMOs to the for-profit form. From 1981 to 1997, the percentage of HMO enrollees in nonprofit plans plummeted from 88 percent to 37 percent.[11] In 1994, the national Blue Cross and Blue Shield Association decided for the first time that for-profit firms could affiliate with the organization, paving the way for a number of regional Blue Cross plans to convert to for-profit status.

Before leaving the subject of the structure of health insurance markets, some mention should be made of the phenomenon of self-insurance. Insurance is fundamentally a way of transferring risk from an individual or group to an insurer, who, by virtue of pooling together large numbers of enrollees with largely independent risks, is better able to accept that risk. For large employers, those with 500 employees or more, pooling within the firm accomplishes much of what an insurer could provide in this regard. Many large employers find it attractive to self-insure—that is, to bear the risks associated with random year-to-year fluctuations in health care utilization—in order to escape some state and federal regulations associated with purchased health insurance and perhaps to gain more control over the insurance they provide and how it is administered.

---

[9]Marsha Gold, "Can Managed Care and Managed Competition Control Medicare Costs?" Health Affairs Web Exclusive, April 2, 2003; Centers for Medicare and Medicaid Services, cms.hhs.gov/statistics/enrollment/.
[10]Centers for Medicare and Medicaid Services, http://cms.hhs.gov/medicaid/managedcare/mmcss02.asp.
[11]Kaiser Family Foundation, Trends and Indicators in the Changing Health Care Marketplace, 2002, Chartbook, www.kff.org/content/2002/3161/marketplace2002_finalc.pdf.

In 2001, half of all covered workers were in self-insured plans, with higher percentages for workers employed by larger firms.[12]

Physicians

In his influential 1974 book on health care and economics entitled *Who Shall Live?*, Victor Fuchs called the physician the "captain of the team" in health care. Although managed care has challenged the physician's preeminent position, Fuchs's characterization remains largely accurate. In addition to the medical and surgical services they provide directly, physicians admit and discharge patients from hospitals, order diagnostic tests, and prescribe drugs, although these tasks are now frequently scrutinized by insurance providers.

About 652,000 medical doctors were active in patient care in 2001, according to American Medical Association data. Fuchs noted that a century ago, two out of three persons employed in health care were doctors. As the health care system developed, with the rise of the modern hospital and the nursing home industry, as well as the introduction of a broad variety of other types of specialized services such as physical therapy and respiratory therapy, employment opportunities vastly expanded for other workers who did not have the breadth and depth of training of a medical doctor. The number of nonphysician health care workers has risen much faster than the number of doctors such that the ratio is now about 14 to 1.[13]

Doctors spend more years in training than almost any other workers. Medical school generally requires 4 years of additional schooling after obtaining a bachelor's degree, and is usually followed by at least 3 additional years in a hospital-based residency program to obtain board certification as a specialist or as a general family practitioner. The need to be accepted by a medical school and then complete this long training period is clearly an important barrier to entry into the medical profession. Some economists have argued that the control exerted by the AMA over the number of medical school slots available and the length of the training period has helped keep doctors' incomes artificially high. The counterargument in favor of supply restrictions and extensive training has been that they promote quality of care, which consumers would find difficult to evaluate in the absence of professional certification.

Medicine continues to be a highly paid profession. According to AMA survey data, median physician income in 2000 was $175,000. An important question for public policy is whether this level is artificially high given the amount of time invested in training, the ability required, and the work effort exerted by the typical doctor. (The AMA also reports that median hours in professional activity for doctors are about 55 per week.) Several studies (unfortunately, none of them are recent) have addressed this question by examining whether the rate of return on the investment in a medical education is unusually high compared with alternatives.[14] An important component of the investment costs are the opportunity costs of foregone earnings during the long training period. The weight of the evidence through about 1985, when the published

---

[12]Jon R. Gabel , Gail A. Jensen and Samantha Hawkins, "Self-Insurance in Times of Growing and Retreating Managed Care," *Health Affairs* 22 (March/April 2003): 202–210.

[13]*Statistical Abstract of the United States: 2002* (Washington, D.C.: U.S. Census Bureau, 2002): Tables 144 and 146, www.census.gov/statab/www/.

[14]See Paul Feldstein, *Health Care Economics*, 5th ed. (Albany, NY: Delmar, 1999), 363–364 for a summary and references.

TABLE 10-2   Doctors in Patient Care by Type of Practice

	1975		1985		1995		2001	
	(in thou-sands)	%	(in thou-sands)	%	(in thou-sands)	%	(in thou-sands)	%
Total	311.9		448.8		582.1		668.9	
Nonfederal								
Office Based	213.3	68.4	329.0	73.3	427.3	73.4	514.0	76.8
Residency or Other Training	53.5	17.2	72.2	16.1	93.7	16.1	92.9	13.9
Hospital Staff	21.0	6.7	30.3	6.8	43.1	7.4	45.4	6.8
Federal	24.1	7.	17.3	3.9	18.1	3.1	16.6	2.5

SOURCE: U.S. National Center for Health Statistics, *Health*, United States, 2003, Table 100, www.cdc.gov/nchs/hus.htm.

studies end, suggests that a medical degree has been an economically attractive invest-ment, with rates of return usually estimated at 13 percent or higher, even after ac-counting for the high costs of acquiring the degree.

Table 10-2 shows the number of medical doctors involved in patient care from 1975 to 2001 and the breakdown by type of practice. Between 1975 and 2001, the num-ber of doctors in patient care increased by about two thirds on a per capita basis, re-sulting primarily from a buildup in medical school capacity that began in the late 1960s and also from an inflow of foreign-trained doctors. For most physicians, the base of practice is in an office rather than in a hospital, and the fraction of doctors who are office based has increased since 1975. About 14 percent of doctors are in residency or other training programs, usually hospital based, and another smaller fraction are em-ployed as full-time hospital staff. Most of the small fraction of physicians who are fed-erally employed are hospital based.

Traditionally, most doctors have been self-employed or partners in small groups. Table 10-3 summarizes data on changes over time in the distribution of office-based physicians by style and size of group. In 1969, the majority of office-based physicians,

TABLE 10-3   Trends in Distribution of Office-Based Physicians by Group Affiliation

	% Distribution of Physicians			Average Size of Group		
	1969	1980	1995	1969	1980	1995
Individual Practice	78.3%	67.2%	51.9%			
Group Practice	21.7	32.8	48.1	6.2	8.2	10.5
Single Specialty	7.1	10.9	20.1	4.1	4.8	6.2
Multispecialty	13.2	20.1	25.8	10.1	15.2	25.4
Family or General Practice	1.5	1.8	2.1	3.5	4.5	5.6

SOURCE: Adapted from Paul J. Feldstein, *Health Care Economics*, 5th ed. (1999), Table 10.2, 247. Albany, NY: Delmar Publishers.

78 percent, were in individual practice, which the AMA defined to include offices with one or two physicians. By 1995, those in individual practice were still in the majority but barely so. By 2001, about 56 percent of doctors were in practices of three or more physicians.[15]

Both single-specialty and multispecialty group practices have grown considerably as a share of all physicians, and, within each type, the average group size has increased. Within physicians' offices, the trend has been toward larger numbers of aides per physician. The number of aides per physician in office-based practice was 1.54 in 1970 and had grown to 2.54 by 1995.[16]

The trend toward larger groups suggests that economic advantages to group practice have increased over time. Some economies of scale exist in production, particularly in the way physicians delegate tasks to allied health workers and use other inputs to production. A group of physicians might be able to utilize a certain type of aide or piece of equipment fully, whereas a solo practitioner could not. Consumers also might prefer to deal with groups for convenience in getting appointments, and because a group can develop a kind of "brand-name" image for quality that the consumer would have more difficulty in assessing at the individual doctor level. Several physicians who share a practice also are likely to experience less variability in workload and income at the individual level than would a solo practitioner, and this risk-spreading feature of groups is valuable.

However, increasing group size also has its disadvantages. For example, if a group of doctors shares the costs of a set of inputs, individual incentives to economize in the use of those inputs are blunted. The distribution of physician group size thus reflects a balancing at the margin of those forces that push in the direction of larger and smaller size, as well as differences in size of market (a small town cannot accommodate a large multispecialty group) and in preferences of doctors and consumers concerning style of practice.

Another reason for doctors to form larger groups could be to position themselves to be responsible for managing all of the health care—or some well-defined subset of it—for a defined population of enrollees, and to accept payment on a capitation basis. Accepting capitation payments is, in effect, acting like a health insurer. The advantage of capitation from the group's point of view is that the group has a greater incentive to manage the total costs of care and can profit from doing so effectively. However, capitation is risky for an individual doctor or a small group because the patient population the group can handle might be too small to predict accurately the level of costs that will be incurred, even if care is managed efficiently. Increasing group size can reduce that risk. In some parts of the country, large groups, sometimes numbering in the hundreds of doctors, contract with managed care plans and sometimes directly with employers on a capitation basis.[17]

The growth of managed care spurred more affiliations of physician practices with hospitals, insurers, or physician practice management companies (PPMCs), although some of those affiliations proved to be short-lived. Doctors or groups that had been in

---

[15]John D. Wassenaar and Sara L. Thran, *Physician Socioeconomic Statistics,* 2003 edition (Chicago, IL: American Medical Association Press).

[16]Feldstein, *Health Care Economics,* 246.

[17]J. C. Robinson and L. P. Casalino, "The Growth of Medical Groups Paid through Capitation in California," *New England Journal of Medicine* 333, no. 25: 1684–1687.

independent practice sometimes sold the physical assets of their practices to a hospital or managed care organization and accepted salaried compensation. Frequently, however, the buyers became dissatisfied with the performance of salaried physicians and found it more advantageous to contract with independent groups. PPMCs, a phenomenon of the 1990s, sometimes bought the assets of groups of doctors and then negotiated contracts with managed care organizations and provided certain management services to the groups in return for a share of net revenues after practice expenses had been paid. A few publicly traded PPMCs grew rapidly in the mid-1990s but seemed to overemphasize expansion at the expense of good management and just as quickly went into decline. MedPartners, FPA Medical, and PhyCor are three PPMCs that grew quickly but have exited the market or gone into bankruptcy.

Despite the development of a variety of business models under which physician practice is organized, most physicians practice as independent professionals, not as employees, and some form of fee-for-service is the predominant method by which they are paid. In the AMA survey of physicians for 2001, 65 percent of nonfederal, nonresident physicians identified themselves as self-employed or as independent contractors, with only 35 percent calling themselves employees.[18] Capitation payments at the level of the individual physician continue to account for only a small share of total physician revenues. Although 88 percent of doctors in 2001 reported at least some managed care contracts (with the percentage varying between 82 percent and 93 percent across the nine census regions), only 7 percent of a doctor's practice revenues, on average, came from capitated contracts. There are also indications that interest in forming large, multispecialty groups has waned recently, perhaps because of difficulties in coordinating the activities of such large groups. Medium-sized (5 to 20 doctors), single-specialty groups are increasingly common.[19]

Hospitals

Hospitals are unusual economic entities. Most are organized as nonprofit firms. In 2001, about 71 percent of community hospital beds were in private nonprofit entities, another 16 percent were in hospitals run by state or local governments, and 13 percent were in for-profit firms. Like any such firm, the nonprofit hospital is not owned by individuals, so no one has a claim to any profits that might accrue to it. Although the administrators are responsible to the hospital's board of trustees, the trustees do not represent ownership in the same way that a private corporation's board of directors does. In addition, decisions about use of a hospital's resources—its beds, employed staff, and equipment—are made to a large extent by its medical staff, meaning doctors who practice in the hospital but generally are not its employees.

Table 10-4 provides data on the evolution of community hospitals since 1946, the year of the passage of the Hill-Burton Act, which allowed for subsidizing the construction and expansion of hospitals. "Community hospitals" is a broad classification used by the American Hospital Association. It includes 84 percent of all hospital beds, excluding only 5 percent that are in federal hospitals and 11 percent in long-term hospitals of various types. Table 10-4 shows that strong expansion in the number of hospitals

---

[18]Wassenaar and Thran, *Physician Socioeconomic Statistics*.
[19]L. P. Casalino et al., "Benefits of and Barriers to Large Medical Group Practice in the United States," *Archives of Internal Medicine* 163, no. 16 (September 8, 2003): 1958–1964.

		Beds (in thousands)	Admissions (in thousands)		Outpatient Visits (in thousands)
Year	Hospitals			Occupancy	
1946	4,444	473	13,655	0.72	n.a.
1950	5,031	505	16,663	0.74	n.a.
1960	5,407	639	22,970	0.75	n.a.
1970	5,859	848	29,252	0.78	133,545
1980	5,830	988	36,143	0.76	202,310
1990	5,384	927	31,181	0.67	301,329
1995	5,194	873	30,945	0.63	414,345
2001	4,908	826	33,814	0.65	538,480

TABLE 10-4   Selected Statistics for Community Hospitals

SOURCE: American Hospital Association, *Hospital Statistics* (Chicago: Health Forum LLC, 2003).

continued until about 1970, and even stronger growth occurred in the number of beds into the 1980s. Hospital admissions grew much faster than the population from 1946 until about 1980 but began to decline thereafter. Since 1995, they have again increased a bit faster than the population.

The average length of a hospital stay began to decline earlier than admissions, as can be inferred from the fact that admissions per bed grew in the 1970s, but occupancy levels declined. The average patient stayed nearly 8 days in 1975 but fewer than 6 in 2001. Optimal occupancy levels for hospitals are a good deal less than 100 percent, as the need for beds fluctuates and it is important to hold some reserve capacity to accommodate periods of peak demand. However, nationwide occupancy levels of less than 70 percent, as have existed since the mid-1980s, are surely indicative of excess bed capacity in the industry.

Table 10-4 also shows rapid growth in the number of outpatient hospital visits. The movement toward shorter hospital stays and substitution of outpatient for inpatient care is driven by technological changes, such as the development of less invasive, laser-assisted surgical techniques, and by changing attitudes about the benefits of prolonged hospitalization. It also has been spurred by cost-containment efforts by managed care organizations, and earlier by Medicare, which focused heavily on the reduction of inpatient care. Inpatient care undoubtedly was overused in the 1960s and 1970s, as doctors and their well-insured patients had little incentive to weigh costs against potential benefits. However, the pendulum might have swung too far in the direction of shorter stays. In the quest to reduce hospital usage because the average cost per patient day is so high, the fact that marginal cost near the end of a stay might be much lower is often insufficiently appreciated.[20] If a bed otherwise would be unoccupied, the incremental cost of extending the stay of a patient needing relatively little care is modest.

Hospitals are multiproduct firms. For inpatient care alone, the Medicare program now recognizes for payment purposes more than 500 diagnosis-related groups (DRGs), which are classifications of patients based on their medical problems. Even

---

[20]Uwe E. Reinhardt, "Our Obsessive Quest to Gut the Hospital," *Health Affairs* 15 (Summer 1996): 145–154.

this large number of categories lumps together patients with widely varying severities of illness and needs for care. Differences across hospitals in average cost per admission are strongly related to differences in the mix of diagnoses among the patients that they treat. Holding patient mix constant, research studies do not indicate substantial economies of scale beyond small hospitals, and any economies probably are exhausted at a size between 200 and 300 beds. In 2001, about 71 percent of community hospitals had fewer than 200 beds. The 29 percent of hospitals that were larger, however, accounted for about 69 percent of admissions.

An Integrated Delivery System (IDS) is a vertically integrated organization that combines some or all of the inputs needed to provide the full range of medical services that an individual might require: hospitals, physicians, outpatient clinics, home health care agencies, nursing homes, and so forth. A group or staff model HMO with its own hospitals is one form of IDS. (Kaiser is the outstanding example.) An IDS also can be organized around a group of physicians. In the 1990s, many hospitals and groups of hospitals sought to create IDSs with themselves at the center. They affiliated with physician groups—sometimes hiring doctors on a salaried basis—and with other elements of the continuum of care. Some hospital-based IDSs met the necessary legal requirements to become HMOs. IDSs also can contract with HMOs or directly with purchasers of care.

From an economic viewpoint, the concept of a hospital-based IDS has a certain appeal. Such an organization seems positioned to take on capitation contracts for the full package of care, potentially cutting out a layer of administrative cost by bypassing middle layers at the insurance level. At least at its top level, the organization has incentives to be conscious of the costs of the resources it uses, substituting, for example, outpatient for inpatient care or preventive for acute care where appropriate.

However, it might be difficult to transmit those top-level incentives to decision makers in other parts of the organization. The success of such an organization depends heavily on the behavior of its affiliated physicians, but if a large part of their compensation is in guaranteed salary, for example, their incentives to work hard and direct the use of other inputs optimally are attenuated. It is not clear from economic theory that a vertically integrated health care organization will outcompete one that purchases most of its inputs through market transactions (e.g., an IPA, HMO, or PPO) and creates incentives through contracts. As the market share of tightly managed care has declined, so also, to some degree, has hospitals' interest in vertical integration. The AHA surveys show a rather sharp decline recently in the share of community hospitals that report having an ownership interest in an HMO, from a peak of 23 percent in 1997 to 15 percent in 2001.

Horizontal integration—affiliating with other hospitals, either in the same market or across markets—is another matter. Hospital markets have become more concentrated since 1980 through reductions in the number of hospitals (evident in Table 10-4) and through the combination of hospitals into systems under common management. If system hospitals operating in the same market are counted as a single hospital, the average number of hospitals per market dropped by about 25 percent between 1981 and 1994, according to one study.[21] In the peak years of the mid-1990s, more than 100 hospital

---

[21]David Dranove, Carol J. Simon, and William D. White, "Is Managed Care Leading to Consolidation in Health-Care Markets?" *Health Services Research* 37, no. 3 (2002): 573–594.

mergers took place per year. Public attention focused heavily on acquisition of non-profit hospitals by for-profit chains, especially by Columbia/HCA, the largest and most aggressive chain. Columbia acquired or negotiated joint venture agreements to manage 35 formerly nonprofit hospitals in 1995 alone. However, for-profit chains became less aggressive about expansion in the wake of a federal government investigation of Columbia, which began in 1997.

In any case, most hospital mergers occur within the nonprofit sector. Consolidation apparently continues. A study of 12 nationally representative communities shows that hospital market concentration increased in all 12 markets from 1996 through 2000.[22]

III.   CONDUCT

Before Managed Care

Physicians

In the postwar, premanaged care period, the markets for physician and hospital care were not characterized by overt price competition. The majority of doctors practiced on a fee-for-service basis. In the early 1960s, before the introduction of Medicare and Medicaid, about 60 percent of payments for physicians' services still came directly from consumer pockets. Doctors were, to some degree, subject to the usual restraint of consumer demand when setting fees. However, obtaining relevant information was difficult for consumers because of the complexity of the set of services that doctors provide and the difficulty of judging quality. It was made more difficult by prohibitions against advertising, which were supported by the AMA and often legally enforced. (Advertising by doctors is no longer prohibited, according to a 1982 Supreme Court ruling.) Thus, even though a large number of doctors practiced in a typical metropolitan area, each individual enjoyed some degree of local monopoly power.

By 1975, the share of physician revenues coming directly from consumers was down to 37 percent, with 35 percent coming from private insurers and 28 percent from public programs. Payments for services were, by then, heavily influenced by the policies of insurers and government payers. Medicare and most insurers adopted the "usual, customary, and reasonable" approach to reimbursement, which paid what the doctor charged unless it was out of line with what that doctor usually charged for the same service, or what was customary for other doctors in the same community. (The "customary" screen was often set at the 75th or 80th percentile of charges in the community.) Such an approach is sensible for an insurer that is a small part of the market and is simply trying to match market rates. As the market becomes dominated by insurers paying in this way, however, this approach tends to freeze in place existing differences in fees across doctors, locations, and types of services, and to encourage a continued upward drift in charges.

Health economists have devoted a great deal of attention to the question of how much control physicians have over the demand for their own services.[23] This question has important implications for the effect of an increase in physician supply, such as the one the United States has experienced since the late 1960s. (See Table 10-2.) Standard

---

[22]Kelly J. Devers et al., "Hospitals' Negotiating Leverage with Health Plans: How and Why Has It Changed?" *Health Services Research* 38, no. 1, part 2 (2003): 419–446.

[23]The Feldstein; Phelps; and Folland, Goodman, and Stano textbooks cited in the Suggested Readings all have extensive discussions of this issue with references to the literature.

economic analysis says that an increase in physician supply leads to lower fees and doctors' incomes, as the supply curve shifts out against a downward-sloping demand curve. However, because patients rely so heavily on them for advice, isn't it possible that doctors who find themselves less busy when the number of competitors rises simply recommend more services, in effect shifting the demand curve outward to match the increase in supply?

Although it strikes most people (especially noneconomists) as plausible that doctors can influence the demand for their services, the importance of the demand-inducement phenomenon eludes precise quantification. Evidence suggests that inducement exists, such as the common finding that doctors' fees are higher in places where physicians are more densely located, but this also might have alternative explanations. Perhaps, for example, consumers are willing to pay more when physicians are more numerous because of greater convenience, shorter waits for services, or more attention from the doctor. The extent of a doctor's power to induce demand thus remains an unsettled area of research. Under tightly managed care, physicians often have financial incentives to recommend fewer rather than more services. As managed care has become less restrictive, the issue of induced demand has gained renewed policy relevance.

Hospitals

In the early 1960s, only about 20 percent of hospital revenues came directly from consumers. By 1969, that share had fallen to less than 10 percent, with 56 percent accounted for by public sources and 20 percent by Medicare alone. Medicare and most private insurers also gave consumers little or no financial incentive to choose less costly over more costly hospitals. If the consumer paid anything out-of-pocket for a hospital stay, the amount was usually the same regardless of the hospital chosen.

A number of theories about the behavior of nonprofit hospitals have been proposed. Some depict the hospital's administration as seeking to maximize a combination of quantity and quality of care. Another model views the hospital as being run in the interest of its staff physicians. Both types of models are broadly consistent with the behavior of hospitals during this period. Hospitals needed physicians to bring in patients, so they made the work environment attractive to the doctors by providing support staff, including interns and residents, and by adding the latest facilities and services. In addition to satisfying the medical staff, these actions signaled that the administrators were running a high-quality institution that the trustees and the community could take pride in. The accommodating payment system of the time, along with advancing technology, provided the other ingredients for increases in expenditures.

Spending growth was even faster for hospitals than for the health care industry as a whole. On average, over the entire period from 1960 to 1979, expenditures in community hospitals rose more than 7 percentage points per year in excess of general inflation.

Such increases could hardly go unnoticed. The states, the federal government, and, to some extent, Blue Cross plans explored a number of regulatory approaches to restraining expenditure growth in hospitals. Certificate-of-Need (CON) regulation is an attempt to control capital investment by requiring that a hospital (or other entity) demonstrate that a need exists in the area before investing in new beds or expensive equipment. This approach was tried in most states, with the earliest adopting it in the 1960s, and it was supported for a time by federal law.

However, economic studies of CON generally conclude that it is ineffective in reducing the growth of total hospital spending: Any expenditure-reducing effects it might have through reductions in the number of beds appear to be offset by higher spending in other areas. Some economists have argued that a regulatory process of this kind is likely to be "captured" by existing hospitals, which have advantages in political clout and control of information, and may be a barrier to potentially valuable innovation.

A number of states also experimented with regulation of the rates at which hospitals were paid for services. The weight of the evidence on rate regulation, from studies that compare hospital spending increases in states that adopted regulation with states that did not, suggests that in some cases it was at least modestly effective in slowing spending growth. Nonetheless, hospital rate regulation was largely abandoned as managed care spread.

A development of great importance to hospitals was Medicare's change in its method of paying for inpatient care beginning in 1983. At that time, Medicare accounted for 28 percent of all hospital revenues and an even higher share in the typical community hospital. The program shifted from reimbursing hospitals on an actual cost basis to paying predetermined rates based on the patient's diagnosis. The new system creates a clear incentive to reduce lengths of stay, as additional days of care add costs but generate no additional revenue.

Hospitals responded strongly to this incentive. Lengths of stay for Medicare patients, which already had been falling slowly, dropped rapidly in the first few years of the Prospective Payment System (PPS). Average length of stay had dropped from 11.2 days in 1975 to 10.3 in 1982, a little less than a day over the course of 7 years, but it then fell an additional 1.7 days over the next 3 years as PPS took effect.

The response to the new system showed that an incentive directed at hospitals could affect their resource use, despite the fact that doctors make the decisions about discharging patients. Medicare remains important for hospitals, accounting for 30 percent of all hospital revenues in 2001. Hospitals respond to the incentives Medicare creates, which, however well-intentioned, are sometimes perverse.

For example, after the PPS began paying hospitals for inpatient care at a fixed rate per case, reimbursement for care provided after discharge in other settings was still done on a cost basis. This created incentives for hospitals to provide skilled nursing care and home care, to discharge patients as early as feasible (sometimes to a different bed in the same facility), and to collect additional revenue from the provision of post-acute care, thereby shifting costs as much as possible to the cost-reimbursed sector. Medicare expenses for skilled nursing care and home care soared. Congress attempted to address the problem in the Balanced Budget Act of 1997, but getting the incentives right while protecting the access of seniors to important medical services is no easy matter.

Health Insurers

As discussed earlier, health insurers in this period largely left the organization and delivery of care to the providers. Commercial insurers did compete with Blue Cross and Blue Shield to sell plans to employers. They made significant inroads, surpassing the Blue plans in total enrollees from the early 1950s onward, despite certain advantages held by the Blues. The Blues were organized as nonprofits and, as such, enjoyed some federal and state tax advantages over for-profit plans. As plans originally organized by hospital associations and medical societies, they also had some advantages in dealing with providers. For example, in some states, Blue Cross received significant discounts on hospital care compared to what was charged to commercial insurers.

Commercial insurers competed by offering an insurance package that was different from that of the Blues, and they priced it differently. The Blues emphasized service benefits and first dollar coverage for hospital care (so individuals faced no co-payments or deductibles for inpatient care) but placed limits on the total number of days covered. These limits left the individual facing large risks in the case of long stays. In contrast, commercial insurers offered major medical insurance covering a wide range of services with deductibles, co-payments, and better coverage for extremely high-cost events. The philosophy of the Blues was also to practice community rating, meaning to set premiums equally across a community in order to spread risks broadly. The problem with community rating in a competitive market for insurance is that groups that expect their health care costs to be lower than the community-wide average have an incentive to split themselves off. Large employers who believed that they had relatively healthy workers turned to commercial insurers (or to self-insurance) to get premiums based on their own experience rather than community rates. As time went on, the Blues responded to competition by behaving more like the commercial insurers—adopting experience rating for large groups.

Managed Care and Conduct

An important contributing factor in the transformation of the health insurance market to managed care in the 1980s and 1990s was the growing concern on the part of employers, especially large ones, with the costs of the insurance. The HMO Act of 1973 promoted HMO growth to some degree, and enrollment grew rapidly from a small base in the 1970s. By the 1980s, the idea of managed care was becoming more familiar, and employers began to look to insurers for ways to gain control over rising premiums, even if it meant placing some restrictions on enrollees' choice of medical providers and access to services.

The PPO concept also emerged in the early 1980s as a less restrictive form of managed care and a more palatable one to many employees. Pressured by employers, health insurers began to compete in new ways, including selectively contracting with hospitals and doctors, negotiating with them for lower payment rates, and implementing other tools of utilization management.

As Figure 10-4 suggests, most health insurance in most parts of the country now incorporates managed care techniques in at least their milder forms. Wide variation still exists across geographic areas in the degree of market penetration of managed care plans, the aggressiveness of price competition among plans, and the extent to which plans have put pressure on providers. Especially in those places where managed care became most aggressive, providers felt pressured to change their behavior or risk being left out of managed care networks, which could considerably reduce demand for their services. Some of their responses involve banding together to become actively engaged in managing care. As discussed earlier, some large physician groups, especially in California, accepted capitation payments and took responsibility for all, or a defined subset of, their enrollees' health care.

More frequently, however, managed care organizations purchase services from providers using some form of fee-for-service, seeking the lowest rates they can get. Rather than being reimbursed for what they consider reasonable costs or charges as they were in the past, hospitals and doctors now often find that payment is determined by what the market will bear. Thus, they find themselves in price competition with their peers to a degree not previously experienced.

Research findings suggest that managed care changed the way hospitals compete. Formerly, hospitals highlighted their quality as a way to attract doctors and patients. Markets with more hospitals might, therefore, experience a "medical arms race," resulting in greater duplication of services and higher unit costs. Evidence from the 1980s and 1990s, however, indicates that when managed care dominates insurance markets, prices of hospital services are lower where competition is more intense, as traditional industrial organization theory predicts.[24]

As would be expected, hospitals and doctors are showing more interest in horizontal combinations (mergers of hospitals, or affiliation with larger physician groups by doctors) to gain bargaining leverage with insurers. At the AMA's annual meeting in June 1999, delegates voted for the first time to support unionization of employed physicians and changes in federal law that would allow collective bargaining groups to represent independent doctors.

IV. PERFORMANCE

How are we to assess the performance of the U.S. health care industry? Rising expenditures, as summarized in Figure 10-2, certainly have been a cause for concern and a driving force behind recent structural changes in the industry. By increasing labor costs, higher health insurance premiums surely spurred employers' interest in managed care. Cost growth in Medicaid and the pressure it placed on government budgets drove state and federal governments in the same direction.

It is important to recognize that rising expenditures on a group of products does not necessarily imply that the industry is performing poorly. For example, if prices fall due to cost-reducing innovations, as with personal computers, an increase in spending will follow naturally if demand is elastic. Total spending also could rise if new, higher-quality but more costly products replace older ones—a more likely scenario for health care. A study analyzing the treatment of heart attack patients between 1983 and 1994 found that although the spending per case was rising, the quality-adjusted price was actually falling about 1 percent per year if improvements in survival were accounted for in a reasonable way.[25]

Still, suspicion is strong that prior to the managed care era, health spending was too high and rose too rapidly. The suspicion stemmed partly from beliefs about the financing system that was in place at the time: Providers of care and well-insured consumers had incentives to expand services, as long as the expected benefits were positive,

---

[24]Reviewed in David Dranove and Mark Satterthwaite, "The Industrial Organization of Health Care," in the *Handbook of Health Economics*. See also Daniel Kessler and Mark McClellan, "Is Hospital Competition Socially Wasteful?" *Quarterly Journal of Economics* 115 (2000): 577–615.

[25]David M. Cutler et al., "Are Medical Prices Declining?" *Quarterly Journal of Economics* (November 1998): 991–1024.

with little regard for costs. Managed care seemed to change that for a time in the mid-1990s, but rapid spending growth has returned.

American health care also needs to be improved in areas other than spending growth. Comparisons of health data across countries, for example, are not particularly flattering to the U.S. system. The United States ranks first by a wide margin in amount spent but is much further down the list in most indicators of population health. Table 10-5 provides comparative data on a few countries, along with median values for a set of 30 (mostly high-income) countries surveyed by the Organisation for Economic Co-Operation and Development (OECD). On a per capita basis, with due allowance for differences in national currencies, the United States spent more than twice as much as the median OECD country and 44 percent more than the second-highest country, Switzerland. Although a strong positive correlation is found between health care spending and income across countries, our spending is high even relative to our incomes. If we compare health care spending as a share of GDP, the United States, at 13.1 percent in 2000, leads all other developed countries by a large margin. Only Germany and Switzerland (at 10.7) have GDP shares greater than 10 percent. Yet despite our high spending, we fare poorly in comparisons of the most common measures of population health, such as infant mortality and life expectancy. The United States ranks 25th in the OECD in infant mortality and 21st in female life expectancy.

We should be cautious, however, about condemning the U.S. health care industry based on the data in Table 10-5. Aggregate measures of population health are influenced in important ways by factors over which the health care system has no direct control. For example, greater income inequality and relatively high poverty rates in the United States, as compared with other developed countries, likely contribute to the high infant mortality rate. Lower mortality, though relatively easy to measure, is also not the only health system output of importance. Alleviation of pain and anxiety, and improvements in physical and mental functioning are among other outputs that should count. Perhaps if we could reliably measure these forms of value-added services, the relative standing of the United States would improve. Still, it is natural to look at the Table 10-5 data and wonder whether the incremental spending in the United States, as compared to other countries, brings with it commensurate benefits.

TABLE 10-5   Health Care Spending and Health in Selected Countries: 2000

	Per Capita	Percent of GDP	Infant Mortality[a]	Female Life Expectancy (in years)
United States	$4,540	13.1%	6.9	79.5
Canada	2,580	9.2	5.3	82.0
Germany	2,780	10.6	4.4	80.7[b]
Japan	1,984	7.6	3.2	84.6
United Kingdom	1,813	7.3	5.6	80.2
OECD median	2,030	8.0	5.1	80.8

[a] *Deaths per 1,000 live births.*
[b] *Data are for 1999.*
SOURCE: Organisation for Economic Cooperation and Development, OECD Health Data 2003, www.oecd.org.

Another phenomenon indicating room for improvement in the American health industry (and probably elsewhere in the world) is the existence of substantial variation across geographic areas in the use of particular types of medical procedures, from relatively simple ones like hernia repair to expensive surgeries such as coronary bypass and hip replacement.[26] Variations in use rates are too large to explain by chance or by variation in illness across areas. Although these variations are not well understood, they seem to indicate that different standards of appropriate treatment somehow get established in different communities, which reflects considerable uncertainty among doctors about the effectiveness of care in many circumstances. The social payoff to getting better information about the most effective treatments and reducing medical practice variations might be large. A recent estimate of deadweight losses from practice variations put them, conservatively, at about $11 billion annually.[27] A good case can be made for a greater government role in expanding knowledge about the effectiveness of medical procedures. A large insurer might gain competitive advantage from investing in research on effectiveness and putting it into practice, but the potential social gains are much larger than what any one firm could expect to capture.

The Institute of Medicine's (IOM) Quality of Health Care in America Committee has recently drawn attention to the related issue of preventable medical errors. The IOM's latest report speaks of a "quality chasm" between what our health care is and what it could be, noting that

> tens of thousands of Americans die each year from errors in their care, and hundreds of thousands suffer or barely escape from nonfatal injuries that a truly high-quality system would largely prevent.[28]

One other common indictment of American health care points to the significant share of the population with neither private nor public health insurance coverage; this amounted to 15.2 percent of the population in 2002. In nearly every other OECD country, virtually 100 percent of the population has insurance coverage. The high uninsured rate in the United States cannot reasonably be blamed on the poor performance of the health care industry, nor can the industry be expected to rectify the situation on its own. If a solution is to be found, collective action through government policy changes will be required.

Effects of Managed Care

Has managed care made a difference in health system performance, and, if so, in what ways? Despite the considerable attention focused on managed care by the media, policy makers, health care interest groups, researchers, and the general public, these questions are surprisingly difficult to answer with confidence. The mid-1990s slowdown of growth in real per capita health spending (Figure 10-2) closely followed the shift in

---

[26]The study of variations in medical practice was pioneered by John Wennberg and his collaborators. See, for example, information about their work on the Dartmouth Atlas of Health Care, www.dartmouthatlas.org.

[27]Charles S. Phelps, "Information Diffusion and Best Practice Adoption," in A. J. Culyer and J. P. Newhouse, eds., *Handbook of Health Economics* (Amsterdam: North-Holland, 2000).

[28]Institute of Medicine, Committee on the Quality of Health Care. *Crossing the Quality Chasm: A New Health System for the Twenty-First Century* (Washington, D.C.: National Academy Press, 2001): 2

health insurance to managed care techniques (Figure 10-4), and the more recent acceleration of spending growth follows the movement toward less-restrictive forms of insurance. It is tempting to infer that managed care was effective in restraining spending growth, but this simple correlation does not necessarily imply a causal link. Researchers have tried to identify the effects of managed care by looking for natural experiments, exploiting the fact that managed care was embraced at different times and to different degrees in different parts of the country. A few studies have shown that health care spending grew less rapidly in places where managed care market penetration was greater, but the evidence is not overwhelming.[29]

A great deal of research also has explored whether and how managed care organizations use resources differently than do traditional insurance providers. Such comparisons must be interpreted carefully: Individuals still exercise some choice in the type of insurance plan they enter; differences observed across types of insurance might reflect differences among the kinds of people who enroll as much as differences in how the plans perform. If, on average, managed care enrollees are younger and healthier, for example, failure to account for this will bias comparisons of plan performance. Second, so much variation exists within managed care plans that it might be difficult to generalize across studies.

Variation extends to what is left of the traditional fee-for-service sector, as well. As Figure 10-4 indicates, unmanaged, conventional health insurance has nearly vanished, at least in the private insurance sector. The blurring of the lines between different forms of health insurance increases the difficulty of doing comparative studies of performance.

Notwithstanding these caveats, most of the evidence points in the direction of lower resource use for HMOs compared with traditional fee-for-service medicine. (Much less evidence is available on the use of resources in the PPO form of managed care.)[30] Studies show fairly consistently that HMOs reduce the use of inpatient hospital care. Evidence is more mixed for physician care outside the hospital, which is not surprising given the conflicting incentives at work. HMOs would be expected to scrutinize the use of all types of services more closely, but they also might provide more preventive care to deter future hospitalizations and substitute less expensive outpatient services for more expensive inpatient ones. Some studies show more use of physician care in HMOs compared with fee-for-service, but the difference is usually not large enough to offset the reduced use of hospital care. Studies that compare HMOs with fee-for-service in the use of particularly expensive services where there is some discretion about use (such as cesarean section in childbirth) indicate that HMOs use these types of services less frequently.

Effects on quality of care are of at least as much interest as those that relate to cost. Here, the evidence is mixed. Robert Miller and Harold Luft find equal numbers of statistically significant results showing higher or lower quality in HMOs.[31] This mix of findings is not so surprising and does not imply that any of the studies were incorrect or poorly executed. A more plausible interpretation is that quality of care is sometimes

---

[29]Evidence on this issue and other aspects of managed-care performance is summarized in Sherry Glied, "Managed Care," in A. J. Culyer and J. P. Newhouse, eds., *Handbook of Health Economics* (Amsterdam: North-Holland, 2000).

[30]Robert H. Miller and Harold S. Luft, "Managed Care Performance Since 1980," *Journal of the American Medical Association* 271 (May 18, 1994): 1,512–1,519; "Does Managed Care Lead to Better or Worse Quality of Care?" *Health Affairs* 16 (September/October 1997): 7–25.

[31]"Does Managed Care Lead to Better or Worse Quality of Care?"

better and sometimes worse in HMOs, depending on the particular organization, type of disease, and other circumstances. One well-conducted study of chronically ill elderly people, for example, found that HMOs provided lower-quality care for physical health but better-quality care for mental health.[32]

An optimistic view of the evidence is that the incentives faced by managed care organizations, at least in the HMO forms, lead them to provide health care at lower cost than traditional fee-for-service arrangements, without systematically adverse effects on quality. Even such a guarded conclusion should be regarded tentatively, and we must be careful not to overgeneralize across the extremely diverse landscape of managed care. If the optimistic view is correct, however, it prompts one to ask why the less restrictive forms of managed care have been gaining ascendancy. Perhaps consumers misperceive quality differences among plans, or perhaps researchers are not capturing all of the aspects of quality that consumers care about. The incentives that consumers typically face when making a choice among plans also might come into play, a subject that we will discuss when we turn to public policy issues.

Managed Care and Provider Compensation

Some observers believe that to the extent that managed care reduced the cost of health insurance, it did so primarily at the expense of providers by exercising market power to force them to accept lower payments. Some indications suggest that insurers successfully used market power to put pressure on providers. A recent study found that average physician real income declined by 5 percent between 1995 and 1999, and it increased 3.5 percent for other skilled professionals.[33] The extent to which this slow growth can be traced to the effects of managed care is not entirely clear. However, one study looking at earlier data from the 1985 through 1993 period found that incomes of primary care doctors grew most rapidly and of hospital-based specialists most slowly in states where managed care market share was growing fastest.[34] Because managed care plans often emphasized (especially during this period) primary care gatekeeping and reductions in inpatient hospital utilization, these findings suggest that demand from managed care plans influenced physician income in ways that health insurers traditionally did not.

A study in Massachusetts, although limited in scope, provides some fascinating information about the effect of managed care on provider payments. David Cutler and his colleagues looked at detailed information on treatment of heart attack patients who had insurance coverage through one large employer (which covered more than 250,000 individuals) during the period between 1993 and 1995.[35] The employees could choose relatively unmanaged indemnity coverage or one of several HMOs. Heart attack care is an interesting case to study: Although enrollees chose their insurance plans, they

---

[32]John E. Ware Jr. et al., "Differences in 4-Year Health Outcomes for Elderly and Poor, Chronically Ill Patients Treated in HMO and Fee-for-Service Systems," *Journal of the American Medical Association* 276 (1996): 1039–1047.

[33]Marie C. Reed and Paul B. Ginsburg, Behind the Times: Physician Income, 1995-99, Data Bulletin, March 24, 2003, Center for the Study of Health System Change, www.hschange.com/CONTENT/544/544.pdf.

[34]Carol J. Simon, David Dranove, and William D. White, "The Impact of Managed Care on the Physician Marketplace," *Public Health Reports* 112 (May-June 1997): 222–230.

[35]David Cutler, Mark McClellan, and Joseph P. Newhouse, "How Does Managed Care Do It?" *Rand Journal of Economics*, 31 (3), Autumn 2000, 526-548.

did so before the attack occurred, and it is unlikely that the healthiness of heart attack patients would differ systematically across insurers. Heart attack survivors also receive different types of procedures of varying cost, and it is frequently claimed that the most expensive procedures, such as coronary bypass surgery, are overutilized in the United States. HMOs might be expected to be more selective than indemnity insurers when it comes to approving such expensive procedures.

Cutler and colleagues found that payments per heart attack treated were only about 61 percent as high in the HMOs ($23,600 compared to $38,500). However, when they placed patients into categories by the type of treatment they received, the costs for HMO patients were lower by a similar ratio in each of the categories, suggesting that the overall difference in cost is not primarily a result of substituting less expensive forms of treatment. At least in this case, it appeared that a large share of the reduction in cost must have come from lower payments to providers. Interestingly, they also could find no difference in quality between the HMOs and indemnity insurers as measured by deaths or rates of hospital readmissions due to complications.

Effects of Consolidation

As noted earlier, one type of provider reaction to pressure from managed care has been to consolidate into larger entities. Much of this activity has been horizontal—physicians forming into groups and hospitals affiliating with other hospitals. Such consolidation could lower costs of production if important economies of scale are achieved. However, actions that increase market concentration always raise questions about effects on prices. It is not hard to believe that a primary aim of many hospital mergers is to gain bargaining power relative to managed care insurers by reducing the insurer's ability to play one hospital against another. These issues have not escaped the notice of U.S. antitrust authorities. The Federal Trade Commission and the Department of Justice held a series of hearings on competition in health care in 2003.[36]

Hospitals increasingly have chosen to affiliate in multihospital systems, frequently with other hospitals in the same local market but also with hospitals in other geographic areas that had not been direct competitors. Some of these affiliations are rather weak, with the individual hospitals remaining largely autonomous but joining forces to achieve some economies in activities such as the purchasing of supplies. Others are formal mergers or acquisitions.

One reason for affiliating with a larger hospital system that extends beyond one's market area is to get access to greater management expertise for coping with rapidly changing market conditions. Other reasons include better access to capital for modernization or expansion, or to gain some benefits (probably small) from shared activities such as joint purchasing. The direct effect on a hospital's local market power from affiliating with hospitals elsewhere is likely to be small.

Mergers with hospitals in the same market could be a different story. We should not expect the merger of two hospitals, unless they were small, to produce significant economies through such avenues as the sharing of overhead functions. However, in a market with underutilized bed capacity or excessive duplication of services—a common

---

[36]A wealth of information from these hearings is posted on the Internet at www.ftc.gov/ogc/healthcarehearings/.

state of affairs for U.S. hospitals today—a merger might facilitate reductions in capacity and more rational planning as new services are added, thereby reducing costs of care. On the other hand, mergers that increase market concentration raise concerns about market power and control over prices.

As with many aspects of the changes wrought by managed care, a consensus view has not emerged about the effects of mergers on hospital prices. A reasonable inference to draw from recent research on hospital mergers is that the opposing effects on prices are present: an efficiency-enhancing or cost-reducing effect that tends to depress prices, and a market power effect that increases them. One study using a large national data set from 1986 to 1994 found that the price-reducing effect tended to be stronger.[37] However, the market power effect, which seems to exist for nonprofit hospitals as well as for for-profits, might be getting stronger over time.[38]

Concentration also has been increasing in markets for health insurance, but we know even less about its effects. Many recent mergers have involved insurers operating in different locations. A larger total enrollment base offers more data that can be used to analyze and improve the effectiveness of techniques for managing care. Although care must be delivered locally, for the most part, if an organization succeeds in developing a wide knowledge base and effective tools for managing care, there could be gains from exploiting this competitive edge in many markets simultaneously. Large, multilocation employers also might find some advantages in dealing with managed care organizations that are similarly far-flung.

Evidence suggests, not surprisingly, that HMO premiums and profits are lower in markets with more HMOs.[39] Mergers of managed care organizations that formerly operated in different areas are not particularly troubling, because they do not increase market power in relevant market areas. Roger Feldman and colleagues found that between 1994 and 1997, concentration in the HMO industry increased at the national level but fell in most local markets.[40] They note that some of the larger mergers—such as Aetna with U.S. Healthcare and FHP with Pacificare in 1996, and Aetna and Prudential in 1999—merged plans that in many cases already were operating in the same markets. The concentration-increasing effect was nonetheless often offset by entry of new HMOs at the same time.

How closely HMOs compete with other forms of insurance such as PPOs is another important question for antitrust policy that is beginning to receive some attention.[41] Even if HMOs and PPOs are viewed as competing in the same market, however, a recent study of 70 metropolitan areas by the AMA found that 87 percent would be considered highly concentrated according to government merger guidelines.[42]

---

[37]Robert A. Connor et al., "Which Types of Hospital Mergers Save Consumers Money?" *Health Affairs* 16 (November/December 1997): 62–74.

[38]E. B. Keeler, G. Melnick, and J. Zwanziger, "The Changing Effects of Competition on Non-Profit and For-Profit Hospital Pricing Behavior," *Journal of Health Economics* 18 (1999): 69–86.

[39]Douglas Wholey, Roger Feldman, and Jon B. Christianson, "The Effect of Market Structure on HMO Premiums," *Journal of Health Economics* 14 (1995): 81–105; M. V. Pauly et al., "Competitive Behavior in the HMO Marketplace," *Health Affairs* 21, no. 1 (2002): 194–202.

[40]R. D. Feldman, D. R. Wholey, and J. B. Christianson, "HMO Consolidations: How National Mergers Affect Local Markets" *Health Affairs* 18, no. 4 (July/August 1999): 96–104.

[41]See the materials from the April 23, 2003, session of the FTC-DOJ hearings referenced previously.

[42]"Competition in Health Insurance: A Comprehensive Study of U.S. Markets," 2nd ed. (January 2003). See the Executive Summary at www.ama-assn.org/ama1/pub/upload/mm/368/execsumfinal.pdf.

V. PUBLIC POLICY ISSUES

The most basic public policy question about the economics of health care concerns market versus nonmarket allocation: Is it best to harness the power of the market for allocating resources as effectively as possible, recognizing and adjusting for the peculiarities of the product and the industry? Or is health care so special that it is better to rely on nonmarket mechanisms, as in the United Kingdom, Canada, and a number of other countries? Compared with other parts of the U.S. economy, the role of government as regulator and purchaser of health care is unusually extensive. Looking across countries, however, our health care system is easily the most market oriented. The comparative data in Table 10-5 lead one to wonder whether we have the right idea.

In a 1963 article generally considered the seminal paper in health care economics, Nobel Laureate Kenneth Arrow argued that uncertainty in the incidence of disease and the effectiveness of treatment, and the institutional adaptations to that uncertainty, largely account for the peculiarities of health care as an economic industry.[43] Uncertainty about illness and the demand for care create a demand for insurance, which may be satisfied through private arrangements or through social insurance programs such as Medicare and Medicaid. Individuals do not want to have to worry about the cost of health care at a time of serious need, and they are willing to pay for insurance to protect them against that eventuality. As taxpayers, we also are willing to provide assistance for the poor to help them in meeting unpredictable medical needs. Arrow also emphasized the patient's uncertainty about the effectiveness of health care and the imbalance of information between doctor and patient. When a health problem presents itself, the doctor is expected to be much better informed than the patient about the consequences of alternative courses of action, and the patient will rely heavily on the doctor's advice.

In the light of these features of health care, there seems to be ample reason for skepticism that unfettered market forces are the answer to resource allocation problems. The usual argument that markets will allocate resources efficiently relies on the discipline imposed by well-informed buyers spending their limited budgets shrewdly, which assures that only sellers who can deliver the best value for the money will survive. Because of the asymmetry of information, however, patients are poorly equipped to play this role. Although health insurance is surely, on balance, a good thing, it brings with it reduced price sensitivity at the time when care is received.

We have long had social institutions, such as licensure and the code of ethics under which physicians practice, to help guard against under provision of services or inferior quality. As insurance coverage grew and technological progress expanded the potential to spend money on health care, we found ourselves with a system that promoted spending growth while creating few incentives to weigh cost against benefit at the margin. *Moral hazard* in this context means "the tendency of the insured to overuse services," which inevitably drives up premiums. This became a serious and persistent problem.

Managed care seemed to change that picture. It swept into the marketplace as purchasers sought new ways to deal with moral hazard. It provided a countervailing force to other features of the system that push in the direction of insufficient attention to cost. However, backlash from consumers and doctors led managed care organizations

---

[43]Kenneth J. Arrow, "Uncertainty and the Welfare Economics of Medical Care," *American Economic Review* 53 (1963): 941–969.

to expand their networks and scale back their intrusion into clinical decisions. Rapid increases in premiums returned, renewing concerns about the costs of health care.[44] Have market forces been given their best shot, only to fail the test?

Advocates of a regulated, single-payer system for the United States would say yes, but those with a stronger faith in markets believe that better institutional arrangements might yet evolve. The best hope for the market is probably some version of managed competition, a concept pioneered and tirelessly advocated by Alain Enthoven, among others.[45] The key idea is that consumers should exercise informed and cost-conscious choice primarily at the point of choosing a health insurance plan, rather than by shopping for actual health care services. Insurers then compete for the consumer dollar, ideally by offering packages that are attractive in terms of cost and quality of care. The insurers play the role of selecting providers and developing effective mechanisms for managing care. Differences in consumer preferences can be accommodated, as long as individuals bear the additional cost of choosing a more expensive plan. Some might be willing to pay for free choice of doctor and comprehensive coverage, while others will accept greater restrictions on choice and benefits in exchange for lower premiums.

To make an analogy, most purchasers of personal computers do not pay much attention to the makers of the component parts, and most would find it difficult to assess the reliability of one hard drive or modem relative to another. They rely more on the incentives of the manufacturer assembling the package, be it a major corporation like Dell or Hewlett-Packard or a local retailer, to make good judgments about quality and cost in selecting components. Performance in this market seems satisfactory.

But choosing a health insurance plan is far different from choosing a personal computer. To begin with, the adverse consequences of a bad choice are potentially much more severe. The proponents of managed competition have always recognized, as the name itself implies, that the environment in which insurance plans compete must be managed or regulated to achieve the best results. In the remainder of this section, we will examine some major public policy issues relating to how competition could be managed and what we can reasonably expect from this strategy.

Cost-Conscious Consumer Choice

Despite the managed care backlash, Enthoven still envisions that in a well-structured system, most consumers would choose a managed care plan organized as an integrated delivery system (IDS), accepting some restrictions on the providers they can see. It has not happened yet, he argues, because few consumers are given the right incentives. Managed competition advocates believe that consumers should select from a variety of health insurance plans, paying the incremental cost of more expensive plans and reaping the financial benefit of choosing less expensive ones.

But for most workers with job-related coverage, this is not the current reality. Most employers who provide coverage offer it through only a single carrier. In 1997, according

---

[44]In addition to increases in health spending per capita (Figure 10-2), increases in insurance premiums are another indicator of rising spending. Following several years of relatively slow growth, average premiums for employer-provided health insurance grew by more than 10 percent each year from 2001 to 2003 (13.9 percent in 2003). See information from the Kaiser Family Foundation Annual Employer Health Benefits Survey, www.kff.org/insurance/.

[45]A recent version of his thinking is contained in "Employment-Based Health Insurance Is Failing: Now What?" Health Affairs Web Exclusive, May 28, 2003, http://content.healthaffairs.org/cgi/reprint/ hlthaff.w3.237v1.pdf.

to a large national survey of employers, only 43 percent of enrollees in job-related insurance plans were offered a choice of plans, and only 23 percent had a choice of insurance carriers. Of those employers who offered a choice of plans, only 28 percent made equal dollar premium contributions regardless of which plan was chosen (as managed competition principles dictate).[46]

Greater consumer choice could be promoted through policies that encourage purchasing cooperatives, which are insurance brokers that pool workers from many firms and offer individuals a wider choice of plans.

Federal tax policy also might be changed to encourage more cost-conscious choices. The open-ended nature of the current tax preference for employer-provided health benefits favors more expensive plans. Instead of excluding all employer payments for health insurance from taxable income, the size of the tax credit an employer or individual receives could be capped, so that high-cost plans are not subsidized at the margin.

Can Consumers Assess Quality?

Many consumers demonstrate a willingness to pay more for higher quality in all kinds of products from coffee to cars, so it would be surprising if they would not do the same for something as important as health care. But do employers and consumers have, or can they get, the information necessary to make reasonable judgments about the quality of health care plans? If those who choose among plans are unable to assess quality, the entire premise of the managed competition strategy is called into question.

Measuring health care plan and health care provider quality is a rapidly evolving field. The National Committee for Quality Assurance (www.ncqa.org) has been reporting on HMO quality since the early 1990s and continues to refine its measures. The Leapfrog Group, an organization of more than 145 Fortune 500 corporations and other large purchasers of health care, was formed to address patient safety concerns and seeks to provide incentives for quality improvement.

Measuring the quality of such a complex product is difficult though. Ideally, we would like to measure a health plan or provider's performance by its impact on the health of the relevant population. However, it is difficult to separate the plan or provider's contribution from other factors that influence health. Hospitals that do poorly in mortality-based measures of quality, for example, consistently object that such measures do not adequately account for how severely ill their patients are. Because quality measures are always imperfect, their use may distort provider behavior. A cautionary recent finding is that after New York and Pennsylvania began publishing hospital and surgeon mortality rates for coronary bypass surgery, surgeons were more reluctant to operate on the sickest patients.[47]

Current measures of health plan performance often focus on structural measures such as the qualifications of network doctors, intermediate outcomes such as the percentage of pregnant enrollees who get prenatal care in the first trimester, and measures of patient satisfaction. Additional research to develop more reliable ways to measure performance in the dimensions that most matter to consumers warrants public support.

---

[46]M. Susan Marquis and Stephen E. Long, "Trends in Managed Care and Managed Competition, 1993–1997," *Health Affairs* 18 (November-December 1999): 75–88.

[47]David Dranove et al., "Is More Information Better? The Effects of 'Report Cards' on Health Care Providers," *Journal of Political Economy* 111, no. 3 (2003): 555–588.

Is Competition Workable?

Aside from demand-side policies to give consumers the incentive to choose in a cost-conscious way among health plans and the information needed to do so wisely, managed competition relies on there being a sufficient supply of health plans to offer consumers a real choice and to make collusion difficult. To consider the potential for competition on the supply side, we should examine the minimum efficient scale of an integrated delivery system, meaning the size required to operate at minimum average cost per enrollee in relation to the size of relevant markets. One study accomplished this by looking at the staffing patterns and use of hospital services in relation to enrollees in large staff model HMOs.[48]

The authors found that a community of 360,000 could support three independent networks of physicians and three hospitals of about 240 beds each, but some types of acute services would not need to be available in all hospitals. A smaller community of 180,000 could still support three independent physician networks but would need to share all hospital inpatient facilities to achieve productive efficiency. The authors noted that 37 percent of the American population lives in health care market areas that are smaller than 360,000 in population, and 29 percent live in markets that are smaller than 180,000. At the other extreme, 42 percent live in markets with a population that is greater than 1.2 million.

We can conclude that in major metropolitan areas, market size is not a serious obstacle to competition among health care plans, but that a significant share of the population lives in areas where several fully independent delivery systems cannot compete and be efficient. Even in areas with a fairly large population base, market power exercised by health plans with substantial market share, combinations of providers, or providers of highly specialized services may still lead to less than optimal results. Vigilant antitrust enforcement will likely be a key component of any market-based approach to health policy, but we are still learning what appropriate antitrust policy entails.

High-Risk Populations and the Uninsured

In any given year, the use of health care resources is highly concentrated among a small part of the population, with 1 percent of the heaviest users accounting for 30 percent of all expenditures and the top 10 percent accounting for 70 percent of spending. To the extent that high usage is predictable on the basis of such factors as age or preexisting conditions, a competitive market in insurance will tend to segregate, with higher-risk groups paying higher premiums. If there are legal restrictions on premium differences or other reasons why they are not practical, health plans will have incentives to attract healthy enrollees and avoid the sick.

This has been a particular concern for the Medicare program when contracting with managed care plans on a capitation basis. Until recently, Medicare paid managed care plans a capitation rate equal to 95 percent of what it would expect to pay for fee-for-service enrollees in the same geographic area. If those who joined managed care plans were typical Medicare beneficiaries, the program could expect to save 5 percent, on average, on each one. However, it appears that managed care plans generally attract relatively healthy Medicare enrollees who would have spent less than 95 percent of the average had they stayed in the fee-for-service system, so the program actually spent more while paying at a discounted rate.

---

[48]Richard Kronick et al., "The Marketplace in Health Care Reform," *New England Journal of Medicine* 328 (January 14, 1993): 148–152.

Payment reforms enacted in 1997 led a number of managed care organizations to stop participating in Medicare. The Medicare reform legislation of 2003 entices them to come back by increasing payments and taking steps to encourage managed competition for health care for seniors. Some analysts are concerned, however, that not enough has been done to prevent private insurers from competing primarily for the healthiest enrollees, leaving the traditional Medicare program to care disproportionately for the least healthy, most costly senior citizens. Any resources devoted to competition for a preferred set of enrollees are wasted from a social perspective; one group or plan's gain comes almost entirely from costs imposed on other groups, plans, or individuals. It also seems unfair that those unlucky enough to be struck with a serious and chronic illness should be burdened further with higher insurance premiums or difficulty in obtaining coverage. The conceptually appropriate solution is clear: Do not vary premiums by risk status (at least for those elements of risk outside the individual's control), but adjust payments to insurers to reflect differences in expected cost. If risk-adjusted payments are made accurately, such a system would be fair to insurance plans and consumers, and would remove incentives for insurers to compete for preferred risks.

Two obstacles stand in the way of widespread adoption of risk-adjustment schemes. One is that despite considerable ongoing research, we are in the early stages of learning to do risk adjustment properly. The second is that to apply risk adjustment widely in the private sector, a mechanism would be needed for pooling premium payments broadly across insured groups and then redistributing them to insurance plans on a risk-adjusted basis. Such a pooling would be possible if most insurance were obtained through purchasing cooperatives, but it is not in the current system.

A large uninsured population, as exists in the United States today, is also not compatible with effective managed competition. Two related problems can be cited. First, the uninsured receive care in emergency situations that often costs more to provide than the recipients are able to pay. Providers must recover the unreimbursed costs of such care in some way, and, to the extent possible, will try to shift the costs into premiums paid by the insured. Because various providers and health plans will not bear the costs of uncompensated care equally due to differences in location and other factors, these extra costs will distort competition among providers and among plans.

Second, in order to survive in the competitive process, providers and plans have incentives to avoid bearing the costs of uncompensated care. The uninsured are likely to find it more difficult to get needed care in a market-driven system than in the earlier world of more passive insurers and employers. For these reasons, advocates of managed competition argue that it will work best if accompanied by government action to assure universal health care coverage.

Technology and Spending Growth

A final question about market mechanisms in health care is whether they can provide the right incentives for new technology and spending growth over time. Managed care creates greater incentives than traditional insurance to adopt innovations that reduce cost and to eliminate those that add cost with no benefit. But what about innovations for which the expected benefits exceed the risks, but at a high cost per unit of benefit? Most health economists believe that the long-term growth of health care spending has been most associated with the adoption of new technologies and treatment techniques offering at least some medical benefit, so this question has important implications for spending growth and consumer welfare. Recent research that attempts to assess the benefits and costs of technological innovations in some important classes of illness concludes that although costs have been high, benefits have been much greater.[49] Therefore, we should guard against constructing a system that creates too little incentive for costly but beneficial innovation.

Yet should we be willing to pay any price for small gains in longevity or quality of life? Should an insurance plan pay for a cholesterol-lowering drug for a healthy 40-year-old with borderline high cholesterol if the cost per expected life year gained is $200,000? What about a $20,000 surgery with a 10 percent probability of adding half a year to a lung cancer patient's life, which on an expected value, cost-benefit basis works out to $400,000 per life year gained? How an insurance plan responds in these situations might depend on its liability to a lawsuit and on how the legal system defines *necessary care*. One can imagine a system in which if the legal environment allows it, some insurance plans are liberal in their coverage of technologies while others offer lower premiums but are much stricter, and consumers choose among them. As a result, individuals with greater ability to pay would gain access to some forms of treatment that others would not. We might or might not be willing to live with the consequences of such a system, which, to some degree, already exists, but the issues are important for public policy to consider.

Conclusion

Dissatisfaction with rising health care spending led to the managed care revolution of the 1990s. That revolution has been rolled back though by no means entirely reversed. A return to rapid spending increases has created a new clamor for change. Enthoven's vision is of a more rationalized market, with consumers choosing among competing, largely self-contained, integrated health care delivery systems that are accountable for quality. This runs counter to recent trends toward broader networks—a trend that seems to indicate that consumers place a high value on free choice of providers at the point of service. Rising costs may yet generate more interest in managed competition ideas and more restricted networks.

If we do not embrace managed competition though, what are the alternatives? One possibility is the eventual adoption of a highly regulated, single-payer system, though such an outcome hardly appears imminent. Employers and insurers lately have shown more interest in consumer-driven models of health care provision.[50]

Consumer-driven health care means different things to different people. In contrast to managed competition, it generally directs its incentives at the point of service rather than at the point of insurance plan choice. One element being tried in a few places is to require substantially higher cost-sharing for access to more costly hospitals. This creates an incentive to be conscious of differences in cost while retaining some choice at the point of service. This cost-tiering idea, already largely in place for prescription drugs, could conceivably be extended to groups of doctors and other health care providers.

---

[49]D. M. Cutler and M. McClellan, "Is Technological Change in Medicine Worth It?" *Health Affairs* 20, no. 5 (September/October 2001): 11–29.

[50]Jon R. Gabel, Anthony T. Lo Sasso, and Thomas Rice, "Consumer-Driven Health Plans: Are They More Than Talk Now?" Health Affairs Web Exclusive, November 20, 2002. www.healthaffairs.org

Movement in this direction makes the development of useful quality information at the level of the hospital or provider group even more important.

In most cases, consumer-driven health plans include, at least as one option, a policy with a large deductible—several thousand dollars or more—above which a catastrophic plan provides full coverage. Advocates argue that until the deductible is spent, individuals will have strong incentives to economize on health care use, as it will be clear that they are spending their own money. High-deductible, catastrophic insurance plans have some serious limitations as a tool of health policy, however. An important one is that given the concentration of health care consumption among a small percentage of users, a large share of total health spending is accounted for by individuals who would exceed even a large deductible. For these individuals (e.g., those undergoing major surgeries or requiring prolonged hospital stays), the catastrophic plan provides no incentive to economize at the margin. Another limitation is that such plans favor the healthy over the sick to a degree that most of us may find unacceptable. Even if premiums are the same, the healthy can expect to pay the premium and little else, while the sick will incur far higher out-of-pocket costs.

Whatever the future holds, interest in controlling the growth of health care spending will not fade away, nor will interest in choice, quality, and equitable access to beneficial care. If we rely heavily on market forces to guide resource allocation, as seems likely for the foreseeable future, getting the incentives created by the legal and regulatory environment right, and supplementing private with public resources where appropriate, will continue to challenge economists and policy makers.

Recommended Readings

Arrow, Kenneth J. 1963. "Uncertainty and the Welfare Economics of Medical Care." *American Economic Review* 53: 941–969.

Cutler, David M. 2003. *Your Money or Your Life: Strong Medicine for America's Health Care System.* New York: Oxford University Press.

Dranove, David. 2002. *The Economic Evolution of American Health Care: From Marcus Welby to Managed Care.* Princeton, NJ: Princeton University Press.

Enthoven, Alain C. 1980. *Health Plan.* Reading, MA: Addison-Wesley.

Fuchs, Victor R. 1974. *Who Shall Live?* New York: Basic Books.

Joskow, Paul L. 1984. *Controlling Hospital Costs.* Cambridge, MA: MIT Press, 1984.

Newhouse, Joseph P. 1984. *Pricing the Priceless: A Health Care Conundrum.* Cambridge, MA: MIT Press.

Starr, Paul. 1982. *The Social Transformation of American Medicine.* New York: Basic Books.

Textbooks

Feldstein, Paul J. 1999. *Health Care Economics,* 5th ed. Albany, NY: Delmar.

Folland, Sherman, Allen C. Goodman, and Miron Stano. 2004. *The Economics of Health and Health Care,* 4th ed. Upper Saddle River, NJ: Prentice Hall.

Getzen, Thomas E. 2003. *Health Economics,* 2nd ed. New York: John Wiley and Sons.

Phelps, Charles E. 2003. *Health Economics,* 3rd ed. Boston: Addison-Wesley.

Technical Paper Collection

Culyer, A. J., and J. P. Newhouse, eds. 2000. *Handbook of Health Economics.* Vols. 1A and 1B. Amsterdam: North-Holland.

CHAPTER 11

Public Accounting

—Philip G. Cottell, Jr.

The scene was striking: A well-dressed man at the pinnacle of his career standing with graven face and hand raised, about to testify before an enraged committee of Congress. Who was this? A crime boss? A furtive financier of terrorists? An illegal drug kingpin? No. It was an accountant and a leading member of a profession that hitherto had been held in the highest regard.

In the fall of 2001, Enron, the seventh-largest corporation in the United States, collapsed after it came to light that it had massive liabilities that were not disclosed on its financial statements. Shortly thereafter, other large firms, notably WorldCom and Tyco, were found to have improper and perhaps fraudulent accounting records. Amidst the maelstrom of scandal surrounding these colossal failures stood an "industry" whose duty is supposed to be protecting the public from these financial disasters. But the person testifying was Joseph Berardino, chief executive of Arthur Andersen, one of the largest public accounting firms in the world and Enron's auditor. His firm, along with four large companies of similar size, stood atop the accounting profession, whose role is to ensure the fidelity of the accounting information, records, and reports that are essential to the functioning of the nation's financial markets.

Just how important is the accounting profession to the economy? One measure is suggested by the increase in ownership of equity securities by the American public. In 1952, when the accounting profession was at or near its high-water mark, approximately 4.1 percent of the population owned equity securities. In 1981, just before consolidation and price competition erupted in the accounting field, ownership of equities had expanded to 14.1 percent of the public. Today, ownership of equities, either directly or through mutual funds, is far more widespread. According to the Investment Company Institute, 49.5 percent of the population now owns equity securities, many through investments in mutual funds. In addition, many participate in pension plans and retirement programs, the returns of which depend on investments in the stocks and bonds of publicly traded firms. Ownership of publicly traded companies, either directly or indirectly, thus hinges on confidence and faith in the veracity of the firms' financial reports.[1]

---

[1] Investment Company Institute, "Equity Ownership in America," available at www.ici.org/statements/res/rpt_02_equity_owners.pdf.

I. HISTORY

Although evidence has been found of accounting records reaching back to biblical times, the earliest record of a public accounting engagement in the United States occurred before the American Revolution. In 1766, Benjamin Franklin asked James Parker to act as his representative in accounting for the final settlement of the sale of a printing business.[2] In 1866, public accounting took the form in which it chiefly operates today when the first accounting partnership, Veysey and Veysey, was established in New York. Two decades later, the predecessors to two of today's Big Four accounting firms emerged when Deloitte, Dever, Griffiths, and Company (forerunner of Deloitte), and Price, Waterhouse, and Company (forerunner of PricewaterhouseCoopers) certified corporate security offerings in 1890.[3]

At the outset, the profession was accorded a special legal status that enabled it to thrive. In 1896, the state of New York granted certified public accounting its first legal recognition. During the period 1896 through 1913, this recognition subsequently spread to 31 states. In the latter year, the sixteenth amendment to the Constitution, which established the income tax, was ratified—a singular event that gave a great boost to the accounting profession owing to the need to define, calculate, and track business and personal income. By 1921, all 48 states had enacted laws giving special recognition to certified public accountants; all the states had recognized the status of public accountants and granted them a special legal "franchise."[4]

The stock market crash in 1929, the financial scandals that subsequently were exposed, and the ensuing depression triggered new growth in the demand for the services of public accounting firms. In instituting reforms for financial reporting, President Franklin Roosevelt signed into law two important new statutes: the Securities Act of 1933 and the Securities Act of 1934.

The 1934 act created a new government agency charged with regulating the nation's financial markets—the Securities and Exchange Commission (SEC). Using the authority provided by these acts, the SEC required all new and continuing registrants of publicly traded securities to have their financial statements audited by independent certified public accountants. During the public hearings on these acts, Col. Arthur H. Carter, senior partner of Haskins and Sells (forerunner of Deloitte) and president of the New York State Society of Certified Public Accountants, averted a complete government takeover of the task of auditing publicly traded companies by persuading the Senate Committee on Banking and Currency not to assign the auditing function to a government agency. Instead, audits were to be performed by firms in the private sector, a development that not only highlighted the importance of the accounting profession but also triggered another quantum leap in the demand for the profession's services.

The accounting field reached the peak of its standing and reputation in the United States beginning in the 1940s and continuing through the mid-1960s. During this era, the public accounting business was practiced as a profession rather than as an "industry." Strong codes of professional ethics among accounting firms discouraged price competition. Partners at accounting firms were rewarded and recognized for the high quality of the audit services they provided to their clients rather than for securing new business. The

---

[2]J. D. Edwards, *History of Public Accounting in the United States* (East Lansing, MI: Michigan State University Press, 1960), 43–44.
[3]Ibid., 48–49.
[4]G. J. Previts, *The Scope of CPA Services* (New York, NY: John Wiley & Sons, 1985), 34–35.

term *Big Eight*, referring to the eight largest public accounting firms, was coined in the 1960s.[5]

As the decade of the 1960s closed, however, new economic forces began to impinge upon public accounting, gradually transforming the biggest firms from organizations that were strongly imbued with professional values to firms that pursued the profit-making goals associated with conventional business success. Until 1972, the partners of the Big Eight firms had kept themselves at the forefront of the process of setting accounting principles, the ways and means by which companies assemble, compute, and report financial information to the public. In 1972, however, the Financial Accounting Standards Board (FASB) was created, and it has been the predominant organization to set standards ever since. This development removed Big Eight partners from center stage in shaping and setting accounting standards; by the 1980s, the Big Eight partners had completely withdrawn from active public dialogue regarding accounting principles.[6]

Another key event occurred in 1977, when the Supreme Court ruled in *Bates v. State Bar of Arizona* that lawyers could advertise and that professional codes of ethics prohibiting advertising by lawyers constituted an illegal restraint of trade in violation of the antitrust laws.[7] The American Institute of Certified Public Accountants (AICPA), which published and enforced the accounting profession's code of ethics, was similarly pressed by the Department of Justice and the Federal Trade Commission (FTC), which charged that parts of the accounting field's ethics codes also illegally restrained trade.

The AICPA succumbed to these pressures and abolished its professional ban on competitive bidding. Then during the 1970s, the FTC compelled the institute to drop rules prohibiting advertising, as well as codes proscribing uninvited solicitation of other accounting firms' clients. In the 1980s, the FTC further pressured the AICPA to eliminate its professional ban on commissions and contingency fees in a change that profoundly altered the climate in which audit firms conducted their affairs. As a result of these developments, accounting firms began actively competing with each other in aggressively pursuing profits, a development that put great strains on traditional professional values[8] and that completed the transformation of accounting from a profession into a profit-driven business.

II. INDUSTRY STRUCTURE

From the 1960s to the mid-1980s, the accounting industry was dominated by the Big Eight accounting firms: Arthur Andersen, Arthur Young, Coopers & Lybrand, Ernst and Whinney, Deloitte Haskins and Sells, Peat Marwick Mitchell, Price Waterhouse, and Touche Ross. During the 1980s, the pressures unleashed by competition compelled these firms to look for new ways to expand their size and profitability. Because large accounting firms found internal growth difficult due to the obstacles associated with the formation of capital in this field, mergers became the prime means by which they expanded.

---

[5]S. A. Zeff, "How the U.S. Accounting Profession Got Where It Is Today: Part I," *Accounting Horizons* 17 (September 2003): 191–195.

[6]Ibid., 195–200.

[7]Philip G. Cottell and Terry M. Perlin, *Accounting Ethics: A Practical Guide for Professionals* (Westport, CT: Quorum Books, 1990), 33.

[8]Zeff, "U.S. Accounting Profession, Part I," 202.

Mergers and Consolidation

The first major merger occurred in 1986 when Peat Marwick Mitchell merged with KMG Main Hurdman to create KPMG Peat Marwick. (The resulting firm has since shortened its name to KPMG.) KMG Main Hurdman had been a U.S. affiliate of Klynveld Main Goerdeler, a large European accounting firm. Because of the extensive network that Klynveld Main Goerdeler had in Europe and elsewhere abroad, the merged firm became the largest accounting firm internationally and the second-largest accounting concern in the United States. The competitive advantages stemming from its extensive European presence induced other accounting firms to seek new growth opportunities, as well.

Thus, in 1989 a blockbuster merger occurred when Ernst and Whinney combined with Arthur Young to form Ernst and Young (Figure 11-1). This was the first consolidation of two Big Eight firms; the resulting organization became the largest accounting firm nationally and internationally. Later that year, the two smallest of the Big Eight firms—Deloitte Haskins and Sells, and Touche Ross—merged to become Deloitte and Touche. This combination created the third-largest firm nationally and internationally; the merged firm subsequently shortened its name to Deloitte.

A third megamerger, between Arthur Andersen and Price Waterhouse, was announced in 1989 but was later called off. Over the next 9 years, several other mergers were proposed but failed to come to fruition. As a result, the industry operated for a decade with six dominant firms, known as the Big Six.

Then in 1998, sixth-ranked Price Waterhouse merged with fifth-ranked Coopers & Lybrand to create the field's second-largest firm, PricewaterhouseCoopers. At this juncture, the industry temporarily stabilized with five major firms. Finally, in 2002, the industry consolidated to the Big Four. Andersen, the fourth-ranked firm, was indicted for obstruction of justice by the Justice Department because of its role as auditor of the collapsed Enron Corporation. This, in turn, triggered a mass exodus of Andersen partners and staff, as well as clients. As a result, Andersen ceased to exist in 2002. These mergers, which collapsed the Big Eight into the Big Four (sometimes cynically referred to as the *Final Four*), are depicted in Figure 11-1.[9]

A Three-Tiered Structure

Thousands of public accounting firms provide auditing services in the United States. However, these firms operate in what is generally recognized as a three-tiered, segmented structure. At the top of this tiered structure sit the Big Four (Table 11-1). These firms are widely recognized as having the capability to audit large, multinational corporations, and they are substantially larger than other accounting firms. They have thousands of partners, tens of thousands of employees, and billions of dollars in annual revenues.

Below the Big Four are the medium-sized accounting firms. The number of firms in this second tier is not universally agreed upon, but most lists would include at least three: Grant Thornton, BDO Seidman, and McGladrey & Pullen. Firms in this second tier have the capability to audit public companies but, as we will see, they operate at a significant competitive disadvantage due to their smaller scale.

The third tier of firms is simply all the rest. This tier contains accounting firms as small as a single practitioner, whose business consists chiefly of tax and write-up work

---

[9]General Accounting Office, "Public Accounting Firms: Mandated Study on Consolidation and Competition" (July 2003): 11.

FIGURE 11-1 Significant Mergers of the 1980s and 1990s

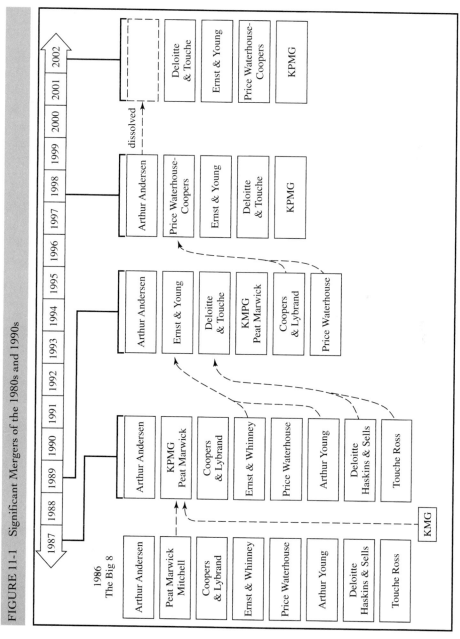

SOURCE: General Accounting Office, Public Accounting Firms: Mandated Study on Consolidation and Competition, July 2003, p. 11.

TABLE 11-1 Firm Size

Firm	FY 02 U.S. Net Revenue (in millions)	FY 02 Global Net Revenue (in millions)	Number of Partners	Nonpartner Professionals	Number of Offices	Total Staff	Practice Mix as a Percentage				Number of SEC Audit Clients
							Audit	Tax	Consulting	Other	
Big Four											
Deloitte	$5,900[a]	$12,500	2,618	19,835	81	28,203	36%	21%	34%	9%	1,193
Ernst & Young	4,515	10,124	2,118	15,078	86	24,162	59	38	-	3	2,528
PricewaterhouseCoopers	4,256	13,782	2,027	16,774	113	24,457	61	23	-	16	2,441
KPMG	3,200	10,720	1,535	10,967	122	17,721	63	37	-	-	1,625
Second Tier											
Grant Thornton	400	1,840	312	2,068	51	3,129	50	34	16	-	424
BDO Seidman	353	2,395	281	1,229	37	1,976	41	41	18	-	283
McGladrey & Pullen	203	1,829	475	1,894	86	2,371	92	8	-	-	107

[a] Public Accounting Report estimated this revenue would be $3,894 million without consulting revenue.
SOURCE: *Public Accounting Report,* "Annual Survey of National Accounting Firms—2003," February 28, 2003.

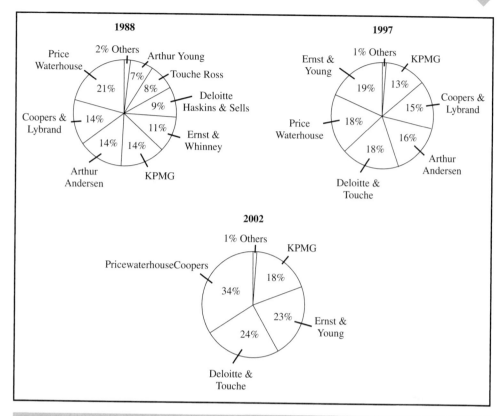

FIGURE 11-2   Percentage of Public Company Audit Market (by Total Sales Audited), 1988, 1997, and 2002

SOURCE: General Accounting Office, Public Accounting Firms: Mandated Study on Consolidation and Competition, July 2003, p. 21.

for small businesses, up to larger regional firms that might provide audit services to non-SEC clients or to an occasional SEC client. Their ability to compete for SEC client work also is severely inhibited, however.[10]

Concentration

Concentration among accounting firms is high and has increased significantly over recent years. Figure 11-2 shows that in 1988, the top four firms (Price Waterhouse, Arthur Andersen, Coopers & Lybrand, and KPMG) audited 63 percent of total public company sales. The next four firms (Ernst and Whinney, Arthur Young, Deloitte Haskins and Sells, and Touche Ross) were significant competitors, auditing 35 percent of total public company sales. By 1997, the top four firms audited 71 percent of public company sales, with two major competitors (Coopers & Lybrand and KPMG) auditing an additional

---

[10]Public Accounting Report, "Public Accounting Report Annual Survey of National Accounting Firms—2003" (February 28, 2003): 3–6.

28 percent. Finally, by 2002, the top four firms audited 99 percent of public company sales with no significant competitors.[11]

Further analysis of the four-firm concentration ratio based on the total number of clients (rather than clients' sales) yields similar results. This measure of concentration increased from 51 percent in 1988, to 65 percent in 1997, reaching 78 percent in 2002. Not surprisingly, the large public segment of the client market is even more concentrated: The Big Four audit approximately 97 percent of all public companies with sales between $250 million and $5 billion, and virtually all public firms with sales greater than $5 billion.[12]

Internationally, the Big Four generate more than $47 billion in global net revenue, with research by foreign regulators suggesting that the markets for audit services for large public companies in other countries are as highly concentrated as in the United States. In recent years, the Big Four audited more than 80 percent of all public companies in Japan, at least 90 percent of all listed companies in the Netherlands, virtually all major listed companies in the United Kingdom, and more than 80 percent of listed companies in Italy.

Another method for measuring concentration is the Herfindahl-Hirschman Index (HHI), which is obtained by summing the squares of the market shares of individual firms. As a general rule, an HHI below 1,000 is considered indicative of a market that is predisposed to behave competitively, whereas an HHI above 1,800 indicates a highly concentrated market in which the firms have the potential to exercise significant market power—meaning the ability to profitably maintain prices above competitive levels for a significant period of time (or lessen competition in other ways, such as product quality, service, or innovation). Figure 11-3 shows that following the merger of Price Waterhouse

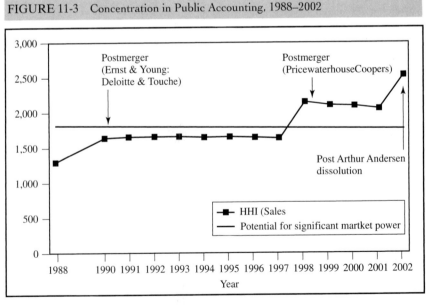

FIGURE 11-3   Concentration in Public Accounting, 1988–2002

SOURCE: General Accounting Office, "Public Accounting Firms: Mandated Study on Consolidation and Competition," July 2003, p. 19.

[11]General Accounting Office, "Public Accounting Firms," 21.
[12]Ibid., 16–22.

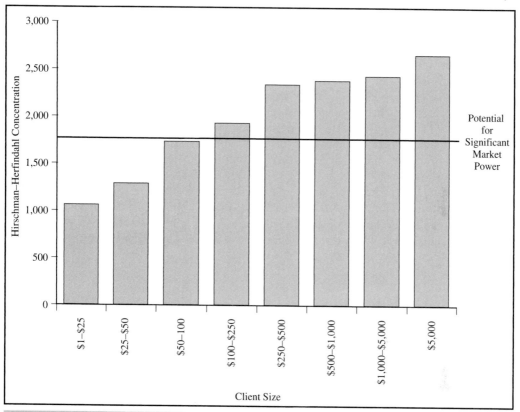

FIGURE 11-4   Concentration by Client Size

SOURCE: General Accounting Office, "Public Accounting Firms: Mandated Study on Consolidation and Competition," July 2003, p. 20.

and Coopers & Lybrand, and the dissolution of Andersen, the market consisted of just a handful of major firms with the potential to exercise significant market power.[13]

Evaluated by client size, Figure 11-4 shows that HHIs (based on number of clients) for firms auditing public companies with total sales between $1 million and $100 million are all below the 1,800 threshold. However, HHIs for companies with sales of more than $100 million are consistently above the 1,800 threshold, again indicating the potential for significant market power in the auditing of larger companies' accounts.[14]

The most dramatic impact of consolidation among accounting firms appears to be the limited number of auditor choices for most large national and multinational public companies should they choose to change auditors. Of the firms that responded to recent surveys, 88 percent indicated that they would not consider using a non-Big Four firm for their audit and attest needs. Additional evidence of reluctance to use non–Big Four firms is provided by data concerning the 1,085 former Andersen clients that changed auditors between October 2001 and December 2002. Only one large public company with assets of more than $5 billion that previously had been audited by Andersen switched to

---

[13]Ibid., 19.
[14]Ibid., 20.

a non–Big Four firm. Thus, for most large public firms, the maximum number of choices available for audit and attest services has declined from eight in 1988 to four today.

Client choices can be limited even further due to potential conflicts of interest, new independence rules (discussed in the public policy section in this chapter), and industry specialization by accounting firms, all of which may limit even more the number of viable auditing alternatives. A hypothetical example illustrates this point: Suppose a large, multinational company that used one Big Four firm for its audit and attest services and another Big Four firm for its outsourced internal audit function seeks to hire a new accounting firm because its board of directors has decided that the company should change auditors every 7 years. In this case, the company would appear to have only two remaining alternatives if it believed that only Big Four firms had the resources needed to audit its operations. However, one of the remaining two Big Four firms might not enter a bid because its market niche in this particular industry encompasses only smaller companies. Consequently, the large, multinational firm would be left with only one alternative. Conceivably, other circumstances could arise in which a company might have *no* viable alternatives for global audit and attest needs.[15]

Barriers to Expansion

In a recent in-depth study, the General Accounting Office (GAO) found five significant barriers to entry and expansion of smaller accounting firms attempting to compete for the audit work of large corporate clients. First, smaller firms generally lack the staff, technical expertise, and global reach to audit the far-flung operations of major multinational companies. Large corporations that responded to a survey affirmed this finding. Of the large companies that stated they would not consider using a non–Big Four auditor, 91 percent said that the capacity of smaller firms was of great or very great importance in their unwillingness to do so.

TABLE 11-2 Gap between First- and Second-Tier Firms

Accounting Firm	Average Real Revenue (in millions)	Average Number of Partners	Average Number of Nonpartner Staff	Average Number of Offices	Average Number of SEC Clients
1988					
Big Eight	$1,566	1,126	10,991	105	1,359
Next Tier	288	364	2,118	57	234
Gap	**1,278**	**762**	**8,874**	**48**	**1,125**
2002					
Big Four	4,468	2,029	15,664	101	2,046
Next Tier	290	292	1,532	47	245
Gap	**4,178**	**1,736**	**14,132**	**54**	**1,801**

SOURCE: General Accounting Office, Public Accounting Firms: Mandated Study on Consolidation and Competition, Washington, D.C., July 2003. Figures differ slightly from the Public Accounting Report data in Figure 11-2 due to the timing of the information and because the GAO added an additional firm—Crowe, Chizek, and Company—to the second tier. The 1988 second-tier firms include Laventhol & Horwath. Crowe, Chizek, and Company replaced this now nonexistent firm in the 2002 data. Average real revenue figures have been adjusted for inflation. Gap figures might not sum due to rounding.

---

[15]Ibid., 25–30.

This problem is particularly daunting with respect to professional staff. As Table 11-1 shows, the smallest of the Big Four has more than three times as many partners, and more than five times as many nonpartner professionals, as the largest second-tier firm. Because of the complexity of large national and multinational firms, it is not uncommon for an audit engagement to require hundreds of staff personnel, which most smaller accounting firms cannot afford to commit to any single client. This limits their ability to compete with the Big Four for large audit clients. Yet, without having large clients, it is difficult to build the capacity needed to attract large clients. In fact, as Table 11-2 shows, the gap between the first and second tier of public accounting firms has widened over the last 15 years. This gap has resulted in a dual market structure—one market where the Big Four compete with several smaller accounting firms for the accounts of medium and small public companies, and another market where essentially only the Big Four compete to audit the largest corporate clients.

A second barrier is reputation. Smaller accounting firms face a challenge in establishing recognition and credibility among large national and multinational public companies, on the one hand, and among capital market participants on the other. Some large corporations surveyed by the GAO reported that although some smaller accounting firms have the capability to provide audit services to large multinational companies, the boards of directors of those concerns might not consider retaining the services of smaller auditing firms as an option. Other respondents stated that despite recent accounting scandals involving the Big Four, many capital market participants and investors continue to expect audit opinions to come from one of the Big Four. Thus, firms seeking to establish or maintain their credibility in the capital markets generally will continue to engage one of the Big Four.

A third barrier to auditing the very largest clients' financial accounts is risk and liability. Many second-tier firms believe that the litigation risks and insurance costs associated with auditing the largest companies make expansion into that segment less attractive. Even if smaller firms were able to purchase additional insurance to manage the increased risk associated with auditing large public firms, they still would lack the size needed to achieve economies of scale by spreading their litigation risk and insurance costs over a larger base. As a result, many second-tier accounting firms believe they have more attractive opportunities for growth in the mid-sized segment of the public company audit market and in the private company audit area, where risk-return prospects are more attractive.

A fourth barrier is capital formation. Large amounts of capital would have to be raised to build the organizational infrastructure required to compete with the Big Four in the large public company audit market. Public accounting firms are effectively prohibited by law from operating under a corporate structure. Thus, the ability to raise outside capital is severely limited because under the partnership structure in which accounting firms must operate, access to equity markets by selling stock is unavailable.

Therefore, to expand their operations, smaller accounting firms must look to other options, such as borrowing, merging with other accounting firms, or tapping the personal resources of their partners and employees. Raising capital through borrowing is difficult though, because accounting firms are professional service organizations whose primary asset is the expertise of their employees; thus, they lack the collateral required to secure loans. Mergers, internal growth, and the personal resources of partners also do not seem to afford viable options for raising the large amounts of capital needed to compete to audit the accounts of large clients.

Finally, state laws and regulations, primarily those dealing with licensing requirements, represent a fifth significant barrier. Firms wishing to expand nationally face the burden and expense of obtaining licenses for staff members in individual states across the country. All 50 states, the District of Columbia, Guam, Puerto Rico, and the U.S. Virgin Islands have varying laws governing the licensing of certified public accountants, including varying requirements for education, examinations, and expertise. Moreover, potential state and federal duplication of regulatory oversight pose a proportionately greater burden for smaller firms than for the Big Four. This barrier might have been compounded by passage of the Sarbanes-Oxley Act, discussed later in this chapter, which calls for greater regulatory oversight of accounting firms' compliance with auditing standards and rules.[16]

III. INDUSTRY CONDUCT

In the heyday of public accounting, the Big Eight refrained from using price as a basis for competition. Instead, the field prided itself on being a profession in which hard competition was considered unseemly and was discouraged. The Big Eight openly charged higher prices than their smaller rivals, justifying their higher fees by insisting that the client was paying for a quality audit. Throughout the 1970s, accounting firms abstained from advertising and instead gained their reputations by taking tough stands on interpretation and enforcement of accounting standards without regard for the consequences, meaning whether they retained or lost their clients. The guiding presumption was that clients wanted their auditors to keep them out of trouble and, therefore, wanted their auditor to object if an accounting practice might lead to problems in the future. In effect, the policy of being tough on accounting standards was the core of what today would be considered an accounting firm's competitive strategy.[17]

The Advent of Price Competition

Several developments induced the profession to abandon the "profession" paradigm and begin to behave more like a conventional, profit-driven industry. We have seen that antitrust actions by the Federal Trade Commission and the Department of Justice forced the profession to repeal its ethics codes that discouraged competitive bidding and direct solicitation of clients. With the fetters of ethics removed, firms began to compete with one another more vigorously. S. A. Zeff related an anecdote exemplifying the sea change in attitude that occurred among the top managers of large accounting firms:

> The arrival of a profoundly altered competitive climate in the practice of public accounting was underscored in a remark attributed to Michael Cook [partner-in-charge of Deloitte and Touche, now Deloitte] in 1985: 'Five years ago if a client of another firm came to me and complained about the service, I'd immediately warn the other firm's chief executive.... Today I try to take away his client.'[18]

At the same time that the large accounting firms began to compete with each other aggressively, opportunities for growth in the market for audit services began to diminish. As a

---

[16]Ibid., 45–52.
[17]A. R. Wyatt, "Accounting Professionalism—They Just Don't Get It!" Address at the annual meeting of the American Accounting Association, Honolulu, Hawaii, August 4, 2003.
[18]S. A. Zeff, "How the U.S. Accounting Profession Got Where It Is Today: Part II," *Accounting Horizons* 17 (December 2003): 272.

result, the top managements of the large accounting firms began to emphasize other services, particularly tax and consulting services, as more lucrative ways to expand. These service lines not only were more profitable, they offered greater growth opportunities, as well.

Merger activity among their corporate clients reinforced these commercial pressures on accounting firms. First, pressure came from merging clients to show healthy earnings in order to demonstrate the success of the mergers and acquisitions they had undertaken. Second, mergers caused accounting firms to lose accounts as two clients merged to form one. Third, merged corporations put further downward price pressure on audit fees. As a result of these factors, by the 1990s, the audit market was saturated and accounting firms competed by looking to other areas for growth and profitability including, most notably, the provision of management consulting services.

As their consulting practices grew, the Big Eight eventually dropped requirements that members of the firms' management qualify as CPAs, the credential that had long been the hallmark of the profession. Because consultants were able to generate higher-margin work, they put pressure on their colleagues in the other two main branches of the industry, audit and tax services. Gradually, the emphasis of those members of the firms also shifted toward profitability. Because audit and tax work did not produce high and growing profits, audit partners were encouraged to bring in consulting work. Cross-selling a range of consulting services to clients became an important criterion in evaluating the job performance of audit partners. Those with technical accounting and auditing skills that were previously considered vital to internal firm advancement found themselves increasingly relegated to marginal roles.

As Wyatt sees it, these attitudinal changes in the auditing field paralleled some less desirable changes in American business more generally:

> Just as greed appears to have been the driving force at many of the companies that have failed or had significant restructurings, greed became a force to contend with in the accounting firms. In essence, the cultures of the firms had gradually changed from a central emphasis on delivering professional services in a professional manner to an emphasis on growing revenue and profitability. The gradual change resulted in the firm culture being drastically altered over the forty years leading up to the end of the century. The historical focus of accounting firms was on quality of service to clients in order to provide assurance to investors and creditors on the fairness of the clients' financial statements. The credibility added to a client's financial statements by the clean audit opinion was the central reason for a CPA firm's existence. This focus gave way to a focus on an ever expanding range of services offered to a client pool fighting to achieve the short term earnings per share growth expected of them in the marketplace.[19]

In an era when competition among accounting firms increasingly focused on consulting services, profits on audit fees became razor thin. Indeed, in many cases they came to be, in effect, loss leaders: Accounting firms were willing to accept lower audit fees because they believed the audit process allowed them to get a foot in the door to do more lucrative consulting work. As a result, in some cases auditors found themselves auditing the very services that their colleagues in the firm had sold to the client—a conflict of interest rife with opportunities for abuse.

---

[19]Wyatt, "Accounting Professionalism."

Following the collapse of Arthur Andersen, however, the behavior of the remaining Big Four has changed significantly. Due to pressure from regulatory authorities as well as from market forces, three of the Big Four have divested themselves of their consulting practices. (Deloitte is the exception.) This, in turn, has ushered in a new era in which firms are expected to engage even more fiercely in price competition in providing their auditing services.

The Behavior of Fees

Audit fees generally remained flat or decreased slightly from the late 1980s through the mid-1990s, but since then they have been rising on an inflation-adjusted basis. It is not possible to isolate the effects of consolidation and competition from several other changes in the economy that have affected the accounting field and how the firms conduct their business. These changes include evolving changes in audit scope (the magnitude of effort firms employ during an audit engagement), technological developments, the growth of management consulting services, evolving audit standards, and legal reforms that have altered audit firms' legal liabilities.[20]

One difficulty in studying price competition in the auditing industry is the paucity of data concerning changes in audit fees over time. One study used a proxy measure—audit revenues for the accounting firm divided by the dollar value of client assets audited—as a surrogate for the audit fee. The results indicated that this price measure fell for merging and nonmerging accounting firms alike.[21]

Another study used audit fees charged to a small sample of companies. This analysis found that the average audit fee per client declined from $3.4 million in 1989 to $2.8 million in 1997 on an inflation-adjusted basis. Although the results were limited due to the small sample size, the study found no evidence that Big Six mergers had produced a permanent increase in audit fees.[22]

In addition, the Manufacturers Alliance conducts a periodic survey of the audit fees paid by 130 firms. This survey indicates a downward trend in audit fees per $100 of public company revenues from 1989 through 1995. (The latter year is important because of enactment of the Private Securities Litigation Reform Act, which limited the liability exposure of accounting firms.) The survey found a slight increase in audit fees from 1995 through 1999 for U.S. and foreign companies; it also revealed that American companies paid lower audit fees than their foreign counterparts during the survey period.

The General Accounting Office used its own proxy—net average audit revenues for top-tier firms as a percentage of total sales audited—to analyze the behavior of audit fees. They also found that audit fees declined slightly from 1989 through 1995, but rose from 1995 through 2001. However, no determination could be made as to whether mergers and consolidation had impacted audit fees negatively or positively in either period.

Although audit fees constitute only a tiny fraction of the revenues of a public company that is being audited, some evidence suggests that these fees have increased most recently, with indications that they might rise further in the years ahead. As we have seen, some experts contend that during the 1980s and 1990s, audit services became loss

---

[20]General Accounting Office, "Public Accounting Firms," 31.
[21]S. Ivancevich and A. Zardkoohi, "An Exploratory Analysis of the 1989 Accounting Megamergers," *Accounting Horizons* 14 (2000): 136–155.
[22]K. Menon and D. Williams, "Long-Term Trends in Audit Fees," *Auditing: A Journal of Practice and Theory* 20 (2001): 115–136.

leaders for accounting firms to gain entry into more lucrative professional service markets, primarily management consulting services. After the new client was secured, the firm would develop a relationship with the client and use it as a basis for selling additional services. Although a low audit fee might not cover the cost of the audit, high-margin fees generated from the additional consulting services could conceivably more than cover shortfalls from audit work. With accounting firms now cutting back on some of these other lines of service, however, they might have to raise their audit fees to make up for these lost profits. For this reason, evidence of flat and low audit fees since 1989 may reveal little about the potential for exercising pricing power in the future.

Market participants, experts, and academics agree that prices are likely to rise further due to new regulatory requirements and related changes in the scope of audit services. Moreover, auditing standards themselves will likely increase the amount of audit work required in an engagement. According to the Public Accounting Report, research shows that audit fees rose a whopping 30.1 percent for Fortune 100 firms in 2001, followed by a 17.8 percent increase in 2002, and experts expect double-digit audit fee growth rates to continue for the foreseeable future.

According to Mark Cheffers, a consultant on auditor liability, more thorough oversight of auditing and greater scrutiny of consulting fees will drive these increases. In addition, firms will find themselves in the position of having to raise rates to compensate for the additional liability risks they face in a post-Enron environment.[23] Because of these complexities, no overall conclusion can yet be reached regarding the influence of market power, high concentration, or anticompetitive behavior on the fees charged by large accounting firms.[24]

Competition in Labor Markets

In addition to competing for clients, the Big Four aggressively compete in the labor market for talented people. Evidence of this abounds on college campuses each fall, where Big Four recruiting efforts take on the tenor of fraternity and sorority rush, including expansive tents where food and clothing with the firms' logos are distributed freely. Nor is competition in the labor market restricted to college campuses. Firms constantly mine their clients and their competitors for qualified people, as well. This is in marked contrast to earlier years when the accounting profession was more stable. In the "good old days," an employee either stayed with the firm for an entire career or, if he or she chose to leave, would not expect to be rehired by the same firm. Contrast that environment with the recent one at Andersen shortly before its collapse: the firm had a "boomerang award" for professionals who were returning, a not uncommon event.

Concern does exist, however, about the accounting profession's ability to continue to attract the best and the brightest. One former national partner has opined that when accounting firms no longer operate in the glamorous consulting business, they will be less able to attract the most talented employees for the more mundane auditing function[25]—a development which, should it come to pass, could adversely affect the quality of audits generally.

---

[23]Public Accounting Report, "Fortune 100 Audit Fees Expected to Increase in 2003 and Beyond," (May 31, 2003): 2.
[24]General Accounting Office, "Public Accounting Firms," 32–35.
[25]Personal interview with David Phillips, October 31, 2003.

IV. INDUSTRY PERFORMANCE

Performance involves an assessment of how efficiently and effectively an industry discharges its economic role. Accounting, however, differs from other industries in an important and unique way. Firms in other industries meet buyer demand by providing a service or producing a product efficiently and profitably. The auditing industry furnishes something that goes far beyond this. Its role is one of ensuring the integrity and accuracy of the financial information on which the entire economy depends. Moreover, those who depend on the services provided by auditors—the public and investors—do not pay for this service. Because of this, the issue of independence is of paramount importance in assessing the performance of this field.

Concentration and Competition

Despite the high degree of concentration among accounting firms, no evidence to date indicates that competition in the field has been impaired. The GAO conducted one set of economic tests to ascertain whether consolidation in the auditing industry has had any discernible anticompetitive effects. They employed a simple model of pure price competition to determine whether the high degree of concentration in the market for audit services was inconsistent with a price-competitive process. (The model is designed to simulate a market driven by pure price competition, in which clients choose auditors solely on the basis of price; neither quality nor reputation, for example, are incorporated in the model.)

The GAO's simulation results suggest that a market driven solely by price competition could result in a high degree of market concentration in accountancy. The model generated simulated market shares that were close to the actual market shares of the Big Four. Specifically, the model predicted that in a purely price-competitive world, the Big Four would audit 64 percent of companies in the sampled market, which is close to the actual market share of 62.2 percent for the companies included in the simulation. Moreover, the GAO's model predicted that the Big Four would audit 96.3 percent of companies in the sample with assets greater than $250 million, compared to the 97 percent of these companies actually audited by the Big Four in 2002.

Although the evidence to date does not appear to indicate that competition in the market for audit services has been undermined, the increased level of concentration, coupled with recently imposed restrictions on the provision of nonaudit services by auditors to their clients, could increase the potential for collusive behavior or the exercise of market power in the future.

The Quality of Auditing

A host of theories has been expounded regarding how competition among accounting firms, auditor tenure, and accounting firm size might impact audit quality. Restatements of financial statements due to accounting improprieties provide one proxy for measuring audit quality. Several recent studies have found financial restatements due to accounting irregularities to have increased over the 1990s, especially for larger corporations. This evidence suggests that audit quality might have been deteriorating. Because larger companies typically employ larger accounting firms, which traditionally have been perceived as providing higher-quality audits, the trend toward larger companies issuing financial restatements further heightens concerns about audit quality. Especially disturbing in this respect is the fact that in some recent high-profile

TABLE 11-3   Financial Reporting and Disclosure Violations

Year End July 31	Violations	Increase	Percent Increase	Cumulative Increase	Cumulative Percent
1998	91	-	-	-	-
1999	61	(31)	(34.1%)	(31)	(34.1%)
2000	110	50	83.3	19	20.9
2001	105	(5)	4.5	14	15.4
2002	149	44	41.9	58	63.7

SOURCE: *Securities and Exchange Commission, Report Pursuant to Section 704 of the Sarbanes-Oxley Act of 2002, Washington, D.C., 2003.* May be found at www.sec.gov/news/studies/sox704report.pdf.

restatement cases, it appears that auditors identified problems but failed to ensure that clients appropriately addressed their concerns, thus raising questions about auditor independence and audit quality.[26]

A recent report by the SEC lends credence to these concerns (Table 11-3): The SEC determined that financial reporting and disclosure violations have risen nearly 64 percent over the 5-year period it examined. Although these increases have not been consistent, the overall trend clearly has been up—yet another disturbing indication of declining audit quality.[27]

The Importance of Independence

Auditor independence and audit quality are inextricably linked. In fact, most would consider auditor independence to be an integral component of the quality of the audit performed. In order to make investment decisions, investors must rely on financial statements published by publicly held corporations. It is the auditor's opinion that furnishes investors with assurance that the client firm's financial statements have been subjected to a rigorous examination by an objective, impartial, and skilled professional, and that investors, therefore, can rely on the auditor's accuracy.[28] In order to perform the auditing function effectively, an auditor must take an unbiased viewpoint when conducting audit tests, when evaluating the results of those tests, and when issuing reports and opinions concerning the client's financial statements.

Independence exists at three distinct levels. At the first and highest level are the honesty, objectivity, and responsibility that enable the auditor to take an unbiased stance. The second level of independence refers to the relationship of the auditor to the client. Here *independence* means avoiding any relationship that would be likely, even subconsciously, to impair the auditor's ability to take an unbiased viewpoint. Thus, the public accountant must avoid personal and business relationships with clients that could cause even the most well-meaning person to compromise his or her professional judgment. On the third level, *independence* means the auditor should avoid any relationship with a client that might suggest to a reasonable observer that a conflict of interest exists.

---

[26]General Accounting Office, "Public Accounting Firms," 36–37.

[27]Securities and Exchange Commission, "Report Pursuant to Section 704 of the Sarbanes-Oxley Act of 2002" (Washington, D.C.: 2003): 1–2, available at www.sec.gov/news/studies/sox704report.pdf.

[28]Securities and Exchange Commission, "Final Rule: Revision of the Commission's Auditor Independence Requirements" (Washington, D.C., 2003), available at www.sec.gov/rules/final/33-7919.htm.

The common terms used in the auditing field to describe these concepts are *independence in fact* and *independence in appearance*.

Independence is one of the most elusive characteristics of professional conduct in the accounting profession. We have little basis to doubt independence in fact in a particular circumstance until the most dramatic of events, an audit failure, comes to light. An audit failure occurs when an independent auditor opines to third parties that a client's financial statements are fairly presented in accordance with generally accepted accounting principles when, in fact, they are not. Investigations following these failures often reveal a lack of independence in fact as a primary contributing factor.[29] A lack of independence in fact on the part of Anderson conceivably contributed to the most dramatic audit failure in history, that of Enron.[30] In the case of other recent high-profile audit failures such as those of Sunbeam Corporation, Xerox, WorldCom, Waste Management, and Adelphia Communications, speculation and charges have swirled around independence of fact issues and questions.

Independence in appearance refers to the perception of others about an auditor's independence. Most of the value of the audit report stems from the belief by investors that an objective, unbiased review has been conducted concerning the financial reports being published. Therefore, if auditors are independent in fact but readers of financial statements or members of the public believe them to be advocates for the client, most of the value of the audit function is lost. Users of financial information can have faith in an auditor's representations only when they are confident that the auditor has acted as an impartial judge. The credibility of the public accounting profession thus ultimately depends on this perception of independence (rather than the fact of independence).[31]

Despite the high profile of failures in the auditing and financial world, these matters should be kept in perspective. When one considers the sheer number of audits conducted by large public accounting firms each year, as well as the immense complexity of the audits of large multinational corporations, the miracle is that so few audit failures occur. The reason financial failures of large companies attract headline news, in other words, is because they are so rare.

The Issue of the Scope of Services Provided

The importance of independence leads to another unique dimension of the performance of this field. This is the "scope of services" issue: whether nonaudit practice is appropriate for a public accounting firm, and whether there is a point at which nonaudit practice, particularly consulting, begins to overwhelm independence on the audit side, thereby jeopardizing audit quality and putting at risk the accounting firm's duty to the public.

As we have seen, the growth of consulting services by the Big Eight began to accelerate rapidly from the mid-1970s onward. Table 11-4 shows the percentage of fees earned by the

---

[29]Cottell and Perlin, *Accounting Ethics*, 29–32.
[30]In pleading guilty in early 2004 to federal charges, Enron's former chief financial officer, Andrew Fastow, said that he "and other members of Enron's senior management fraudulently manipulated Enron's publicly reported financial results. Our purpose was to mislead investors and others about the true financial position of Enron and, consequently, to inflate artificially the price of Enron's stock and maintain fraudulently Enron's credit rating." John R. Emschwiller and Thaddeus Herrick, "Fastow Plea Deal May Boost Cases against Enron's Ex-CEOs," *Wall Street Journal* (January 15, 2004): A3.
[31]Cottell and Perlin, *Accounting Ethics*, 33.

TABLE 11-4	Percentage of Gross Fees According to Accounting and Auditing/Tax/Management Consulting Work			
	1975	**1990**	**2000**	
Arthur Andersen & Co.	66/18/16	35/21/44		Arthur Andersen & Co./Andersen Consulting
		48/38/14	43/31/26	Arthur Andersen & Co.
Price Waterhouse & Co.	76/16/8	51/26/23		
			33/18/49	PricewaterhouseCoopers
Coopers & Lybrand	69/19/12	56/19/25		
Peat Marwick Mitchell	68/21/11	53/27/20	45/38/17	KPMG
Ernst & Ernst	73/17/10			
		53/25/22	44/30/26	Ernst & Young
Arthur Young & Company	69/17/14			
Haskins & Sells	74/15/11			
		57/23/20	31/20/49	Deloitte & Touche
Touche Ross & Co.	62/24/14			

SOURCES: 1975: *The Accounting Establishment* (1976): 30.

1990: *International Accounting Bulletin*, Issue No. 84 (March 1991), p. 13, and the firms' annual reports for 1990 to the SEC Practice Section of the AICPA's Division for CPA Firms.

2000: The firms' annual reports for 2000 to the SEC Practice Section of the AICPA's Division for CPA Firms.

largest public accounting firms in their three primary lines of business: accounting and auditing, tax services, and management consulting. Note that in 1975 all of the Big Eight generated more than 60 percent of their gross revenues from accounting and auditing practice. By 2000, however, none of the Big Five generated even half of their gross revenues from accounting and auditing. The most dramatic change occurred at PricewaterhouseCoopers. Its predecessor, Price Waterhouse & Co., was known as the firm that shunned management consulting work prior to the mid-1970s, but its percentage of gross revenue from consulting grew from 8 percent at that time to nearly 50 percent by 2000.[32]

By 1994, the SEC grew increasingly alarmed about this trend toward consulting and away from traditional auditing. One SEC concern was the threat this development posed to auditor independence and objectivity; another concern was the expanding role of nonaudit personnel, who are not bound by the accounting profession's code of ethics, at the top management levels of accounting firms. These concerns grew as the decade of the 1990s progressed. At the same time, there was also growing concern about a phenomenon known as the "intimidation factor"—the inability of an individual auditor to withstand pressure from an aggressive client.[33]

Following the collapse of Andersen and in response to public outcry, the Big Four recently have taken steps to address these concerns. Three of the Big Four have spun off their consulting wings; today, Deloitte remains the only large accounting firm with a significant consulting business, although two of the leading second-tier firms continue to maintain consulting practices. In addition, developments indicate that large public accounting firms are taking steps to disassociate themselves from clients they suspect might cause potential problems. As Table 11-5 shows, 30.4 percent of the audit changes

[32]Zeff, "Accounting Profession, Part II," 270.
[33]Ibid., 269–280.

TABLE 11-5 Dismissals and Resignations: 2003 Third Quarter

Auditor	Audit Client Changes	Dismissals	Voluntary Resignations	Percent Change Due to Resignation
Deloitte	31	24	7	22.6%
Ernst & Young	54	35	19	35.2
KPMG	21	17	4	19.0
PricewaterhouseCoopers	47	34	13	27.7
BDO Seidman	7	4	3	42.9
Grant Thornton	30	17	13	43.3
McGladrey & Pullen	4	4	0	—
Totals	194	135	59	30.4

SOURCE: Public Accounting Report, November 15, 2003.

experienced by the Big Four and the second tier are attributable to voluntary resignation by the auditing firm rather than to dismissal by the client. The trend toward a rising resignation rate began in the late 1990s and has jumped substantially since 2001. Accounting firms also have become focused on the risk profiles of their clients. They increasingly scrutinize the strength of the client's audit committees, the independence of its board of directors, and its practices concerning financial reporting generally.[34] From a performance perspective, however, the accounting firms' decision to abandon high-risk clients has important but conflicting implications. On the one hand, it has the desirable effect of motivating client companies to clean up their operations and procedures. The inability to retain an auditor is expensive in terms of finding a new auditor and, more importantly, in the capital markets where it may raise the firm's cost of obtaining capital. On the other hand, abandoned clients might obtain audits of lesser quality, thereby potentially depriving the investing public of better financial information.

V. PUBLIC POLICY

Over the 40 years following enactment of the Securities Acts of 1933 and 1934, the public accounting profession thrived as a self-regulated institution. The SEC, which had the authority to regulate the industry, took a hands-off approach. This arrangement worked well, chiefly because accountants took great pride in their professionalism. Although they lived comfortably, the temptation to amass great wealth was seemingly lacking. Moreover, the profession held market forces at bay with a code of ethics which, as we have seen, discouraged aggressive competition.

By law, accounting standards—the rules that guide the preparation of corporate financial statements—are the province of the SEC, which has, however, traditionally delegated this responsibility to accounting practitioners. Until 1972, the profession performed the function of setting accounting standards through the American Institute of Certified Public Accountants (AICPA). However, in the early 1970s, controversy arose about the AICPA's standard-setting body, the Accounting Principles Board (APB). Critics claimed that the APB was dominated too strongly by the Big Eight, which, in turn, were believed to be susceptible to influence by their clients in setting accounting standards.

---

[34]Public Accounting Report, "Largest Firms Taking Proactive Stance to Dumping Clients" (November 15, 2003): 1, 7.

As a result of these concerns, the AICPA was compelled to yield that function to a newly created body, the Financial Accounting Standards Board (FASB), in 1972. Since then, accounting standards described as Generally Accepted Accounting Principles (GAAP) have been established by the FASB through its Statements on Financial Accounting Standards and historically have been supported by the SEC. Although the AICPA lost its influence in setting financial accounting standards, it retained its authority to establish standards and guidelines governing the conduct of audits, a role it retained until the recent eruption of corporate financial scandals. Since then, the role of the AICPA in this area, too, has begun to erode with greater public and government scrutiny of the functions and duties of external auditors.

The SEC and Independence

During the 1990s, the SEC became increasingly concerned about the independence issue. With criticism of the auditing industry growing, the AICPA appointed an Advisory Panel on Auditor Independence to examine the situation. This panel expressed dissatisfaction with the practice of the Big Five in expressing their clients' views before the FASB in its standard-setting deliberations, because it seemed to violate the principle of independence in appearance. In 1996, SEC Chairman Arthur Levitt issued a stern warning to the profession:

> I'm deeply concerned that "independence" and "objectivity" are increasingly regarded by some [in the accounting profession] as quaint notions…. I caution the [accounting] industry, if I may borrow a Biblical phrase, not to "gain the whole world, and lose [its] own soul."[35]

In its role of providing regulatory oversight to the public accounting industry, the SEC has issued rules governing the independence of auditors. In 2003, the SEC issued a significant modification of these rules entitled "Final Rule: Revision of the Commission's Auditor Independence Requirements."[36] These new rules encompass four key principles for identifying relationships that impermissibly render an accountant not independent of an audit client in the eyes of the SEC.

The first principle involves financial and employment relationships. Prior to modification, the rule attributed to an entire auditing firm the ownership of stock shares held by each and every partner in the firm, including managerial employees and their families. Interpretation of this rule tended to be captious. For example, suppose the spouse of a partner in a national accounting firm living in Des Moines owned 100 shares of the Cyclops Corporation, headquartered in Buffalo. Before the Buffalo office of the accounting firm could acquire Cyclops as an audit client, the spouse in Iowa would have had to divest those shares. The rule was extremely unpopular with partners in the Big Four, because it severely restricted investment opportunities. The latest revision narrowed the application of this rule by constricting the circle of firm personnel whose investments are imputed to the auditor. The SEC stated its belief that independence will be protected and the rule made more workable by focusing only on those persons who can actually influence an audit, rather than encompassing all the partners in the entire accounting firm.

---

[35]Zeff, "Accounting Profession, Part II," 278.
[36]Securities and Exchange Commission (2003a), "Final Rule: Revision of the Commission's Auditor Independence Requirements," Washington, D.C. Available www.sec.gov/rules/final/33-7919.htm.

The second principle deals with the provision of nonaudit services. Here the SEC adopted a policy that for the first time identifies specific nonaudit services as rendering the auditor not independent of the client. In so doing, the SEC has effectively banned nine kinds of consulting services from being provided by accounting firms to their audit clients: (1) bookkeeping or other services related to the audit client's accounting records or financial statements, (2) financial information systems design and implementation, (3) appraisal or valuation services and fairness opinions, (4) actuarial services, (5) internal audit services, (6) management functions, (7) human resources services, (8) broker-dealer services, and (9) legal services. In each of these nonaudit service lines, the SEC concluded that there is a potential impermissible influence of nonaudit relationships on audit objectivity, or that investor confidence would be adversely affected by reasonable concerns about nonaudit services compromising audit objectivity.[37]

The third principle addresses quality controls and requires accounting firms to have policies and systems in place to ensure that the rules on independence are not violated. The accounting firm also must provide means to remedy independence violations promptly upon discovery.

The final principle requires public disclosure of nonaudit services. The amendments require registrants to disclose in their proxy statements their audit fees, fees for financial information systems design and implementation, and fees for other nonaudit services rendered by the principal accountant to a company. In addition, the SEC requires companies to disclose whether their audit committees have considered if the provision of financial information systems and other nonaudit services by the company's principal accountant are compatible with maintaining the principal accountant's independence.

Within the purview of these principles, the SEC has issued a number of rules that specifically pertain to audit partners and accounting firms, and are intended to prevent abuses uncovered following the collapse of Enron, Worldcom, and others. Thus, an audit partner cannot be compensated on the basis of how much nonauditing service he or she sells to a client; the top two accounting partners on a client's audit are required to rotate off every 5 years and must wait a minimum of 5 years before returning to that client's work; audit professionals must wait a year before accepting employment with a client and overseeing the auditing firm's work; and audit firms must disclose how much revenue they obtain from their nonauditing operations.[38]

The Sarbanes-Oxley Act

The Sarbanes-Oxley Act (SOA), passed in 2002, is perhaps the single most important piece of legislation affecting corporate governance, financial disclosure, and the practice of public accounting since the U.S. securities laws were first enacted in the 1930s. The act establishes a Public Company Accounting Oversight Board (PCAOB), a private sector, nonprofit corporation created to oversee the auditors of public companies to protect the interests of investors and promote the public interest in the preparation of informative, fair, and independent audit reports. With the establishment of the PCAOB, several major responsibilities that formerly rested with the profession are moved closer to the governmental sector. Section 103 provides that the PCAOB shall (1) register public accounting firms; (2) establish or adopt by rule "auditing, quality

---

[37]Ibid
[38]Public Accounting Report, "SEC Passes New Rules" (January 31, 2003): 1, 4.

control, ethics, independence, and other standards relating to the preparation of audit reports for issuers"; (3) conduct inspections of accounting firms; (4) conduct investigations and disciplinary proceedings, and impose appropriate sanctions; (5) perform such other duties or functions as necessary or appropriate; (6) enforce compliance with the act, with the rules of the board, with professional standards, and with the securities laws relating to the preparation and issuance of audit reports, including the obligations and liabilities of accountants with respect thereto; and (7) set the budget and manage the operations of the board and the staff of the board.[39]

The PCAOB must cooperate on an ongoing basis with designated professional groups of accountants and any advisory groups convened in connection with standard setting for auditing, and although the board can "to the extent that it determines appropriate" adopt auditing standards proposed by those groups, the board will have authority to amend, modify, repeal, and reject any auditing standards suggested by the groups. The board also must report on its standard-setting activity to the SEC on an annual basis, a provision that removes from the accounting profession the authority to establish standards governing the ways and means by which audits of publicly held firms are conducted.

The Sarbanes-Oxley Act also requires the PCAOB to adopt an audit standard to implement the internal control review required by Section 404(b) of the act. (Internal control refers to the means by which companies ensure the integrity of their accounting and financial records.) The required internal control standard must oblige the auditor to evaluate whether the internal control structure and procedures include records that accurately and fairly reflect the transactions of the issuer, provide reasonable assurance that transactions are recorded in a manner that will permit the preparation of financial statements in accordance with Generally Accepted Accounting Principles, and provide a description of any material weaknesses in the client's internal controls.

Sarbanes-Oxley further requires that accounting firms be inspected regularly. Section 104 calls for annual quality reviews to be conducted for firms that audit more than 100 client companies; firms that audit fewer companies must be reviewed every 3 years. This section also gives PCAOB the authority to discipline wayward auditors. The board can impose sanctions on an accounting firm that has failed to supervise reasonably any associated person with regard to auditing or quality control standards, or that has violated any other approved audit standards. The board's findings and sanctions are subject to review by the SEC. Moreover, the act gives the SEC broad oversight of the PCAOB. The SEC may assign it additional responsibilities, review its actions, and discipline the board itself if it does not fulfill its responsibilities.

Sarbanes-Oxley requires the accounting profession to pay for the board created to oversee it. Thus, in order to audit a public company, a public accounting firm must register with the PCAOB. The board shall collect a registration fee and an annual fee from each registered public accounting firm, in amounts that are sufficient to recover the costs of processing and reviewing applications and annual reports. The PCAOB also shall establish by rule a reasonable "annual accounting support fee" as may be necessary to maintain the board.[40]

Finally, Title II of Sarbanes-Oxley addresses auditor independence. Among its various provisions are requirements for auditor rotation, definitions of conflict of interest,

---

[39]American Institute of Certified Public Accountants, "Summary of Sarbanes-Oxley Act of 2002" (2003), available at www.aicpa.org/info/sarbanes_oxley_summary.htm.
[40]Ibid.

and codification of services prohibited by auditors. (The SEC was assigned broad authority to issue rules to ensure auditor independence. These rules, discussed in the previous section, were issued in 2003.)

Clearly, an outcropping of new regulatory rules and laws has been proliferated in responding to the recent rash of accounting and financial scandals. (A similar regulatory reaction appears to be commencing in the European Community in response to the scandalous collapse in 2003 of the huge Parmalat firm, in what has been called the greatest fraud in European financial history.)[41] Ultimately, however, the high level of concentration in the accounting field may pose an insuperable challenge to tough regulation: Any severe sanction could put one of the Big Four firms out of business, thereby strengthening the dominance of the remaining majors and further concentrating the field. Already, the dominance of the Big Four threatens to render unworkable a concept the Securities and Exchange Commission has been considering to enhance independence by requiring companies to rotate audit firms every 5 years. More generally, this raises the question of whether the Big Four have reached a point where they are too big, too important, and too few in number for any one of them to be allowed to fail. If so, this would essentially place them beyond the reach of effective regulation.[42]

Conclusion

Public accounting firms perform a vital function in a capitalist economy in which financial markets depend upon accurate financial information in allocating trillions of dollars of funds. External auditors cannot ensure perfect information, but they can provide assurance to others that the financial statements they audit are fairly and accurately representative of the financial position of the reporting entity. This "attest" function is one on which the financial markets place immense weight; as recent events show, the consequences can be catastrophic when auditing firms fail to perform it effectively.

In its first 4 decades, the practice of accounting was accomplished in a relatively sheltered profession. After the profession was opened to market forces, however, dysfunctional behavior began to appear as profit maximization led the industry to seek profits and growth beyond its traditional auditing base. Ironically, actions by the antitrust agencies to promote competition in the field may have paved the way to an industry with greater concentration and less competition in the long run. Although forcing the profession to abandon its ethics codes had the short-run effect of stimulating competition, those competitive forces, in turn, might ultimately have generated a tight oligopoly with significant barriers to entry.

Today the profession stands at a crossroad: Either the practice of accounting will accept far-reaching reform, or it will cease to exist in its present form. The only other alternative, it seems, would be for the profession to cede its auditing functions to a government agency, a development that could render accounting even more politicized. In *The Fellowship of the Ring,* Galadriel tells the fellowship, "But this I will say to you: Your Quest stands upon the edge of a knife. Stray but a little and it will fail, to the ruin of us all. Yet hope remains while the company is true." The Big Four accounting firms would do well to take these words to heart.

---

[41]"Special Report: Europe's Corporate Governance," *Economist* (January 17, 2004): 59–61.
[42]Paula Dwyer, "The Big Four: Too Few to Fail?" *Business Week* (September 1, 2003): 34.

Suggested Readings

American Institute of Certified Public Accountants. 2003. "Summary of Sarbanes-Oxley Act of 2002." Available at www.aicpa.org/info/sarbanes_oxley_summary.htm.

Cottell, P. G., and T. M. Perlin. 1990. *Accounting Ethics: A Practical Guide for Professionals.* Westport, CT: Quorum Books.

Edwards, J. D. 1960. *History of Public Accounting in the United States.* East Lansing, MI: Michigan State University Press.

Emerson's Professional Services Review. Published bimonthly. Emerson Company.

Levitt, Arthur. 2002. *Take on the Street.* New York: Pantheon.

Public Accounting Report. Published semi-monthly. Atlanta, GA: Aspen Publishers, Inc.

Securities and Exchange Commission. 2003a. "Final Rule: Revision of the Commission's Auditor Independence Requirements." Available at www.sec.gov/rules/final/33-7919.htm.

Securities and Exchange Commission. 2003b. "Report Pursuant to Section 704 of the Sarbanes-Oxley Act of 2002." Available at www.sec.gov/news/studies/sox704report.pdf.

U.S. General Accounting Office. 2003. "Public Accounting Firms: Mandated Study on Consolidation and Competition." July.

Zeff, S. A. 2003. "How the U.S. Accounting Profession Got Where It Is Today: Part I." *Accounting Horizons* 17 (September): 189–205.

_____. 2003. "How the U.S. Accounting Profession Got Where It Is Today: Part II." *Accounting Horizons* 17, December. pp. 267–286.

CHAPTER 12

College Sports

—JOHN L. FIZEL AND RANDALL W. BENNETT

S ports are big business in the United States. Nike, Inc.—the maker of athletic footwear, apparel, and equipment—reported more than $10 billion in revenue for 2002. The Washington Redskins National Football League team was sold in 1999 for $800 million, and the Boston Red Sox baseball club was sold in 2002 for $700 million. Alex Rodriguez signed a $252 million, 10-year contract to play baseball for the Texas Rangers from 2001 through 2010—a value exceeding the $250 million owner Tom Hicks paid to buy the team in 1998.

Big business is not confined to athletic companies or professional sports. In 2001, National Collegiate Athletic Association (NCAA) Division I and II members generated more than $4.4 billion in revenue. The big-time collegiate programs (Division I-A) alone produced more than $2.8 billion, more than 2.5 times the $1.07 billion generated in 1989. Major college football coaches, such as Bob Stoops of the University of Oklahoma and Dennis Franchione of Texas A&M University, have compensation packages that exceed $2 million annually, ranking them as the highest-paid public employees in each state. Coaches often earn additional income through sports camps, media shows, and endorsement contracts with athletic apparel companies. CBS paid $6 billion for television rights to the NCAA Division I basketball tournament for 2003 through 2013.

College sports are a lucrative and growing business, but are not without turmoil. Reports of athletes obtaining cash payments, cars, and falsified academic credentials are widespread. Between 1977 and 1985, some football players at Texas Christian University were paid between $35,000 and $40,000 apiece to attend the school. In 1998, a former office manager at the University of Minnesota admitted to completing more than 400 pieces of course work for 20 basketball players over the years from 1993 through 1998. A booster of the University of Michigan basketball program gave more than $600,000 to at least four members of the team in the 1990s. The president of St. Bonaventure University in upstate New York admitted a junior college basketball player from a nonacademic program in welding over the objection of the school's compliance director; the resulting scandal over the ineligible player cost the president his job during the 2002–2003 season.

Why is there such tremendous controversy in collegiate sports? The NCAA depicts itself as a beleaguered organization waging a noble fight against dishonest coaches, lax administrators, and greedy athletes who violate the rules against under-the-table payments and other special favors. However, the situation is better analyzed by examining the economic incentives associated with a cartel: The universities operating college athletic programs are cartel members, and the NCAA is the cartel manager. A cartel is a group of rivals that suppresses economic competition by agreeing to coordinate their individual behavior and to follow rules and practices that maximize their economic benefits. Walter Byers, executive director of the NCAA from 1951 to 1987, describes the NCAA as a cartel that is "operated by not-for-profit institutions contracting together to achieve maximum financial returns."[1] The success of the NCAA cartel is such that Harvard University economist Robert Barro has called the NCAA the most effective monopoly in America.[2]

Although cooperation among cartel members increases group profits, each member has an incentive to circumvent the group rules to increase its individual share of the collective profits. For example, if one university pays signing bonuses to the best high school athletes, it might be able to win more games, increase attendance at games, enhance private donations from excited fans, and reap the dollar rewards from appearing in a postseason tournament or bowl game. Yet, if many members cheat, the increased competition will cause an escalation in bonus payments, smaller profits, and less certain and surely more limited benefits for all. Thus, the successful cartel must limit autonomous behavior by enforcing and monitoring its rules. However, the rules themselves are political, and no matter what policies the cartel promulgates, they reflect a compromise among divergent views. As with any compromise, some cartel members will be more satisfied than others. Therefore, churning within the industry will occur as members constantly weigh the benefits of joint versus individual action.

I. HISTORY

The original incentive for forming the NCAA, as well as the impetus for its early growth, was not based on financial goals related to cartel behavior. Instead, the catalyst for the development of the NCAA was the violence and lack of standard playing rules in college football. In the late 1880s, football was a cross between rugby and soccer, retaining some rules from each of its ancestors, as well as utilizing additional rules of its own. College teams constantly looked for new tactics to win in this evolving sport. Many of the successful strategies involved increasingly violent player behavior: In 1905 alone, the college football season resulted in 18 player deaths and 159 serious injuries.

As the number of injuries and deaths grew, fan appeal fell. Some colleges attempted to limit violent tactics only to lose on the field to the universities that continued to employ them. The industry was facing the classic "prisoner's dilemma": All colleges had much to gain from cooperatively banning violent play, but each college continued to have an individual incentive to use unilaterally successful tactics. Little could be done without some formal agreement or means to punish aberrant behavior.

President Theodore Roosevelt reacted to the carnage by calling on colleges to reform athletics. He organized a meeting with representatives of several schools in hopes of creating a cooperative plan to limit brutal and destructive play. No agreement could be reached. Shortly thereafter, a number of colleges dropped football as a sanctioned sport. A new sense of urgency developed, and a second meeting was called. From this

---

[1]Walter Byers, *Unsportsmanlike Conduct: Exploiting College Athletes* (Ann Arbor: University of Michigan Press, 1995): 374.
[2]"The Best Little Monopoly in America," *Business Week* (December 9, 2002): 22.

latter meeting came the Intercollegiate Athletic Association of the United States, which underwent a name change to the NCAA in 1910.

Implementation of standardized rules and prohibition of violence in football quickly reduced the rate of injury. At the same time, the popularity of the game increased. NCAA membership grew rapidly as more schools sought the benefits of cooperation, and increasing acceptance of the NCAA allowed the organization to standardize rules for other college sports. However, the NCAA and its membership soon recognized that cooperation in the area of rules could be expanded to other areas of competition, and the NCAA turned its attention from standardizing rules to instituting the foundations for cartel control of college sports.

Input Controls

Cartel development began with the effort to limit competition for athletic talent. Contending that colleges should be limited to amateur athletics, the NCAA worked to remove professionals from collegiate sports. Many teams were packed with "hired guns," players who were not students, often had no link to the college, and participated for a paycheck. The NCAA declared that eligible athletes must be full-time students. In addition, eligibility was limited to 3 years. (Freshmen were ineligible.) The NCAA also made the following declaration:

> No student shall represent a college or university in any intercollegiate game or contest . . . who has at any time received, either directly or indirectly, money, or any other consideration.[3]

To facilitate implementation of the rules, the NCAA recommended in 1919 that members should schedule games only with opponents who abided by NCAA rules.

Predictably, the result was widespread cheating, because no enforcement mechanism was in place to police adherence to the amateurism and athletic compensation rules. Colleges that disregarded the rules and offered lucrative contracts to talented athletes reaped the financial rewards of a winning program. With lax enforcement and great incentives for noncooperative behavior, the labor restraint rules were largely ineffective.

These shortcomings were addressed in the Sanity Code of 1948. It established standards for financial aid to student athletes and created an enforcement apparatus to deal with rule violations. In pursuit of amateurism, the NCAA enacted rules stating that athletes and nonathletes were to be treated identically: Aid could be based upon need or academic merit but not on athletic ability; need-based grants were to make no distinction between athletes and other students. Student athletes in the top 25 percent of their high school class or who had a grade point average (GPA) of B or better in college were eligible to receive merit aid even if no need was demonstrated.

The Sanity Code also established the NCAA Compliance Committee to handle allegations of rule violations. This first attempt to crack down on schools that violated the rules was hindered, however, because the only penalty available was to revoke membership: The rule breaker would be tossed out of the NCAA if two thirds of NCAA members voted for expulsion. In fact, in 1950 the Compliance Committee voted to expel seven schools, the so-called "Seven Sinners" (Villanova, Boston College,

---

[3]Byers, 40.

Virginia, Maryland, Virginia Military Institute, The Citadel, and Virginia Polytechnic Institute), for rule violations. However, the two-thirds vote of all NCAA members needed to confirm the expulsions was not obtained, indicating the reluctance of the NCAA membership to punish rule violators, at least when faced with the imposition of such a drastic penalty. This lack of will led to the abolition of the Sanity Code in 1951, and the Compliance Committee died the following year.

In 1953, the NCAA enacted a range of penalties that were less severe than termination of membership in an attempt to improve enforcement. In 1954, it established the Committee on Infractions to deal with rules violations. For the first time, the NCAA had the means and the ability to enforce athletic labor market restraints.

Output Controls

Having restrained competition for athletic talent, the NCAA began an effort to control industry output by asserting jurisdiction over all aspects of contract negotiations for college football telecasts. The NCAA Television Plan consisted of exclusive contracts with the television networks that limited the number of telecasts and the number of appearances by individual college members over a specified period of time, and also stipulated the times at which games could be televised. The financial gains from restricting output quickly became apparent: The initial television contract (1952) generated $1.15 million; by 1962, the contract went for $5.1 million; in 1972, $12 million; and in 1992, $59 million.

This spectacular growth in broadcast revenues, combined with the NCAA's process for distributing these fees, created tensions within the organization. The few members that had football teams with sufficient fan interest to generate substantial broadcasting fees were sharing those fees with the large number of member schools whose teams enjoyed far more limited fan support. The revenue-generating members became disgruntled with the cartel's allocation mechanism. To save the cartel, the NCAA would have to address the diverse interests of its members.

In 1973, the NCAA responded by creating three subgroups within the organization: Divisions I, II, and III. By having a common commitment to athletics and common revenue-generating capacity within divisions, more of the broadcasting fees earned within a given division could be distributed among the members of each division.

Several of the elite schools were not placated, though. They threatened to leave the cartel unless they were provided even greater sovereignty within the organization. The response was more restructuring. Division I was further subdivided according to the size of football programs: I-A, I-AA, and I-AAA. Division I basketball remained unchanged. This divisional split brought stability to the cartel, at least temporarily.

The NCAA thus began as an organization dedicated to creating uniformity in playing rules and reining in brutal play. After members began cooperating on these issues, however, there was little additional cost to determining how to control competition for inputs and outputs within the college sports industry. In short, the evolution of the NCAA provides a classic example of the genesis of a cartel.

II. STRUCTURE

Colleges in the United States can belong to one of two organizations that oversee male and female intercollegiate athletics: the NCAA and the National Association of Intercollegiate Athletics (NAIA). All big-time college athletic programs belong to the

NCAA, and the size diversity of NCAA membership is illustrated by the football attendance figures in Table 12-1. The major football programs of Division I-A schools play before tens of thousands of fans, led by the University of Michigan with a 2002 average home game attendance of 110,576.

The next level, Division I-AA, has fewer athletic scholarships available and generally includes smaller schools. The average attendance is 10,000 or fewer, with Jackson State University leading the way with a 2002 average attendance of 23,691 per home

TABLE 12-1 Attendance at NCAA Football Games

Division I-A

Year	No. of Teams	Total Attendance	Per-Game Attendance
1982	97	24,770,855	43,869
1987	104	25,471,744	41,963
1992	107	25,402,046	41,170
1997	112	27,565,959	42,085
2002	117	34,384,264	44,367

Division I-AA

Year	No. of Teams	Total Attendance	Per-Game Attendance
1982	92	5,655,519	11,709
1987	87	5,129,250	11,151
1992	88	5,057,955	10,429
1997	118	5,212,048	8,118
2002	123	5,525,250	7,893

Division II

Year	No. of Teams	Total Attendance	Per-Game Attendance
1982	126	2,745,964	4,443
1987	107	2,424,041	4,481
1992	129	2,733,094	4,251
1997	142	2,349,442	3,309
2002	149	2,647,038	3,381

Division III

Year	No. of Teams	Total Attendance	Per-Game Attendance
1982	195	2,002,857	2,223
1987	209	1,982,506	2,021
1992	228	2,032,336	1,884
1997	209	1,730,400	1,746
2002	228	1,999,663	1,759

SOURCES: National Collegiate Athletic Association, *NCAA Football,* various issues; National Collegiate Athletic Association, *NCAA News,* various issues.

football game. NCAA Division II schools are allowed even fewer scholarships and average 5,000 or fewer in attendance per game, led by Tuskegee University with 11,851 fans per 2002 home game. NCAA Division III schools are not allowed to give athletic scholarships and average about 2,000 fans per game, with St. John's of Minnesota averaging a division-leading 5,717 spectators per football game in 2002. The NAIA comprises a homogeneous group of smaller schools that do not place great emphasis on intercollegiate sports or have large fan bases, and so are similar to NCAA Division III schools. In sum, as noted by Fleisher, Goff, and Tollison, "(f)or all practical purposes, the NCAA today directs and controls all major revenue-producing collegiate athletic events."[4]

Entry and Entry Barriers

Unfortunately for the NCAA, its success at restricting competition and increasing profits has resulted in a clamor for admittance to membership by outsiders that are eager to share in the cartel's profits. Rapid entry has resulted in divergent interests and potential rule breaking. The situation has been exacerbated by heterogeneity in revenue-generating capability. Also, monitoring and enforcing rules for member behavior has become more difficult. In short, the stability of the cartel is jeopardized.

The NCAA had 1,006 college members in 2003. Multiply this by the number of coaches, players, potential recruits, alumni, and fans at each institution and it quickly becomes apparent that monitoring all potential rule-breaking activities would be prohibitively expensive, if not impossible. If monitoring is impossible, then cheating should be rampant. Although the NCAA cannot closely monitor each rule-related activity, it can use probabilistic evidence to infer when a member's behavior might deviate from the rules.[5]

This process compares current performance with the historic performance of its members: If a significant improvement in current performance is observed, then suspicion is raised that the college has cheated. Resources can be allocated to launch a more intense investigation to determine whether cheating actually has occurred.

If cheating cannot be controlled, the cartel will disintegrate. The NCAA, however, can apply sanctions to punish cheaters who are caught, and these sanctions have become increasingly severe in recent years. For instance, the NCAA can reduce the number of athletic scholarships a college can grant. The NCAA also can limit television appearances and prohibit a college from appearing in lucrative postseason tournaments. Because an appearance in a Bowl Championship Series (BCS) game such as the Rose, Sugar, Orange, or Fiesta Bowl is worth more than $13 million per team, the NCAA clearly has powerful means to enforce adherence to its rules.

Although violations of NCAA rules are often cast in terms of legality or illegality, these rules are not public law. The NCAA is a private organization governed by rules that have been adopted by representatives of its member institutions. Although it is not illegal for a college athlete to sign a product endorsement contract, it might be an

---

[4]A. Fleisher, B. Goff, and R. Tollison, *The National Collegiate Athletic Association: A Study in Cartel Behavior* (Chicago: University of Chicago Press, 1992): 55.
[5]For details, see Fleischer, Goff, and Tollison.

NCAA violation to accept a job that is linked to his fame as a collegiate athlete. The perception that NCAA rules are law does, however, aid in enforcement. The "legal" ramifications of their actions may deter potential perpetrators of rule violations.

Recently, however, NCAA rules have begun to seep into the legal system. In addition to the NCAA punishing an athlete and a college if an agent pays an athlete, many states now consider it a felony for an agent to offer something of value to anyone as a means of inducing a student athlete to sign with an agent. To provide uniformity across states, the NCAA has been promoting the Uniform Athlete Agent Act (UAAA) to state legislatures. This legislation has been enacted into law in 22 states as of June, 2003, with 9 more states currently considering adoption. Only 17 states had no regulation of sports agents as of June 2003. In addition to criminal sanctions, the UAAA allows the athlete and the school to sue the sports agent for civil damages if violations of the act cause harm. Various proposals also have been made at the federal level to address sports agent behavior. Although other students on campus and other workers in general are allowed to seek legal advice and representation as they see fit, athletes are not. The NCAA's influence seems to be creeping beyond the narrow confines of college sports.

Entry considerations traditionally have focused on keeping peace within the ranks. With so many member colleges in the NCAA, the concern always has been that a disgruntled group of members could form a new, separate league of their own. (We will discuss later the rise and fall of the College Football Association [CFA] as an example of this course of action.) To be effective, the number of seceding teams must be sufficient to form an alternative league with a full slate of games and potential postseason play. However, as indicated previously, the creation of subgroups within the NCAA increases the homogeneity of colleges within each division and reduces incentives for cheating. Thus, Division I-A football colleges can enact rules that apply only to them; they need not be impeded by the legislative dictates of the smaller, less sports-oriented colleges.

The entry barriers that do exist consist primarily of limiting admission to various NCAA divisions, especially Division I-A football. A Division I-A football entrant must offer at least 16 varsity sports (male and female), play at least 5 home games against other Division I-A members, average more than 17,000 in paid attendance per home game, grant an average of 90 percent or more of the maximum allowable football scholarships for each 2-year period, and give at least 200 total athletic scholarships or spend at least $4 million on athletic scholarships for all sports each year. The NCAA also requires Division I-A conferences to have at least 8 members.

Until August 2, 2003, a college could meet these minimum standards and be accepted for 3 years as a provisional member of Division I-A. Provisional entrants comply with division rules, but they do not receive division benefits. Currently, a change of division membership requires an exploratory year plus 4 more provisional years. The number of provisional entrants was 96 in 1995, 67 in 1998, 59 in 2001, and 28 in 2002. The NCAA clearly has slowed migration between divisions in an attempt to retain divisional homogeneity.[6]

---

[6] The slowing of entry into Division I programs despite profit incentives prompted R. Sandy and P. Sloan to ask, "Why don't all colleges that can possibly beg or borrow the money start Division I-A programs?" See "Why Do U.S. Colleges Have Sports Programs?" in *Economics of College Sports,* ed. John Fizel and Rod Fort (Westport, CT: Praeger, 2004).

III. CONDUCT

Although the market share of the NCAA is nearly 100 percent, the specter of disharmony among the large number of members and the growing threat of new entrants put severe strains on the cartel. The stresses are so serious that much of the output control once held by the NCAA is being eroded. The NCAA today is better viewed as an input cartel, but even its labor controls are being tested.

Output Control

Control of broadcasting rights to college football telecasts is one key dimension of output control. As noted earlier, this control initially generated large, rapidly rising broadcasting fees. Increased dissension about the distribution of these fees, however, fueled a restructuring of the NCAA. The resulting split into divisions in 1973 was only a temporary solution to the growing disparity in revenue generation across the membership, and dissatisfaction soon returned.

The College Football Association (CFA), founded in 1977, was an outgrowth of this dissension. The CFA included most of the Division I-A schools except those from the Big Ten and PAC Ten conferences. (Originally, the CFA members threatened complete secession from the NCAA but stopped short when they did not have the support of the Big Ten and PAC Ten schools.) Instead, the CFA focused solely on gaining control of football telecast revenues. The CFA also planned to garner more television appearances and generate more television revenue for its member schools.

In 1981, the CFA signed an agreement with NBC that fulfilled these goals. The NCAA immediately threatened penalties that would apply to football and other sports. Later that year, the University of Oklahoma and University of Georgia filed suit against the NCAA, alleging that the NCAA Television Plan, by limiting television exposure for any one team, was an illegal restraint of trade in violation of the antitrust laws.

The 1983 Television Plan allowed 2 networks, ABC and CBS, each to air 14 telecasts annually. These telecasts could be a mixture of national and regional games, but each network was required to telecast at least 82 different teams over a 2-year period. ABC and CBS together had to show at least 115 different teams over the 2-year life of the plan. The NCAA also mandated that teams be limited to 4 national appearances and 6 total appearances during this period. Finally, all teams involved in a telecast received equal remuneration, regardless of the attractiveness of the game to viewers and fans or the number of stations that broadcast the game. In some years, for example, Oklahoma, University of Southern California (USC), Appalachian State, and the Citadel each received the same compensation, even though the Oklahoma–USC game was broadcast over 200 stations but the Appalachian State–Citadel game was broadcast on only 4.

The NCAA acknowledged that its Television Plan restrained trade but pointed out that professional sports often had been granted exemptions from prosecution when restrictive business practices were necessary to promote competitive balance. The NCAA asserted that if colleges were given the right to negotiate their own contracts, a proliferation of telecasts would ensue, with most appearances being awarded to traditional football powers. Because television appearances are a key aid in recruiting top athletes, a distribution of appearances skewed toward the traditional powers would accentuate inequality among football programs; existing powers would prosper, and nonpowers would suffer.

Nevertheless, in 1984, the Supreme Court held that the NCAA Television Plan restricted output and fixed prices in violation of the Sherman Antitrust Act.[7] The ruling granted individual colleges the property right to their college football telecasts—a right the schools had an option to sell or assign at their discretion.

The demise of NCAA television control had three significant outcomes. Soon after the Court's ruling, colleges, conferences, and select organizations of colleges frenetically pursued local, regional, national, and cable outlets to televise their games. The number of network games doubled shortly after the ruling, and the price per network game dropped from $2.3 million to $0.6 million.

Also, Bennett and Fizel as well as Fort and Quirk found that competitive balance on the field has been enhanced by the Court's decision.[8] Contrary to the NCAA's argument, NCAA control over television was not necessary to generate more equality of playing strength among Division I football teams.

Finally, the case initially was a coup for the CFA and its partial secession from the NCAA. However, over time, the CFA began to face internal pressures similar to those experienced by the NCAA. Eventually, several prominent members left the CFA; in 1997, the CFA ceased operations.

In response to the development of the CFA and the future threat of similar alliances by major Division I programs, the NCAA changed its Division I structure of governance in 1997 from one school/one vote to a representative system based upon conference votes. The Division I-A conferences now have a majority of votes on the Division I board of directors and the Division I Management Council, even though more schools are in Divisions I-AA and I-AAA. The votes of the former members of the CFA now have a larger impact on NCAA policy, with the less than surprising result that the NCAA is now allocating a higher percentage of revenues to these institutions.[9]

One area that escapes NCAA control is postseason play in Division I-A football. Currently, 117 Division I-A football schools participate in the only sport for which the NCAA does not sponsor a national championship. Why would the NCAA ignore championship play in the sport that generates the largest revenue for the typical Division I-A school? The answer lies in the historical development of the postseason bowl system. Since the University of Michigan defeated Stanford University 49–0 in the 1902 Rose Bowl, a system of postseason bowls has developed as a reward for a successful football season: The Rose Bowl was first played in 1902, the Orange and Sugar Bowls in 1935, the Sun Bowl in 1936, the Cotton Bowl in 1937, the Gator Bowl in 1946, the Liberty Bowl in 1959, and the Fiesta Bowl in 1971. By 2002, the number of Division I-A postseason bowl games had grown to 28.

The mythical national champion of Division I-A football historically has been determined by polls of sportswriters or coaches, not by performance on the playing field as is done for Divisions I-AA, II, and III football. Dissatisfied with this arrangement,

---

[7]See *The National Collegiate Athletic Association v. Board of Regents of the University of Oklahoma and University of Georgia Athletic Association,* 468 U.S. 85 (1984).

[8]Randall W. Bennett and John L. Fizel, "Telecast Deregulation and Competitive Balance," *American Journal of Economics and Sociology* 54 (1995): 183–200; R. Fort and J. Quirk, "Introducing a Competitive Economic Environment into Professional Sports," in *Advances in the Economics of Sports,* ed. W. Hendricks (Greenwich, CT: JAI Press, 1997): 11.

[9]For a detailed analysis of the restructuring, see Joel Maxcy, "The 1997 Restructuring of the NCAA: A Transaction Cost Explanation" in *Economics of College Sports,* ed. John Fizel and Rod Fort (Westport, CT: Praeger, 2004).

the major football programs began tinkering with the bowl system in 1991 in an attempt to arrange for the number 1 and number 2 teams in the coaches' and press polls each year to play in a national championship game at an existing bowl. This initial bowl coalition became the bowl alliance for the 1995 season, in a system whereby the Orange Bowl, Sugar Bowl, and Fiesta Bowl would trade off as hosts for this national championship game.

This game was not, however, a true national championship, because the finalists were determined through the polls and not by a playoff system; in addition, two major conferences, the Big Ten and PAC Ten, were not involved initially. These conferences were not ready to sever the lucrative arrangement that tied their conference champions to the Rose Bowl—the bowl with the biggest payout—for the chance to play for the national championship. The Big Ten, PAC Ten, and the Rose Bowl did join the bowl alliance for the 1998 season, however, forming the Bowl Championship Series (BCS).

The championship game now rotates among the Orange, Sugar, Fiesta, and Rose Bowls. The compromise that brought the Big Ten and PAC Ten into the BCS allows their champions to still meet in the Rose Bowl when it is not hosting the championship game, and when they are not involved in the championship game in other years.

Bowl directors and major conference commissioners—not the NCAA—administer the BCS. The administrators have reduced the emphasis on polls to determine the championship game participants by relying on a combination of (1) team record, (2) Associated Press and ESPN/*USA Today* poll rankings, (3) computer rankings, and (4) a measure of strength of schedule based on opponent performance. The 1999 Fiesta Bowl hosted the first BCS game, in which the University of Tennessee was crowned national champion after defeating Florida State 23 to 16. Other BCS champions include Florida State in 2000, Oklahoma in 2001, Miami in 2002, and Ohio State in 2003.

A true playoff system would likely be much more lucrative than the current bowl system. One proposal from the late-1990s was for a 16-team Division I-A football playoff tournament to pay the NCAA about $380 million per year for 8 years, an amount that is much larger than the $168 million the bowls paid out following the 2002 season. DeLoss Dodds, the athletic director of the University of Texas at the time, said that colleges are "leaving $2 million a year, per school, on the table" by not going to a playoff system.[10]

Although many argue that college revenues would be enhanced if the NCAA could gain control of postseason play in football, others offer counterarguments. One weakness of the argument for playoffs is that they would lengthen the college football season. The aforementioned proposal would have played the championship game the week before the Super Bowl in mid-January. Graham B. Spanier, Penn State president and chairman of the NCAA Division I Board of Directors at the time, said:

> There is a great concern about commercialization, professionalism, and extending the season, and I can tell you that most of the presidents I've spoken with are not persuaded by the money that's potentially on the table.[11]

The existing bowls oppose a postseason tournament because they fear they would lose autonomy or even be eliminated entirely by a playoff system. Arguments that con-

---

[10]Welch Suggs, "Can $3-Billion Persuade Colleges to Create a Playoff for Football?" *Chronicle of Higher Education* (August 6, 1999): 2.
[11]Ibid., 3.

ference commissioners make against playoffs are that they would reduce the importance of the regular season for most teams, hurt or destroy existing bowls, and possibly eliminate the opportunity for postseason bowl play for many teams. Almost half of the 117 teams that played Division I-A football in 2002 participated in a bowl game. If a 16-team playoff destroys the minor bowl games, many fewer teams will earn postseason play.

Walter Byers, former executive director of the NCAA, argued that major college football programs do not want a playoff system because they do not want the money generated from postseason play to be funneled through the NCAA, where it is likely that funds will flow to nonparticipating schools and to the NCAA itself. Currently, as Figure 12-1 shows, the power football conferences receive more than 90 percent of the revenue from BCS games.[12]

There is no doubt that the NCAA will work diligently to develop a proposal for a postseason football tournament/playoff. But can the NCAA design a proposal that overcomes the academic concerns of college presidents, the distribution concerns of institutional football powers, and the lobbying that will inevitably come from bowl administrators?

Two recent and related responses to the BCS have generated additional uncertainty about the future of a football playoff system. First, Congressional hearings have been

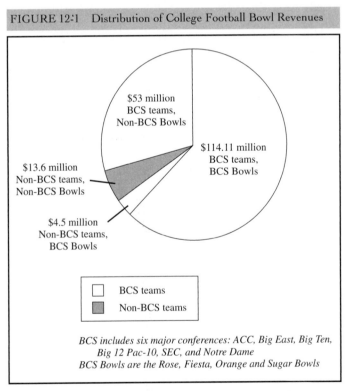

FIGURE 12-1   Distribution of College Football Bowl Revenues

$53 million
BCS teams,
Non-BCS Bowls

$114.11 million
BCS teams,
BCS Bowls

$13.6 million
Non-BCS teams,
Non-BCS Bowls

$4.5 million
Non-BCS teams,
BCS Bowls

☐ BCS teams
▨ Non-BCS teams

*BCS includes six major conferences: ACC, Big East, Big Ten,
Big 12 Pac-10, SEC, and Notre Dame
BCS Bowls are the Rose, Fiesta, Orange and Sugar Bowls*

SOURCE: *Chris Isidore, "Flushing Money Down the Bowls," CNN/Money.com,
December 8, 2003.*

---

[12]Maxcy, "The 1997 Restructuring of the NCAA."

held to discuss the antitrust implications of the BCS. Critics contend that the BCS has shut all teams but those from the six power conferences out of the hundred million–per–year arrangement (Figure 12-1). Such action, they argue, is a restraint of trade and illegal. Second, college football is packed with an increasing number of bowl games. These games are conducted under the auspices of the NCAA and include teams that are members and nonmembers of the BCS. According to Independence Bowl Director Glen Krupica, as bowls scramble for attractive teams,

> the line between a bowl-eligible team and a bowl-deserving team is getting blurrier and blurrier. . . . I think the integrity of the bowl system is at stake in this.

With TV and sponsor budgets practically exhausted, bowls are asking for and often receiving taxpayer subsidies. Debate about the suitability of using public money to finance these profitable ventures is ongoing.[13]

Input Control

A cartel in the output market increases profits by enabling members to limit output and increase prices collectively. A cartel in the input market increases profits by enabling members to collectively *lower* the price paid for the input. The NCAA has created a voluminous system of rules aimed at controlling the cost of inputs in collegiate sports, with most of the regulations being directed at the recruitment and compensation of athletes.

The NCAA contends that the proliferation of its recruiting controls enhances competitive balance by standardizing rules within the organization. Yet an examination of some of the rules shows that they are effective monopsonistic methods to reduce recruiting expenditures: Potential recruits are limited in the number of on-campus and off-campus contacts they can have with representatives of a college's athletic program. Direct contact also is limited to certain months of the year. Each of these stipulations reduces the per-recruit cost of recruiting.

The total costs of recruiting are further diminished because colleges are limited in the number of athletic scholarships they can award. A Division I-A college can grant in any year a maximum of 85 scholarships in football and 13 in basketball. Scholarship limits are applied to other sports, as well. Freshman eligibility also reduces the total costs of recruiting by giving colleges 4 rather than 3 years of service by the athlete and by reducing the number of costly ventures into the recruiting fray. Recruits sign a National Letter of Intent to indicate their chosen college. Once signed, the recruit cannot enroll in another institution without forfeiting 2 years of athletic eligibility. Once signed, the chosen college and all other colleges can terminate expenditures for wooing this particular athlete immediately.[14]

Despite the importance of recruiting rules, the predominant feature of the NCAA cartel is the compensation package paid to athletes. Under the guise of "amateurism,"

---

[13]"BCS Proponents and Critics Prepare for Senate Hearing," *USA Today* (October 21, 2003): 9C; "More Bowls, More Problems," *USA Today* (September 8, 2000): 2C; "College Bowls Dip into Public Funds," *USA Today* (September 8, 2000): 1A.

[14]Dan Wetzel, "Letter of Intent Benefits Schools, Not Athletes," CBS SportsLine (November 12, 2001).

the NCAA has severely limited athletes' compensation relative to their value to the institution, while coupling the ability to receive compensation with a variety of changing academic standards.

In 1956, the NCAA initiated athletic scholarships that were independent of need or academic merit. The scholarships were limited to tuition, room, board, and incidentals "not to exceed the cost of attendance at the school." In almost 50 years, these compensation limits have changed little. If anything, compensation has decreased over time. The NCAA now allows athletes to hold limited jobs to cover the difference between the full cost of attending college and the value of the athletic scholarship. NCAA President Myles Brand has even said he approves of the concept of giving athletes an additional $2,000 to $3,000 per year to meet the scholarship-cost differential. State legislators also find athletic scholarships limiting and have initiated legislation to have schools pay athlete expenses beyond tuition, room, board, and book fees.[15]

The NCAA strictly enforces the existing compensation limits. Departures from the rules, no matter how slight, can bring severe penalties. For example, UCLA's basketball team was prohibited from playing in the postseason tournament because recruits were given free UCLA shirts and the team received a free Thanksgiving dinner from an athletic booster. These perks were violations because they were available to basketball players but not to students on the campus at large.

The shrinking compensation paid to athletes occurs as the revenues of the NCAA are skyrocketing. College athletic programs are generating annual revenues greater than $1 billion in ticket sales and television receipts. The bowls following the 2002 football season alone paid out $168 million, and the 2002 men's basketball tournament brought in more than $500 million in television revenue. A winning basketball or football team can provide enough revenue to finance a college's entire athletic program. Clearly, monopsonistic exploitation is profitable.

A number of methods exist for assessing the extent to which athletes are underpaid relative to the revenue stream they generate. What if competition for athletic services were introduced across the entire NCAA? When this happened in major league baseball, player salaries increased to 50 percent to 60 percent of total team revenues. If 50 percent of the Division I-A football revenue were allocated among the football players in this division, each player would receive about $35,000 to $40,000 per year.

What if compensation followed the revenue-sharing rules of the National Basketball Association (NBA)? Charlie Bell played in three NCAA Final Fours and won a national basketball championship during his Michigan State University basketball career (1998 to 2001). His annual scholarship and aid package was worth an estimated $10,000. If the NCAA used the NBA formula, Bell would have made about $1.3 million in his 4-year career, or $345,666 per season, according to calculations made by ESPN.com.

What if athletes were paid an amount equal to their economic value to an athletic program? Marginal revenue product analysis offers similar conclusions concerning the appropriate average compensation of athletes and suggests that monopsonistic exploitation is even greater for star players. Brown and Jewell concluded that the annual

---

[15]Doug Tucker, "Many Big 12 Coaches Favor Paying Players," *Kansas City Star Telegram* (September 22, 2003); "Extra Money for Athletes Gaining Steam," *USA Today*, (September 19, 2003): 1C.

marginal revenue product of individual college football and basketball stars is at least $400,000 and $1 million, respectively.[16]

The NCAA argues that amateurism is an essential part of the product it sells, and that these compensation rules are necessary to minimize commercialization of collegiate sports. Nevertheless, the NCAA does not prohibit other competitive and commercial activities: Athletes are courted with lavish stadiums, training facilities, locker rooms, and specially outfitted athletic dormitories. Customers are wooed with college brand apparel, videos, logos, and advertisements. Business interests are exploited with stadium billboards, electronic ads on scoreboards, sponsorship of bowl games, logos on team uniforms, and exclusive apparel/equipment contracts. Only the athletes seem to be barred from reaping the benefits of big-time college sports.

In 1965, the NCAA began developing academic eligibility standards in response to the accusation that colleges were accepting ill-prepared student athletes who had little chance of academic success. These standards also reinforced the NCAA claim that amateur sports required that educational objectives supercede profit-making objectives. The success of academic standards, however, has been limited legally and practically.

The initial academic standard was the 1.6 rule, which restricted freshman athletic scholarships to those who could expect a freshman grade point average of 1.6 or above, based upon high school academic performance and standardized SAT or ACT scores. The 1.6 rule continued through the 1960s and early 1970s, when campus upheaval led many colleges to relax admission standards for all students. In 1973, the NCAA voted to rescind the 1.6 rule and to let colleges set their own admission standards for athletes. This led to a period of declining graduation rates, followed by college presidents leading a fight to reinstate academic requirements for incoming student athletes.

The result was enactment of Proposition 48 in 1983. Freshman eligibility under Proposition 48 required that a student be a high school graduate, obtain at least a 700 on the SAT or a 15 on the ACT, and earn at least a 2.0 grade point average in 11 core high school courses. Students who did not meet these standards were not eligible to practice or play during their freshman year of college and had only 3 years of eligibility left.

Proposition 16 was passed by the NCAA in 1996, replacing Proposition 48. It required college freshmen to have a high school diploma and a minimum grade point average in 13 core high school courses, with this GPA linked to standardized test scores by a sliding scale: The higher the high school GPA is, the lower the allowable standardized test score is. For instance, a student with a 2.0 GPA in these core courses needed to score 1,010 or higher on the SAT in order to achieve freshman eligibility; an SAT score of less than 820 rendered the student ineligible for his or her freshman year regardless of high school GPA.

The standards were revised in 2002 for all students entering college after August 1, 2003. The number of core high school courses has been raised to 14, and the sliding scale relating the GPA in these courses to the standardized test score has been extended so as to eliminate the minimum SAT score. Now, a potential athlete can score a 400,

---

[16]R. Brown and R. T. Jewell, "Measuring Marginal Revenue Product in College Athletics: Updated Estimates," in *Economics of College Sports*, ed. John Fizel and Rod Fort (Westport, CT: Praeger, 2004).

the lowest possible score on the SAT, and still be eligible as long as he or she has a core GPA of at least 3.55.

The NCAA combined this easing of entrance standards for poor standardized test takers with new rules that will make it more difficult for athletes to retain eligibility throughout their college years: Athletes must now complete at least 24 semester hours of course work prior to their second year of college and then complete at least 18 semester hours each academic year and complete at least 6 semester hours each term. The new standards also require that athletes attain at least 90 percent of the minimum cumulative GPA needed to graduate by the beginning of their second year, at least 95 percent by the start of their third year, and 100 percent by the start of each succeeding year.

The standards governing the percent of degree requirements completed each year also were strengthened: Students will need to finish 40 percent rather than 25 percent of their degree requirements prior to the beginning of their junior year, 60 percent rather than 50 percent prior to their fourth year, and 80 percent rather than 75 percent by the beginning of their fifth year. Failure to meet these standards will make the athlete ineligible to play.

Despite the SAT and high school course requirements, athletes continue to have average SAT scores below those of other students.[17] The initiation of these propositions might have reduced differences between the academic backgrounds of athletes and nonathletes, but measurable differences continue to exist. These data are consistent with admission policies that pave the way to recruit excellent athletes who are marginal students but also create a situation where the student athlete often will be at a disadvantage in competing with his or her peers in the classroom. Athletes also appear to opt for less rigorous curricula and are significantly slower in obtaining an academic degree. Thus, the Knight Commission reports that graduation rates in Division 1-A schools were only 48 percent for football players and 34 percent for men's basketball players, and that these rates have fallen in recent years. The graduation rate for white football players was 55 percent, the lowest rate in several years, and 42 percent for black football players compared to an overall graduation rate of 75 percent for all students who enroll full time immediately after high school graduation and continue at the same college for up to 5.5 years.[18]

The market for coaches provides a stark contrast to the market for athletes. Head coaches operate in a market that is close to the competitive ideal. They are free to accept whatever salary and fringe benefits they are offered in the open competition for their services by colleges. The existence of potential National Football League or National Basketball Association assistant and head coaching positions intensifies the college-level competition for coaches. Many star basketball and football coaches are earning annual salaries that exceed $1 million.

In 1991, however, the NCAA instituted a restricted-earnings rule that limited the income of assistant coaches: Restricted-earnings assistant coaches could be paid a maximum of $16,000 per year and faced other limitations. For example, the third assistant coach for a Division I men's basketball team could receive only $12,000 in salary with

---

[17]J. Fizel and T. Smaby, "Participation in Collegiate Athletics and Student Grade Point Averages," in *Economics of College Sports,* ed. John Fizel and Rod Fort (Westport, CT: Praeger, 2004).

[18]Knight Foundation Commission on Intercollegiate Athletics, *Ten Years Later* (Miami: Knight Foundation, 2001).

up to $4,000 in additional summer earnings but was prohibited from off-campus re-cruiting and could hold this job for a maximum of 5 years. The NCAA's stated intentions were to provide low-cost, entry-level positions for young and inexperienced coaches, and to prevent a bidding war for assistant coaches that would result in a competitive imbalance as the sports powerhouses outbid others for the best assistants. A group of restricted-earnings coaches disagreed, however, and sued the NCAA, alleging that the rule limiting their pay was an illegal restraint of trade in violation of antitrust law.

The NCAA argued that the restricted-earnings rule was a reasonable restraint of trade, similar to other restraints the courts have allowed. For instance, the NCAA is allowed to limit the size of coaching staffs, the number of games played per season, and financial aid to athletes in order to foster competitive balance. The NCAA also argued that the rule was enacted as an alternative to eliminating these coaching positions completely in order to reduce costs.

In 1995, a U.S. district court found that the restricted-earnings rule did indeed violate antitrust law and ordered the NCAA to cease and desist from setting assistant coaches' pay levels. After the appellate court upheld the verdict in 1998, a jury awarded damages of $11.2 million for restricted-earnings basketball coaches and $11.1 million for coaches in other sports that were affected by the restricted-earnings rule. These damages of $22.3 million were then tripled under antitrust law to nearly $67 million. After an appeal that ended in March 1999, the NCAA settled the case for $54 million.

This decision prompts once again the question: Why are restricted earnings illegal when applied to coaches but not when applied to the players?

IV. PERFORMANCE

Most college sports lose money. This is an assertion that is commonly made by representatives of collegiate athletic departments and the NCAA, and it is increasingly believed by the media.[19] For example, officials at Michigan and UCLA have regularly claimed financial shortfalls in their athletic budgets, yet these schools play football in stadiums that seat more than 100,000, they traditionally have strong basketball teams that play to sell-out crowds, they compete regularly in the NCAA postseason tournament, they do well in minor sports as well as football and basketball, and they are located in heavily populated metropolitan areas. Their revenues typically exceed $20 million. These schools also are supported by the NCAA's power to control pricing of output and payments to inputs. How is it that these schools operate in the red? The information in Table 12-2 indicates a 50 percent increase from 1989 to 2001 in the number of athletic programs reporting budget deficits when non-athletic institutional support is excluded, lending credence to the sports-lose-money claim.

Yet despite these deficits, schools are in a race to build new and ever-more-luxurious stadiums and arenas. In the 7 years prior to 2001, capital expenditures at Division 1-A institutions increased by 250 percent. The increasing prevalence of deficits has even caused athletic departments to ask for financial support from the general fund,

---

[19]See *USA Today* (August 15, 2003): 1C, 11C, 16C; *USA Today* (July 15, 1999): 16C; J. Schulman and W. Bowen, *The Game of Life: College Sports and Educational Values* (Princeton, NJ: Princeton University Press, 2001).

TABLE 12-2 Athletic Department Budget Deficits: Division IA

Year	No. of Teams	Percentage of Programs with Deficit When Institutional Support Excluded	Percentage of Programs with Deficit When Institutional Support Included
2001	114	65	32
1999	104	54	29
1997	98	56	31
1995	87	52	14
1993	85	49	24
1989	87	40	40

SOURCE: Daniel L. Fulks, *Revenues and Expenses of Divisions I and II Intercollegiate Athletic Programs* (Indianapolis, IN: NCAA Publications, 2001).

capital fund, or other non-athletic revenue resources of the university. Table 12-2 shows that in 2001, 65 percent of all Division 1A athletic departments reported deficits. However, when university-wide financial support of athletic operations is included in the computation, only 32 percent of athletic departments continued to show deficits in that year. (In 1989 there was no institution-wide financial support of athletic departments, so the percentage of athletic programs showing deficits is the same in the last row of columns 3 and 4 in Table 12-2.)

These data, however, misrepresent the true profitability of college athletics because they are derived using accounting practices that cause reported profits to dramatically understate true economic profits. The two most important of these practices are overestimating the cost of athletes and omitting the positive promotional effects sports teams have on admissions and financial contributions to colleges.

Consider first the data reported by the NCAA for the major revenue sports—Division I-A football and Division I basketball. (See Table 12-3.) These profit statistics differ dramatically from media reports that imply athletic department losses. The revenue growth from 1989 to 2001 was approximately 152 percent for football and 122 percent for basketball. During the same period, expenses for football and basketball grew by only 98 percent and 108 percent, respectively. The result of this disparity in growth rates is a tripling or quadrupling of profits per team. In other words, accounting profits are escalating.[20]

Also, the reported expenses overstate the true economic expenses of each athlete. This report indicates costs of approximately $62,000 per football player and $164,000 per basketball player. However, the NCAA sets the maximum allowable payment to athletes to cover all in-kind and direct payments for the "cost of attending school." Brown claims that the ceiling for such payments is $20,000.[21] If correct, the total expenses for

---

[20]R. Brown, "Measuring Cartel Rents in the College Basketball Recruitment Market," *Applied Economics* 26 (1994): 27–34; R. Brown, "An Estimate of the Rent Generated by a Premium College Football Player," *Economic Inquiry* 31 (1993): 671–684.

[21]R. Brown, "Measuring Cartel Rents in the College Basketball Recruitment Market," *Applied Economics* 26 (1994): 27–34; R. Brown, "An Estimate of the Rent Generated by a Premium College Football Player," *Economic Inquiry* 31 (1993): 671–684.

TABLE 12-3 Revenues and Expenses of Division I-A Football and Basketball

Division I-A Football

Year	Average Revenue per School	Average Expenses per School	Average Expenses per Player
2001	$10,920,000	$6,170,000	$61,700
1999	9,040,000	5,260,000	52,600
1997	7,630,000	4,425,000	44,250
1995	6,440,000	4,099,000	40,099
1993	6,300,000	4,013,000	40,130
1989	4,340,000	3,112,000	31,120

Division I-A Basketball

Year	Average Revenue per School	Average Expenses per School	Average Expenses per Player
2001	$3,640,000	$1,970,000	$164,166
1999	3,160,000	1,580,000	131,666
1997	2,850,000	1,298,000	108,166
1995	2,500,000	1,219,000	101,583
1993	2,120,000	1,091,000	90,917
1989	1,640,000	948,000	79,000

SOURCE: Daniel L. Fulks, *Revenues and Expenses of Divisions I and II Intercollegiate Athletic Programs* (Indianapolis, IN: NCAA Publications, 2001).

football players are about one third and the total expenses for basketball players about one eighth of what the NCAA claims. Granted, however, travel expenses and capital allocations must be added to this per-player expense.

The story concerning the expenses allocated per athlete is still incomplete though. Thus far, we have considered only the potential average cost of the athletes rather than the marginal cost to the college of enrolling these students. Given that few colleges operate at full capacity, the marginal cost of admitting an additional student is near zero. The colleges will not hire new faculty or build new classrooms to educate the athlete. Booster contributions, rather than college resources, finance many of the scholarships. When scholarship payments are based on marginal costs, athletic department profits increase substantially.

Sheehan and Goff each estimated the impact on athletic budgets if appropriate economic costs for employment of athletes were used. Sheehan found 16 percent and Goff found 10 percent of athletic programs in deficit (see Table 12-4), a far cry from the 65 percent indicated by the NCAA data in Table 12-2.[22]

Athletic department accounting practices also underestimate the revenue attributable to the signing of athletes. In addition to providing games for consumption, athletic departments also can be construed as a public relations branch of the college.

---

[22]R. Sheehan, *Keeping Score* (South Bend, IN: Diamond Communication, 1996); B. Goff, "Effects of University Athletics on the University," in *Economics of College Sports,* ed. John Fizel and Rod Fort (Westport, CT: Praeger, 2004).

TABLE 12-4 Adjusted Profits for Top 109 Athletic Departments

Profits/Losses (millions of dollars)	Percent of Athletic Programs	
	Sheehan	Goff
Unprofitable Programs		
< −1.0	7%	0%
−1.0 to −0.1	9	10
Profitable Programs		
0.0 to 0.9	13	11
1.0 to 1.9	13	7
2.0 to 3.9	20	24
4.0 to 6.9	17	22
7.0 to 9.9	7	11
> 9.9	14	15
Median Program Profits	$2.5	$3.9

SOURCE: Adapted from R. Sheehan, *Keeping Score* (South Bend, IN: Diamond Communications, 1996); B. Goff, "Effects of University Athletics on the University," in *Economics of College Sports*, ed. John Fizel and Rod Fort (Westport, CT: Praeger, 2004).

Athletic events provide a large amount of advertising for the colleges. Such promotions can increase student applications, as well as enhance endowments and gifts from boosters. Each can be a significant source of income for the institution.

In short, collegiate sports are profitable. Appropriate cost and revenue adjustments turn apparent deficits into million-dollar profits. Skousen and Condie demonstrated that Utah State athletics that publicly reported a loss of $700,000 actually turned a $360,000 profit.[23] Borland, Goff, and Pulsinelli showed that the alleged loss of $1.5 million in the athletic department at Western Kentucky was actually a $700,000 net gain to the college.[24] Noll provided evidence that a $3 million deficit at the University of Michigan should more accurately be interpreted as a $5 million profit.[25] Institutions might want to mask these surpluses as they pump boosters or college presidents for money to support the sports "arms race" and continue financing bigger stadiums, more elaborate training facilities, and amenities such as chartered jets to attract athletes. However, the facts indicate that sizable cartel profits continue to flow.

V. PUBLIC POLICY

College athletics has clashed with a number of public policies legislated by Congress, and the courts have become increasingly embroiled in determining violations of these laws and appropriate remedies. Recent cases have held that NCAA rules have violated antitrust laws enacted to promote competition and prevent anticompetitive practices. Recent judicial decisions also have held that NCAA rules have violated antiracial discrimination

---

[23]C. Skousen and F. Condie, "Evaluating a Sports Program: Goalposts v. Test Tubes," *Managerial Accounting* 60: 43-49.

[24]M. Borland, B. Goff, and R. Pulsinelli, "College Athletics: Financial Burden or Boon?" in *Advances in the Economics of Sports*, ed. G. Scully (Greenwich, CT: JAI Press, 1992).

[25]R. Noll, "The Economics of Intercollegiate Sports," in *Rethinking College Athletics*, ed. J. Andre and D. James (Philadelphia: Temple University Press, 1991).

laws. Battles concerning gender equity and athlete compensation are apt to be the next major legal challenge faced by collegiate athletics. How these challenges are resolved will have a significant impact on the structure and functioning of the college sports cartel.

Title IX

Perhaps no issue has caused more controversy for athletics departments and the NCAA than gender equity or Title IX compliance. As Cedric Dempsey, the past president of the NCAA has said

> I do not know of any topic in college athletics that brings emotions to the surface more quickly than Title IX. People from all perspectives on this issue have assailed me. It is absolutely impossible to engage this topic without frustrating or even angering somebody.[26]

Title IX of the Education Amendments of 1972 states the following:

> No person in the United States shall, on the basis of sex, be excluded from participation in, be denied the benefits of, or be subjected to discrimination under any education program or activity receiving federal funds.[27]

Uncertainty about what Title IX meant was clarified by the U.S. Supreme Court in 1984, when it ruled that violations of Title IX affected only federal money going to areas directly involved in the violation.[28] Because college athletics receive few federal funds, movement toward Title IX compliance was slowed due to the lack of effective penalties.

This changed dramatically, however, with the 1988 enactment of the Civil Rights Restoration Act, which barred institutions that violate civil rights laws from receiving any federal money in *any* area of their entire operation. The particular activity need not receive federal funds; it is enough that the institution receives federal funds for any of its activities to be covered under Title IX.

The impact of Title IX on women's athletics has been immense: The number of women's sports offered and the number of female athletes participating in sports have skyrocketed. At the high school level, female participation in athletics has catapulted from fewer than 300,000 participants before the passage of Title IX to 2.8 million today, an increase of more than 800 percent. Prior to Title IX, fewer than 32,000 women participated in intercollegiate athletics. This number has risen by 400 percent to the more than 160,000 women who participate today.[29]

The NCAA had no interest in women's athletics prior to Title IX. The Association of Intercollegiate Athletics for Women (AIAW) was the primary organization for women's athletics at the time. Title IX forced the NCAA to take more interest in women's sports. The AIAW was in trouble after the NCAA started sponsoring intercollegiate

---

[26]"NCAA's Commitment to Title IX Still Strong," *NCAA News* (March 15, 1999): 2; also available at www.ncaa.org/news.

[27]20 U.S.C. section 1681 (a).

[28]See *Grove City College v. Bell*, 465 U.S. 555, 573–574 (1984).

[29]Donna de Varona and Julie Foudy, Minority Views on the Report of the Commission on Opportunity in Athletics (February 2003): 2, also available at www.savetitleix.com/minorityreport.pdf.

championships for women's sports in the early 1980s, because the NCAA funds most of the expenses associated with participating in its championships. This was something the poorer AIAW could not afford, and the organization folded in 1983.

The conflicts arising from Title IX are mainly due to disputes about how compliance with the law should be determined. The Civil Rights Office of the Department of Education, which enforces Title IX, has promulgated three criteria for determining compliance with the law. If at least one of these three criteria is fulfilled, compliance is met.

The first is the "proportionality" test. This test requires that the participation of women and men in intercollegiate sports should reflect the gender proportions of the full-time undergraduate student body at the institution. A school with 60 percent women and 40 percent men should have women comprise approximately 60 percent of the school's intercollegiate athletes. Athletic scholarships and other forms of support also should reflect the gender proportion of students.

The second compliance test is to show a continuing expansion of programs for the underrepresented sex that is "responsive to developing interests and abilities of that sex."[30] If programs for the underrepresented sex are expanding fast enough to satisfy the student body, then the school is complying with Title IX.

The third test for compliance is to show that existing programs have satisfied the underrepresented group's "interests and abilities" in intercollegiate sports.

A recent court case illustrates these tests in action. In 1991, Brown University sponsored 16 men's sports and 16 women's sports. Brown decided to cut university funding for four sports: men's golf and men's water polo, and women's gymnastics and women's volleyball. Members of the women's teams sued the university for violating Title IX. The 1990–1991 school year's athletic participation was 63 percent men and 37 percent women, but the student body was 51 percent women. Brown argued that the disparity was due to a lower level of interest by women in athletics and that the school was complying with Title IX by matching offerings with interests. A survey of potential students found that 50 percent of the men and 30 percent of the women had an interest in playing intercollegiate sports. It also was noted that eight times as many men as women participated in intramural sports at Brown.[31]

In 1995, the district court ruled that Brown had violated Title IX. The court said that Brown did not meet any of the three criteria set by the Office for Civil Rights: The participation relative to enrollment numbers violated the proportionality standard; the demotion of two women's programs did not correspond to expanding opportunities; and the two demoted programs had the necessary interest of women students because Brown was able to field teams in them.

Brown appealed this decision to the U.S. Court of Appeals for the First Circuit in Boston, which upheld the lower court's finding. The court said that:

> To assert that Title IX permits institutions to provide fewer athletics participation opportunities for women than for men, based upon the premise that women are less interested in sports than are men, is (among other things) to ignore the fact that Title IX was enacted in order to remedy discrimination that results from stereotyped notions of women's interests and abilities. . . .

[30]"Comment: Use of Proportionality Test Is Out of Control," *NCAA News* (April 12, 1999): 4; also available at www.ncaa.org/news.
[31]Walter Olson, "Title IX from Outer Space," *Reason* (February 1998): 50–51.

Interest and ability rarely develop in a vacuum; they evolve as a function of opportunity and experience. . . . [W]omen's lower rate of participation in athletics reflects women's historical lack of opportunities to participate in sports.[32]

This ruling makes it difficult to demonstrate Title IX compliance on any basis other than proportionality.

The U.S. Supreme Court declined to review this decision in 1997, and Brown settled the case the following year. It agreed to maintain women's sports participation within 3 percentage points of the women's undergraduate student body percentage.

The focus on proportionality is typical. In 1996, the Office of Civil Rights in the Department of Education declared that proportionality was a *safe harbor*, meaning that a school is presumed to be in compliance with Title IX if the criterion of proportionality is met. This primacy of proportionality led to a lawsuit by the National Wrestling Coaches Association, which was later joined by organizations representing other so-called minor sports, alleging that proportionality is in reality an illegal quota system that has resulted in the elimination of many men's college sports teams.

Adding women's sports and cutting men's sports has been common in the era of Title IX. This, in turn, has provoked heated protest by those involved with men's non-revenue sports. They charge that athletic departments facing limited budgets and the Title IX proportionality standard expand women's programs by eliminating non-revenue men's sports. Statistics offer some support. The 1984–1985 season was the peak for male athletic participation, with NCAA members averaging 254 male athletes per school, and Division I schools averaging 318. For the 2001–2002 season, NCAA members averaged 205 male athletes, almost a 20 percent decrease from 1984–1985. Division I schools averaged 264 male athletes in 2001–2002, a reduction of almost 17 percent from 1984–1985. Over the same period, the number of female athletes increased from an average of 98 to 150 per school for the NCAA as a whole, and from 115 to 205 for members of Division I—a 53 percent increase for all schools and a 78 percent increase for Division I members.[33]

The numbers indicate that proportionality has not yet been attained. Women made up about 42 percent of all NCAA athletes in 2001–2002, which is up substantially from the almost 28 percent figure for 1984–1985. However, it is still far short of proportionality, because the majority of undergraduate students are women. The preceding numbers also make clear that the movement toward proportionality has been achieved by increasing opportunities for women and decreasing opportunities for men.

In June 2002, the U.S. Department of Education established the secretary of education's Commission on Opportunity in Athletics to study Title IX. The commission's recommendations were issued in February 2003, accompanied by a separate minority report submitted by two commissioners and advocates of women's athletics. Recommendations of the commission included a request that the Department of Education clearly explain that each of the three criteria for meeting Title IX are independent methods of compliance, that reducing the number of men's teams to attain compliance is a disfavored practice, that the

---

[32]"Brown Title IX Decision Upheld on Appeal," *NCAA News* (December 2, 1996): 2; also available at www.ncaa.org/news..

[33]Welch Suggs, "Cutting the Field: As Colleges Eliminate Teams, the Lessons Athletes Learn Are Losing Out to Commercial Interests," *Chronicle of Higher Education* (June 6, 2003): A37.

Department of Education should establish standards regarding private funding of particular teams facing elimination of university funding, that walk-ons be excluded from proportionality calculations, that schools could conduct interest surveys to help demonstrate compliance, and that proportionality would no longer be a "safe harbor."

Mike Moyer, the executive director of the National Wrestling Coaches Association, especially welcomed the recommendations that would give flexibility in meeting the requirements of Title IX and the elimination of safe harbor status for the proportionality test.[34] The two dissenting commissioners, Donna de Varona and Julie Foudy, argued in their minority report that the majority recommendations would weaken Title IX and reduce opportunities for women athletes. Rod Paige, Secretary of Education, initially declared that the department would only consider implementing the recommendations that were passed by consensus. In July 2003 the Education Department announced there would be no changes in the way that Title IX is enforced. Women's rights advocates lauded the announcement, while those who criticized the use of proportionality predicted that reductions in men's sports would continue as schools attempt to conform to Title IX.

The attack on proportionality was primarily aimed at reducing the elimination of nonrevenue men's sports. The argument seems logical: Facing a need to allocate funds to satisfy Title IX proportionality, the athletic director has little alternative but to add nonrevenue women's sports at the expense of nonrevenue men's sports. However, as compelling as the argument might seem, the facts tell a different tale. If Title IX requirements place an undue burden on athletic budgets, one would expect the ax to fall disproportionately on Division III men's nonrevenue sports because neither men's football nor basketball generate profits to subsidize their continued existence. In contrast, profits from football and basketball in Division I-A can be used to spare the demise of nonrevenue men's sports.

However, a profitable football program is no guarantee that men's or women's sports will receive adequate funding. Table 12-5 presents data compiled by the Women's Sports Foundation on the change in the number of men's sports between 1978 and 1996. In contrast to expectations, the data show that the offerings of men's sports declined in Divisions I-A and I-AA, but increased in Divisions I-AAA, II, and

TABLE 12-5 Changes in Men's Sports (1978–1996)

NCAA	Number of Sports Added	Number of Sports Deleted	Net Change
I-A	22	113	−91
I-AA	68	129	−61
I-AAA	93	56	+37
II	344	286	+58
III	400	269	+131
Total	927	853	+74

SOURCE: Adapted from D. Marburger and N. Hogshead-Makar, "Is Title IX Really to Blame for the Decline in Intercollegiate Men's Non-Revenue Sports?" *Marquette Law Review* (Forthcoming).

[34]Kay Hawes, "Title IX Report Shares Center Stage with Dissenting View," *NCAA News* (March 3, 2003): 4, also available at www.ncaa.org/news/2003/20030303/active/4005n01.html.

III. The largest net decrease was in Division I-A. Similarly, Leeds et al. found that Division I-A football programs have an almost uniformly negative impact on offerings for women. They predicted that, on average, premier football programs drain approximately $184,000 per year from women's sports. It thus appears that many collegiate athletic departments view violating Title IX as congruent with profit maximization: . Athletic directors in Division I have an incentive to dedicate a greater portion of their budgets to football and basketball because the marginal benefit of a dollar spent on these programs exceeds the marginal benefit of a dollar spent on football and basketball in Division II or III or on nonrevenue sports. In practice, the athletic director cannot eliminate all nonrevenue sports because the NCAA requires a minimum number of varsity sports to be a member of Division I, and Title IX insulates women's nonrevenue sports from the budgetary ax. Thus, the athletic director slows the growth of nonrevenue women's programs and cuts nonrevenue men's programs. As a result, we can expect the continuation of reverse gender discrimination lawsuits against universities in addition to the gender discrimination lawsuits filed by female athletes.[35]

Eliminate the Monopsony

Current NCAA policies governing athletic compensation violate the spirit of antitrust laws, but the NCAA claims that these policies are needed to protect the competitive balance and amateur status of collegiate sports. These defenses may no longer be valid, if they ever were.

The NCAA has used the competitive balance argument in previous cases involving restrictive practices. This argument failed in the NCAA's attempt to maintain control over college football telecasts. Without control of telecasts, the NCAA claimed that broadcasts would be skewed in favor of the traditional football powers, allowing them to recruit more successfully and thereby increasing the on-field disparity between the traditional powers and their lesser rivals. The Supreme Court rejected this claim and assigned control of telecasts to the individual schools. Empirical evidence suggests that competitive balance has increased, not declined, since the telecast restrictions have been lifted.

The competitive balance argument also failed when the NCAA imposed a salary cap on assistant coaches. Without the salary cap, the NCAA claimed that the best coaches would all be drawn to just a few schools and destroy competitive balance. However, the fact is that with or without a salary cap, the coaches already had an incentive to go to the best sports schools because these programs provide better training and exposure.

A change in the compensation structure does not affect competitive balance, but it does change the allocation of resources: A salary cap transfers monies from coaches to the colleges. The same is true for college athletes: Compensation restrictions transfer monies from the players to the colleges without affecting competitive balance.

The NCAA's second line of defense is that it provides amateur sports contests. If athletes were paid and collegiate sports were commercialized, the NCAA claims, demand for college sports would decline. This argument is commonly and uncritically accepted, but for most colleges that engage in big-time sports, the game is not now broadly viewed as amateur. Audiences do not view the players as student athletes; they

---

[35]M. Leeds, Y. Suris, and J. Durkin, "College Football and Title IX," in *Economics of College Sports,* ed. John Fizel and Rod Fort (Westport, CT: Praeger, 2004).

accept the commercialization of college sports. Billions of dollars in NCAA revenues indicate that acceptance, too. We agree with Noll, who stated:

> College sports are already professionalized at universities that house their athletes separately, that advertise themselves as preparatory schools for a career in professional sports, and that fail to graduate nearly all of their players. America wants big-time sports, professional and collegiate, and as long as they do, colleges will supply it . . . the damage of professionalism has been done, and is probably irreversible even if one wanted to undertake the task of changing the system.[36]

It is also doubtful that colleges would lose a significant portion of their audience and revenue if the athletes were paid. Fan support has been growing steadily even as the sport has become commercialized. Boosters, the biggest supporters of college sports, are typically the ones attempting to pay athletes to recruit them to play on their teams. Perhaps popularity and demand would even accelerate if the hypocrisy tainting the amateur status of collegiate sports were removed. Certainly, the Olympics has lost none of its appeal and has generated increased revenues since it abandoned the requirement that its participants be amateurs.

Occasionally, supporters of the NCAA monopsony will argue that underpayment is a temporary phenomenon, with athletes soon to make millions as professionals. The soon-to-be-rich athletes are subsidizing the less fortunate. This claim is invalid on two counts: First, fewer than 1 percent of all collegiate athletes actually make it to the professional ranks. Second, collegiate athletes typically come from poorer households than the average college student; often they come from disadvantaged backgrounds. Thus, the NCAA not only blocks the functioning of this labor market, it does so in a regressive way that hurts poorer, less-advantaged students the most.

The question remains: How should athletes be paid? Several alternatives have been suggested. The players could unionize. A fundamental factor in the NCAA's current power is that colleges do not recognize athletes as employees. If athletes were viewed as employees, then they would be eligible to unionize and bargain for pay. They also would be eligible for workers' compensation for injuries sustained in practice and play. (Athletic department concern over worker's compensation is a major deterrent to athlete pay.) This arrangement would be similar to that in professional sports, where an alliance of teams bargains with a union of players to establish rules and compensation packages linked to the marginal revenue product of the athletes. An athlete compensation fund could be set up for each college, with limits determined by an estimation of monopsony rents. Colleges could then distribute the funds among the players as they saw fit: They could pay athletes a signing bonus to enroll, pay rewards for competitive performance, or establish trust funds. To emphasize the concept of the student athlete, athlete compensation could be linked to graduation: If athletes do not graduate, they forego a portion of their agreed-upon remuneration.

Player compensation does have its side effects. If a college currently uses profits from its basketball and football programs to subsidize nonrevenue sports, the nonrevenue programs might suffer unless they can obtain financial support from the college or other sources. Many colleges might drop some sports due to the diminished profits. The basic issue is whether athletes in profitable sports should bear the cost of

---

[36]Noll, "The Economics of Intercollegiate Sports," 208.

supporting less-profitable programs. An increase in the cost of athletic talent also might precipitate a significant decline in the salaries of coaches. However, fans might get to view higher-quality collegiate sporting contests as the top athletes continued to play college sports rather than jumping early to professional leagues. Most important, collegiate athletes would earn a competitive salary in exchange for the value of their services.

Conclusion

The NCAA and its member schools have created a vast college sports cartel that pays its most important resources, the athletes, far below what they would earn in a competitive market. The NCAA operates behind a veil of amateurism as its members generate revenues comparable to those of professional sports teams, practice and play in facilities that rival those found in professional sports, and pay their top coaches salaries comparable to those paid to coaches of professional teams. Only the student athletes are bound to amateur status and prevented from sharing in the bounty generated by their play.

Yet, ironically, as the wealth of the cartel increases, its strength might be eroding. A recent string of losing court battles is stripping away the veil of amateurism. Gender equity requirements are causing serious profit allocation difficulties. The specter of competing leagues portends the possible necessity of bidding competitively for human resources. Employee rights may soon be granted to athletes. Meanwhile, points of conflict multiply with the ever-increasing size and diversity of NCAA membership.

The NCAA has responded to threats in the past by expanding its reach—in membership as well as in its rules and regulations. Yet NCAA regulations have done little to promote amateurism and little to improve on-the-field competitiveness. Depken and Wilson reported that such regime changes as the Sanity Code, the minimum GPA, the dividing of the NCAA into multiple divisions, and the BCS have had a negative influence on the competitive environment of NCAA sports. Likewise, NCAA rule-enforcement policies also often harm competitive balance.[37]

The NCAA is facing large legal and political challenges from outside the organization. Its rules and enforcement policies exacerbate internal tensions. Once again, the college sports cartel is beginning to crack, and only the future will reveal its response to these latest challenges.

Suggested Readings

Byers, W. 1985. *Unsportsmanlike Conduct: Exploiting College Athletes.* Ann Arbor: University of Michigan Press.

Fizel, J., and R. Fort, eds. 2004. *The Economics of College Sports.* Westport, CT: Praeger.

Fleisher, A., B. Goff, and R. Tollison. 1992. *The National Collegiate Athletic Association: A Study in Cartel Behavior.* Chicago: University of Chicago Press.

Fort, R., and J. Quirk. 1999. "The College Football Industry." In *Sports Economics: Current Research.* Ed. J. Fizel, E. Gustafson, and L. Hadley, 11–26. Westport, CT: Praeger Publishers.

---

[37]C. Depken and D. Wilson, "Institutional Change in the NCAA and Competitive Balance in Intercollegiate Football," and "The Impact of Cartel Enforcement in Division I-A Football," both in *Economics of College Sports,* ed. John Fizel and Rod Fort (Westport, CT: Praeger, 2004).

Knight Foundation Commission on Intercollegiate Athletics, Ten Years Later. 2001. Miami: Knight Foundation.

Koch, J. 1982. "The Intercollegiate Athletics Industry." In *The Structure of American Industry.*, ed. Walter Adams, 325–346. New York: Macmillan Publishing Co.

Noll, R. 1991. "The Economics of Intercollegiate Sports." In *Rethinking College Athletics.* Ed. J. Andre and D. James, 197–209. Philadelphia: Temple University Press.

Schulman, J., and W. Bowen. 2001. *The Game of Life: College Sports and Educational Values.* Princeton, NJ: Princeton University Press.

Sperber, M. 1990. *College Sports, Inc.* New York: Henry Holt.

_____. 2000. *Beer and Circus: How Big Time College Sports Is Crippling Undergraduate Education.* New York: Henry Holt.

CHAPTER 13

Public Policy in a Free-Enterprise Economy

—JAMES W. BROCK

Controlling power in a free society and guarding against its abuse is the crux of the American political-economic experience. Indeed, the American nation was forged from the colonists' protest against the arbitrary power of the British Crown.

Once liberated, the nation's founders understood that in creating a governance structure for a free society, they must provide for a government that is strong enough to prevent individuals from infringing on the liberties of one another. At the same time, they recognized that additional safeguards were required to prevent government itself from being transmuted into an instrument of oppression. Throughout their deliberations, the founders displayed a profoundly dyspeptic view of human nature. They understood (as Thomas Burke put it in 1777) that "power of all kinds has an irresistible propensity to increase a desire for itself"; that "power will sometime or other be abused unless men are well watched, and checked by something they cannot remove when they please"; and that the "root of the evil is deep in human nature."

Their solution for resolving this dilemma was incorporated in the Constitution and predicated on two transcending principles: First, it is the *structure* of government, not the personal predilections of those who govern, that is paramount. Second, in Thomas Jefferson's words, "It is not by the consolidation or concentration of powers, but by their distribution, that good government is effected." Their master plan was to construct a system of checks and balances—a Newtonian mechanism of countervailing powers—that operate harmoniously in mutual frustration. The goal was to prevent what the founders considered the ultimate evil: the concentration of power and the abuses that flow from it.

As James Madison observed in *Federalist Paper 51:*

> It may be a reflection on human nature that such devices should be necessary to control the abuses of government. But what is government itself, but the greatest of all reflections on human nature? If men were angels, no government would be necessary. If angels were to govern men, neither external nor internal controls on government would be necessary. In framing a government which is to be administered by men over men, the great difficulty lies in this: you must first enable the government to control the governed; and in the next place oblige it to control itself. A dependence on the people is, no doubt, the primary control on the government; but experience has taught mankind the necessity of auxiliary precautions.

I. THE AMERICAN ANTITRUST TRADITION

Subsequent events demonstrated that in a free society, the power problem is not confined to the political realm. A century after the Constitution was ratified, during the post–Civil War era, an explosion of pools, trusts, cartels, and monopolies demonstrated the need to control economic as well as political power. To guard against excessive private as well as governmental concentrations of power, Americans recognized the necessity of preventing autocrats of trade from ensnaring them in a new kind of industrial feudalism. "If we will not endure a king as a political power," Ohio Republican Senator John Sherman warned, "we should not endure a king over the production, transportation, and sale of any of the necessaries of life." Unless Congress addressed the problem of private economic power, he urged, there would "be a trust for every production and a master to fix the price for every necessity of life."[1]

In theory, Adam Smith showed how the competitive marketplace regulated and neutralized economic power—how it dispersed economic decision-making power in the hands of a multitude of rivals and compelled each to perform well in the public interest, thereby transforming the private vice of self-interest into a public virtue. He showed how in theory a competitive market system would harness private economic decision making and channel it into socially beneficial outlets by compelling innovation, progress, and efficiency in allocating resources in accordance with society's preferences. Also in theory, Smith showed how a competitive market system would maintain economic freedom and opportunity for all while rendering private economic decision making accountable to the public.

In reality, however, the corporate combination and trust movement of late nineteenth-century America showed that as an effective system of economic governance, the competitive market is neither self-perpetuating nor an immutable artifact of nature. Events demonstrated that without strictly enforced rules, the competitive market can be eroded and subverted through cartel agreements not to compete, as well as through mergers and monopolization by dominant firms.

Maintaining competition as the primary regulator of America's economic affairs is the central objective of the antitrust laws. Like the Constitution, American antitrust laws provide for a structure of governance—a social blueprint for organizing economic decision making and for guarding against its abuse. Like the Constitution, the goal of the antitrust laws is to disperse power into many hands rather than allowing it to be concentrated in the hands of a few. Just as the purpose of the Constitution is to prevent any one political faction from monopolizing the coercive power of the state, so the basic objective of the antitrust laws is to prevent private organizations from monopolizing society's economic decision making.

The Sherman Act, the nation's first antitrust statute, was enacted in 1890; it outlaws two major types of interference with competitive free enterprise: cartels and monopolization. Section 1 of the Sherman Act, which deals with cartels, states: "Every contract, combination . . . or conspiracy in restraint of trade or commerce among the several States, or with foreign nations, is hereby declared illegal." As interpreted by the courts, this makes it unlawful for businesses to engage in such collusive actions as agreeing to fix prices, agreeing to restrict output or productive capacity, agreeing to divide markets

---

[1]Hans B. Thorelli, *The Federal Antitrust Policy: Origination of an American Tradition* (Baltimore: Johns Hopkins University Press, 1955), 180.

or allocate customers, or agreeing to exclude competitors by systematically resorting to oppressive tactics and predatory practices. In short, it enjoins agreements among competitors aimed at controlling the market and short-circuiting its regulatory discipline.

Section 2 of the Sherman Act, which addresses structural concentrations of economic power, provides that: "Every person who shall monopolize or attempt to monopolize, or combine or conspire to monopolize any part of the trade or commerce among the several States, or with foreign nations, shall be deemed guilty ... and ... punished." Section 2 makes it unlawful for firms to obtain a stranglehold on the market, either by forcing rivals out of business or by absorbing or controlling them. Further, it prohibits a single firm (or group of firms acting jointly) from dominating an industry or market. Positively stated, Section 2 encourages a decentralized economic structure in which a sufficient number of independent rivals operate to ensure effective competition.

The Sherman Act's proscriptions are general, perhaps even vague, and essentially negative. Directed primarily against *existing* dominant firms and *existing* trade restraints, the Sherman Act proved incapable of addressing specific practices that could be used to realize the proscribed results. Armed with the power to dissolve existing monopolies, the enforcement authorities could not, under the Sherman Act, attack the growth of a monopoly in advance and prior to its realization. For this reason, Congress enacted supplementary legislation in 1914 in order "to arrest the creation of trusts, conspiracies and monopolies in their incipiency and before consummation." In the Federal Trade Commission Act of 1914, Congress established an independent commission to police the economic field against "all unfair methods of competition," as well as to undertake expert studies of conditions of competition and monopoly in the economy.

In the Clayton Act of the same year, Congress targeted four specific practices that had historically been favorite means for creating monopoly positions: (1) price discrimination (that is, cutthroat competition and predatory price cutting), (2) tying contracts and exclusive dealership agreements, (3) mergers and acquisitions, and (4) interlocking boards of directors among rival firms. Emphasizing their preventive purpose, these practices were declared unlawful, not in and of themselves but where their effect "might be to substantially lessen competition or tend to create a monopoly."

Price discrimination, for example, would be illegal only if used systematically as a device for destroying competition, as it was in the hands of the Standard Oil and American Tobacco trusts. Similarly, the Clayton Act's merger provisions (as amended by the Celler-Kefauver Act in 1950) prohibit any business merger or acquisition whose effect may be to lessen competition substantially or to tend to create a monopoly in any line of commerce in any region of the country. The emphasis in the Clayton Act is on preventing anticompetitive problems from arising in the first place rather than struggling with how to remedy them after they become entrenched.

The essence of American antitrust policy has perhaps been most cogently articulated by Judge Charles Wyzanski:

> Concentrations of power no matter how beneficently they appear to have acted, nor what advantages they seem to possess, are inherently dangerous. Their good behavior in the past may not be continued; and if their strength were hereafter grasped by presumptuous hands, there would be no automatic check and balance from equal forces in the industrial market. And in the absence of this protective mechanism, the demand for public regulation, public ownership, or other drastic measures would become irresistible in time of crisis. Dispersal of private

Economics of a Free Market

Producers   Consumer

Economics of Security

Mergers
Price Fixing
Patent Pool

Producers   Consumer

FIGURE 13-1   The Free Enterprise Challenge

SOURCE: Thurman W. Arnold, Cartels or Free Enterprise? Public Affairs Pamphlet 103, 1945.

economic power is thus one of the ways to preserve the system of private enterprise ... [Moreover,] well as a monopoly may have behaved in the moral sense, its economic performance is inevitably suspect. The very absence of strong competitors implies that there cannot be an objective measuring rod of the monopolist's excellence ... What appears to the outsider to be a sensible, prudent, nay even a progressive policy of the monopolist, may in fact reflect a lower scale of adventurousness and less intelligent risk-taking than would be the case if the enterprise were forced to respond to a stronger industrial challenge.

Progress, Wyzanski wrote, "may indeed be in inverse proportion to economic power; for creativity in business as in other areas, is best nourished by multiple centers of activity, each following its unique pattern and developing its own esprit de corps to respond to the challenge of competition."[2]

---

[2]*United States v. United Shoe Machinery Corp.*, 110 F. Supp. 295 (1953), affirmed per curiam, 347 U.S. 521 (1954).

II. ANTITRUST UNDER FIRE

Over the years, these traditional precepts have been attacked from both ends of the political-economic spectrum.

The Challenge from the Left

On the left, an antitrust regime of competition enforced by law has long been dismissed as a barbaric and counterproductive anachronism. Instead, concentration and market dominance are believed to be the inevitable product of industrial advance. The left advocates more direct social control—comprising negotiation and compromise among representatives of industry, labor, and government—as the preferred policy.

This was true of the consolidation and trust wave at the turn of the last century. Pioneer labor leader Samuel Gompers, for example, rejected antitrust policy (the early enforcement of which had been directed against labor unions): "We have seen those who know little of statecraft and less of economics urge the adoption of laws to 'regulate' interstate commerce, 'prevent' combinations and trusts," he charged, but the state "is not capable of preventing the legitimate development or natural concentration of industry."[3] Strong unions, Gompers believed, would neutralize the power of the trusts and enable workers to bargain for a fairer share of the benefits of industrial giantism and market concentration.

Herbert Croly, a leading progressive of the day, was certain that monopolistic trusts marked "an important step in the direction of the better organization of industry and commerce." He advocated scrapping the antitrust law in favor of a national policy aimed at fostering "a more positive mode of action and more edifying habit of thought" among corporate and labor leaders.[4]

Socialists, meanwhile, asserted with biblical certitude that we "have left the Egypt of competition . . . and are now wandering in the desert of monopoly, which we must pass through to reach the promised land of universal co-operation."[5]

Criticism of antitrust from the left reemerged during the 1930s and became the touchstone for the National Industrial Recovery Act of 1933. The National Industrial Recovery Administration (NRA) was created to launch a new economic regime of "constructive cooperation," which, it was believed, would lift the country from the depths of the Great Depression: Business would get self-government, relief from "destructive" competition, and immunity from the antitrust laws. Labor leaders believed the NRA would usher in the kind of social planning and industrial self-government they had long advocated, including the right of workers to organize and bargain collectively with business. Progressive government leaders like Rexford Tugwell held that the NRA would demonstrate that "cooperation not conflict" was a superior principle for restoring confidence and getting the economy moving again.[6] These goals, many New Deal

---

[3]Quoted in Joseph Dorfman, *The Economic Mind in American Civilization*, vol. 3 (New York: Viking Press, 1949), 217.

[4]Herbert Croly, *The Promise of American Life*, Harvard Library ed. (Cambridge, MA: Harvard University Press, 1965), 358–59, 397.

[5]Quoted in Jack Blicksilver, *Defenders and Defense of Big Business in the United States, 1880–1900* (New York: Garland, 1985), 68.

[6]See Ellis W. Hawley, *The New Deal and the Problem of Monopoly* (Princeton, NJ: Princeton University Press, 1966), 19–33.

proponents believed, could be achieved only by replacing competition with a system of national planning along individual industry lines—sectoral planning jointly undertaken by business and labor, and overseen by government in the public interest.

In the 1980s, the anemic performance of the U.S. economy, coupled with the specter of a world-triumphant "Japan Inc.," sparked another major resurgence of cooperation and coalitionism from the left, under the rubric of industrial policy, as an alternative to America's antitrust tradition. Pointing to a flood of foreign imports into American markets, lagging U.S. productivity and savings, and stubbornly rising unemployment levels, industrial policy advocates charged: "What used to work won't work. For the world has changed."[7] The only viable course, they contended, lay in a consciously constructed national industrial policy comprising tripartite planning, negotiation, and compromise among management, labor, and government. They pointed to postwar economic miracles in Japan and other East Asian nations as what they considered proof of the superior results such cooperation could achieve. They also derided traditional antitrust concerns about disproportionate economic size and market power as antiquated and destructive in a new global age. According to Thurow, industry policy advocates "don't care whether General Motors is the only car manufacturing company. It's still in a competitive fight for its life with the Japanese and Germans. And it doesn't make sense to hamstring General Motors or anybody else with antitrust laws since they must operate in an international competitive environment . . ."[8]

As a guide for economic policy, however, the left's infatuation with "cooperationism" and organizational giantism suffers from a number of fatal flaws. The first drawback is the inevitable tendency toward the coalescence of power among organized groups, which are predisposed to protect their parochial private interest rather than promote the public well-being. Advocates of "coalition capitalism" assume that powerful private groups will act in ways, and toward ends, that will promote good economic performance. However, such power blocs might instead recognize their mutual interest in preserving the status quo and aggrandizing their power and influence at the public's expense.

This is not idle conjecture. The consequences of the National Recovery Administration, for example, were scarcely what its proponents promised: The NRA enabled business groups to cartelize industries and labor groups to raise wages while government rubber-stamped their self-serving schemes. Yet in 1934, at the conclusion of congressional hearings on the NRA, Senator Gerald Nye was "forced to the conclusion that the power of monopoly has been greatly increased during the stay of the NRA; that invitation to monopoly in the United States is greater than ever before. In view of what amounts to suspension of the antitrust laws, the small independent producers, the small business man generally, whether buyer from, competitor of, or seller to large monopolized industries, and the great mass of ultimate consumers, are seemingly without protection other than that given by the NRA. And the NRA is not giving this protection. On the contrary, it has strengthened, not weakened, the power of monopoly."[9]

---

[7]U.S. Congress. House. Subcommittee on Economic Stabilization. Hearings: Industrial Policy, Part 1, 98th Cong., 1st sess., 1983, 173.

[8]Lester C. Thurow, "Abolish the Antitrust Laws," *Dun's Review* (February 1981): 72. See also Thurow, *The Zero-Sum Solution* (New York: Simon & Schuster, 1985).

[9]Quoted in Leverett S. Lyon et al., *The National Recovery Administration: An Analysis and Appraisal* (Washington, D.C.: Brookings Institution, 1935), 709. See also Barbara Alexander, "The Impact of the National Recovery Act on Cartel Formation and Maintenance Costs," *Review of Economics and Statistics* 76 (May 1994): 245–254.

In the steel industry, corporate giants and organized labor honed cooperative industry control into a fine art form. For decades, Big Steel and the United Steelworkers union coalesced to engineer a record of sustained price-wage-price inflation in a key industrial commodity. When foreign competition threatened to disrupt their cozy coalition, they cooperated to lobby government to impose restraints on imports, most recently in 2002. These restraints serve the narrow interests of steel management and labor. However, by inflating steel prices by 30 percent or more, they jeopardize the competitiveness of the vast constellation of American steel-using firms and the far greater number of workers they employ (12.8 million steel-using jobs versus 226,000 steelmaking jobs, according to one estimate).[10] At the same time, management and labor collectively negotiated billions of dollars of pension and retirement programs -"legacy costs"- that the companies cannot afford and which the industrial-labor complex in steel has shoved onto society by having the government assume financial responsibility for (to the tune of $7 billion as a result of the bankruptcies of steel giants LTV, Bethlehem, and National).[11]

In airlines, collective bargaining between the largest carriers and organized labor (especially the powerful pilots' union) has driven the giants' costs sky high and pushed them to the brink of bankruptcy and beyond (including employee-owned United, which collapsed into bankruptcy in 2002).[12] The management-labor complex in airlines, like that in steel, also is shifting the legacy costs of the pension and retirement programs they collectively bargained with each other to society and the government's pension insurance fund instead. They, too, privatize their gains while socializing their losses.

In professional sports, mutual accommodation between players and owners has enabled the sports-industrial complex to blackmail communities by threatening to relocate teams unless they are provided a lavish bounty of public subsidies. Billions of dollars of professional sports welfare provide magnanimous profits for owners, astronomical salaries for players, and palatial stadiums for both, while depriving local communities of desperately needed funds for education, transportation, and genuine job development.[13]

In telecommunications, organized labor and management battle fiercely at the bargaining table but cooperate to lobby government to maintain barriers to new competition and maximize the profits to be divided between them.[14]

In defense weapons procurement, intimate cooperation between the Pentagon as a buyer of weapons and the defense contractors that supply them—including the notorious revolving door by which the same officials occupy influential positions in organizations on *both* sides of the market—is scarcely a model of economic rectitude. It has tainted the award of billions of dollars of reconstruction contracts in post–Saddam Iraq. It is malodorously evident in the scandal surrounding the Pentagon's recent procurement of aerial refueling aircraft from Boeing, where a purchasing official for the Pentagon was negotiating for the Air Force on the buyer side while simultaneously

---

[10]Gary Clyde Hufbauer and Ben Goodrich, "Steel Policy: The Good, the Bad, and the Ugly," International Economics Policy Brief 03-1, Institute for International Economics, January 2003; Consuming Industries Trade Action Coalition, "Steel-Consuming Jobs vs. Steel-Producing Jobs, 1999," available at www.citac-trade.org.

[11]Amy Borrus, "Will the Bough Break?" *Business Week* (April 14, 2003): 62–63. On the steel industry generally, see Walter Adams and James W. Brock, *The Bigness Complex: Industry, Labor, and Government in the American Economy*, 2d. ed. (Palo Alto, CA: Stanford University Press, 2004), chapters 19 and 21.

[12]See Steven Greenhouse, "Unions Are a Victim of Their Own Success at the Nation's Airlines," *New York Times* (April 26, 2003): B3.

[13]See Adams and Brock, *Bigness Complex*, chapter 22.

[14]Matt Richtel, "A Marriage, and Divorce, of Convenience at Verizon," *New York Times* (August 8, 2003): C4.

negotiating for an executive position with Boeing on the selling side. In this case, Senator McCain has charged, "the Air Force appeared not so much to negotiate with Boeing as to advocate for it, to the point of appearing to allow the company too much control not only over pricing and the terms and conditions of the contract, but perhaps also over the aircraft's capabilities."[15]

Antitrust critics on the left also harbor a misplaced faith in the virtues of corporate giantism. General Motors (GM) has long stood as the world's largest automotive concern, with annual revenues exceeding the gross national product of all but a handful of nations. Yet GM has perennially suffered from the bureaucratic sclerosis endemic to mastodonic organizational size. It strains credulity to suggest that GM's afflictions are somehow due to its being too small, when only by substantially paring its size in recent years has the firm been able to improve its economic performance, and when the megamerger of Chrysler and Daimler has generated unenviable results.

In steel, a century of merger-induced corporate bigness did not produce paragons of efficiency or technological innovativeness. Instead, America's steel giants became backward, hide-bound bureaucracies that lost sales, market share, and hundreds of thousands of jobs when confronted first by competition from abroad, and later by hyper-efficient U.S. minimills—small, state-of-the-art producers that have revolutionized the field and won markets from such supposedly invincible suppliers as "Japan, Inc." and South Korea.

In the pharmaceutical drug industry, a decade of mergers that have consolidated the field into the hands of fewer, more massive firms has been justified in the name of promoting the research, development, and commercialization of new, life-saving medicines. At the same time, however, the new product pipelines of the merged giants have dried up, and they are turning increasingly to smaller, more advanced firms for their new breakthrough medicines.[16]

In airlines, it is the largest carriers that have incurred the biggest losses during the period leading up to and following the 9/11 terrorist attacks, but the smaller carriers (Southwest, Jet Blue, AirTran) have remained profitable throughout.

More generally, megamergers throughout the economy (including the consolidation of AOL and TimeWarner, AT&T's acquisition of cable giant TCI, Tyco's serial acquisition of dozens of companies, WorldCom's purchase of 70 firms, and massive combinations among the nation's biggest banks) have failed to enhance the merged giants' performance and, more often than not, have harmed it.[17]

---

[15]On Iraq, see Jane Mayer, "Contract Sport," New Yorker (February 16 and 23, 2004): 80-91. On Boeing's tanker program, see Senator McCain's opening statement, U.S. Congress. Senate. Committee on Commmerce, Science, and Transportation. Hearing: Lease of Boeing Tankers to U.S. Air Force, September 3, 2003; U.S. Congressional Budget Office, Assessment of the Air Force's Plan to Acquire 100 Boeing Tanker Aircraft, Washington D.C., August 2003; Anne Marie Squeo, and J. Lynn Lunsford, "How Two Officials Got Caught by Pentagon's Revolving Door," *Wall Street Journal* (December 18, 2003): 1. For an earlier analysis of coalescing power in the defense field, see Walter Adams and James W. Brock, *The Bigness Complex* (New York: Pantheon, 1987), chapter 24 and the sources therein.

[16]Adams and Brock, *Bigness Complex*, 2d. ed., chapter 4.

[17]See, for example, Gary Hamel, "When Dinosaurs Mate," *Wall Street Journal* (January 22, 2004): A12; Alex Barenson, "Big Mergers Have Long History of Failure and Troubles," *New York Times* (January 15, 2004): C8; David Henry, "Mergers: Why Most Big Deals Don't Pay Off," *Business Week* (October 14, 2002): 70; Robert Frank and Robin Sidel, "Firms That Lived by the Deal in '90s, Now Sink by the Dozens," *Wall Street Journal* (June 6, 2002): 1; Leslie P. Norton, "Merger Mayhem," *Barron's* (April 20, 1998): 33–37. In addition, see Sara B. Moeller, Frederik P. Schlingemann, and Rene M. Stulz, "Do Shareholders of Acquiring Firms Gain from Acquisitions?" NBER Working Paper No. 9523, February 2003, finding that shareholders lose the most when large firms make large acquisitions.

Nor are these infirmities and failures of corporate bigness unique to the United States. Abroad, merger-induced giantism failed to provide economic salvation for West European nations (especially Britain and France), which became enthralled with the corporate bigness mystique during the 1950s and 1960s. The putative national champions that they urged to merge so they could dominate their national industries (including British Leyland in automobiles, British Steel, and Bull in French computers) came to be recognized as lame ducks in the 1970s and 1980s. Suffering chronic losses, they became dependent on economic life support from their home governments. According to Paul Geroski and Alexis Jacquemin, these "new super firms did not give rise to a new competitive efficiency in Europe. Indeed, by creating a group of firms with sufficient market power to be considerably sheltered from the forces of market selection, the policy may have left Europe with a population of sleepy industrial giants who were ill-equipped to meet the challenges of the 1970s and 1980s."[18]

As for East Asia, advocates of coalition capitalism seem to have ignored an important strength of Japan's postwar economic miracle, while celebrating what events in Japan and South Korea have revealed to be a serious weakness of intimately cooperative industry-banking-government relationships.

The strength of Japan's postwar performance is due in important part to a competitive domestic market structure that was put into place by American occupation authorities during the years immediately following World War II. Under the leadership of General Douglas McArthur, a massive deconcentration program was implemented: 16 of Japan's largest holding companies were dissolved outright, 26 were dissolved and reorganized, and another 19 firms with "excessive concentration" were dismembered. The 2 largest Japanese holding companies, Mitsui and Mitsubishi, were divided into hundreds of successor firms, and an accompanying divestiture program forced the sale of perhaps as much as half of the 1945 paid-in value of all Japanese corporate securities.[19] Later, during the 1950s and 1960s, concentration trends in Japan and the United States diverged, with average market concentration drifting downward in Japan but rising in the United States. In fact, Japanese industrialists strenuously resisted government efforts to promote oligopoly giantism by limiting major industries to a few national champions. In automobiles, for example, Honda overcame government efforts to limit the field to the two incumbent firms, while in electronics, Sony overcame Ministry of International Trade and Industry (MITI) efforts to stifle it by impeding the then unknown firm's efforts to procure transistor rights in the United States.[20] Conversely, Japan's recent decade-long slump has to an important degree been aggravated by corporate giantism and the debilitating consequences of coalescing power, including the collapse of banks that are as weak as they are big, and incestuous relationships between banking giants and government financial regulators.[21]

---

[18]Paul A. Geroski and Alexis Jacquemin, "Industrial Change, Barriers to Mobility, and European Industrial Policy," *Economic Policy* (November 1985): 175.

[19]Walter Adams and James W. Brock, "The Bigness Mystique and the Merger Policy Debate: An International Perspective," *Northwestern Journal of International Law & Business* (Spring 1988): 36–43.

[20]Christopher Wood, *The End of Japan Inc.* (New York: Simon & Schuster, 1994), 77.

[21]See James Brooke and Ken Belson, "Japanese Plan to Overhaul Banks Hits a Stone Wall," *New York Times* (October 23, 2002): C1; Sheryl WuDunn, "A New Acid Test for Tokyo as It Tackles Banking Crisis," *New York Times* (September 1, 1998): C4; Jathon Sapsford and Robert Steiner, "Japan's Banks Struggle with Many Problems," *Wall Street Journal* (January 22, 1997): 1; Michael Williams, "Many Japanese Banks Ran Amok While Led by Former Regulators," *Wall Street Journal* (January 19, 1996): 1.

"*Keiretsu*" arrangements of cross-corporate stock holdings among industrial firms and banks—sanctioned by government—have over the 1990s also been revealed as a trap. In Japan, these families of interconnected industrial and financial firms became dependent on each other for subsidies and financial bailouts, and their reliance on easy sales to corporate family members may have rendered them complacent and vulnerable to competition from abroad.[22] In South Korea, huge conglomerates ("*chaebol*") came to be perceived as too big to be allowed to fail: Allotted the lion's share of financial capital in a futile effort to forestall their collapse, their dominance hamstrung banks and starved the Korean economy of investment capital. Only the crisis of the Asian meltdown of 1997 through 1998 compelled the Korean government to begin to free itself from the chaebol by forcing these giants to shrink their size and to focus their operations and improve their performance. At the same time, the government liberated banks to redirect their lending toward smaller, more vibrant firms.[23]

At bottom, the Achilles heel of the cooperative capitalism that is advocated on the left is the problem of power and interest-group politics. As Henry C. Simons pointed out long ago, "Bargaining organizations will contest over the division of the swag, but we commonly overlook the fact that they have large common interests as against the community and that every increase of monopoly power on one side serves to strengthen and implement it on the other." To promote such coalescing power, Simons warned, would be to "drift rapidly into political organization along functional, occupational lines—into a miscellany of specialized collectivisms, organized to take income away from one another [but] incapable of acting in their own common interest or in a manner compatible with general prosperity."[24]

The Challenge from the Right

On the right, economic Darwinists have long deprecated America's traditional antitrust philosophy, urging that it be supplanted by a policy of laissez-faire. This, they claim, would enhance economic performance by unleashing the benefits of natural selection of the economically fittest.

Concentration of power in the trusts, William Graham Sumner insisted a century ago, "is indispensable to the successful execution of the tasks which devolve upon society in our time . . . The concentration of power (wealth), more dominant control, intenser discipline, and stricter methods are but modes of securing more perfect integration. When we perceive this we see that the concentration of wealth is but one feature of a grand step in societal evolution." Monopolists, he believed, are "the naturally selected agents of society for certain work. They get high wages and live in luxury, but the bargain is a good one for society."[25]

---

[22]"Fall of a Keiretsu: How Giant Mitsubishi Group Lost Its Way," *Business Week* (March 15, 1999): 90.

[23]See Michael Schuman and Namju Cho, "Troubles of Korean Conglomerates Intensify, Signaling End of an Era," *Wall Street Journal* (March 25, 1997): A11; "The Giants Stumble," *Economist* (October 18, 1997): 67; Meredith Woo-Cumings, "How Industrial Policy Caused South Korea's Collapse," *Wall Street Journal* (December 8, 1997): A24; "The Chaebol That Ate Korea," *Economist* (November 14, 1998): 67; Jay Solomon, "Back from Brink, Korea Inc. Wants a Little Respect," *Wall Street Journal* (June 13, 2002): 1. See also Kwangshik Shin, "The Treatment of Market Power in Korea," *Review of Industrial Organization* 21 (September 2002): 113.

[24]Henry C. Simons, *Economic Policy for a Free Society* (Chicago: University of Chicago Press, 1948), 119, 219.

[25]William Graham Sumner, "The Concentration of Wealth: Its Economic Justification," in *On Liberty, Society, and Politics: The Essential Essays of William Graham Sumner* (Indianapolis, IN: Liberty Fund, 1992), 149–150, 155.

John D. Rockefeller, father of the Standard Oil monopoly, put it in botanical terms: "The growth of a large business is merely a survival of the fittest. The American Beauty rose can be produced in the splendor and fragrance which bring cheer to its beholder only by sacrificing the early buds which grow up around it. This is not an evil tendency in business. It is merely the working-out of a law of nature and a law of God."[26]

A leading modern-day exponent of this view, Robert Bork, sees a striking analogy between a free-market system and Darwinian evolution: "The familiarity of that parallel, and the overbroad inferences sometimes drawn from it, should not blind us to its important truths. The environment to which the business firm must adapt is defined, ultimately, by social wants and the social costs of meeting them. The firm that adapts to the environment better than its rivals tends to expand. The less successful firms tend to contract— perhaps, eventually, to become extinct." There is little justification, Bork contends, to interfere with the natural operation of a free-market system. Laissez-faire, he argues, can be trusted to produce optimal results. Private monopoly and market power should be of no social concern because neither has any durability: "A market position that creates output restriction and higher prices will always be eroded if it is not based upon superior efficiency."[27] As the neo-Darwinists see it, "[t]he only important source of long-lasting monopoly is the government," especially today, when global competition and technological change "are making market competition a more potent force for prosperity and progress and undermining any justification there ever was for government to pursue an active antitrust policy."[28]

Alas, this doctrine, too, suffers from a number of congenital defects. First, it is based on a *post hoc ergo propter hoc* fallacy: The mere existence of a monopolist, oligopolist, or corporate giant proves that it must have achieved its position solely because of superior performance. This is no more than an assertion—devoid, more often than not, of any empirical substantiation. In fact, although economic Darwinism makes superior economic performance the centerpiece of its policy position, its advocates concede that such economic performance is difficult, if not impossible, to measure scientifically. Judge Bork, for example, admits "the real objection to performance tests and efficiency defenses in antitrust law is that they are spurious. They cannot measure the factors relevant to consumer welfare, so that after the economic extravaganza was completed we should know no more than before it began."[29]

Likewise, Judge Frank Easterbrook urges us "to avoid econometric [i.e., empirical] answers when we can," because "[t]hey are expensive as well as potentially indeterminate."[30] These modern-day Darwinists despair the possibility of evaluating economic performance, even though they posit it as the transcending goal of public policy.

---

[26]Quoted in Richard Hofstadter, *Social Darwinism in American Thought*, rev. ed. (Boston: Beacon Press, 1955), 45.

[27]Robert H. Bork, *The Antitrust Paradox*, rev. ed. (New York: Free Press, 1993), 118, 133. In fairness, Judge Bork has found Microsoft's monopoly of computer operating software to be an exception to his general laissez-faire rule. See Robert H. Bork, "There's No Choice: Dismember Microsoft," *Wall Street Journal* (May 1, 2000): A34.

[28]Harold Demsetz, "The Trust behind Antitrust," in *Industrial Concentration and the Market System*, ed. Eleanor M. Fox and James T. Halverson (Chicago: American Bar Association, 1979), 51; Dwight R. Lee and Richard B. McKenzie, "Technology, Market Changes, and Antitrust Enforcement," Center for the Study of American Business, Policy Study No. 155, February 2000, 16.

[29]Bork, *Antitrust Paradox*, 124.

[30]Frank H. Easterbrook, "On Identifying Exclusionary Conduct," *Notre Dame Law Review* (1986): 979; Easterbrook, "Ignorance and Antitrust," in *Antitrust, Innovation, and Competitiveness*, ed. Thomas M. Jorde and David J. Teece (New York: Oxford University Press, 1992), 119.

Second, economic Darwinism is concerned primarily with static, managerial efficiency rather than dynamic social efficiency. It thus falls victim to the sin of suboptimization: The relevant question is not whether GM or Ford produces gas-guzzling sport utility behemoths at the least average total cost but whether they should be producing such gas-guzzlers at all. The relevant policy question is not whether Microsoft writes operating software at lowest cost but whether other, fundamentally different operating software systems would be the preferred choice of computer users if software rivals were free from Microsoft's monopoly power to innovate and compete.

Third, economic Darwinism assumes that any firm that no longer delivers superior performance will be displaced by newcomers automatically. This ignores the ability of powerful, established firms to build private storm shelters—or to lobby government to build public storm shelters for them—in order to shield themselves from Schumpeterian gales of creative destruction. It ignores the difference between the legal freedom of entry and the economic realities that deter the entry of potential newcomers into concentrated industries.

The airline industry provides a case in point: After deregulating the field in the 1980s to allow competition to better regulate economic decision making, a laissez-faire policy subsequently permitted mergers to concentrate the industry into a tight-knit oligopoly of giants that command formidable fortress hub monopolies. A laissez-faire policy has permitted these carriers to replicate their domestic dominance on a global scale through a constellation of alliances with their major potential foreign rivals, while allowing them to predatorily drive new competitors from their air routes at home. A laissez-faire policy has produced subpar performance that sparks perennial pleas for an air passenger bill of rights.

Fourth, proponents of laissez-faire overemphasize the disciplining influence of international competition in the new global market. They underestimate the capacity of powerful domestic firms, once they become dominant, to subvert foreign competition at home and abroad. In recent years, for example, the Justice Department has uncovered and prosecuted a host of global cartels, collecting more in fines during the past decade than over the department's entire 100-year history. Recent antitrust prosecutions of the world's leading producers of food preservatives, animal feed additives, and vitamins have revealed vividly the ability of global rivals to fix world prices, rig global market shares, and eliminate global competition. (In the case of the global citric acid cartel, the president of the Archer Daniels Midland Company assured his foreign conspirators that "[o]ur competitors are our friends and our customers are our enemies."[31]) Transnational alliances and mergers, in addition to or in lieu of world cartels, also can short-circuit the discipline of the global marketplace. As Sir Alfred Mond, the organizer of Imperial Chemical Industries, the giant British chemical combine, observed long ago, "The old idea of the heads of great businesses meeting each other with scowls and shaking each other's fists in each other's faces and . . . trying to destroy each other's business may be very good on the films, but it does not accord with any given facts."[32]

---

[31]For in-depth analyses of these global cartels, see Kurt Eichenwald, *The Informant* (New York: Broadway Books, 2000); John M. Connor, *Global Price Fixing* (Boston: Kluwer Academic Publishing, 2001).

[32]Quoted in George Stocking and Myron Watkins, *Cartels in Action* (New York: Twentieth Century Fund, 1946), 429.

Fifth, economic Darwinists decry counterproductive government policies which, they say, are the prime evil to be avoided. However, they ignore the fact that in a representative democracy, government does not operate in a vacuum, and that the anticompetitive government policies they condemn are the product of political lobbying by powerful economic groups bent on manipulating the state. They ignore the fact that in a representative democracy, disproportionate economic size inherently entails disproportionate influence in the political arena, as corporate giants mobilize the vast political resources at their command—executives and labor unions, suppliers and subcontractors, governors and mayors, senators and representatives, Democrats and Republicans—in their efforts to pervert public policy to serve their antisocial ends. Thus, corporate bigness complexes can lobby for government import restraints to immunize them from foreign competition (as the steel industry has done repeatedly) at exorbitant expense to the economy. They can obtain billions of dollars in government subsidies by whipsawing states and communities against one another in bidding to attract or retain their plants and facilities. They can violate their defense contracts with government, immune from the "death sentence" disbarment penalty meted out to smaller firms for committing similar illegalities.[33] They can fail to innovate while lobbying government for legislation to penalize the innovativeness of others (as GM has done in the case of hybrid automobiles pioneered by Toyota and Honda).[34] They can placate labor by negotiating munificent retirement programs, then dump them on the government's Pension Benefit Guaranty Corporation when they decide the pensions they negotiated are too burdensome (as recently has been the case with collapsing steel and airline giants).[35] They are accorded privileged treatment in these ways and others because, as Federal Reserve Chairman Alan Greenspan has said of merged megabanks, they "are entities that create the potential for unusually large system risks in the national and international economy should they fail."[36]

As shown by government bailouts of Lockheed, Chrysler, Long Term Capital Management, big banks with souring loans in Mexico and East Asia, and major airlines in the post–9/11 period, large firms can survive not because they are better but because they are bigger, not because they are fitter but because they are fatter.[37] Because they permit economic size and power but ignore its larger political ramifications, the economic Darwinists are like Henry David Thoreau's neighbors who, he observed, "invite the devil in at every angle and then prate about the garden of Eden and the fall of man."

Finally, economic Darwinists fail to make the critical distinction between individual freedom and a free economic *system*. As Jeremy Bentham recognized, it is not enough to shout "Laissez-faire!" and oppose all government intervention: "To say that a law is contrary to natural liberty is simply to say that it is a law: for every law is established at the expense of liberty—the liberty of Peter at the expense of the liberty of Paul."[38] If individual rights were absolute and unlimited, they would (as Thomas Hobbes understood 4 centuries ago) provide license to commit the grossest abuses

---

[33]Anne Marie Squeo, "Are Firms Too Big to Debar?" *Wall Street Journal* (June 10, 2003): A4.

[34]Harry Stoffer, "Toyota, Honda Lose out on Hybrid Credits," *Automotive News* (December 1, 2003): 1.

[35]U.S. General Accounting Office, "Pension Benefit Guaranty Corporation's Single-Employer Insurance Program: Long-Term Vulnerabilities Warrant 'High Risk' Designation," Washington, D.C., July 23, 2003.

[36]"The Evolution of Bank Supervision" (remarks by Alan Greenspan, American Bankers Association, Phoenix, AZ, October 11, 1999).

[37]In the case of banking, for example, see Gary H. Stern and Ron J. Feldman, *Too Big to Fail: The Hazards of Bank Bailouts* (Washington, D.C.: Brookings Institution, 2004).

[38]J. Bowring, ed., *The Works of Jeremy Bentham*, vol. 3 (Edinburgh: W. Tait, 1843), 185.

FIGURE 13-2   The Public Policy Choice

SOURCE: Thurman W. Arnold, Cartels or Free Enterprise? Public Affairs Pamphlet 103, 1945.

against society, including destroying the freedoms of others. Considered in this light, the Darwinian admonition not to penalize the winner of the race is irrelevant for public policy purposes. Rather, the relevant challenge is how to reward the winner without including in its trophy the right to impose disabling handicaps on putative competitors, or the power to determine the rules by which future races shall be run—or the discretion to eliminate the institution of racing altogether.

Conclusion

The purpose of American antitrust policy is to maintain the structural prerequisites for effective competition. The transcending goal is to protect the decentralized decision-making system of the competitive market from encroachment by central planning, whether by the state or by private monopolists, oligopolists, and cartels. The objective is to maintain regulatory control by the invisible hand of the competitively structured marketplace, and to guard it from the depredations of private economic power blocs operating as despotic governments, free from competitive checks and balances and accountability, and with no assurance that their private decision making promotes the public good. The spectacular revelations of fraud, deception, and looting in the wake of Enron, WorldCom, Tyco, Arthur Anderson, Merrill Lynch, Citigroup and others are stark reminders of the continuing challenge of checking economic decision-making power in a free society and guarding against its abuse.

Suggested Readings

Acs, Zolton J. 1999. *Are Small Firms Important?* Boston: Kluwer Academic Publishers.

Adams, Walter, and James W. Brock. 1991. *Antitrust Economics on Trial: A Dialogue on the New Laissez-Faire.* Princeton, NJ: Princeton University Press.

_____. 2004. *The Bigness Complex*, 2d. ed. Palo Alto, CA: Stanford University Press.

Bork, Robert H. 1993. *The Antitrust Paradox*, rev. ed. New York: Free Press.

Brandeis, Louis B. 1934. *The Curse of Bigness.* New York: Viking.

Breit, William, and Kenneth G. Elzinga. 1996. *The Antitrust Casebook*, 3d. ed. New York: Dryden Press.

Brock, James W., and Kenneth G. Elzinga. 1991. *Antitrust, the Market, and the State: The Contributions of Walter Adams.* Armonk, NY: M.E. Sharpe.

De Jong, H. W., ed. 1993. *The Structure of European Industry*, 3d. ed. Boston: Kluwer Academic Publishers.

Dewey, Donald. 1990. *The Antitrust Experiment in America.* New York: Columbia University Press.

Edwards, Corwin D. 1949. *Maintaining Competition.* New York: McGraw Hill.

Fetter, Frank A. 1931. *The Masquerade of Monopoly.* New York: Harcourt, Brace and Co.

Fox, Eleanor M. 2002. *The Competition Law of the European Union.* Eagan, MN: West Group.

Friedman, David. 1988. *The Misunderstood Miracle: Industrial Development and Political Change in Japan.* Ithaca, NY: Cornell University Press.

Galbraith, John Kenneth. 1978. *The New Industrial State,* 3d. ed. Boston: Houghton Mifflin.

Graham, Otis L. 1992. *Losing Time: The Industrial Policy Debate.* Cambridge: Harvard University Press.

Hadley, Eleanor M. 1970. *Antitrust in Japan.* Princeton, NJ: Princeton University Press.

Hall, Thomas E. 2003. *The Rotten Fruits of Economic Controls.* New York: University Press of America.

Hawley, Ellis. 1966. *The New Deal and the Problem of Monopoly.* Princeton, NJ: Princeton University Press.

Hofstadter, Richard. 1944. *Social Darwinism in American Thought.* Boston: Beacon Press.

Johnson, Peter. 2003. *Industries in Europe: Competition, Trends, and Policy Issues.* Northampton, MA: Edward Elgar.

Katz, Richard. 1998. *Japan: The System That Soured.* Armonk, NY: M.E. Sharpe.

Kwoka, John E., and Lawrence J. White, eds. 2004. *The Antitrust Revolution,* 4th ed. New York: Oxford University Press.

Lippman, Walter. 1937. *The Good Society.* Boston: Little, Brown.

Lowi, Theodore. 1979. *The End of Liberalism,* 2nd. ed. New York: Norton.

Machlup, Fritz. 1952. *The Political Economy of Monopoly.* Baltimore: Johns Hopkins University Press.

May, James. 1989. "Antitrust in the Formative Era: Political and Economic Theory in Constitutional and Antitrust Analysis, 1880–1918." *Ohio State Law Journal* 50: 257–395.

Olson, Mancur. 1982. *The Rise and Decline of Nations.* New Haven, CT: Yale University Press.

Peritz, Rudolph J. R. 1996. *Competition Policy in America, 1888–1992.* New York: Oxford University Press.

Peterson, Wallace C., ed. 1988. *Market Power and the Economy.* Boston: Kluwer Academic Publishers.

Porter, Michael E. 1990. *The Competitive Advantage of Nations.* New York: Free Press.

Reich, Robert B. 1991. *The Work of Nations.* New York: Knopf.

Rosenbaum, David I. 1998. *Market Dominance.* Westport, CT: Praeger.

Seager, Henry R., and Charles A. Gulick, Jr. 1929. *Trust and Corporation Problems.* New York: Harper.

Shepherd, William G. 1997. *The Economics of Industrial Organization,* 4th ed. Upper Saddle River, NJ: Prentice Hall.

Simons, Henry C. 1948. *Economic Policy for a Free Society*. Chicago: University of Chicago Press.

Spencer, Herbert. 1982. *The Man versus the State*. Indianapolis: Liberty Fund.

Stiglitz, Joseph E. 2003. *The Roaring Nineties*. New York: W.W. Norton.

Stocking, George W., and Myron W. Watkins. 1946. *Cartels in Action*. New York: Twentieth Century Fund.

_____. *Cartels or Competition?* New York: Twentieth Century Fund, 1948.

_____. *Monopoly and Free Enterprise*. New York: Twentieth Century Fund, 1951.

Sullivan, Lawrence A., and Warren S. Grimes. 2000. *The Law of Antitrust*. Eagan, MN: West Wadsworth.

Sumner, William Graham. 1992. *On Liberty, Society, and Politics*. Robert C. Bannister, ed. Indianapolis: Liberty Fund.

Thorelli, Hans B. 1955. The Federal Antitrust Policy: Origination of an American Tradition. Baltimore: Johns Hopkins University Press.

Thurow, Lester C. 1985. *The Zero-Sum Solution*. New York: Simon & Schuster.

Waldman, Don, and Elizabeth J. Jensen. 2000. *Industrial Organization*, 2nd. ed. New York: Addison Wesley.

Whittaker, D. H. 1997. *Small Firms in the Japanese Economy*. Cambridge: Cambridge University Press.

Name Index

Subject Index